Microsoft® Office
for WINDOWS® 95
Tutorial & Applications

William R. Pasewark, Sr., Ph.D.

Professor Emeritus, Texas Tech University

Office Management Consultant

William R. Pasewark, Jr., Ph.D., C.P.A.

University of Houston

JOIN US ON THE INTERNET

WWW: http://www.thomson.com
EMAIL: findit@kiosk.thomson.com

A service of I(T)P®

SOUTH
WESTERN
EDUCATIONAL
PUBLISHING

I(T)P® An International Thomson Publishing Company

Cincinnati • Albany • Bonn • Boston • Detroit • London • Madrid • Melbourne • Mexico City
• New York • Philadelphia • Pacific Grove • San Francisco • Singapore • Tokyo • Toronto • Washington

Editor-in-Chief: Robert E. First
Managing Editor: Janie Schwark
Project Manager: Dave Lafferty
Art Director: John Robb
Consulting Editor: Custom Editorial Productions, Inc.
Marketing Manager: Kent Christensen
Production: Custom Editorial Productions, Inc.

ISBN: 0-538-71090-5

1 2 3 4 5 6 7 8 9 10 PR 00 99 98 97 96 95

Printed in the United States of America

International Thomson Publishing

South-Western Educational Publishing is a division of International Thomson Publishing, Inc. The ITP trademark is used under license.

PREFACE

• • • • • • • • • • • • • • • • • • • •

This preface has two sections: one for the student and one for the teacher.

To the Student

Computers affect our daily lives. For example, they schedule television programs and advertisements; operate cash registers; print newspapers, books, and documents; keep records of athletic events; control telephone communications; monitor automobile engine performance; and generate course schedules and grade reports for schools.

You may already have a working knowledge of computers, or you may have little or no computer experience at all. In either case, *Microsoft Office for Windows 95: Tutorial and Applications* will help you further develop your level of computer competency.

Microsoft Office for Windows 95—An Integrated Software Package

Microsoft Office for Windows 95 is an *integrated* software package. The Professional Edition combines five popular computer applications: Word, Access, Excel, Schedule+, and PowerPoint. These can be used for many applications, such as writing letters or research papers (Word), making lists of names and addresses (Access), recording income and expenses (Excel), scheduling appointments (Schedule+), and making presentations (PowerPoint). You can easily combine documents and information from the various applications.

Integrated software is commonly used in academic, business, career, and personal settings to help you complete routine tasks more quickly and accurately, thus improving your efficiency and productivity.

Microsoft Office for Windows 95: Tutorial and Applications—Learn and Apply

The authors planned this book to provide a realistic, complete, and successful learning experience for you. Objectives listed at the beginning of each chapter give you an overview of the chapter. Short segments of text explain new information and tell why it is important. Then, activities with numbered steps guide you through the computer operation. These activities give you a chance to practice the concepts you have just learned. The book includes many illustrations and activities to simplify complex concepts and operations. A summary, true/false and completion questions, and applications at the end of each chapter help you review the chapters.

Within *Microsoft Office for Windows 95: Tutorial and Applications,* the authors share with you their enthusiasm about how powerful a tool a computer can be in your life.

Student's Guide for Using This Book

Reading this guide before starting work in this book will help you to learn faster and easier.

The following terminology and procedures are used in this book:

■ *Text* means words, numbers, and symbols that are printed.

■ *Keying* (also called keyboarding) means entering text (also called data) into a computer. The terms *keying* and *typing* are sometimes used interchangeably.

■ After computer concepts are explained in the text, you will practice the concepts in a hands-on activity that will involve using the keyboard and the mouse.

The different type styles used in this book have special meanings:

■ Individual keys that you will press are in bold type:

> **Esc, Ctrl, Tab**.

■ Text you will key into the computer is in bold type:

> Key **Grade** as the field name.

■ Filenames are italicized in upper- and lower-case letters:

> Open *Activity 14-1* from the template disk.

■ Words in this book that you will also see on the screen are in italics:

> Click in the box beside *Personal Information* and click **OK**.

■ Key terms (words defined in the text and listed in the glossary) are in bold and italics:

> **Word processing** is using a computer and software program, such as Microsoft Word, to produce documents such as letters and reports.

To the Teacher

In today's world, understanding computer concepts and knowing how to apply computer skills are essential for every student. Students enter computer courses with widely varying levels of skill and knowledge. Some may already know several software packages; others may not have been exposed to computers at all.

Microsoft Office for Windows 95: Tutorial and Applications is designed for new and experienced learners as they develop computer competency using an integrated computer software package. The tutorial can be structured for courses of study from thirty to forty-five class meetings in length, making it easily adaptable to a variety of curriculum patterns.

System Requirements

Microsoft Office for Windows 95 has the following computer requirements:

- Microsoft Windows 95 operating system or Microsoft Windows NT Workstation version 3.51 or later.

- Multimedia PC (includes 386DX or higher processor—486 recommended) or equivalent PC with multimedia PC upgrade kit (includes CD-ROM drive and audio board).

- Microsoft MS-DOS CD-ROM Extensions (MSCDEX) version 2.2 or later (provided with CD-ROM).

- 8 MB of memory required; 12 MB of memory required to run Microsoft Access on Windows 95; 16 MB of memory required to run Microsoft Access or two other programs on Microsoft Windows NT Workstation; more memory required to run additional programs simultaneously on Windows 95 or Windows NT Workstation.

- One CD-ROM drive.

- Approximately 40 MB of free space on hard disk for compact install; 87 MB for typical installation; 126 MB for maximum (custom) installation.

- VGA or higher-resolution video adapter (SVGA 256-color recommended).

- Mouse or other pointing device.

- Any Windows-compatible printer.

Microsoft Office 95—An Integrated Software Package

Microsoft Office for Windows 95 is an integrated software package. Contained within the Professional Edition are five programs:

- Microsoft Word, with graphics capability

- Microsoft Excel, with charting capability

- Access, with reporting capability

- Schedule+

- PowerPoint

These programs can be used independently or in any combination. For example, you can easily integrate a chart from Excel into a letter from Word, or attach a list from Access to a memo created in Word.

Integrated computer software packages increase efficiency and productivity, and are becoming common in the workplace. Exposure to this type of software package is a definite advantage to students in their academic, personal, and career lives.

Students who learn any Microsoft Office 95 program will benefit from the enormous amount of transfer of learning that will occur when they use any other Microsoft product such as Works.

Teaching and Learning Aids

This instructional package is designed to simplify instruction and to enhance learning with the following learning and teaching aids:

TEXTBOOK—THE TUTORIAL

Learning objectives listed at the beginning of each chapter give students an overview of the chapter.

Step-by-step instructions for specific operations allow students to progress independently. When the same operations are repeated, instructions are "faded"; that is, fewer specific instructions are included, challenging the student gradually to perform the operations without prompting.

Computer activities immediately follow the presentation of new concepts and instructions. The activities give students the opportunity to apply what they have just learned.

The **integration and simulation** sections at the ends of each unit teach students how to merge Word, Excel, Access, and PowerPoint.

Illustrations, including numerous screen captures, explain complex concepts and serve as reference points when students complete activities.

Chapter summaries provide quick reviews for each chapter, entrenching the main points in the student's mind.

True/False and Completion questions and **computer reinforcement applications** follow each chapter to gauge students' understanding of the chapter's information and operations. The applications offer minimal instruction so students must apply concepts previously introduced.

Appendices A and B briefly describe and provide practice using Bookshelf '95 and Encarta '95. Appendix C gives an overview of Microsoft Exchange.

The **glossary** is a list of common computer terms and definitions.

A **comprehensive index** supplies quick and easy accessibility to specific parts of the tutorial.

THE TEACHER'S MANUAL

The comprehensive teacher's manual includes a variety of aids for planning the course of study, presenting information, and managing the classroom. All are designed to ensure a successful and enjoyable teaching experience. The manual includes the following features:

Guidelines for **scheduling students** with varying abilities.

General teaching suggestions include strategies for effective instruction with a minimum of stress.

Specific teaching suggestions are presented for each chapter.

Reproducible short-answer chapter tests with answers, and production tests with solutions are included in the manual.

An **Application Progress Record** can be reproduced for each student, and a realistic **Grading Scale for Documents,** which is a business-oriented guide for evaluating students' work, is also included.

THE TEMPLATE DISKS

The template disks contain pre-keyed text and graphics for activities and applications, and may be copied for students. Four template disks are provided. Two contain only files for use with Access. The other two disks contain files for use with all other Office 95 programs. These disks allow students to use more class time learning computer operations rather than keying large amounts of text into the computer.

THE SOLUTIONS DISKS

The solutions disks contain solutions to selected activities and all applications so that you can verify formatting and students' disks.

STUDENTS' REPRODUCIBLE EXERCISES

This $8\frac{1}{2} \times 11$-inch unbound packet contains duplicates of the true/false questions, completion questions, and reinforcement applications at the end of each chapter in the student's book.

Transfer of Learning Among Microsoft Programs

Screens, commands, and operations for Microsoft Office 95 programs are similar to and sometimes identical with those for many versions of other Microsoft products such as Works. Therefore, students who learn any Microsoft program will benefit from the enormous amount of *transfer of learning* that occurs when they use other Microsoft programs.

The Authors' Commitment

In writing *Microsoft Office for Windows 95: Tutorial and Applications*, the authors dedicated themselves to creating a complete and appealing instructional package to make teaching and learning an interesting, successful, and rewarding experience for both teachers and students. The authors assembled in one resource all the materials and aids a teacher needs to create a learning experience in which students can successfully master skills that will serve them in their academic and career endeavors, as well as in their personal lives.

Acknowledgments

The authors thank Stephen Collings, Rhonda Davis, Todd Knowlton, Laura Melton, and Dawna Walls for their dedicated and effective contributions to this and other publications. We also value and appreciate their commitment to produce "books that will help our students to live better lives."

Many professional South-Western sales representatives make educationally sound presentations to teachers about our books. The authors know of and appreciate very much a sales representative's valuable function as a "bridge" between authors and teacher.

Some Other Books by the Same Authors

The Microsoft Windows books listed below are available exclusively from South-Western Educational Publishing. Also available are Macintosh and DOS versions of Microsoft Works books as well as a ClarisWorks tutorial.

Windows 3.0, 3.1, and 3.11

TUTORIAL AND APPLICATIONS SERIES
Microsoft Works (2.0) for Windows: Tutorial and Applications (High School)
Microsoft Works (2.0) for Windows: A Practical Approach (College)
Microsoft Works 3.0 for Windows: Tutorial and Applications
Microsoft Office Professional 4.3: Tutorial and Applications

QUICK COURSE SERIES
Microsoft Works 3.0 for Windows: Quick Course

APPLICATIONS FOR REINFORCEMENT SERIES
Microsoft Works 2.0/3.0 for Windows: Applications for Reinforcement

Windows 95

TUTORIAL AND APPLICATIONS SERIES

Microsoft Works 4.0 for Windows 95: Tutorial and Applications
Microsoft Office for Windows 95: Tutorial and Applications

QUICKTORIAL SERIES

Microsoft Works 4.0 for Windows 95: QuickTorial
Microsoft Office for Windows 95: QuickTorial

APPLICATIONS FOR REINFORCEMENT

Microsoft Works 4.0 for Windows 95: Applications for Reinforcement

Other Titles

Desktop publishing books include PageMaker 5.0, PageMaker 6.0, Express Publisher, PFS: First Publisher, and Publish It!

Texty Award

The Pasewarks and South-Western Educational Publishing won the Textbook and Academic Authors Association *Texty Award* for the best computer book in 1994.

JOIN US ON THE INTERNET VIA WWW, FTP, OR E-MAIL

WWW: http://www.thomson.com
FTP: ftp.thomson.com
E-MAIL: findit@kiosk.thomson.com

South-Western Educational Publishing is a partner in *thomson.com*, an on-line portal for the products, services, and resources available from International Thomson Publishing (ITP). Through our site, users can search catalogs, examine subject-specific resource centers, and subscribe to electronic discussion lists.

South-Western Educational Publishing is also a reseller of commercial software products. See our printed catalog or view this page at:

http://www.swpco.com/swpco/comp_ed/com_sft.html

For information on our products visit our World Wide Web at:

WWW: http://www.swpco.com/swpco.html

To join the South-Western Computer Education discussion list, send an e-mail message to: **majordomo@list.thomson.com**. Leave the subject field blank, and in the body of your message key: SUBSCRIBE SOUTH-WESTERN-COMPUTER-EDUCATION <your e-mail address>.

A service of I(T)P®

Table of Contents

UNIT 3

MICROSOFT EXCEL

UNIT 4

MICROSOFT ACCESS

UNIT 5

MICROSOFT SCHEDULE+ AND MICROSOFT POWERPOINT

UNIT 6

SIMULATION

U N I T

1

INTRODUCTION

MICROSOFT WINDOWS 95 BASICS

CHAPTER

1

OBJECTIVES

When you complete this chapter, you will be able to:

1. Understand the background and advantages of a graphical user interface.

2. Start Microsoft Windows 95.

3. Perform common mouse operations.

4. Be familiar with the Windows 95 desktop.

5. Move, resize, scroll through, maximize, minimize, and close windows.

6. Use menus and dialog boxes.

7. Use Windows 95 Help.

8. Understand the concept of My Computer, Windows Explorer, and the Recycle Bin.

Introduction to Windows 95

When the IBM®[1] PC was introduced in 1981, it was not nearly as powerful as today's computers. The operating system, known as *DOS* (**d**isk **o**perating **s**ystem), could process a limited number of commands that the user had to key. A simple operation such as copying a file required the user to know the DOS command COPY, to know where the file to be copied was located, and to be able to tell the computer where it should be copied to. This process usually meant accurately keying letters, numbers, and symbols, and carefully checking to be sure the file wasn't going somewhere it shouldn't.

---

[1]IBM is a registered trademark of International Business Machines Corporation.

As computer **hardware,** the physical components of a computer, became more advanced, computer **software,** the lists of instructions that computers follow to perform specific tasks, progressed too. IBM PCs and PC compatibles still relied on the DOS operating system to interpret commands from the user, and users still had to key these commands on a keyboard. But computer programs became easier to use as programmers built in better ways for the user to interact with the computer.

In 1985, Microsoft Corporation introduced the first version of Windows, a new way for PC users to communicate with their computers. Windows is a *graphical user interface (GUI).* This means that the user actually interacts with the computer by means of graphics, or pictures. Instead of using the keyboard to enter commands, a user can use a mouse to point at pictures or words that tell the computer to do specific tasks. In earlier versions of Windows, DOS still ran in the background. But Windows 95 replaces the previous combination of DOS and Windows with one new operating system.

You can see how a GUI (pronounced "gooey") would be much easier to use. Instead of memorizing the DOS instructions for opening an application, you can simply point at a pictorial representation of the application and Windows 95 will launch it for you.

Also, all programs designed for Windows 95—and for earlier versions of Windows that will work in Windows 95—have similar features: Files are opened, saved, and printed in the same way; many commands are the same from program to program; even the screen looks the same from program to program. After you have learned one Windows 95 program, you can easily learn others.

If you have never used Windows 95 before, this chapter will teach you what you need to know to feel comfortable using Office 95.

Starting Windows 95

If Windows 95 is already installed, it should start automatically when you turn the computer on. If your computer is on a network, you may have a few other steps, which your instructor can help you with.

ACTIVITY

Starting Windows 95

1. Turn on the computer.

2. After a few moments, Microsoft Windows 95 appears.

When Windows 95 starts up, the first window you see is the desktop. The *desktop* is the space where you do your work. It has icons that allow you to access and work with programs and files. Windows 95 lets you customize and organize your desktop by creating files, folders, and shortcuts. Later, you will explore the desktop. First, you need to make friends with a mouse.

Partners with a Mouse

Graphical user interfaces such as Windows 95 speed the work of the user by teaming the user with a mouse. A *mouse* is a device that rolls on a flat surface and has one or more buttons on it (see Figure 1-1). (You may use a *trackball,* which is an alternative form of a mouse. It has an embedded ball for your fingers and palm to rotate.) The mouse allows you to communicate with the computer by pointing to and manipulating graphics and text on the screen. The *pointer,* which appears as an arrow on the screen, indicates the position of the mouse.

The four most common mouse operations are point, click, double-click, and drag. These operations are outlined in Table 1-1. Once these operations *click* in your mind, you will see the *point* of using a mouse, and your computer will never again be a *drag* to use.

FIGURE 1-1
A mouse makes user interface easier by providing a way to point to and manipulate graphics and text on the screen.

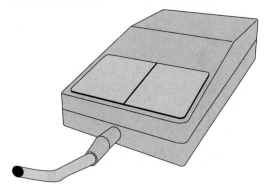

TABLE 1-1
Common mouse operations.

OPERATION	DEFINITION
Point	Moving the mouse pointer to a specific item on the screen
Click	Pressing the mouse button and quickly releasing it while pointing to an item on the screen. (The term *click* comes from the noise you hear when you press and release the button.)
Double-click	Clicking the mouse button twice, quickly, while keeping the mouse still
Drag	Pointing to an object on the screen, pressing and holding the left mouse button, and moving the pointer while the button is pressed. Releasing the button ends the drag operation.

The Desktop

igure 1-2 illustrates a typical desktop screen. Your screen may vary slightly from the figure. For example, your screen may display shortcut icons. Or you may have Microsoft Plus installed on your computer, which provides extra features for Windows 95, including creative and whimsical desktops. The main features of the desktop screen are labeled on the figure and discussed below:

- The *Start* button brings up menus that give you a variety of options, such as starting a program, finding help, or shutting down the computer.

- The *taskbar,* located at the bottom of the screen, tells you the names of all open programs. Figure 1-2 shows that Microsoft Word is open.

- *My Computer* is a program that allows you to see what files and folders are located on your computer.

- The *Recycle Bin* is a place to get rid of files or folders that are no longer needed.

- Other *icons,* or small pictures, represent programs waiting to be opened.

FIGURE 1-2
The desktop is organized to help you work productively.

Icons

Start button

Taskbar

Using the Mouse to Explore the Desktop

1. Move the mouse around on your desk (or mouse pad) and watch the pointer move on the screen. Do not press the mouse buttons yet.

2. Point to the **Start** button.

3. Click the left mouse button. A menu of choices appears above the Start button as shown in Figure 1-3.

4. Point to **Settings** without clicking. Another menu appears.

5. Click **Control Panel.** A new window appears. The title bar at the top tells you that *Control Panel* is the name of the open window.

6. Leave this window on the screen for the next activity.

FIGURE 1-3
Clicking the Start button brings up a menu of choices.

Using Windows

Whether a window is a program window or a document window, you can change its shape, size, and location.

Moving and Resizing Windows

Sometimes you will have several windows on the screen at the same time. To work more effectively, you may need to move or change the size of a window. To move a window, click the title bar and drag the window to another location. You can resize a window by dragging the window borders. When you move the pointer to a horizontal border, it changes to a vertical two-headed arrow. When you move the pointer to a vertical border, it changes to a horizontal two-headed arrow. You can then click and drag the border to change the width or height of the window. It is also possible to resize two sides of a window at the same time. When you move the pointer to a corner of the window's border, it becomes a two-headed arrow pointing diagonally. You can then click and drag to resize the window's height and width at the same time.

ACTIVITY

Moving and Resizing Windows

1. Move the Control Panel window by clicking on the title bar and holding the left mouse button down. Continue to hold the left mouse button down and drag the Control Panel until it appears centered on the screen. Release the mouse button.

2. Point anywhere on the border at the bottom of the Control Panel window. The pointer turns into a vertical two-headed arrow.

3. While the pointer is a two-headed arrow, drag the bottom border of the window down to enlarge it.

4. Point to the border on the right side of the Control Panel window. The pointer turns into a horizontal two-headed arrow.

5. While the pointer is a two-headed arrow, drag the border of the window to the right to enlarge it.

6. Point to the lower right corner of the window border. The pointer becomes a two-headed arrow, pointing diagonally.

7. Drag the border up and to the left to resize both sides at the same time until the window is about the same size as the one shown in Figure 1-4.

8. Leave the window on the screen for the next activity.

FIGURE 1-4
It is possible to resize two sides of a window at the same time.

As you can see from the activity you just completed, the pointer is not always the same arrow. The shape of the pointer indicates what the computer is doing. For example, sometimes the pointer turns into an hourglass to indicate that the computer is temporarily busy. When the hourglass pointer appears, wait for the pointer to change back to an arrow, which should not take long depending on the speed and memory capabilities of your computer.

Scroll Bars

A *scroll bar* appears on the edges of a window any time there is more to be displayed than a window can show at its current size. A scroll bar can appear along the bottom edge (horizontal) and/or along the right side (vertical) of a window. Scroll bars appeared in the last step of the previous activity because the window was too small to show all the icons at once.

Scroll bars are a convenient way to move quickly to another part of the window's contents you want to view. On the scroll bar is a sliding box called the *scroll box.* The scroll box indicates your position within the window's contents. When the scroll box reaches the bottom of the scroll bar, you have reached the end of the window's contents. *Scroll arrows* are located at the ends of the scroll bar. Clicking on a scroll arrow moves the window in that direction over the contents of the window.

ACTIVITY

1-4 Scrolling

1. On the horizontal scroll bar, click the scroll arrow that points to the right. The contents of the window shift to the left.

2. Press and hold the mouse button on the same scroll arrow. The contents of the window scroll quickly across the window. Notice that the scroll box moves to the extreme right end of the scroll bar.

3. You can also scroll by dragging the scroll box. Drag the scroll box on the horizontal scroll bar from the extreme right to the extreme left.

4. Drag the scroll box on the horizontal scroll bar to the middle of the scroll bar.

5. Drag the scroll box on the vertical scroll bar to the middle of the scroll bar.

6. Another way to scroll is to click on the scroll bar. Click the horizontal scroll bar to the right of the scroll box. The contents scroll left.

7. Click the horizontal scroll bar to the left of the scroll box. The contents scroll right.

8. Scroll the Control Panel window until the horizontal scroll box is at the extreme left of the scroll bar.

9. Scroll the Control Panel window until the vertical scroll box is at the top of the scroll bar.

10. Resize the Control Panel until the scroll bars disappear.

Other Window Controls

Three other important window controls, located on the right side of the title bar, are the *Maximize button,* the *Minimize button,* and the *Close button* (see Figure 1-5). The Maximize button enlarges a window to full size. The Minimize button shrinks a window to a button on the taskbar. The button on the taskbar is labeled and you can click it any time to make the window reappear. The Close button is used to close a window.

When a window is maximized, the Maximize button is replaced by the Restore button (see Figure 1-6). The *Restore button* returns the window to the size it was before the Maximize button was clicked.

FIGURE 1-5
The Maximize button, Minimize button, and Close button provide efficient window handling.

FIGURE 1-6
The Restore button returns a maximized window to its regular size.

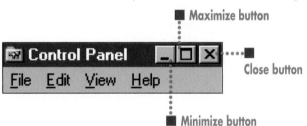

■ Maximize button

■ Close button

■ Minimize button

■ Restore button

ACTIVITY

Maximizing, Restoring, Minimizing, and Closing Windows

1. Click the **Maximize** button. The window enlarges to fill the screen.

2. Click the **Restore** button on the Control Panel window (see Figure 1-6).

3. Click the **Minimize** button on the Control Panel window. The window is reduced to a button on the taskbar.

4. Click the **Control Panel** button on the taskbar to open the window again.

5. Click the **Close** button to close the window.

Menus and Dialog Boxes

To see what a restaurant has to offer, you look at the menu. You can also look at a *menu* on the computer's screen to discover what a computer program has to offer. Menus in computer programs show what your options are and let you choose one of the options. One way menus can be accessed is from the Start button on the desktop, as you have already learned.

When you click the Start button, a menu is displayed with a list of options. If you choose a menu option with a right-pointing arrow, another menu opens that lists additional options. A menu item followed by an ellipsis (…) indicates that a dialog box will appear. A *dialog box,* like the Shut Down Windows dialog box shown in Figure 1-7, appears when more information is required before the command can be performed. You may have to key information, choose from a list of options, or simply confirm that you want the command to be performed. To back out of a dialog box without performing an action, press Esc, click the Close button, or choose Cancel (or No).

FIGURE 1-7
When a dialog box appears, you must provide additional information so the command can be performed.

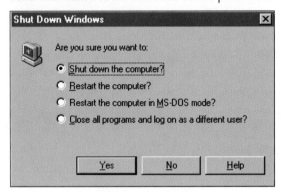

ACTIVITY

Using a Dialog Box

1. Click the **Start** button. A menu appears.

2. Click **Shut Down.** The Shut Down Windows dialog box appears, as shown in Figure 1-7.

3. Click **No** to back out of the dialog box without shutting down.

When a Windows program is open, menus can also be accessed from a menu bar (see Figure 1-8). A *menu bar* appears beneath the title bar at the top of the screen in each Windows program and consists of a row of menu titles. Each title in the menu bar represents a separate pull-down menu. A *pull-down menu* is a list of commands that appears below each title in the menu bar. Pull-down menus are convenient to use because the commands are in front of you on the screen, as shown in Figure 1-8. As you do with a menu in a restaurant, you can view a list of choices and pick the one you want.

You can give commands from pull-down menus using either the keyboard or the mouse. Each item in the menu bar and pull-down menus has an underlined letter called a *mnemonic.* To access a pull-down menu using the keyboard, press Alt + the mnemonic letter shown on the menu title. Using the mouse, place the pointer on the menu title and click the left button.

Just as with the Start button menus, pull-down menus also have items with right-pointing arrows that open other menus and ellipses that open dialog boxes. Choosing an item without an ellipsis or a right-pointing arrow executes the command. To back out of a menu without choosing a command, press Esc or click with the left mouse button somewhere on the screen other than the menu.

FIGURE 1-8

The menu bar at the top of the screen in a program contains menu titles that represent pull-down menus.

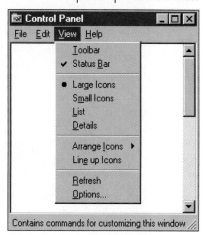

ACTIVITY

1-7   Using Menus

● ●

1. Open the Notepad accessory by clicking **Start, Programs, Accessories, Notepad** (See Figure 1-9).

2. Click **Edit** on the menu bar. The Edit menu appears.

3. Click **Time/Date** to display the current time and date.

4. Click **File** on the menu bar. The File menu appears (see Figure 1-10).

5. Click **Exit.** A Save prompt box appears.

6. Click **No.** The Notepad window disappears and you return to the Windows 95 desktop.

FIGURE 1-9
Menus can be opened by clicking the Start button.

FIGURE 1-10
The File menu offers an alternative
way to exit a program.

Windows 95 Help

This chapter has covered only a few of the many features of Windows 95. For additional information, Windows 95 has an easy-to-use Help system. Use the Windows 95 Help system as a quick reference when you are unsure about a function. Windows 95 Help is accessed through the Help option on the

Start menu. Then, from the Help Topics dialog box, you can choose either to see the table of contents, as shown in Figure 1-11, or to search the Help system using the Index or the Find command. If you are working in a Windows 95 program, you can get more specific help about topics in that program by accessing Help from the Help menu.

FIGURE 1-11
The Help program is a convenient source
of information about Windows 95.

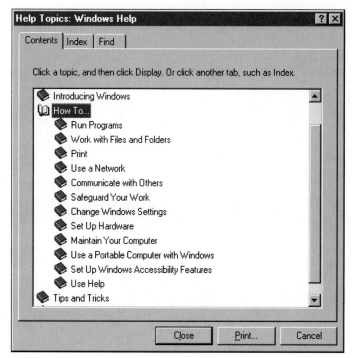

The Contents tab in the Help Topics dialog box is useful if you want to browse through the topics by category. Double-click a book icon to see additional help topics. Double-click a question mark to display a window with detailed help information.

Use the Index tab when you want to search for help on a particular topic by keying a word. Windows will search alphabetically through the list of Help Topics to locate an appropriate match, as shown in Figure 1-12. When you double-click an item in the list, a Topics Found dialog box will appear that displays topics related to the item. Double-click the topic you want to see explained in a Help window.

The Find tab is similar to the Index tab, but will perform a more thorough search of the words or phrases that you key. Using the Find command, you can display every occurrence of a particular word or phrase throughout the Windows 95 Help system. Double-click the topic that seems to be most similar to what you are looking for and a Help window on the subject will appear.

FIGURE 1-12
Key the topic you need help with in the Index.

There are several additional ways to get help. If you are using an Office 95 application, choose Answer Wizard from the Help menu. After you key your question, the Answer Wizard will search for and display a list of topics to help give you an answer. If you are in a dialog box, click the question mark next to the Close button on the title bar, then click the item you would like more information about. A pop-up box appears that displays a brief help message about the item. If you forget what a toolbar button is for, point the pointer at the button for a few seconds and the button name will be displayed.

If you need assistance using the Windows 95 Help program, choose *How To, Use Help* from the Contents tab.

ACTIVITY

Using Help

1. Open the Windows 95 Help program by clicking **Start, Help.**

2. Click the **Contents** tab if it is not already selected.

3. Double-click **How To.** Your screen should appear similar to Figure 1-11. Then double-click **Use Help** in the resulting list.

4. Double-click **Finding a topic in Help.**

5. Read the Help window; then click **Help Topics** at the top of the window.

6. Click the **Index** tab.

7. Begin keying **Close button** until *Close button* is highlighted in the list of index en-tries. Your screen should appear similar to Figure 1-12.

8. Click the **Display** command button at the bottom of the box.

9. Click **Quitting a program** if it is not already highlighted; then click **Display.**

10. Read the Help window; then close the Help program by following the instructions you read in the Help window.

Other Features

There are several other features of Windows 95 that you must know before moving on, including My Computer, Windows Explorer, and the Recycle Bin.

My Computer

As you learned earlier, there is an icon on your desktop labeled My Computer. Double-clicking on this icon brings up the My Computer window, which looks similar to the one shown in Figure 1-13. The My Computer program is

My Computer

helpful because it allows you to see what is on your computer. First double-click the icon for the drive you want to view. A window appears, with that drive's name in the title bar, displaying all the folders and files on that drive.

Because computer disks have such a large capacity, it is not unusual for a floppy disk to contain dozens of files or for a hard disk to contain hundreds or thousands of files. To organize files, a disk can be divided into folders. A *folder* is a place where files are stored on a disk. They help keep things organized on disk just as folders do in a file cabinet. Folders group files that have something in common. You can also have folders within a folder. For example, you could create a folder to group all of the files you

FIGURE 1-13
My Computer shows you the drives, folders, and files located on your computer.

are working on in computer class. Within that folder, you could have several other folders that group files for each tool or each chapter.

When you double-click on a folder in My Computer, the contents of that folder are displayed. There are two types of files—program files and data files. Double-clicking on a program file icon will open that program. Double-clicking on a data file icon opens that document and the program that created it, if it is not already open.

Windows Explorer

Another way to view the folders and files on a disk is to use the Windows Explorer program. To open, click Start, Programs, Windows Explorer. The Explorer window is split into two sides, as shown in Figure 1-14. The left side shows a hierarchical, or "tree," view of how the folders are organized on a disk and the right side shows the files and folders located in the folder that is currently selected on the left side.

Explorer is a useful tool for organizing and managing the contents of a disk because you can create folders and rename, delete, move, and copy files.

Recycle Bin

Another icon on the desktop that you learned about earlier is the Recycle Bin. It looks like a wastebasket and is a place to get rid of files and folders that you no longer need. Until you empty the Recycle Bin, items that have been thrown away will remain there and can still be retrieved.

Now that you have learned the basics of Windows 95, you will get to know Office 95 in the next chapter.

FIGURE 1-14
Clicking a folder on the left side of the Explorer's window will display its contents on the right side of the window.

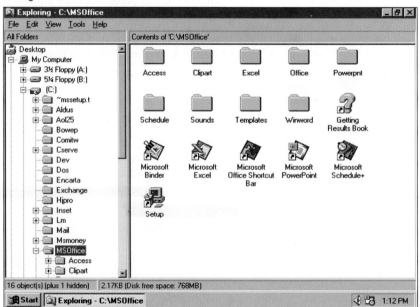

Summary

■ Windows 95 is a graphical user interface (GUI) for IBM and compatible computers. A graphical user interface makes it easier to use a computer. The desktop organizes your work and the Start button brings up menus that give you a variety of options.

■ In Windows 95, program and document windows can be moved, resized, opened, and closed. If all the contents of a window cannot be displayed in the window's current size, scroll bars appear to allow you to move to the part of the window you want to view. Windows can be maximized to fill the screen or minimized to a button on the taskbar.

■ Menus are an important part of Windows 95. Menus allow you to choose commands to perform different actions. Menus are accessed from the Start button on the desktop or from a program's menu bar near the top of the window. When you choose a menu command with an ellipsis (…), a dialog box appears that requires more information before performing the command.

■ The Windows 95 Help program provides additional information about the many features of Windows 95. You can access the Help program from the Start button and use the Contents, Index, or Find tabs to get information. You can also get help from the Help menu within Windows programs.

■ Folders group files that have something in common. To organize a disk, it can be divided into folders where files and other folders are stored.

■ Other useful features of Windows 95 include My Computer, which lets you see what is on your computer; Windows Explorer, which helps organize and manage your files; and the Recycle Bin for deleting unneeded files or folders.

● ● ● ● ● ● ● ● ● ● ● ● ● ●

REVIEW ACTIVITIES

TRUE/FALSE

Circle T or F to show whether the statement is true or false.

T F   1. Windows 95 replaces the previous version of Windows and DOS with one operating system.

T F   2. When Microsoft Windows 95 starts, the desktop appears.

T F   3. Sliding describes the action of holding a mouse button while moving the mouse on a flat surface.

T F   4. The taskbar indicates the position of the mouse.

T F   5. Scroll bars appear when all items in the window are visible.

T F   6. To maximize a window, click the Restore button.

T F   7. A menu item followed by a right-pointing arrow indicates that a dialog box will appear.

T F   8. Each item in the menu bar and pull-down menus has an underlined letter called a mnemonic.

T F   9. The Help system is available from the Start menu.

T F   10. A folder is a place where files and other folders are stored on disk.

COMPLETION

Write the correct answer in the space provided.

1. Name one factor that makes graphical user interfaces easier to use than non-graphical user interfaces, such as DOS.

_____

_____

2. Describe the drag mouse operation.

_____

_____

3. What does it mean when the mouse pointer becomes an hourglass?

_____

_____

4. What button do you click to have the option of starting a program, finding help, or shutting down the computer?

_____

_____

5. How do you move a window?

_____

_____

6. Where is the Close button located?

_____

_____

7. What does the Minimize button do?

_____

_____

8. What is a pull-down menu?

_____

_____

9. What tab would you choose in the Help Topics dialog box to browse through Help topics by category?

_____

_____

10. What is the purpose of the Recycle Bin?

_____

_____

OFFICE 95 BASICS

CHAPTER

2

OBJECTIVES
When you complete this chapter, you will be able to:

1. Explain the concept of an integrated software package.

2. Start an Office 95 application from Windows 95.

3. Understand how to use the Microsoft Office Shortcut Bar.

4. Open an existing document.

5. Save and close an Office 95 document.

6. Know the shortcuts for opening recently used documents.

7. Quit an Office 95 application.

Introduction to Office 95

Office 95 is an integrated software package. An ***integrated software package*** is a program that combines several computer applications into one program. The professional version of Office 95 consists of a word processor application, a spreadsheet application, a database application, a presentation application, a schedule application, and an organization application.

The word processor application (Word) enables you to create documents such as letters and reports. The spreadsheet application (Excel) lets you work with numbers to prepare items such as budgets or to determine loan payments. The database application (Access) organizes information such as addresses or inventory items. The presentation application (PowerPoint) can be used to create slides, outlines, speaker's notes, and audience handouts. The schedule application (Schedule+) increases your efficiency by keeping track of appointments, tasks, contacts, and events.

Because Office 95 is an integrated program, the applications can be used together. For example, numbers from a spreadsheet can be included in a letter created in the word processor or be used in a presentation.

Starting an Office 95 Application

An Office 95 application can be started in several ways: from the Program menu, using the Shortcut Bar, and from the Start menu, among others.

Opening an Office 95 Application from the Programs Menu

To open an Office 95 application from the Programs menu, choose Start, Programs, and then click the name of the application you want to open.

Opening an Office 95 Application Using the Shortcut Bar

Displayed at the top right of the screen is the Microsoft Office Shortcut Bar, shown in Figure 2-1. Using the Shortcut Bar is another way to access an Office 95 application or document quickly. To start an Office 95 application and open a new document at the same time, click the Start a New Document button.

The default buttons on the Shortcut Bar also allow you to open a document that already exists by clicking the Open a Document button; open Microsoft Exchange to send an e-mail message; or open Schedule+ to make an appointment, add a task, or add a contact. With the Office 95 CD-ROM in its

FIGURE 2-1

You can use the Microsoft Office Shortcut Bar to open an Office 95 application and create a blank document at the same time.

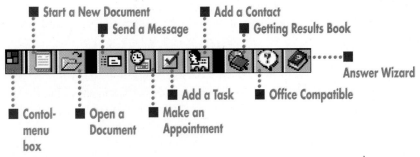

drive, you can click the Getting Results Book button to get instructions and explanations about Office 95 applications, or you can click the Office Compatible button to see a demonstration of products that work well with Office 95 applications. The Answer Wizard button opens the Help program where you can get answers to specific topics by keying a question.

You can customize the Microsoft Office Shortcut Bar to meet your needs by changing, adding, or removing buttons. If you don't want the Shortcut Bar displayed, double-click the Control-menu box on the left to remove it from the screen.

FIGURE 2-2
You can open a new document in an Office 95 application from the Start menu.

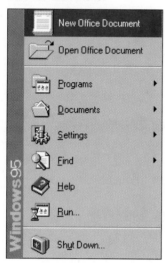

Opening an Office 95 Application from the Start Menu

To open an Office 95 application and create a new blank document within the application at the same time, click the Start button. Then, click New Office Document on the Start menu, as shown in Figure 2-2. In the General section of the New dialog box that appears (see Figure 2-3), double-click the icon for the type of blank document you want to create. The application for that type of document opens and a new blank document is created. For example, if you double-click the Blank Presentation icon, PowerPoint will open and a blank presentation will be displayed on the screen.

FIGURE 2-3
In the General section of the New dialog box you can choose the type of blank Office 95 document you want to open.

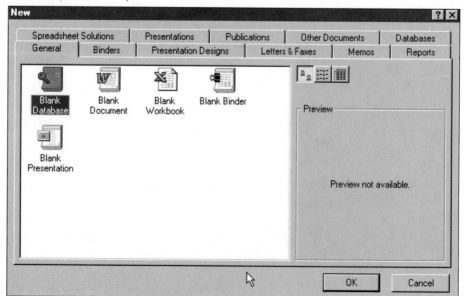

ACTIVITY

Starting Office 95 Applications

• •

1. Click the **Start** button to open the Start menu.

2. Click **Programs;** then **Microsoft Excel.** Excel opens.

3. Click the **Minimize** button on the title bar to reduce Excel to a button on the taskbar.

4. Click the Start button; then click **New Office Document** (see Figure 2-2).

5. The New dialog box appears, as shown in Figure 2-3.

6. Click the **General** tab, if it is not already selected.

7. Double-click the **Blank Document** icon.

8. Word starts and a blank document appears.

9. Leave Word on the screen for use in the next activity.

Opening, Saving, and Closing Office 95 Documents

In Office 95 applications, you *open, save,* and *close* files in the same way. Opening a file means loading a file from a disk onto your screen. Saving a file stores it on disk. Closing a file removes it from the screen.

Opening an Existing Document

There are several ways to open an existing document. You can choose Open from an application's File menu, choose Open Office Document from the Start menu, or click Open a Document on the Shortcut Bar. Any of these methods will display the Open dialog box (see Figure 2-4).

The Open dialog box enables you to open a file from any available disk and folder. The Look in box, near the top of the dialog box, is where you select the disk drive that contains the file you want to open. Below that is a list that shows you what folders are on the disk. Double-click a folder to see the files and folders contained within. To see all the files or Office 95 documents in the

FIGURE 2-4

The Open dialog box can open a file from any available disk and folder.

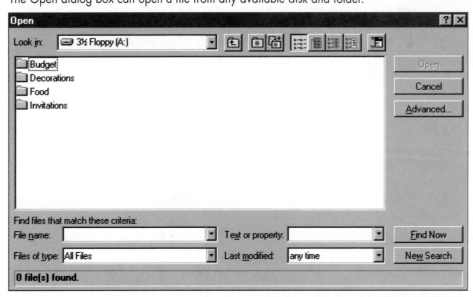

folder instead of just those created with a particular application, choose All Files or Office Files from the Files of type box near the bottom left of the Open dialog box.

ACTIVITY

Opening an Existing File from the File Menu

1. With Word on the screen, choose **Open** from the **File** menu. The Open dialog box appears.

2. Insert your template disk into drive A.

3. Click on the down arrow at the right of the Look in box to display the available disk drives.

4. Click **3½ Floppy (A:).** Your Open dialog box should resemble the one partially shown in Figure 2-5.

5. Double-click the **Employees** folder. The folders within the Employees folder will appear (see Figure 2-6).

6. Double-click the **Rita** folder. The name of the Word file in the Rita folder is displayed.

7. In the Files of type box, click the down arrow and click **All Files.** The names of all files in the Rita folder are displayed.

8. Click on **Schedule Memo.**

FIGURE 2-5
The list below the Look in box shows what folders and files are on the disk.

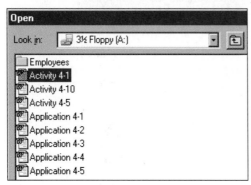

FIGURE 2-6
Within the Employees folder are several additional folders.

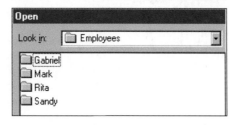

9. Click **Open** to open the file.

10. Leave the file open for the next activity.

You can see how folders can help organize and identify documents. In the same folder as the memo to Rita is a spreadsheet with the work schedule for the first two weeks in September. In the next activity, you will open the spreadsheet that goes with the memo.

ACTIVITY

Opening a File from the Start Button

1. Click the **Start** button.

2. Click **Open Office Document.**

3. With your template disk in drive A, click on the down arrow at the right of the Look in box.

4. Click **3½ Floppy (A:).**

5. Double-click the **Employees** folder; then double-click the **Rita** folder.

6. Click on **September Schedule.**

7. Click **Open** to open the file. *September Schedule* appears on the screen.

8. Leave the file on the screen for the next activity.

Saving a File

Saving is done two ways. The Save command saves a file on a disk using the current name. The Save As command saves a file on a disk using a new name. The Save As command can also be used to save a file in a new location.

Filenames

Unlike programs designed for the early versions of Windows and DOS, Windows 95 does not limit you to eight characters when naming your files. With Office 95, a filename may contain up to 255 characters and may include spaces. Rarely, however, will you need this many characters to name a file. Name a file with a descriptive name that will remind you of what the file contains. The authors of this book have chosen names that are descriptive and easy to use. Follow their examples in naming your files. The filename can include most characters found on the keyboard with the exception of those shown in Table 2-1.

TABLE 2-1
Characters that cannot be used in filenames.

CHARACTER	NAME	CHARACTER	NAME
*	Asterisk	<	Less than
\	Backslash	.	Period
[ ]	Brackets	;	Semicolon
:	Colon	/	Slash
,	Comma	"	Quotation mark
=	Equal	?	Question mark
>	Greater than			Vertical bar

ACTIVITY

2-4 Saving a File with a Different Name

1. *September Schedule* should still be on the screen from the last activity.

2. Take the template disk out of drive A and insert your data disk.

FIGURE 2-7
Use the Save As command to save a file with a new name.

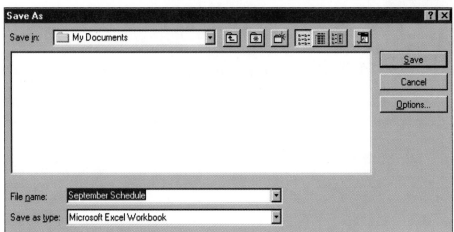

3. Choose **Save As** from the **File** menu. The Save As dialog box appears, as shown in Figure 2-7.

4. In the File name box, key **Sept Work Sched**.

5. Click the down arrow at the right of the Save in box.

6. Click **3½ Floppy (A:).**

7. Choose **Save** to save the file on your data disk with a new name.

NOTE: *If your screen displays an error message, press Esc to clear the screen and continue the Save operation. This message appears because Windows 95 expects the template disk to be in the drive.*

8. Leave the file on the screen for the next activity.

Closing an Office 95 Document

You can close an Office 95 document either by choosing Close from the File menu or by clicking the Close button on the right side of the menu bar. If you close a file, the application will still be open and ready for you to open or create another file.

Closing Office 95 Documents

1. Choose **Close** from the **File** menu. *Sept Work Sched* closes.

2. Click the **Microsoft Word** button on the taskbar to bring it to the screen. *Schedule Memo* should be displayed.

3. Click the **Close** button (X) in the right corner of the menu bar to close *Schedule Memo*.

Shortcuts for Loading Recently Used Files

Office 95 offers you two shortcuts for opening recently used files. The first is to click Documents on the Start menu. A menu will open listing the fifteen most recently used documents. To open one of the recently used files, double-click on it. If the file is on a floppy disk, you must be sure that the correct disk is in the drive.

The second shortcut can be found on each Office 95 application's File menu. The bottom part of the File menu shows the filenames of the four most recently opened documents. The filename with the number 1 beside it is the most recently opened document. When a new file is opened, each filename moves down to make room for the new number 1 file. To load one of the files, you simply choose it as if it were a menu selection. If the document you are looking for is not on the File menu, use Open to load it from the disk.

Quitting an Office 95 Application

The Exit command on the File menu provides the option to quit Word or any other Office 95 application. You can also click the Close button (X) on the right side of the title bar. Exiting an Office 95 application takes you back to the Windows 95 desktop. Always remove your data or template disk before turning off the computer.

ACTIVITY

Quitting Office 95 Applications

1. Word should be on your screen. Pull down the **File** menu. Notice the files listed toward the bottom of the menu. These are the four most recently used files mentioned in the previous section.

2. Choose **Exit.** Word closes and Excel is displayed on the screen.

3. Click the **Close** button in the right corner of the title bar. Excel closes and the desktop appears on the screen.

4. If any other applications are open, click their buttons on the taskbar to display them and then close them.

If You Do Not Finish Before the End of Class

If you need to exit an Office 95 application while working on an activity, save your work on your data disk and exit the application. When you resume work, open the document from your data disk and continue.

Summary

- Microsoft Office 95 is an integrated software package. The professional version consists of a word processor application, a spreadsheet application, a database application, a presentation application, and a schedule application. The documents of an integrated software package can be used together.

- Office 95 applications can be started in several ways: from the Program menu, using the Shortcut Bar, and from the Start menu, among others.

- The Microsoft Office Shortcut Bar provides an easy way to open an application and create a document. Other default buttons also enable you to click to perform tasks quickly. You can customize the Shortcut Bar to meet your needs or you can remove it from the screen.

- You can open an existing document from the File menu, the Start button, or by clicking a button on the Shortcut Bar. The Open dialog box will be displayed, enabling you to open a file from any available disk or directory.

- No matter which Office 95 application you are using, files are opened, saved, and closed the same way. Filenames may contain up to 255 characters and may include spaces.

- Recently used files can be opened quickly by choosing the filename from the bottom of the File menu. Or, choose Documents from the Start menu to list the fifteen most recently used files. To exit an Office 95 application, choose Exit from the File menu or click the Close button (X) on the title bar.

• • • • • • • • • • • • • •

REVIEW ACTIVITIES

TRUE/FALSE

Circle T or F to show whether the statement is true or false.

T F   **1.** An integrated software package is a computer program that combines common applications into one program.

T F   **2.** Office 95 applications are started from the File menu.

T F   **3.** You can customize the Microsoft Office Shortcut Bar by changing, adding, or removing buttons.

T F   **4.** In all Office 95 applications, you open, save, and close files the same way.

T F   **5.** A filename can contain a maximum of eight characters.

T F   **6.** The Save As command saves a file on disk using the current name.

T F   **7.** You can close an Office 95 document from the File menu or by clicking the Close button.

T F   **8.** Choosing Documents from the Start menu will open a menu listing the ten most recently used documents.

T F   **9.** The bottom of the Open menu shows the filenames of the four most recently opened documents.

T F   **10.** Quitting an Office 95 application takes you back to the Windows 95 desktop.

COMPLETION

Write the correct answer in the space provided.

1. List four of the applications that are included in the professional version of Office 95.

   _____

   _____

2. How would you start an Office 95 application from the Programs menu?

   _____

   _____

3. How would you open an Office 95 application and create a new document at the same time?

   _____

   _____

4. Which section *(or Tab)* of the New dialog box do you choose to open a blank document?

_____

5. To open a document that already exists, which button would you click on the Shortcut Bar?

_____

6. What does the Open dialog box enable you to do?

_____

_____

7. In the Open dialog box, how can you tell which files and folders are contained in a folder?

_____

_____

8. What is the difference between the Save and Save As commands?

_____

_____

9. What does closing a file do?

_____

_____

10. Which menu provides the option to exit an Office 95 application?

_____

U N I T

MICROSOFT WORD

WORD PROCESSING BASICS

OBJECTIVES
When you complete this chapter, you will be able to:

1. Identify parts of the Normal view screen.

2. Switch between documents.

3. Enter text.

4. Move the insertion point with the keyboard.

5. Edit text using a variety of Word features.

6. Save a document.

7. Preview a document.

8. Print a document.

Introduction to Word Processing

Word processing is using a computer and software program, such as Microsoft Word, to produce documents such as letters and reports. These documents can be used in your school, career, personal, and business activities. Thanks to today's advanced computers and easy-to-use software, word processing can be done by almost anyone who can use a computer.

Documents created using word processing can be corrected easily before being printed. In addition, word processing allows you to store documents for future use.

One of the most popular word processing programs is Microsoft Word. Word can be used to create simple documents, such as memos, as well as complex documents, such as newsletters with pictures.

The Word chapters contain hands-on activities for you to complete using a computer and Word. After completing all of the activities, you will be able to create and revise your own word processing documents.

Creating a New Word Document

Word processing documents include reports, letters, memos, and outlines. You can create a new Word or Office 95 program document anytime—even if you already have one document open on your screen.

As you learned in Chapter 2, Word can be started from the Office 95 New Office Document button. The New dialog box appears, where you can choose to start any program in Office 95. To start Word, click on Blank Document and click OK.

A screen displaying copyright information will appear briefly, followed by the blank page in Normal view as shown in Figure 3-1. Normal view is where documents are created and edited.

FIGURE 3-1
The Normal view screen appears after you start Word.

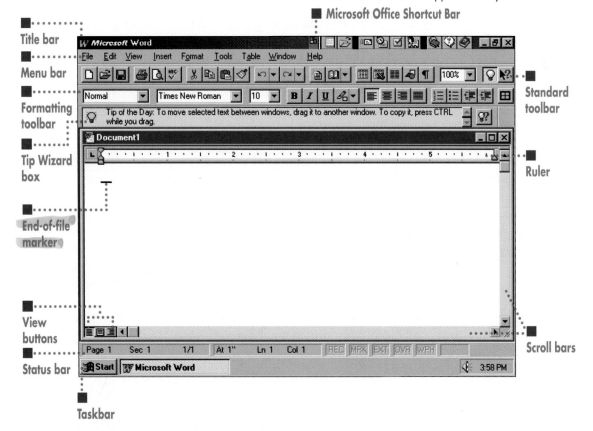

Microsoft Office Shortcut Bar

Title bar

Menu bar

Formatting toolbar

Tip Wizard box

End-of-file marker

View buttons

Status bar

Taskbar

Standard toolbar

Ruler

Scroll bars

Creating a New Document

1. With Windows 95 running, click **Start** on the taskbar.

2. At the top of the Start menu, click **New Office Document.** The New dialog box appears.

3. Click the **Blank Document** icon and click **OK.** Microsoft Word opens and a blank

Normal view screen appears, as shown in Figure 3-1. The document is titled *Document1* until you save it with a new name.

4. Leave the document open on your screen for use in the next activity.

The Normal View Screen

Look carefully at the parts of the Normal view screen labeled in Figure 3-1, then find them on your screen. Many of these elements appear in other Office applications as well, and you will want to become familiar with them. The most important features of the Normal view screen are discussed below.

At the very top of the screen is the ***title bar*** where the name of the program is located. The ***Microsoft Office Shortcut Bar*** is located in the right portion of the title bar. The Shortcut Bar allows you to access other Office 95 documents quickly. The ***menu bar*** is the horizontal bar at the top of the Normal view window. It contains menu titles from which you can choose a variety of word processing commands. The ***standard toolbar,*** located directly below the menu bar, contains buttons you can use to perform common tasks, such as printing and opening documents. The ***formatting toolbar*** contains buttons for changing character and paragraph formatting, such as alignment and type styles. The toolbars use ***icons,*** or small pictures, to remind you of each button's function. If you do not know the function of a toolbar button, move the mouse pointer to the button, but do not click. The name of the function will appear below the button.

The ***TipWizard*** box gives you a Tip of the Day and suggests other tips to help you work faster and more efficiently. Using the ***ruler,*** located directly below the document's title bar, you can quickly change indentions, tabs, and margins. The ***end-of-file marker*** is a horizontal line that shows the end of the document. Just above the end-of-file marker is the blinking insertion point, which shows where text will appear when you begin keying.

The *view buttons* at the lower left corner of the document window allow you to quickly change between Normal, Page Layout, and Outline view. The *scroll bars,* located at the bottom and right sides of the window, allow you to move quickly to other areas of the document. Located at the bottom of the window is the *status bar.* The message in the status bar gives you directions on how to access menus and briefly summarizes the actions of commands that you choose. The Windows 95 *taskbar* is located at the bottom of the screen. It shows all open programs, and the Start button lets you open programs on your computer.

The mouse pointer looks like an I-beam in the text area of the window, but when you move it out of the text area toward the toolbars, it becomes an arrow. It allows you to easily point and click on toolbar buttons and menu names.

Switching Between Documents

One of the most useful features of Word is its ability to open more than one document at a time. While you are working on one document, you can create a new document and work on it. You can switch back and forth as often as you like. Suppose, for example, you are creating a resumé in one document. While the resumé document is on the screen, you can create a new document in which to key the cover letter you will send with the resumé. If you want to send two different cover letters, you can even open a third document in which to key the second cover letter. All the programs in Office 95 allow you to open new documents while you are working on other documents, as you will see later in this book.

Opening a new document is very simple. You click the New button on the toolbar and Word displays the new document on top of the document that is already open. The new document window becomes the active window. The title bar of the active window is a different color or intensity than the title bar of the inactive window. It is easy to move back and forth between documents: Just click on the title bar—or any other visible part—of the document you want to work on, and it will become the active window and move to the front of the screen. You can also choose a document you want to become active in the Window menu. You can enter text only in an active window.

Switching Between Documents

1. Click the **New** button on the toolbar. Another word processing document named *Document2* appears on top of *Document1*, as shown in Figure 3-2. Notice that the title bar of *Document2* is a different color than the title bar of *Document1*, and *Document1* is almost hidden behind *Document2*. This means *Document2* is the active window.

2. Click on the *Document1* title bar and notice that it becomes the active window. *Document2* disappears from the screen because it is now behind *Document1*.

3. To bring *Document2* to the front again, click the **Window** menu. At the bottom of the menu, you will see your two documents listed, with a check mark beside *Document1*. Click **2 Document2.** The menu closes and *Document2* will once again be the active window.

4. Choose **Close** from the **File** menu. The *Document2* window closes and the *Document1* window remains on the screen.

5. Leave the *Document1* window on the screen for the next activity.

FIGURE 3-2
Word lets you easily switch back and forth between documents.

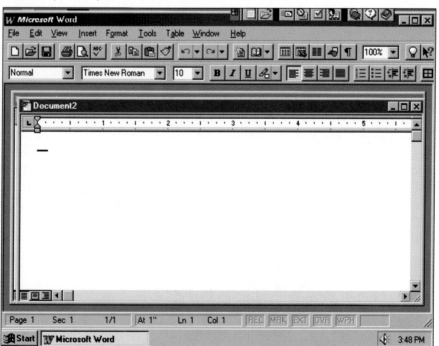

Text Entry and Word Wrap

To enter text in a new document, you begin keying at the insertion point. As you key, the insertion point moves to the right and data in the status bar changes to show your current position on the line. If the text you are keying goes beyond the right margin, it automatically moves to the next line. This feature is called *word wrap* since words are "wrapped around" to the next line when they will not fit on the current line.

Press Enter only to end a line at a specific place or to start a new paragraph. To insert a blank line, press the Enter key twice.

ACTIVITY

 **Keying Text to Observe Word Wrap**

1. Key the text from Figure 3-3 below and watch how the words at the end of each line wrap to the next line as they are keyed.

2. If you key a word incorrectly, Word may underline it with a wavy red line. Just keep keying. You will learn how to correct errors later in this chapter.

3. Leave the text on the screen for use in the next activity.

FIGURE 3-3

> Each day, you should take time to plan and organize the day's work. You can avoid wasted effort and meet your goals when a daily time plan is made.
>
> When making a daily time plan, list all tasks to be completed that day and rank the tasks in order of importance. Record tasks that must be completed that day on a calendar and draw a line through each task as it is completed.
>
> Weekly and monthly time plans also can help you get organized and avoid wasting time. Weekly and monthly time plans can be made following the same steps as those you used for completing a daily time plan.

Moving the Insertion Point

To correct errors, insert new text, or otherwise change your existing text, you need to know how to relocate the insertion point in your document. You can move the insertion point in a document using either the mouse or keyboard commands. For short documents, you may find it faster to move the insertion point using the mouse. To relocate the insertion point, place the I-beam where you want the insertion point to be, then click the left mouse button. The blinking insertion point appears.

When working with a long document, you may find it tedious to use the mouse pointer to move the insertion point as scrolling through a document of several pages can take a long time. In this case, it is faster to use the keyboard to move your insertion point. Table 3-1 shows the keys you can press to move your insertion point both short and long distances.

TABLE 3-1
Keyboard shortcuts for moving the insertion point.

PRESS	TO MOVE THE INSERTION POINT
Right arrow	Right one character
Left arrow	Left one character
Down arrow	To the next line
Up arrow	To the previous line
End	To the end of a line
Home	To the beginning of a line
Page Down	To the next screen
Page Up	To the previous screen
Ctrl+right arrow	To the next word
Ctrl+left arrow	To the previous word
Ctrl+End	To the end of the document
Ctrl+Home	To the beginning of the document

ACTIVITY

3-4 Moving the Insertion Point

1. Move the mouse pointer to the end of the first line in the first paragraph. Click once. The insertion point moves to the end of the line.

2. Move the insertion point to the end of the document by pressing **Ctrl+End.**

3. Move the mouse pointer to the left of the first word in the document. Click once.

4. Move to the fourth word in the first line by pressing **Ctrl+right arrow** four times.

5. Leave the document on the screen for use in the next activity.

Highlighting Text

Highlighting a block of text may also be called *selecting.* Blocks can be as small as one word or as large as an entire document. Once you have selected a block of text, you can edit the entire block at once. This speeds operations such as large deletions and changes to line spacing. You can highlight text using the mouse, combining keys on the keyboard with the mouse, and using the Edit menu.

To highlight text with a mouse, position the I-beam to the left of the first character of the text you want to highlight. Hold down the left button on the mouse, drag the pointer to the end of the text, and release the button. To remove the highlighting, click the left mouse button.

Shortcuts for highlighting text are also available by double-clicking and triple-clicking the left mouse button. *Double-clicking* is when you press the left mouse button two times rapidly. *Triple-clicking* is pressing the left mouse button three times in a row quickly.

Other shortcuts are available by simultaneously using the mouse and pressing a key on the keyboard. *Shift-clicking* is holding down the Shift key while clicking the mouse. You will use shift-clicking in a later chapter to highlight two or more drawing objects. You can also use the Select All command from the Edit menu to highlight an entire document. Table 3-2 lists ways to highlight text.

TABLE 3-2
Methods of highlighting text.

TO HIGHLIGHT THIS	DO THIS
Word	Double-click the word
Line	Click one time in the left margin beside the line
Sentence	Press and hold down Ctrl and click in the sentence
Paragraph	Triple-click anywhere in the paragraph or Double-click in the left margin of the paragraph
Multiple paragraphs	Double-click in the left margin beside the paragraph, then drag to highlight following paragraphs
Entire document	Triple-click in the left margin or Hold down the Ctrl key and click one time in the left margin or Choose Select All from the Edit menu
Objects (two or more)	Press Shift and click on the objects

ACTIVITY

3-5 Highlighting Text

1. Click once to the left of the word *Each* to highlight the first line.

2. Click once anywhere in the document to remove the highlighting.

3. Double-click the word *Each* to highlight it.

4. Click anywhere to remove the highlight.

5. Triple-click the word *Each* to highlight the paragraph.

6. Remove the highlight.

7. Position the insertion point before the *y* in the word *you* in the first sentence. Click and drag to highlight the words *you should take time*.

8. Remove the highlight.

9. Choose **Select All** from the **Edit** menu to highlight the entire document.

10. Remove the highlight.

11. Leave the document on the screen for use in the next activity.

Editing Text

Unless you are an extremely accurate keyboarder, your documents will probably contain a few typographical errors. You may also find, as you read over your text, that you would like to add, delete, or change a word. Microsoft Word offers several ways to make such changes. You can use Cut, Copy, and Paste; AutoCorrect; Automatic Spell Checking; the Backspace and Delete keys; Overtype; and Undo and Redo.

Cutting, Copying, and Pasting Text

At some point when you are editing a document, you will probably wish you had put a certain paragraph last or a specific sentence first. If you do not like where a paragraph is, you can follow a couple of simple steps to move it to a better location. If you especially like the way a sentence reads, you can copy it to other locations using only a few steps.

The feature that makes these moving and copying operations so easy is the Clipboard. The *Clipboard* is a temporary storage place in memory. You send text to the Clipboard by using either the Cut or Copy command from the Edit menu, or by clicking the Cut or Copy buttons on the toolbar. Then you can retrieve that text by using the Paste command. You can paste the Clipboard text as many times as you want. The Clipboard will store the text you send to it until you send another block of copy or until you clear the Clipboard. The Clipboard does not provide long-term storage, as saving a file does. When you turn off the computer, the text in the Clipboard is lost.

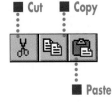

When you want to move text from one location to another, you use the Cut and Paste commands. The Cut command removes the selected text from your document and places it on the Clipboard. The Paste command removes the text from the Clipboard and pastes it at the location of the insertion point in the document. If this sounds like the kind of editing you used to do with scissors, you're right. This operation is often referred to simply as *cutting and pasting*. But it is far easier to do it on the screen than with paper, scissors, and glue.

Cutting and Pasting Text

1. Highlight the first paragraph.

2. Choose **Cut** from the **Edit** menu. The paragraph you selected disappears from the screen. It has been placed on the Clipboard.

3. Position the insertion point at the end of the last sentence of the last paragraph.

4. Insert a blank line.

5. Choose **Paste** from the **Edit** menu. The paragraph appears.

6. Leave the document on your screen for use in the next activity.

The Copy command is similar to the Cut command. When you choose the Copy command, however, a copy of your highlighted text is placed on the Clipboard while the original text remains on the screen. Use the Paste command, as before, to retrieve the copied text from the Clipboard.

Copying Text Using the Toolbar

1. Highlight the first sentence of the last paragraph, which begins, *Each day ...*

2. Click the **Copy** button on the toolbar.

3. Position the insertion point at the beginning of the first paragraph.

4. Click the **Paste** button on the toolbar. Adjust the spacing between the sentences, if necessary.

5. Leave the file on your screen for use in the next activity.

Using Drag and Drop to Copy or Move Text

When copying or moving text a short distance within a document, you can use a quick method called *drag and drop.* To use this method to move text, highlight the text you want to cut. Move the mouse pointer into the highlighted text, then click and hold down the mouse button. A small box appears below the pointer. Using the mouse, drag the text to the location where you want to move or copy the text. As you begin dragging, a dotted insertion point appears. Place this dotted insertion point in the place where you want the data to appear and release the mouse button.

To use the drag and drop method to copy text, perform the same steps as when cutting text but hold down the Ctrl key while dragging. A box with a + (plus) sign will appear below the pointer. When you release the mouse button, the text is placed at the dotted insertion point location, while the originally highlighted text remains unchanged.

ACTIVITY

Using Drag and Drop to Move and Copy Text

1. Highlight the last sentence of the document.

2. Position the pointer over the highlighted text.

3. Click and hold. A dotted insertion point will appear at the pointer and a box will appear below the pointer.

4. Drag the pointer to the end of the second paragraph. Position the pointer after the period ending the paragraph and release the mouse button. The sentence is moved.

5. Highlight the first sentence of the second paragraph.

6. Position the pointer over the highlighted text, then click and hold.

7. Hold down **Ctrl** and drag to place the dotted insertion point after the word *work* at the end of the last paragraph. Then release the mouse button and the Ctrl key. The sentence is copied.

8. Leave the document on your screen for the next activity.

Using AutoCorrect and Automatic Spell Checking

AutoCorrect is a feature of Microsoft Word that automatically corrects errors as you type. It corrects capitalization errors and common spelling errors. It also changes the case of letters used incorrectly in a word. By default, this feature is turned on. You can turn it off in the AutoCorrect dialog box by choosing

FIGURE 3-4
Choose the word from the list of correctly spelled alternatives.

plan, list all tasks to be completed that day and rank the
that must be completed on a calendar and draw a line thro

| completed |
| complied |
| competed |
| computed |
| complete |
| Ignore All |
| Add |
| Spelling... |

pleted task, you will g   shment, wh

plans also can help yo   oid wasting
made following the s   used for cor

AutoCorrect from the Tools menu and removing the check marks beside each automatic correct feature.

Automatic Spell Checking identifies misspellings and words that are not in its dictionary by underlining them with a wavy red line immediately after you key them. To correct a misspelled word that is underlined, position the pointer on the word and click with the *right* mouse button. A list of correctly spelled words appears in a pull-down menu, as shown in Figure 3-4. Click with the left mouse button on the suggestion that you want, and it replaces the misspelled word.

ACTIVITY

3-9 Correcting Words with AutoCorrect and Automatic Spell Checking

1. Place your insertion point before the *E* in the first word of the document.

2. Key the following phrase (with the misspelled word, *beginin*): **at the beginin of**. Notice that AutoCorrect automatically capitalized *At* as the first word in a sentence immediately after you keyed it. The Automatic Spell Checking also detected the misspelled word and underlined it in red.

3. Insert one space between the words *of* and *Each* if there's not one already.

4. Position the I-beam on the underlined misspelled word and click the right mouse button. A pull-down menu appears.

5. With the left mouse button, click on *beginning*, the correct spelling. The misspelled word is replaced with the correctly spelled word and the wavy red underline disappears.

6. Correct any words in your document that are underlined in red.

7. Leave the document open for use in the next activity.

Using the Backspace and Delete Keys

There are two ways to delete characters: by using the Backspace key or the Delete key. Pressing the Backspace key deletes the character to the left of the insertion point; pressing the Delete key removes the character to the right of the insertion point. If you hold down either of these keys, it will continue to remove characters until you release the key. You can also easily remove a number of words or characters by highlighting them, then pressing either Backspace or Delete.

Using the Backspace and Delete Keys

1. Place the insertion point after the *E* in the word *Each* in the first sentence.

2. Press **Backspace** to delete *E*. Key **e** in its place.

3. Place the insertion point after the word *should* in the first sentence of the document.

4. Press **Backspace** until *you should* and the extra blank space before the *y* disappear.

5. In the second sentence, highlight the words *that day.*

6. Press **Delete.** The words disappear.

7. Use the Backspace and Delete keys to correct any additional mistakes you have made.

8. Leave the document open for use in the next activity.

Using the Overtype Mode

In *Overtype* mode, the text you key replaces existing text, or "types over" it. The Overtype mode is especially useful for correcting misspelled words or for replacing one word with another one of the same length. For example, you can replace the *ie* in *thier* with *ei* to correct the spelling of *their* without having to insert or delete any letters or spaces.

Use the Insert key to turn Overtype mode on or off. The Insert key is a *toggle key*—press it once to turn the mode on; press it again to turn the mode off. When Overtype is on, *OVR* will appear in black on the right side of the status bar, as shown in Figure 3-5. After replacing text, turn off the Overtype mode so you do not key over any text you want to keep.

Using Undo and Redo

When editing a document, you will sometimes delete text accidentally or change your mind about a deletion immediately after you have pressed the Delete key. This is when the Undo command is useful. The Undo command reverses a previous command to

FIGURE 3-5
Using the Overtype mode, you can replace text without having to first delete it.

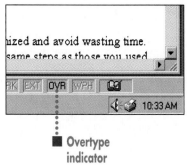

■ Overtype indicator

delete text or change the format of text. The Undo command on the Edit menu, however, will reverse only the most recent change. To use the Undo command, choose Undo from the Edit menu or press Ctrl+Z.

The Undo command on the toolbar is a bit different from the Undo command on the Edit menu. It lists all your recent actions. When you click the arrow next to the Undo button, a drop-down list of your recent actions appears. You can then choose the action you want to undo. Keep in mind that if you choose one from the list, Word will also undo all actions listed above it on the list.

The Repeat command in the Edit menu is similar to the Undo command. Use this command to repeat the action you just performed. The command name changes to reflect the most recent action. Located next to Undo on the toolbar, Redo reverses the Undo command. Like the Undo command, when you click Redo a list of recent actions appears. Choose the action you want to Redo. If you choose an action from the list, Word will redo all actions above it.

ACTIVITY

Using Overtype, Undo, and Redo

1. Position the insertion point after the period at the end of the first paragraph.

2. Insert a blank line and key the following text:

   As you mark off each performed task, you will feel a sense of accomplishment, which will motivate you to complete more tasks.

3. Press **Insert** to turn on the Overtype mode. *OVR* appears in the status bar.

4. Move the insertion point back to the left of the *f* in the word *feel* in the sentence you just keyed. Key **gain**.

5. Move the insertion point to the *p* in *performed* in the same sentence. Key **completed**.

6. Press **Insert** to turn off the Overtype mode.

7. Click the arrow beside the **Undo** button on the toolbar. A drop-down list appears.

8. Scroll down the list and choose **Typing c.** The word *completed* changes to *performed*.

9. Click the arrow beside the **Redo** button on the toolbar. A drop-down list appears.

10. Scroll down the list and choose **Typing d.** The word *performed* changes back to *completed*.

11. Leave the document open for use in the next activity.

Saving a File

The document you see on the screen is temporarily stored in the computer's *random access memory (RAM).* When the computer is turned off, the document is erased from RAM. Therefore, you must save the document to a disk if you want to retrieve it later. When you choose the Save As command, Word stores the document on a hard or floppy disk, where it remains until you remove it. It is a good practice to save the document at intervals (every ten to fifteen minutes) to avoid accidentally losing your work and wasting time redoing a document. However, Word has an Autosave feature that automatically saves your document every ten minutes.

When you save a file for the first time, choose Save As from the File menu or click the Save button on the toolbar. The Save As dialog box appears, as shown in Figure 3-6. The next time you want to save your changes, you can click the Save button on the toolbar or choose Save from the File menu. These commands update the file and do not bring up the dialog box.

To save a file for the first time using the Save As dialog box, click the down arrow to the right of the Save in box and click the drive where you will save your file. Highlight the contents of the File name box, key a filename, and choose Save. In this course, you will save all files to your *data disk* unless your instructor tells you otherwise. This disk should be formatted and blank before you begin to store information on it.

We will assume your computer has a hard disk that is labeled C: and that Drive A will be your floppy disk drive (if not, make the appropriate substitution throughout this book).

FIGURE 3-6

The Save As dialog box lets you choose where and how to save a document.

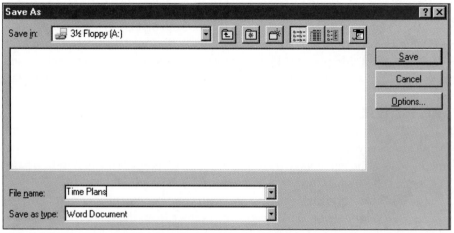

Saving a Document

1. Place your data disk in Drive A.

2. Click the **Save** button on the toolbar.

3. Click on the down arrow at the right of the Save in box to display the available disk drives.

4. Choose Drive A, where you want to save the file, by clicking on the icon labeled **3½ Floppy (A:).**

5. In the File name box, highlight the current entry and key **Time Plans**.

6. Choose **Save.**

7. Word returns you to the document screen. Leave the document on the screen for use in the next activity.

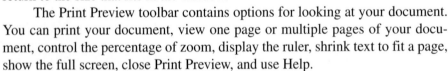

Previewing Your Document

The Print Preview command enables you to see how a document will appear when printed. You can access the Print Preview command from the File menu, or you can click on the Preview button on the toolbar. As shown in Figure 3-7, the pointer changes to a magnifying glass with a plus (+) sign in the middle that allows you to look at the text up close to find mistakes before you print your document. Simply position the magnifying glass where you want to view text up close and click. The screen will be enlarged. The magnifying glass changes to a minus (-) sign. Click on the document again and the document will return to the size that fits in the window.

The Print Preview toolbar contains options for looking at your document. You can print your document, view one page or multiple pages of your document, control the percentage of zoom, display the ruler, shrink text to fit a page, show the full screen, close Print Preview, and use Help.

The Print button allows you to print your document using default settings. The Magnifier button changes the pointer from the magnifying glass to the regular pointer. The One Page button shows one page in Print Preview. The Multiple Pages button lets you choose to view from one to six pages in Print Preview.

FIGURE 3-7

Print Preview has many options for viewing a document before it is printed.

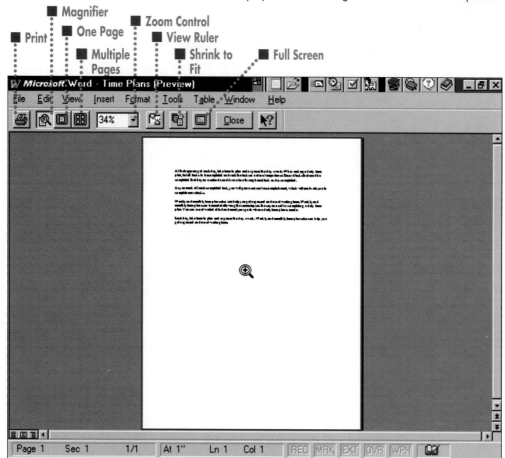

Zoom Control lets you choose from a drop-down menu a percentage of magnification in which to view your document. You can view one page at as much as 200 percent and you can view as many as eleven pages at 10 percent. The Whole Page option lets you view one page; the Two Pages option lets you view two pages at a time. The Page Width option shows the document at its actual width.

The View Ruler button displays the ruler on the Print Preview screen. You can use this ruler to set margins, set tabs, and adjust indents. The Shrink to Fit button changes the type size of a document so that more text will fit on a page.

The Full Screen button maximizes the window so that you can view an entire page on the screen at a larger percentage of magnification than the regular Whole Page view. The Close button exits Print Preview and returns you to your document view. Click the Help button when you need help using these buttons.

ACTIVITY

3-13 Previewing Your Document

1. Choose **Print Preview** from the **File** menu.

2. Click on the text part of the page with the plus sign magnifying glass. The page is enlarged.

3. Click with the minus sign magnifying glass. The page returns to full page view.

4. Click the **View Ruler** button.

5. Click the **Full Screen** button. The window is maximized.

6. Click the **Full Screen** button again. You are returned to full page view.

7. Click the down arrow beside **Zoom Control.** Click **50%**.

8. Click the down arrow again and click **150%**.

9. Click the down arrow again and click **Whole Page.** You are returned to full page view.

10. Choose **Close** on the toolbar to return to the Normal view screen.

Printing Your Document

Y ou can print a full document, a single page, or multiple pages from a document on the screen at any time. The Print dialog box, shown in Figure 3-8, appears when you choose Print from the File menu. The Print dialog box has various options for printing files. You can also print by clicking the Print button on the toolbar in the Normal view screen or in Print Preview, but the Print dialog box won't appear. Clicking the button causes Word to skip the Print dialog box and begin printing immediately.

To print certain pages of a document, simply click the Pages option in the Page range box, then key the range of pages you want to print separated by a hyphen. For example, to print pages 3 through 5 of a document, key *3-5*. When you want to print individual pages, separate them with a comma. For example, to print only pages 3 and 5, key *3,5*. Choose the Current page option to print the page where the insertion point is located. Click the Selection option to print only the highlighted text.

FIGURE 3-8

The Print dialog box contains options for printing parts or all of a document.

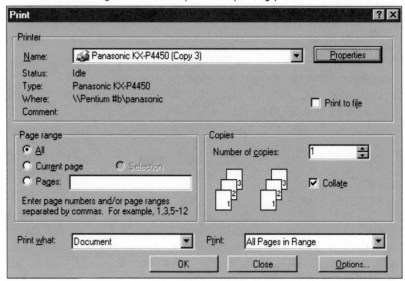

The Copies box allows you to specify the number of copies of the document or pages you are printing. Click the Collate check box to print the first copy of the pages in order (for example, from 1 to 5), then to start the second copy of pages (from 1 to 5). Turn off this option if you want to print all copies of page 1, then all copies of page 2, and so on.

The Print box in the lower right portion of the dialog box allows you to choose to print All Pages in Range, only the Odd Pages, or only the Even Pages.

A C T I V I T Y

Printing a Document

● ●

1. Choose **Print** from the **File** menu. The Print dialog box appears.

2. Print the document by choosing **OK.**

3. Close the document by clicking its Close box.

4. Choose **Exit** from the **File** menu to quit Word.

Summary

- Microsoft Word is a word processing program that can be used to create documents such as letters, memos, and forms. When you start Word, the Normal view screen appears. When text is entered, the word wrap feature automatically wraps words around to the next line when they will not fit on the current line. When corrections or additions need to be made, the insertion point can be placed anywhere within a document using the keyboard or the mouse.

- It is easy to move back and forth between documents: Just click on the title bar of the document you want to work on, and it will become the active window and move to the front of the screen. You can also choose a document you want to become active in the Window menu.

- You send text to the Clipboard by using either the Cut or Copy command from the Edit menu or toolbar. Then you can retrieve that text by using the Paste command. When copying and moving text a short distance, you can use a quick method called drag and drop.

- Automatic Spell Checking identifies misspellings and words that are not in its dictionary by underlining them in red immediately after you key them. AutoCorrect automatically corrects capitalization and common spelling errors as you type. You can delete text using the Backspace key and the Delete key. The Overtype mode allows you to replace existing text with the new text that is keyed. Overtype is especially useful for correcting misspelled words.

- The document that appears on the screen is stored in the computer's RAM. Therefore, it must be saved to a floppy or a hard disk if it is to be retrieved later.

- The Print Preview command enables you to look at a document as it will appear when printed. An entire document or part of a document can be printed at any time.

- The Print dialog box appears when you choose Print from the File menu. You can also print by clicking the Print button on the toolbar in the Normal view screen or in Print Preview, but the Print dialog box won't appear. Clicking this button causes the document to skip the Print dialog box and begin printing immediately

● ● ● ● ● ● ● ● ● ● ● ● ●

REVIEW ACTIVITIES

TRUE/FALSE

Circle T or F to show whether the statement is true or false.

T F **1.** Each time Word is started, a Normal view screen appears.

T F **2.** Parts of the Normal view screen include the insertion point, status bar, and ruler.

T F **3.** When keying text, press the Enter key at the end of each line.

T F **4.** Highlighting blocks of text speeds editing operations.

T F **5.** Overtype is used to correct errors that are underlined in red.

T F **6.** Pressing the Backspace key deletes the character to the left of the insertion point.

T F **7.** You should save your file once every hour.

T F **8.** When a document is saved to a disk, it is stored there permanently and remains there until it is removed.

T F **9.** The Full Screen button in Print Preview allows you to see your document at 150%.

T F **10.** An entire document, one page, or a range of pages can be printed at any time.

COMPLETION

Write the correct answer in the space provided.

1. Which menu is used to switch between documents?

   _____

2. What is the purpose of word wrap?

   _____

   _____

3. What are two ways of positioning the insertion point within a document?

   _____

   _____

4. What is Overtype?

   _____

   _____

5. Which two keys can be used to delete mistakes?

_____

_____

6. How do the Cut and Copy commands differ?

_____

_____

7. Why must documents be saved on a disk if they are to be retrieved later?

_____

_____

8. How do you enlarge a document in Print Preview?

_____

_____

9. Why is Print Preview useful?

_____

10. Which menu contains the Print command?

_____

REINFORCEMENT APPLICATIONS

application 3 - 1

1. Start Microsoft Word.

2. Key the following text:

   The Statue of Liberty was designed as a gift to America. The people of France contributed the $250,000 cost of the statue to memorialize the alliance of France and the U.S. during the American revolution.

3. Use Automatic Spell Checking to correct any words you misspelled while keying.

4. Place the insertion point before *d* in *designed*. Turn on Overtype and key **created**. Use the Delete key to delete the extra *d*. Turn off Overtype.

5. Delete the word *America* in the first sentence and key the words **the United States**.

6. Delete the abbreviation *U.S.* and key the words **United States**.

7. Save the document on your data disk as *Liberty*.

8. Print and close the document.

9. Exit Word.

application 3 - 2

1. Start Word.

2. Key the following text:

   The following list contains ten words that are commonly misspelled:

   business

   address

   environment

   manual

   column

   February

   calendar

   grammar

   noticeable

   receive

3. Use Automatic Spell Checking to correct any words you misspelled while keying.

4. Save the document on your data disk as *Word List*.

5. Preview the document. Close the preview window.

6. Print the document.

7. Exit Word.

application 3 - 3

1. Start Word.

2. Key the following text:

Preparing for a Job Interview

A job interview gives you the chance to sell yourself to a possible employer. To make a good impression, you should prepare for the interview in advance. First, you should learn about the company you are interviewing with and prepare any questions you have about the company.

Prepare a folder containing information you may need during the interview such as names and addresses of former employers, names and addresses of references, a copy of your resume, school records, and your Social Security card.

3. Use what you've learned to correct any mistakes you made when keying.

4. Use the Save command to store the document on your data disk as *Interview.*

5. Preview, print, and close the document.

6. Exit Word.

application 3 - 4

1. Start Word and open *Application 3-4* from the template disk at the same time.

2. Move the Mozart data to the end of the document. Leave one blank line between the Beethoven and Mozart data.

3. Copy the words *German composer* in the first line of the Bach paragraph to the first line (after the date) of the Beethoven paragraph using the drag and drop method.

4. Save the document on your data disk as *Composers*.

5. Print and close the document.

BASIC FORMATTING

OBJECTIVES

When you complete this chapter, you will be able to:

1. Change font, font style, size, color, and case of text.

2. Align text.

3. Change the margins of a document.

4. Adjust indents and line spacing.

5. Set and use tabs.

6. Sort text and numbered lists.

7. Insert Date and Time and use Auto Formatting.

8. Insert page breaks.

9. Insert headers and footers.

Using Fonts

Designs of type are called *fonts*, or typefaces. Just as clothing comes in different designs, fonts have different designs. Like clothing, type can be dressy or casual. When you are creating a document, you should consider what kind of impression you want the text to make. Do you want your document to look dressy or formal? Or do you want it to look casual or informal? The fonts shown in Figure 4-1 would result in four very different looking documents.

It is possible to use many different fonts in one document. However, using more than two or three fonts makes a document look cluttered and hard to read. The fonts available to you are those that are supported by your printer or installed on your computer. Because there are hundreds of different kinds of

FIGURE 4-1
Fonts can give text very different appearances.

This font is called Arial.

This font is called Impact.

This font is called Brush Script.

This font is called Times New Roman.

FIGURE 4-2
Serifs are the small lines at the ends of characters.

■ Serifs

Serif Font: Aa Bb Cc Dd

Sans Serif Font: Aa Bb Cc Dd

printers in use, the fonts mentioned in this book may not be available on your printer. If you do not have some of the fonts suggested for use in this book, use the fonts available to you.

If you look closely at the first line in Figure 4-2, you can see small lines at the ends of the characters. These lines are called *serifs*. If a font has these serifs, it is called a serif font. If a font does not have serifs, it is called a *sans serif* font. Serif fonts are generally considered to be "dressier" than sans serif fonts and are often used for the body of a document. Sans serif fonts are often used for titles, headings, and page numbers.

Changing the Font

Word offers two ways to change the font: using the Font dialog box and using the Font box on the formatting toolbar. To display the Font dialog box, shown in Figure 4-3, choose Font from the Format menu. Click the Font tab to access the Font section of the dialog box. In the box under Font is the current font. Below that, other fonts are listed. Use the scroll bars to locate the font you want, then click on it. The text in the Preview box will change to the chosen font. Click OK.

FIGURE 4-3
The Font dialog box has all the options for changing the appearance of text.

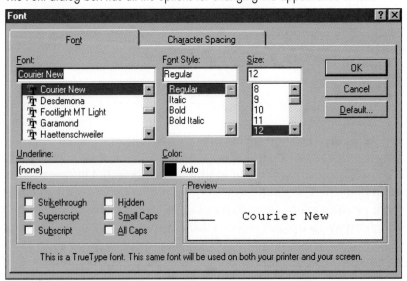

Times New Roman

To change the font using the Font box on the formatting toolbar, simply click the down arrow at the right of the box, scroll to the font of your choice, and click it.

You can change the font of text already keyed by highlighting it first, then choosing a new font. Or, change the font of text not yet keyed by first choosing the font, then keying the text.

A C T I V I T Y

4-1 Changing the Font

1. Open *Activity 4-1* from the template disk.

2. Choose **Select All** from the **Edit** menu to select all the text.

3. Choose **Font** from the **Format** menu. The Font dialog box appears.

4. In the Font box, click **Times New Roman.** You may have to use the scroll bar to locate this font. If Times New Roman is not available, choose a font that looks similar to the text used in this book.

5. Choose **OK.** The text in your document changes to Times New Roman.

6. Click anywhere in the document to remove the highlight.

7. Highlight the title of the document.

8. Click the arrow to the right of the Font box in the formatting toolbar. A list of fonts appears. (If the Font box is not on your screen, choose Toolbars from the View menu. Then, choose Formatting and click OK.)

9. Choose a sans serif font, such as Arial, from the list of fonts. The title appears in the selected font. Click the mouse button to remove the highlight.

10. Save the document on your data disk as *Diet*.

11. Leave it open for use in the next activity.

Changing Font Style

Not only can you change the font, but you can also change the font style. *Font style* refers to certain standard changes in the appearance of a font. Common font styles are bold, italic, and underline. These styles can be applied to any font. You may also combine styles, creating bold italics, for example. Figure 4-4 illustrates some of the styles available in Word.

When you begin keying a document, you are using a regular style. This is the style you will most likely use for the body of your document. However, you

FIGURE 4-4
Fonts can appear in different styles such as regular, bold, italic, and underline.

> This is Times New Roman normal.
> **This is Times New Roman bold.**
> *This is Times New Roman italic.*
> This is Times New Roman <u>underlined.</u>

■ Bold ■ Underline
■ Italic

will probably want to use other styles for particular features in your document. For example, you may want to emphasize your title by applying a bold style to it.

Word allows you to change font styles using the Font dialog box, the toolbar buttons, or shortcut keys. The easiest way to change the style is to highlight the text and click the Bold, Italic, or Underline button on the toolbar. The style will be applied to, or removed from, the selected text. To combine styles, click two buttons in succession, such as Bold and then Italic to create bold italics.

Highlight the text and choose Font from the Format menu to change the font style using the Font dialog box. Click the Font tab if it isn't already chosen. Under Font Style, click one of the styles listed. The text in the Preview box changes to the chosen font style. Choose OK. While the toolbar buttons may be the fastest way to change font style, using the Font dialog box can save you time because you can change the font, font style, size, and other characteristics of text at the same time.

Another way to change font style is to use keyboard shortcuts. Table 4-1 shows keyboard shortcuts that can be used to change font styles.

TABLE 4-1
Keyboard shortcuts for choosing font style.

TYPE STYLE	PRESS
Bold	Ctrl+B
Italic	Ctrl+I
<u>Underline</u>	Ctrl+U
Regular	Ctrl+Spacebar

ACTIVITY

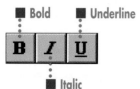
4-2 **Changing the Font Style**

● ●

1. Highlight the title.

2. Choose **Font** from the **Format** menu. Under Font Style, click **Bold.**

3. Choose **OK.** The title changes to bold style.

4. Highlight the word *fat* in the first paragraph, second sentence.

5. Click the **Italic** button on the toolbar. The text changes to italic.

6. Save the document. Leave the document open for use in the next activity.

Changing Font Size

Font size is determined by measuring the height of characters in units called *points*. There are 72 points in an inch. A standard font size for text is 12 point. The higher the point size, the larger the characters. Figure 4-5 illustrates the Arial font in 10, 14, and 18 point. You can change font size by using the Font Size box on the toolbar or in the Font dialog box.

FIGURE 4-5
Different sizes can be selected
within the same font.

> This is Arial 10 point.
>
> ## This is Arial 14 point.

ACTIVITY

4-3   Changing the Font Size

1. Select the entire document.

2. Choose **Font** from the **Format** menu. Under Size, scroll down and click on **14.**

3. Choose **OK.** Remove the highlight.

4. Highlight the title.

5. Click the arrow to the right of the **Font Size** box in the toolbar. A list of font sizes appears.

6. Choose **18.** The title appears in 18 point size. Remove the highlight.

7. Save the document and leave it open for use in the next activity.

Changing Text Color

Word allows you to change the color of text on your screen. Colors are fun to use and can add interesting effects to your documents. If you have a color printer, you can even print your document as it appears on your screen. If you have a printer with black ink or toner only, the document will print in black and shades of gray.

To change the color of text on your screen, highlight the text and choose Font from the Format menu. You can choose the color you want in the Color box.

ACTIVITY

4-4 Changing the Color of Text

● ●

1. Highlight the title.

2. Choose **Font** from the **Format** menu. The Font dialog box appears.

3. Click the arrow under **Color.** A list of colors appears. Scroll down and click **Red.** Notice the characters in the Preview box change to red.

4. Click **OK.** Remove the highlight. The title appears in red.

5. Save the file. Leave it open for use in the next activity.

Changing Case

Case refers to whether letters are capitalized or not. Uppercase letters are capitalized. Lowercase letters are not capitalized. To convert the case of text, simply highlight the text and choose Change Case from the Format menu. The Change Case dialog box, shown in Figure 4-6, appears, listing five choices for changing case. *Sentence case* changes highlighted text to look like a sentence, capitalizing the first letter of the first word and lowercasing the rest of the text. The *lowercase* option lets you change all highlighted text to lowercase; the *UPPERCASE* option lets you change all highlighted text to uppercase. The *Title Case* option changes highlighted text to initial caps—each word in the title is capitalized and other characters are lowercased. The *tOGGLE cASE* option reverses the case of the highlighted text. All capital letters are lowercased and all lowercase text is uppercased. To choose a case option, click the appropriate option button.

FIGURE 4-6
The Change Case dialog box gives you five options for changing the case of text.

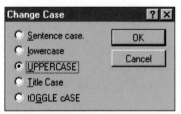

ACTIVITY
4-5 Changing the Case of Text

● ●

1. Highlight the title.

2. Choose **Change Ca<u>s</u>e** from the **F<u>o</u>rmat** menu. The Change Case dialog box appears.

3. Choose **<u>T</u>itle Case.**

4. Choose **OK.** All words begin with a capitalized letter.

5. Highlight the words *In The* in the title.

6. Choose **Change Ca<u>s</u>e** from the **F<u>o</u>rmat** menu. The Change Case dialog box appears.

7. Choose **<u>l</u>owercase.**

8. Choose **OK.** The capitals change to lowercase letters.

9. Save the document and leave it open for use in the next activity.

Aligning Text

Alignment refers to how text is positioned between a document's margins. As Figure 4-7 shows, text can be aligned left, center, right, or justified. Left alignment is the default setting. The type of alignment you use can significantly alter a document's appearance.

Documents are normally aligned left or justified. Long documents are easier to read when aligned left. Centering is often used for invitations, titles, and headings. Right alignment may be used for page numbers and dates.

FIGURE 4-7
Text can be left-aligned, centered, right-aligned, or justified.

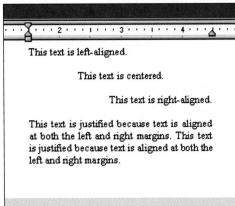

To align text, choose Paragraph from the Format menu. In the Paragraph dialog box, shown in Figure 4-8, choose an alignment from the drop-down list in the Alignment box. However, the easiest way to change alignment is to click the alignment buttons on the toolbar.

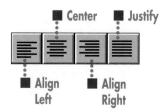

FIGURE 4-8
The Paragraph dialog box allows you to change alignment and other text characteristics.

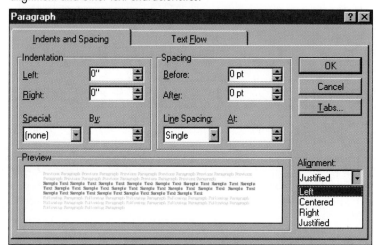

Aligning Text

1. Highlight the title.

2. Choose **Paragraph** from the **Format** menu. The Paragraph dialog box appears, as shown in Figure 4-8.

3. Under Alignment, click the down arrow beside *Justified.* Click on **Centered.**

4. Choose **OK.** The title is centered.

5. Highlight the date above the title.

6. Click the **Align Right** button on the toolbar. The date is right-aligned.

7. Insert a blank line between the date and the title.

8. Highlight the paragraph that begins *Today ...*

9. Click the **Align Left** button on the toolbar. The paragraph is aligned left.

10. Save the document and leave it open for use in the next activity.

Changing Document Margins

Margins are the blank spaces around the top, bottom, and sides of a page. If you do not specify the amount of space to use as margins, Word will set the space to a standard setting, called the *default margins.* Sometimes, however, you will want different margins. For example, if you plan to bind a document along the left side of the page, you will need a larger left margin to make room for the binding.

The margins of a document are changed in the Page Setup dialog box, shown in Figure 4-9. Notice how the Page Setup dialog box is divided into four sections. Each section has a tab you can click to access it. You can change settings in more than one section before clicking OK.

To change the margin settings, highlight the current entry beside Top and key a new measurement. Press Tab to go to Bottom, the next setting. As you press Tab, notice the Preview document's margins change to show the new margin settings. After you change the measurements for Top, Bottom, Left, and Right, click OK.

FIGURE 4-9

The Page Setup dialog box contains the settings for a document's margins.

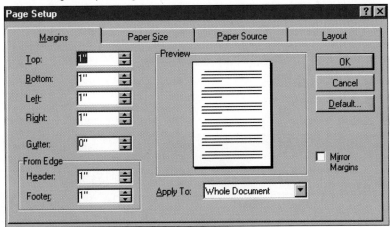

ACTIVITY

4-7 Setting Margins

1. Preview the document to see the margins. Close Print Preview.

2. Choose **Page Setup** from the **File** menu. The Page Setup dialog box appears.

3. Change the Top margin to 1.25 inches by keying **1.25**.

4. Press **Tab** to go to the Bottom margin setting. Notice the sample document's margins change as you press Tab.

5. Key **1.25** in the Bottom margin setting.

6. Using the instructions in steps 3–5, change the Left margin setting to **1.5** and the Right margin setting to **1.25**.

7. Choose **OK.**

8. Preview the document. Close Print Preview.

9. Save and leave the document open for the next activity.

Changing Indents and Spacing

An *indent* is the space you place between text and a document's margin. You can indent text either on the left margin, right margin, or on both the left and right margins. You can indent text by using the indent markers on the ruler, shown in Figure 4-10.

FIGURE 4-10
The indent markers are located on the ruler.

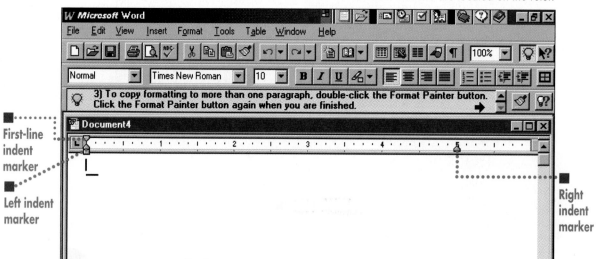

First-line indent marker

Left indent marker

Right indent marker

The first-line indent marker is the upper triangle at the left edge of the ruler. The lower triangle is the left indent marker. The right indent marker is the lower triangle located at the right edge of the ruler. To indent text, position the cursor in the text you want to indent, then simply drag one of these markers to the desired point on the ruler.

The first-line indent and the left indent are often used together, so they sometimes move at the same time. To move them at the same time, click the rectangle below the left indent marker, then drag. To move the left indent marker without moving the first-line indent marker, click the left indent marker and drag.

Setting a First-Line Indent

Changing the first-line indent gives you many different ways to vary the look of your text. Using the first-line indent marker, you can indent paragraphs as you enter text, as shown in Figure 4-11.

Setting a Hanging Indent

You can also create *hanging indents* in which the first full line of text is followed by indented lines, as shown in Figure 4-12. To set a hanging indent, drag the left indent marker to the right of the first-line indent marker.

FIGURE 4-11

You can create indented paragraphs automatically using the first-line indent marker.

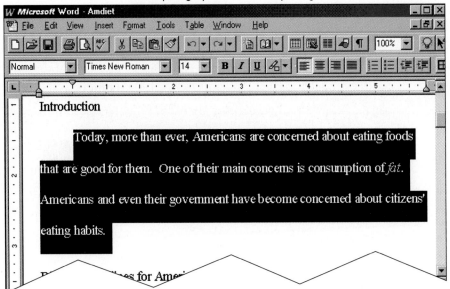

FIGURE 4-12

You can create hanging indents using the first-line indent marker and the left indent marker.

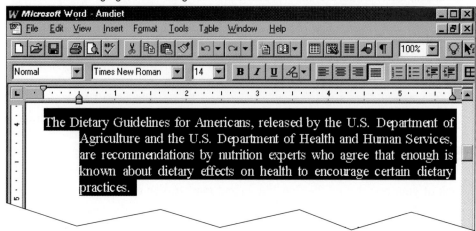

Indenting from Both Margins

Indenting from both margins, as shown in Figure 4-13, is useful for setting off paragraphs from the main body of text.

FIGURE 4-13

You can indent from both margins by moving all the indent markers.

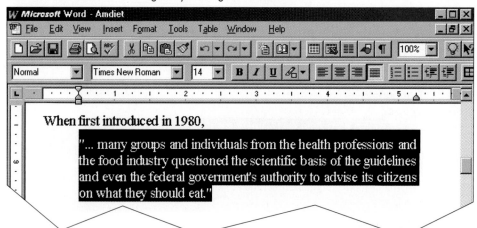

ACTIVITY

4-8 Indenting Text

● ●

1. Highlight the first paragraph.

2. Click on the first-line indent marker and drag it to the $\frac{1}{2}$-inch mark. You have created a first-line indent.

3. Click anywhere in the document to remove the highlight.

4. Highlight the next paragraph after the *Dietary Guidelines for Americans* heading.

5. Click and drag the left indent marker to the $\frac{1}{2}$-inch mark. You have created a hanging indent.

6. In the next paragraph, place the insertion point after the space following *1980,* and press **Enter.**

7. Now place the insertion point after the space following *eat."* and press **Enter.**

8. Highlight the quotation.

9. Click on the rectangle below the left indent marker and drag both the first-line indent and left indent markers to the $\frac{1}{2}$-inch mark. You have created a left indent.

10. Drag the right indent marker to the $5\frac{1}{4}$-inch mark. You have created a right indent.

11. Save the document. Leave it open for use in the next activity.

Adjusting Line Spacing

Line spacing refers to the amount of space between lines of text, as shown in Figure 4-14. By default, Word single-spaces text. Single-spacing

FIGURE 4-14
Word offers a number of spacing options.

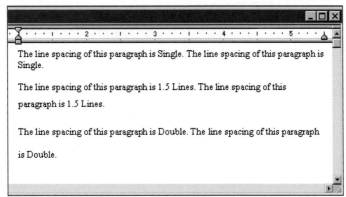

does not leave extra space between each line. Single-spacing is often used for business letters.

To make text more readable, you can add space between lines of text. Double-spaced text has a full blank line between each line of text.

You can change spacing by choosing Paragraph from the Format menu to add any amount of space you want, or you can change to a common line space by using the keyboard shortcut keys shown in Table 4-2.

Another way to increase the readability of a page is to add spaces between the paragraphs. Word lets you add space before or after paragraphs, and you can decide how much space in each place. To add paragraph space, you must access the Paragraph dialog box and change the values in the Before or After box of the Spacing area.

TABLE 4-2
Spacing keyboard shortcuts.

LINE SPACE OPTIONS	SHORTCUT
1	Ctrl+1
1½	Ctrl+5
2	Ctrl+2

ACTIVITY

4-9 Changing Line Spacing

1. Highlight the first paragraph.

2. Choose **Paragraph** from the **Format** menu. The Paragraph dialog box appears.

3. In the Spacing box under Line Spacing, click the arrow beside *Single*.

4. Click on **Double**.

5. Choose **OK**. The paragraph is double-spaced.

6. Highlight the two paragraphs under the *Dietary Guidelines for Americans* heading.

7. Choose **Paragraph** from the **Format** menu. The Paragraph dialog box appears.

8. In the Spacing box beside *Before*, click the up arrow; *0 pt* should change to *6 pt*.

9. Choose **OK**. The extra space is inserted before each paragraph.

10. Save the document and close it.

Setting Tabs

Tabs mark the place where the insertion point will stop when the tab key is pressed. Tabs are useful for creating tables or aligning numbered items. Default tabs in Word are set every half inch. Text can be aligned with decimal, left-aligned, right-aligned, or centered tabs, as shown in Figure 4-15. Notice that different tab symbols appear over the different types of tab settings.

FIGURE 4-15
Use tabs to align columns in a table or list.

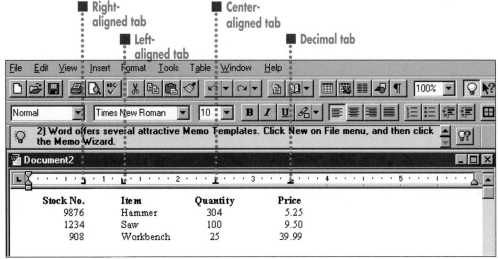

A tab may be preceded by a line of periods or dashes called *dot leaders,* which begin at the end of text and extend to the tab setting. Sometimes these are used with tables of contents. Dot leaders can be used with any tab.

To set tabs, highlight the text you want to be affected by the tab and choose Tabs from the Format menu. The Tab dialog box appears, as shown in Figure 4-16. Key the tab stop position, choose a tab alignment, then choose what kind of leader you want. Click Set to set the tab. After setting the tabs you want, click OK.

The Clear button allows you to clear a tab listed in the Tab Stop Position box. Use the Clear All button to clear all the tabs listed.

Another way to set tabs is by clicking the tab box at the far

FIGURE 4-16
The Tabs dialog box allows you to specify exactly where you want your tabs to appear.

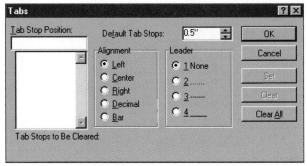

left of the ruler. Each time you click, it changes to another type of tab—left, right, center, and decimal. When it changes to the tab you want, click on the ruler at the measurement where you want to set the tab. The tab appears at the place you click on the ruler.

ACTIVITY 4-10 **Setting Tabs**

1. Open *Activity 4-10* from the template disk.

2. Display the ruler, if it isn't showing already, by choosing **Ruler** from the **View** menu.

3. Highlight all data except the title.

4. Choose **Tabs** from the **Format** menu. The Tabs dialog box appears as shown in Figure 4-16.

5. Choose **Clear** to clear the -0.5 tab.

6. Set a left tab at 2 inches by keying **2** in the Tab Stop Position box.

7. In the Alignment box, choose **Left** if it isn't chosen already, and in the Leader box, choose **None** if it isn't chosen already.

8. Choose **Set.**

9. Key **4.25**.

10. In the Alignment box, choose **Decimal** and in the Leader box, choose **2.**

11. Choose **Set.**

12. Choose **OK.** The dialog box disappears and the items in the document are lined up at the tabs you set.

13. Save the document as *Wish List.*

14. Leave the document open for use in the next activity.

Sorting Text in a Document

Sorting arranges a list of words in ascending order (*a* to *z*) or in descending order (*z* to *a*). It can also arrange a list of numbers in ascending (smallest to largest) or in descending (largest to smallest) order. Sorting is useful for putting lists of names in alphabetic order.

To sort text in a document, choose Sort Text from the Table menu. The Sort Text dialog box appears, as shown in Figure 4-17. In this dialog box, you can choose the options for the sort.

FIGURE 4-17
You can sort text and numbers using the Sort Text dialog box.

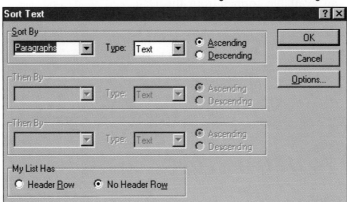

ACTIVITY

4-11 Sorting a List

1. Highlight the list. Do not highlight the title.

2. Sort the list in ascending order by price, following these steps:
   a. Choose **Sort Text** from the **Table** menu. The Sort Text dialog box appears.
   b. In the Sort By box, choose **Paragraphs** if it isn't chosen already.
   c. In the Type box, choose **Number.**
   d. Choose **Ascending** if it's not already selected.
   e. Click **OK.** The list is sorted in ascending order by price and the list is now single-spaced. (Several blank lines may be added between the list and the title.)

3. Sort the list in ascending alphabetic order following these steps:

   a. With the list still highlighted, choose **Sort Text** from the **Table** menu. The Sort Text dialog box appears.
   b. In the Sort By box, choose **Paragraphs** if it isn't chosen already.
   c. In the Type box, choose **Text** if it isn't chosen already.
   d. Choose **Ascending** if it isn't chosen already.
   e. Click **OK.** The list is sorted in ascending alphabetic order.

4. Delete all but one blank line between the title and the list.

5. Save the document.

6. Print and close the document.

Inserting the Date and Time

You can insert the current date and time into your word processing documents easily by choosing Date and Time from the Insert menu and choosing an available format from the Date and Time dialog box, shown in Figure 4-18. Being able to insert the current date and time is especially useful for including the date in a letter or memo—each time you open the document, the current date will be shown.

FIGURE 4-18
The Date and Time dialog box contains many different formats for the current date and time.

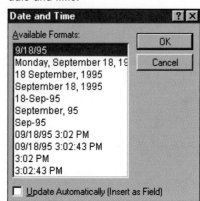

Using Automatic Formatting

When you use the AutoFormat As You Type feature, Microsoft Word automatically applies built-in formats to text as you type. For example, if you type the number 1, a period, press Tab, then key text, Word automatically formats the text for a numbered list. Similarly, if you type a bullet, press Tab, and key text, Word formats that text as a bulleted list. Word also changes fractions and numbers such as *3/4* to $\frac{3}{4}$ and *31st* to *31st* as you key.

You can turn AutoFormat As You Type on and off using the Options command in the Tools menu. AutoFormat As You Type is on by default.

ACTIVITY

4-12 AutoFormatting Text As You Type

1. Start a new Word document.

2. Make sure AutoFormat As You Type is on by choosing **Options** from the **Tools** menu.

3. Click the **AutoFormat** tab. Below Show Options For, click the button beside *Auto-*

Format As You Type if it isn't chosen already.

4. In the Apply As You Type box, click to insert a check mark (if it's not there already) in the boxes beside *Automatic Numbered Lists* and *Automatic Bulleted Lists*. The Borders box may also be checked.

5. Click **OK.**

6. Key **To Do List--**. (The two hyphens may be converted to a dash automatically.)

7. Choose **Date and Time** from the **Insert** menu. The Date and Time dialog box appears.

8. Highlight the second choice in the list (for example *Friday, September 15, 19--*). Click **OK** and press **Enter.**

9. Key **1.** and press **Tab.** Key **Go to the bank**.

10. Press **Enter.** Notice how Word automatically formats the text for a numbered list.

11. Key the remaining items in the To Do List shown below. Notice that you do not have to key the numbers.

    2. **Pick up dry cleaning.**
    3. **Meet Terry for lunch.**
    4. **Study for Spanish test.**

12. After you key the fourth item, press **Enter** twice to stop the numbered list formatting.

13. Key **Test** and press **Enter.**

14. Key ***** and press **Tab.** Key **Conjugate verbs.**

15. Press **Enter.** Notice how Word automatically changes the asterisk to a bullet and formats the text for a bulleted list.

16. Key the remaining items under *Test* shown below. You do not have to key the bullets.

    • **Work on accents.**
    • **Practice conversation.**

17. After keying the third item in the list, press **Enter** twice to stop the bulleted list formatting.

18. Save the document as *Auto Format Lists*.

19. Leave the document on the screen for use in the next activity.

If you choose to turn off AutoFormat As You Type, you can still apply the numbered and bulleted list formats using AutoFormat buttons on the toolbar. Simply highlight data you want to change and click the Numbering or Bullets button on the toolbar.

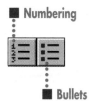

■ Numbering

■ Bullets

ACTIVITY 4-13 Using AutoFormats

1. Choose **Options** from the **Tools** menu. The Options dialog box appears.

2. Click the **AutoFormat** tab.

3. In the Apply As You Type box, click in the box to remove the checkmark beside *Automatic Numbered Lists*. Apply As You Type (Automatic Numbered Lists) is now turned off.

4. Click **OK**.

5. Key **Grocery List** and press **Enter.**

6. Key **1.** and press **Tab.** Key **Bananas** and press **Enter.** Notice that Word does not automatically format the list.

7. Key the remaining items in the Grocery List shown below.

   2. **Orange juice**

   3. **Bread**

   4. **Butter**

8. Highlight the four items in the list. Do not highlight the title, *Grocery List.*

9. Click the **Numbering** button on the toolbar. Word formats the list using the Numbered List AutoFormat.

10. Save the document.

11. Print and close the document.

Inserting Page Breaks

When a document has more text than will fit on one page, Word must select a place in the document to end one page and begin the next. The place where one page ends and another begins is called a ***page break.*** Word automatically inserts page breaks where they are necessary. You also can insert a page break manually. You would want to do this when an automatic page break separates a heading from the text that follows it. To insert a page break manually, choose Break from the Insert menu, then choose Page Break. To delete manual page breaks, highlight the page break line and press the Backspace or Delete key.

In Normal view, an automatic page break is a dotted line across the page. A manual page break is also shown by a dotted line across the page, but it has the words *Page Break* in the middle, as shown in Figure 4-19.

FIGURE 4-19
Page Breaks separate one page from another.

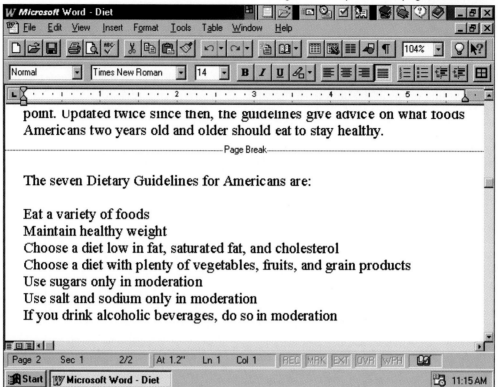

Inserting Page Breaks

1. Open *Diet* from your data disk.

2. Place the insertion point on the blank line before the list that begins, *The seven Dietary Guidelines …*

3. Choose **Break** from the **Insert** menu. The Break dialog box appears.

4. In the Insert box, **Page Break** should be selected. Choose **OK.** The dotted line with

the words *Page Break* in the middle indicates that a manual page break has been inserted. The list is now on page 2 of the document.

5. Save the document. Leave it open for the next activity.

Inserting Headers and Footers

Headers and footers allow you to repeat information, such as your name and the page number, on each page of a document. Word has many header and footer options. You can even create separate headers and footers for even and odd pages. A *header* is text that prints at the top of each page; a *footer* is text that prints at the bottom of the page, as shown in Figure 4-20.

FIGURE 4-20
Headers contain text that is printed at the top of a page, whereas footers are printed at the bottom of a page.

J&D Enterprises Annual Report   September 8, 199-

Page 1

Insert headers and footers by choosing Header and Footer from the View menu. Headers and footers have their own formatting toolbar that appears when you choose the Header and Footer command. The toolbar, shown in Figure 4-21, contains formatting buttons you can use to insert the date, time, and page numbers. Other buttons make it easy to access the Page Setup dialog box and to switch between the header and footer.

FIGURE 4-21
The Header and Footer toolbar contains many options for creating headers and footers.

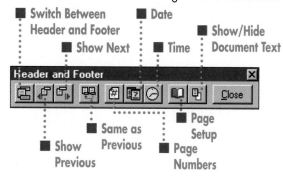

ACTIVITY

4-15 Working with Headers and Footers

1. Move the insertion point to the beginning of the document.

2. Choose **Header and Footer** from the **View** menu. Your document is changed to Page Layout view and your insertion point is in the header pane. A Header and Footer toolbar appears. Your document should look similar to Figure 4-22.

3. Click the **Page Setup** button on the Header and Footer toolbar. The Page Setup dialog box appears.

4. Click the **Margins** tab. Change the left margin to 1.25 inches. Click **OK.**

5. Key **Your Name** in the header. (You may need to move the Header and Footer toolbar out of your way, to the top of the window. Just click the title bar and drag.)

6. Press **Tab.** Click the **Date** button on the Header and Footer toolbar. The Date appears.

FIGURE 4-22
The Header and Footer toolbar lets you add options to your header or footer.

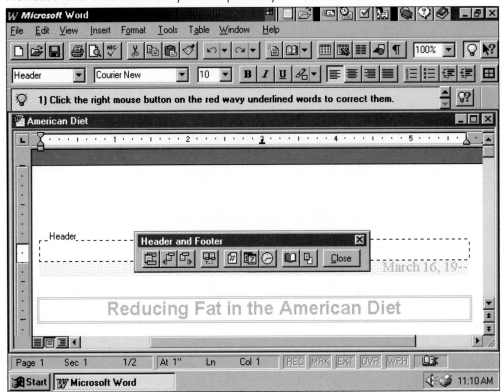

7. Press **Tab.** Click the **Page Number** button on the Formatting toolbar. The number *1* is inserted.

8. Switch to the Footer pane by clicking the **Switch Between Header and Footer** button. The insertion point appears in the footer pane.

9. Press **Tab** to move the insertion point to the centered tab.

10. Key **American Diet**.

11. Highlight the footer data you just keyed. Change the font to Times New Roman 10 point.

12. Click the **Switch Between Header and Footer** button to go back to the header. Change the font of the header data to Times New Roman 10 point.

13. Click the **Close** button on the toolbar.

14. Choose **Page Layout** from the View menu.

15. Scroll to the top and bottom of the page. The header and footer text you keyed is shown in light gray text.

16. Save and print the document.

17. Close the document and exit Word.

Summary

- If you do not specify the amount of space to use as margins, Word will set the space to a standard setting, called the default margins.

- Serif fonts are generally considered to be "dressier" than sans serif fonts and are often used for the text portion of a document. Sans serif fonts are often used for titles, headings, and page numbers. Common font styles are bold, italic, and underline. These styles can be applied to any font. Font size is measured in points. A point is about $1/72^{nd}$ of an inch. The higher the point size, the larger the characters. Changing case changes the case of highlighted text.

- You can align text by choosing Paragraph from the Format menu or by clicking the buttons on the toolbar. Single-spacing does not have extra space between each line. Double-spacing leaves one full line space between each line of text.

- Text can be aligned with decimal, left-aligned, right-aligned, or centered tabs. Dot leaders can be used with any kind of tab. Sorting arranges a list of words or numbers in ascending order or in descending order.

- The date and time command is especially useful for including the date in a letter or memo. AutoFormat As You Type automatically applies built-in formats to text as you type. If you choose to turn off AutoFormat As You Type, you can still apply the numbered and bulleted list formats using the toolbar. You can indent text either on the left or right margin, or on both the left and right margins.

- Word automatically inserts page breaks where necessary. You also can insert a page break manually. To do this, choose Break from the Insert menu and choose Page Break.

- Headers and footers have their own formatting toolbar that appears when you choose the Header and Footer command. The Header and Footer toolbar contains formatting buttons you can use to insert the date, time, and page numbers.

● ● ● ● ● ● ● ● ● ● ● ● ●

REVIEW ACTIVITIES

TRUE/FALSE

Circle T or F to show whether the statement is true or false.

T   F   **1.** The higher the point size, the smaller the characters.

T   F   **2.** Serif fonts usually are used for titles and headings.

T   F   **3.** Double-spacing leaves one full blank line between each line of text.

T   F   **4.** Default tabs in Word are set every inch.

T   F   **5.** Ascending order means sorting text from *a* to *z*.

T   F   **6.** If you do not specify the amount of space to use as margins, Word will set the space to a standard setting, called the default margins.

T   F   **7.** You can turn off AutoFormat As You Type in the Options dialog box of the Tools menu.

T   F   **8.** The right indent marker is the lower triangle located at the left edge of the ruler.

T   F   **9.** A manual page break is shown by a dotted line with the words *Page Break* in the middle.

T   F   **10.** The Header and Footer toolbar allows you to access the Print command.

COMPLETION

Write the correct answer in the space provided.

1. What are the units of measurement that determine type size?

_____

2. What are margins?

_____

3. What is the easiest way to align text?

_____

4. What is a hanging indent?

_____

5. What are dot leaders?

_____

6. In what menu is the Sort Text command?

_____

7. What are the steps for inserting the date and time into text?

_____

8. What are two things AutoFormat As You Type changes as you key?

_____

9. What do automatic page breaks look like in Normal view?

_____

10. What is the difference between headers and footers?

_____

▼REINFORCEMENT APPLICATIONS

application 4-1

1. Open *Application 4-1* from the template disk.
2. Select all the text.
3. Change the font to Times New Roman.
4. Change the font size to 11 point.
5. Bold the first word of the document, *Friends*.
6. Italicize the last sentence of the document.
7. Save the document as *Friends* on your data disk.
8. Print and close the document.

application 4-2

1. Open *Composers* from your data disk.
2. Select all the text.
3. Change the font size to 12.
4. Highlight the title and change it to 14 point.
5. Change the case of the title to all uppercase letters.
6. Change the font of the title to Arial or another sans serif font.
7. Change the color of the title to blue.
8. Bold each composer's full name.
9. Change all the margins to 1.5 inches.
10. Save the document as *Great Composers* on your data disk.
11. Print and close the document.

a p p l i c a t i o n 4 - 3

1. Open *Application 4-3* from your template disk.

2. Left-align the entire document.

3. Center and boldface the title.

4. Double-space the first paragraph.

5. Indent the first line of the first paragraph .25 inches.

6. Leave one blank line after the second paragraph, and key the following items using Auto-Format As You Type to format the bulleted list:

   Social Security card
   names and addresses of former employers
   names and addresses of references
   a copy of your resume
   school records

7. Highlight the bulleted list and sort the text in ascending order.

8. Save the document on your data disk as *Interview Preparation.*

9. Print and close the document.

a p p l i c a t i o n 4 - 4

1. Open *Application 4-4* from your template disk.

2. Replace *(Insert Your Name)* with your name. Follow the handwritten instructions on Figure 4-23 to format this document.

3. Save the document as *Johnson Memo.*

4. Print and close the document.

FIGURE 4-23

Change top margin
to 1.5 inches

Insert right-aligned tab
at 1 inch and left-aligned tab   MEMORANDUM   ← Change to 12 pt bold
at 1.25 inches

Bold ⌐ To: (Insert Your Name)
       From: Janice Johnson
       Date: Friday, July 11, 19-- ←   ⌐ Double-space
       Subject: Things To Do Next Week ⌐ Insert current date

Bold → Monday
1. Finish formatting financial report and send to finance department.
2. Proofread job announcement and fax to the newspaper.
3. Write a letter to Office Products Etc. about receiving the incorrect toner cartridges.
4. Attend the marketing meeting at 10 a.m. and take notes.
5. Key notes taken at marketing meeting.

Tuesday
1. Write a news release about the vice president's speech and send to publications department for the newsletter.
2. Attend Professional Partners lunch and take notes for me.
3. Key notes taken at lunch.

Wednesday
1. Prepare two hours of training for the new word processing operator who comes in on Thursday.
2. Send memo to mail room about misdirected mail.
3. Develop a list of phone numbers and extensions for entire office so we don't have to keep spending time looking these up.
4. Have list of questions and messages ready for me when I call at 11 a.m. Give me highlights from Monday's marketing meeting.

Thursday
1. Make photocopies of phone list and distribute in office.
2. Call Paper Plus and order copy paper.
3. Research the prices for a new high-speed copier and prepare a brief report.
4. Order new stapler and paper clips from Office Supply House.

Friday
1. Key and distribute letters to partners about new parking arrangements.
2. Pick me up from the airport at 3:38 p.m. Let me know if there are any important items I need to take care of before 5 p.m.

Format each numbered list
using the Numbering AutoFormat

a p p l i c a t i o n   4 - 5

1. Open *Application 4-5* from your template disk.

2. Center the first three lines of the document (including the date).

3. Highlight the line that begins, *The members of ...*

4. Create a left indent at 2 inches.

5. Insert a footer with your initials and the date left-aligned. Insert the page number at the 6-inch right tab.

6. Change the font and size of the footer text to Times New Roman 10 point.

7. Close the footer.

8. Save the document as *Meeting Minutes*.

9. Print and close the document.

Advanced Word Processing Features

CHAPTER 5

OBJECTIVES
When you complete this chapter, you will be able to:

1. Format text into columns.
2. Draw and manipulate objects.
3. Insert and scale clip art.
4. Add borders and shading to text.
5. Create and use a template.

Creating Columns

Sometimes a document can be more effective if the text is in multiple columns. A newsletter is an example of a document that often has two or more columns. Columns are easy to create in Word. Choose Columns from the Format menu; the Columns dialog box appears, as shown in Figure 5-1. In this dialog box, specify the number of columns you want and how much space you want between them. You can also specify whether you want a line separating the columns.

The columns will not appear side by side in Normal view. To see the columns side by side, choose Page Layout from the View menu.

FIGURE 5-1
The Columns dialog box allows you to specify how
many columns you want in your document.

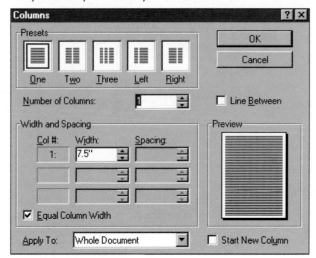

ACTIVITY

Creating Columns in a Document

1. Open *Activity 5-1* from your template disk.

2. Use Print Preview to view the document. Close Print Preview.

3. Choose **Columns** from the **Format** menu. The Columns dialog box appears as shown in Figure 5-1.

4. In the Presets box, click the **Two** option.

5. In the Width and Spacing box under Spacing, delete the current data and key **.6**.

6. Click in the box beside *Line Between* to insert a check mark. Click **OK.**

7. Choose **Page Layout** from the **View** menu. The document is shown in two columns.

8. Use Print Preview to view the columns. Close Print Preview.

9. Save the document on your data disk as *Glenview Newsletter*. Leave the document open for use in the next activity.

Drawing and Manipulating Graphics

Microsoft Word allows you to enhance documents by adding graphics. *Graphics* are pictures that help illustrate the meaning of the text, make the page more attractive, or make the page more functional. Word includes drawing tools that enable you to create your own graphics and add them to your documents.

Figure 5-2 shows a document created with Word. The letter takes on a more professional appearance with the addition of a letterhead that includes a graphic created with Word's drawing tools.

FIGURE 5-2
The graphic created in Word is a great addition to this letterhead.

PRIMARY CHILD CARE

1223 Canyon Trail   Amarillo, TX 79120-1222   806-555-1002

10 March 1998

Mr. Jeremiah Washington
450 Buffalo Road
Amarillo, TX 79120-4500

Mr. Washington

Our records indicate that your March child care payment for $250 is past due. If we do not receive payment by March 15, a late payment fee of $25 will be added to your bill.

I'm sure this is just an oversight on your part. Please remit your payment as soon as possible to avoid the late fee. We do have some flexible payment plans I'd be glad to go over with you.

Drawing Objects

To draw graphics, you must be in Page Layout view. When you are ready to create your graphic, click the Drawing button on the toolbar to display the drawing toolbar at the bottom of the document window. The drawing toolbar, shown in Figure 5-3, contains buttons for drawing and manipulating objects, such as lines, arcs, squares, circles, and freeform shapes.

FIGURE 5-3

The drawing toolbar contains tools you can use to draw and manipulate objects.

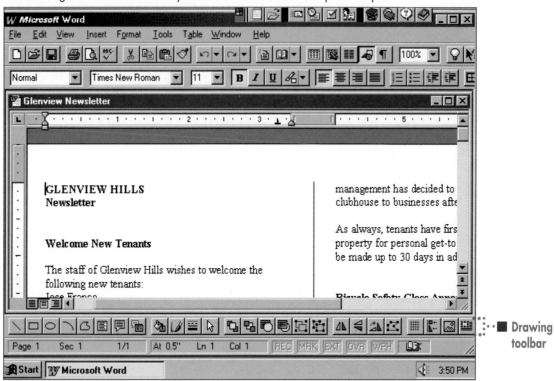

■ Drawing toolbar

5-2 Displaying the Drawing Toolbar

● ●

1. Highlight the second block of text under the heading *Independence Day Parade* ... that begins with *Keep children and animals* ... and ends with ... *will be towed*.

2. Click the **Bullets** button on the toolbar.

3. Position the insertion point on the first blank line after the paragraph about bicycle

safety, under the *Bicycle Safety Class Announced* heading.

4. Click the **Drawing** button on the toolbar. The drawing toolbar appears.

5. Leave the document on the screen for use in the next activity.

The drawing toolbar contains many tools. Some are used for drawing, and some buttons are used for manipulating or modifying what you've drawn. Table 5-1 summarizes the main tools that appear in the drawing toolbar.

TABLE 5-1
Drawing tools.

BUTTON	NAME	FUNCTION
	Rectangle tool	Draws rectangles and squares. To use, click and hold the left mouse button, then drag to draw. To create a perfect square, hold down the Shift key as you drag.
	Line tool	Draws straight lines. To use, position the pointer where you want the line to begin, then click and hold the mouse button and drag to where you want the line to end.
	Ellipse tool	Draws ovals and circles. To use, click and hold the mouse button, then drag to draw the oval or circle. To create a perfect circle, hold down the Shift key as you drag.
	Arc tool	Draws arcs. To use, click and hold the mouse button, then drag to draw.
	Freeform tool	Draws polygons and freehand objects. To draw straight sections, click at each endpoint or vertex. To draw freehand, drag and double-click to end a line. You can mix straight sections and freehand drawing in the same object.
	Select Drawing Objects	Lets you select and manipulate objects. To use, click on the arrow. The insertion point will assume the pointer shape.

Inserting a Frame

A *frame* is a special rectangle you draw that allows you to position a graphic within text. A frame allows the text to "wrap" around the object. To insert a frame, click the Insert Frame button located at the far right of the drawing toolbar. The insertion point changes to a crosshair or plus (+) sign. Drag to create a frame for your drawing.

Changing Default Settings

When you draw objects, you can specify a color for each line and fill. (You will learn more about colors later in this chapter.) Word uses the last specified colors as its defaults. A *default* is a setting used unless another option is chosen. For this chapter, you need to change these defaults before you begin drawing. To do this, choose Drawing Object from the Format menu. The Drawing Defaults dialog box appears, as shown in Figure 5-4. The Fill and Line tabs allow you to choose new settings.

FIGURE 5-4
The Drawing Defaults dialog box allows you to change the default fill and line colors.

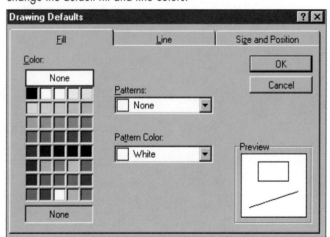

ACTIVITY

5-3 Inserting a Frame and Drawing a Graphic

1. Click the **Insert Frame** tool. Your mouse pointer will change to a crosshair.

2. Position the crosshair pointer on the right side portion of the paragraph about bicycle safety.

3. Press and hold the mouse button and drag to draw an upright rectangle about 1½ inches tall and ¾ inch wide. Some of the lines of text will wrap to make room for the frame you are drawing between the margin and the text. Release the mouse button when your rectangle frame is approximately the same size and in the same position as the one in Figure 5-5.

4. Choose **Drawing Object** from the Format menu.

5. Click the **Fill** tab if it isn't chosen already.

6. Under Color, click **None.**

7. Under Patterns, None should be chosen; under Pattern Color, White should be chosen.

8. Click the **Line** tab.

9. Under Line, choose **Custom** if it isn't chosen already.

10. Under Color, Black should be chosen; under Weight, 1 pt should be shown.

11. Choose **OK.**

12. Click the **Rectangle** tool.

13. Click and drag to draw a rectangle (the beginning of a traffic light) inside your frame like the one in Figure 5-6.

FIGURE 5-5
A frame allows you to position a graphic in text.

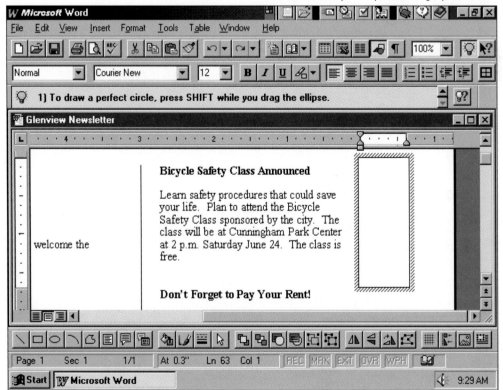

FIGURE 5-6
You can draw many different objects using the drawing tools.

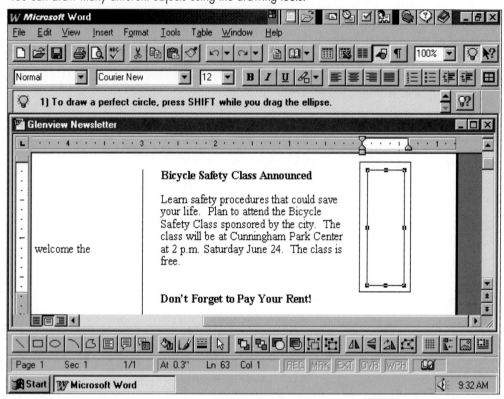

14. Click the **Ellipse** tool.

15. Hold down the **Shift** key. Beside the rectangle, draw a perfect circle with a diameter of about ½ inch.

16. Leave the document on the screen for use in the next activity.

Selecting an Object

When you first drew the objects in Activity 5-3, you probably noticed the little squares that appeared at the edges of the graphic when you released the mouse button. These small squares are called *handles.* They indicate that the object is selected and allow you to manipulate the selected object. When you choose another tool, the selection handles around an object disappear. Before you can copy, move, delete, or manipulate an object, you have to select it.

To select an object, use the Select Drawing Objects tool. When you choose the Select Drawing Objects tool, the pointer becomes an arrow pointer. Click on the object you want to select. The selection handles appear around the object, and you can then manipulate the object.

To deselect an object, click on another object or anywhere in the window. To delete an object, select it and press the Delete or Backspace key.

Resizing an Object

Handles do more than indicate that an object is selected. They also allow you to resize an object. Often during the process of creating a drawing, you will realize that the line, rectangle, or circle you just drew isn't quite the right size. Resizing is easy. You simply select the object to make the handles appear, and then drag the handles inward or outward to make the object smaller or larger.

Cutting, Copying, and Pasting Objects

You can cut, copy, and paste objects like text. The Cut and Copy commands place a copy of the selected image on the Clipboard. Pasting an object from the Clipboard places the object in your drawing. You can then move it into position.

ACTIVITY

Selecting, Resizing, and Using Copy and Paste

1. Click the **Select Drawing Objects** tool and select the circle you drew by clicking on its line.

2. Drag the circle into the rectangle. Then drag the circle's handles to resize it, until the circle fits snugly inside the bottom of the rectangle, as shown in Figure 5-7.

3. With the circle still selected, click the **Copy** button on the toolbar.

4. Click the **Paste** button on the toolbar. A copy of the circle appears.

5. Click the **Paste** button again. Another copy of the circle appears.

6. Click the **Select Drawing Objects** tool.

7. The last circle you pasted is still selected. Place the pointer on the circle's line, then press and hold down the mouse button. Drag the circle into the rectangle and place it above the first circle. When you release the mouse button, the selection handles will reappear.

8. In the same manner, drag the remaining circle into place above the second circle. Your screen should look like Figure 5-8. If necessary, adjust the size of your rectangle so that all three circles fit in it snugly.

9. Save and leave the document open for the next activity.

FIGURE 5-7
You can move an object to a new location.

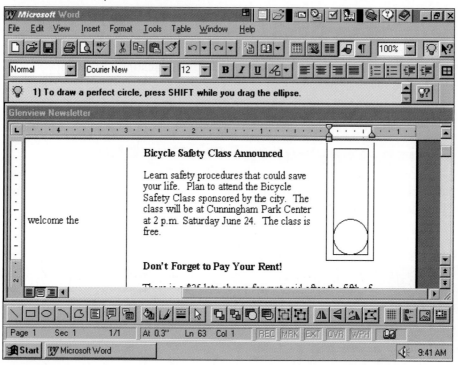

FIGURE 5-8
Use Copy and Paste to add identical objects.

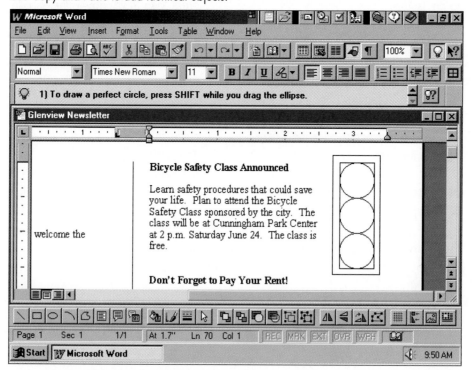

Changing the Appearance of Objects

Color adds life to your drawings. Word allows you to easily fill objects with color or change the color of lines. Since you changed it earlier, the default fill color is none and the default line color is black. To change these defaults, select the object you want to fill or the line you want to change, and click the Fill Color button or the Line Color button on the drawing toolbar. When you click one of these buttons, a color box appears, as shown in Figure 5-9.

To choose a color from the color box, simply click the color you want. Your selected object appears in this color. To find out the name of the colors in the color box, click and hold the mouse button and drag the mouse pointer over the colors without releasing the mouse button. The color name appears at the bottom of the color box.

FIGURE 5-9
The color box contains many different colors and shades of gray you can use to add color to your drawings.

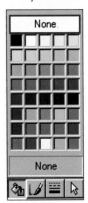

Another way to change the appearance of drawings is to change the line style. You can change the style of a line or the lines that make up an object such as a rectangle. Word gives you many choices for line styles including thick and thin lines, dotted lines, and arrows. To change the line style, select the line you want to change and click the Line Style button on the drawing toolbar. When you click the Line Style button, a box of line styles appears. The choices in the line style box are slightly different depending on whether you want to change the line style of a line or an object, as shown in Figure 5-10. Click a line style and your selected line or object's line will change to your choice.

FIGURE 5-10
The line style box gives you choices for changing the lines of selected lines or objects.

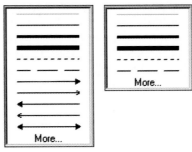

ACTIVITY

5-5 Adding Color to Your Drawing and Changing Line Style

1. Select the top circle on your drawing of a traffic light.

2. Click the **Fill Color** button on the drawing toolbar. The color box appears.

3. Click and hold the mouse button on the **Red** color square. The word *Red* appears in the bottom of the color box.

4. With the color Red still selected, release the mouse button. The top circle in your drawing appears in red.

5. Select the second circle on your drawing.

6. Click the **Fill Color** button on the drawing toolbar and click the color **Yellow.** The second circle becomes yellow.

7. Select the third circle on your drawing and fill it with the color **Green** or **Dk Green.**

8. Select the rectangle you drew.

9. Click the **Line Color** button on the drawing toolbar. The color box appears.

10. Click the color **Dk Gray** in the lower right corner of the color box.

11. Click the **Line Style** button. A box of line styles appears.

12. Click the thickest one, which is the fourth line from the top. The line on your drawing thickens.

13. With the rectangle still selected, fill the rectangle with the color **Black** in the upper left corner of the color box. Your drawing of the traffic light is complete, with three colored circles and a black background. (If your black rectangle covers your colored circles, click the Send to Back button one time.)

14. Save the document and leave it on your screen for the next activity.

Understanding Layering

Send to Back

Bring to Front

Each object you create can be changed, moved, or deleted at any time. This is an advantage of drawing on a computer rather than on paper. The computer allows you to lift your mistakes right off the screen and try again. The objects you create are laid on top of each other. When you create an object, it is placed on top of other objects that already have been drawn. Sometimes you will need to rearrange the order in which objects are layered. Word provides two commands for doing this: Send to Back and Bring to Front. Both buttons are on the drawing toolbar. The Send to Back command moves the selected object or objects to the bottom layer. The Bring to Front command moves the selected object or objects to the top layer.

When you draw an object without a frame, you can draw on top of text. Word allows you to change the stacking order of text and objects. Just as its name suggests, the Bring to Front of Text button places the selected object in front of text. The Send Behind Text button sends the selected object behind the text.

ACTIVITY 5-6 Layering Objects

1. Select the red circle.

2. Click the **Send to Back** button on the drawing toolbar. The red circle is sent behind the black rectangle.

3. With the red circle still selected, click the **Bring to Front** button on the drawing toolbar. The red circle is brought to the front of the black rectangle.

4. Position the cursor at the beginning of the document.

5. Click the **Fill Color** button and choose **None.**

6. Click the **Line Style** button and choose the second style from the top.

7. Without inserting a frame, draw a rectangle approximately 3½ inches wide and ¾ inches tall on top of the text as shown in Figure 5-11.

8. Change the Fill Color to **10% Gray** and change the Line Color to **10% Gray.** The text disappears.

FIGURE 5-11
Word lets you draw objects on top of text.

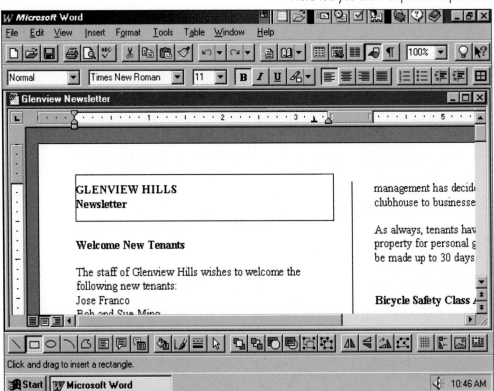

9. With the rectangle still selected, click the **Send Behind Text** button. The text appears in front of the gray rectangle.

11. Save and leave the document open for the next activity.

10. Highlight the title, *GLENVIEW HILLS*, and change the font size to 14 point.

Selecting More Than One Object

Sometimes you will want to select more than one object. Word gives you two ways to do this. The first is called *Shift-clicking.* The second method is to draw a selection box around a group of objects.

SHIFT-CLICKING

To Shift-click, hold down the Shift key and click each of the objects you want to select. Use Shift-clicking when you need to select objects that are not close to each other, or when the objects you need to select are near other objects you do not want to select. If you select an object by accident, click it again to deselect it.

DRAGGING A SELECTION BOX

Using the Select Drawing Objects tool, you can drag a selection box around a group of objects. Objects included in the selection box will be selected. Use a selection box when all of the objects you want selected are near each other and can be surrounded with a box. Be sure your selection box is large enough to enclose all the selection handles of the various objects. If you miss a handle, that item will not be selected.

COMBINING METHODS

You can also combine these two methods. First, use the selection box, then shift-click to include objects that the selection box may have missed.

Grouping Objects

Ungroup

Group

As your drawing becomes more complex, you will find it necessary to "glue" objects together into groups. Grouping objects allows you to work with more than one object as though they were one object. To group objects, select the objects you want to group and click the Group button from the Drawing toolbar. Objects can be ungrouped using the Ungroup button.

ACTIVITY 5-7

Selecting and Grouping Your Objects

1. Scroll back to the traffic light drawing. Hold down the **Shift** key.

2. Select the gray and black rectangle by clicking on the gray line in the top right corner.

3. While continuing to hold down the **Shift** key, click in the center of each circle. Don't worry if some of the selection handles disappear.

4. Release the **Shift** key.

5. Click the **Group** button on the toolbar. Your drawing is now grouped into one object instead of four separate objects.

6. Save your document and leave it open for the next activity.

Flipping and Rotating Objects

You can modify an object by flipping or rotating it. Flipping reverses the orientation or direction of the selected object. Word has two flipping options on the drawing toolbar: Flip Horizontal changes the orientation of an object from right to left, and Flip Vertical reverses the orientation from top to bottom. The Rotate Right button on the drawing toolbar moves a graphic in 90-degree increments to the right. To flip or rotate an object, simply select it and click the appropriate button on the toolbar.

Flip Horizontal

Flip Vertical

Rotate Right

ACTIVITY 5-8

Flipping and Rotating Objects

1. Select the traffic light object.

2. Click the **Rotate Right** button on the Drawing toolbar. The traffic light rotates 90 degrees to the right and is now on its side.

3. Click the **Flip Horizontal** button. The object doesn't appear to move, but it has reversed its position and the red light is now on the far left instead of on the right.

4. Click the **Flip Horizontal** button again. The red light is now on the right.

5. Click the **Rotate Right** button. The object rotates to the right and the traffic light is now upside down with the red light on the bottom.

6. Click the **Flip Vertical** button. The object doesn't appear to move, but it

has reversed position and the red light is now on the top again.

7. Leave the document on the screen for the next activity.

Using Grid Snap

One of the most difficult parts of drawing with a computer drawing program is aligning and sizing objects. To help, Word provides an invisible grid on your screen. Objects automatically align to the nearest grid line. This feature is called *grid snap*. This makes it easy, for example, to draw three lines that are an equal distance apart. You can place each line one grid distance from the next. The result is perfectly spaced lines.

There will be times, however, when you want to place an object more precisely. For example, when you are drawing the details on your graphic, grid snap may not allow you to place two objects as close together as you would like. To allow for more precise alignment, the program provides a way to turn off grid snap. Choose the Snap to Grid button on the drawing toolbar. The Snap to Grid dialog box, shown in Figure 5-12, allows you to toggle grid snap on or off. If the command has a check mark beside it, grid snap is on.

FIGURE 5-12
Snap to Grid is a toggle command.

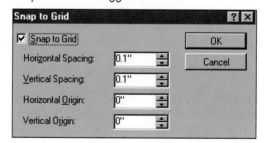

1. Select the traffic light and drag it to the right, out of the frame. Notice how the object seems to snap to position.

2. Click the **Snap to Grid** button on the Drawing toolbar. The Snap to Grid dialog box appears.

3. Click to remove the check mark beside **Snap to Grid.** Choose **OK.** Grid snap is off.

4. Select the traffic light and drag it back into the frame. Notice how it slides smoothly, rather than snapping into place.

5. Click the **Snap to Grid** button on the drawing toolbar. The Snap to Grid dialog box appears.

6. Click to insert the check mark beside **Snap to Grid.** Choose **OK.** Grid snap is now on again.

7. Leave the document on the screen for the next activity.

Exploring on Your Own

Other features are available when you are creating your own drawings. You may want to experiment with the drawing toolbar commands not presented in this chapter. Use the Help menu if you need some additional instruction.

Inserting and Scaling Clip Art

You may sometimes want to use art from another source rather than drawing it yourself. Graphics that are already drawn and available for use in documents are called *clip art.* Clip art libraries offer artwork of common objects that can speed up and possibly improve the quality of your work. Figure 5-13 illustrates how clip art adds flair to a zoo poster.

To insert clip art, choose Object from the Insert menu. The Object dialog box appears. Click Microsoft ClipArt Gallery in the list and choose OK. The Microsoft ClipArt Gallery will appear with many different clip art images. If you get a message that asks if you want to add clip art files from Office, choose Yes. You can even add clip art from other sources to the ClipArt Gallery. To insert an image from the Gallery, simply click on the object you want and choose Insert. The image will appear on your screen at the location of your insertion point.

Although the graphics you use are already created, you can alter the way they appear on the page. When you resize a graphic using the handles, the length and width may not maintain the same proportions. To change the size, or *scale,* of a graphic so that its proportions are correct, choose Picture from the Format menu. In the Picture dialog box, you can key an exact size or percentages of length and width scale.

FIGURE 5-13
Clip art adds a professional look to this poster.

Welcome to
Mason City Zoo

Home of Zimba

Inserting and Scaling Clip Art

• •

1. Click the **Select Drawing Objects** tool to deselect it.

2. In the first column, scroll down to the blank lines below the paragraph about amusement park tickets. Place the insertion point on the first blank line below that paragraph.

3. Choose **Object** from the **Insert** menu. The Object dialog box appears.

4. Under Object Type, click Microsoft ClipArt Gallery.

5. Choose **OK.** The Microsoft ClipArt Gallery dialog box appears.

6. Under Categories, click **Entertainment.**

7. Click the picture of the roller coaster, as shown in Figure 5-14. (Your screen may look slightly different from Figure 5-14.) At the bottom of the ClipArt Gallery, the Description of the clip art is *Risk*.

8. Click **Insert.** The roller coaster appears in your document.

FIGURE 5-14
The Microsoft ClipArt Gallery allows you to easily insert a clip art picture.

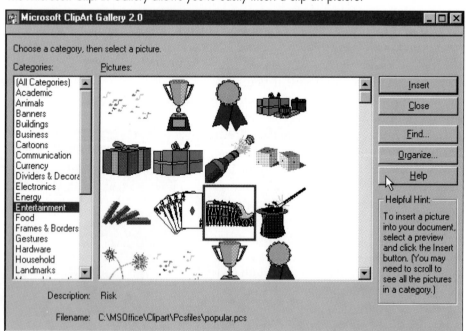

9. With the object selected, scale down the size of the clip art slightly by choosing **Picture** from the **Format** menu. The Picture dialog box appears.

10. In the Scaling box beside Width, key **80**.

11. Press **Tab.** Key **80** beside Height in the Scaling box. Press **Tab.**

12. In the Size box, the Width should be 3.2 inches and the Height should be 1.69 inches. If your Size box has different measurements, delete the current data and key these measurements.

13. Click **OK.** The clip art is smaller, as shown in Figure 5-15.

14. Save the document and leave it open for the next activity.

FIGURE 5-15
Scaling clip art allows you to keep the original proportions.

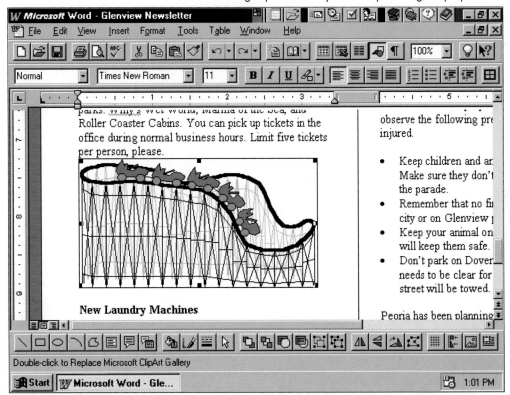

Using Borders and Shading

Borders and shading add interest and emphasis to text. However, be sure to use them sparingly and wisely. Too many borders or shades on a page can make it look cluttered and hard to read.

Adding Borders to Paragraphs

Borders are single, double, thick, or dotted lines that appear around one or more paragraphs and are used to emphasize the text. You can specify whether the border appears on all four sides like a box, on two sides, or only on one side of the paragraph. Another option is the shadow border, which makes the paragraph look three-dimensional. Highlight the text you want to border and choose Borders and Shading from the Format menu. In the Paragraph Borders and Shading dialog box, shown in Figure 5-16, specify the type of border, size of line, and color for your border in the Borders section. After selecting your options, you can see a sample in the Border box.

FIGURE 5-16
The Paragraph Borders and Shading dialog box allows you to change the style of borders.

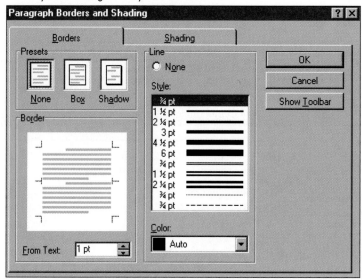

Adding Shading to Paragraphs

You can also add *shading*—grays or colors—or patterns, such as diagonal stripes, to paragraphs or lines of text. However, to maintain readability of a paragraph that contains several sentences, it is best to add only light shades (25 percent or less) to text. You can create interesting effects by adding patterns to short titles or names. Simply highlight the text you want to shade and access the Shading section of the Paragraph Borders and Shading dialog box. From here, you can choose the shade or pattern you want, and the foreground and background colors. Think of foreground and background colors as two layers: the foreground layer on top, and the background layer on bottom. You could, for example, have a solid red background and a 75 percent blue foreground. The result would be a shade that is 75 percent blue and 25 percent red. The Preview box shows you what your choices will look like.

ACTIVITY

5-11 Adding Borders and Shading

1. Highlight the heading *Don't Forget to Pay Your Rent!*, the blank line, and the sentence below it.

2. Choose **Borders and Shading** from the **Format** menu. The Paragraph Borders and Shading dialog box appears.

3. Click the **Borders** tab if it's not chosen already.

4. In the Presets box, click the **Box** option.

5. In the Line box under Style, click the **1½pt** single-line style.

6. In the Color box, choose **Blue.** A blue single-lined border appears around the heading and text, as shown in the Border preview box.

7. Click the **Shading** tab. In the Fill box, click the **20%** pattern.

8. In the Foreground box, choose **Yellow.** In the Background box, choose **White.**

9. Click **OK.** In addition to the border, the text now contains a yellow 20% shade, as shown in Figure 5-17.

10. Save the document.

11. Print and close the document.

FIGURE 5-17
Borders and shading are useful when you want to emphasize text.

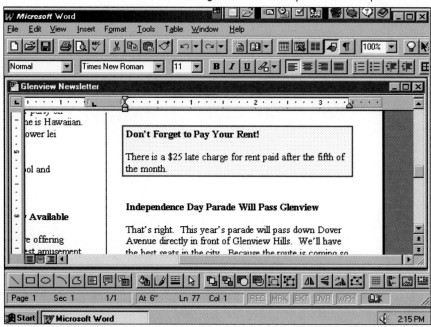

Using Templates

Suppose you are a traveling sales representative and you must file a report each week that summarizes your sales and the new contacts you have made. Parts of this report will be the same each week, such as the document's format and the headings within the report. It would be tedious to recreate the document each week. Word solves this problem by allowing you to create a template or use an existing Word template for documents that you use frequently. A *template* is a file that contains page and paragraph formatting and text that you can customize to create a new document similar to, but slightly different from, the original. A report template would save all formatting, font choices, and text that does not change, allowing you to fill in only the new information each week.

Do not confuse the Word templates with the template disk that you use with this book. Both use the word *template* because they both involve taking an unfinished document and completing it.

Opening an Existing Template

Word contains many templates you can use to create documents. To open an existing Word template, choose New from the File menu. The New dialog box contains existing templates in categories, such as Memos and Reports, as shown in Figure 5-18. You can use a template as is, or modify it and save it as a new template. To open a template you want to use as is, click the icon and choose OK. Replace the data in the template with your own data and save. To open a template and modify it, click the icon, click the Template option button, and click OK.

FIGURE 5-18
The New dialog box contains existing Word templates you can use to create new documents.

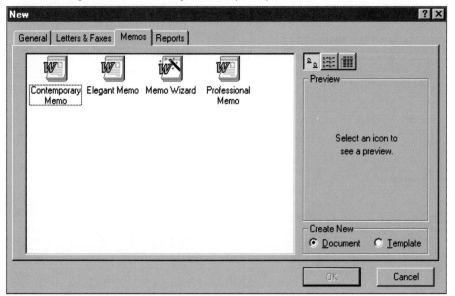

ACTIVITY

Opening a Template to Use As Is

1. Choose **New** from the **File** menu. The New dialog box appears.

2. Click the **Memos** tab.

3. Click the **Contemporary Memo** icon and choose **OK.** The Contemporary Memo template appears on your screen.

4. Beside To: click and key **Paul Williams**.

5. Beside CC: click and key **Jane Yen**.

6. Beside From: key your name.

7. Beside Re: key **How to Use Memo Templates**.

8. Save the file on your data disk as *Memo Document.*

9. Print and close the document.

Creating a Template

As stated previously, you can create a template by modifying an existing one, or you can create a template from your own document. To create a template using a new, blank document, choose New from the File menu. In the General section, click the Blank Document icon, then click the Template option at the lower right corner of the dialog box. When you save your new document, it will be saved as a template in the Template directory on the hard drive. The Template directory has different categories or subdirectories where you can save your templates. These subdirectories (Letters & Faxes, Memos, and Reports) correspond with the tabs in the New dialog box. You must save template files in the Template directory in order to use them as templates.

ACTIVITY

Creating a Letterhead Template

1. Choose **New** from the **File** menu.

2. Click the **General** tab.

3. Click the **Blank Document** icon and click the **Template** option button.

4. Click **OK.** A blank template document will appear on your screen.

5. Choose **Object** from the **Insert** menu.

6. Under Object Type, click Microsoft ClipArt Gallery. Click **OK.** The Microsoft ClipArt Gallery appears.

7. Under Categories, choose **Animals.**

8. Choose the dove picture with the Description: *Dove Love Peace.* Choose **Insert.** The clip art appears in the document.

9. Select the picture and click the **Center** align button on the toolbar to center the graphic.

10. Select the graphic and choose **Picture** from the **Format** menu. The Picture dialog box appears.

11. Key **25** in the Scaling Width box. Press **Tab.** Key **25** in the Scaling Height box. Press **Tab.** In the Size box, the Width should be 1 inch and the Height should be

0.93 inches. If your measurements are different, replace them with these. Click **OK.** The graphic is scaled down to the appropriate size for use in a letterhead.

12. Using whatever fonts are available to you, create a letterhead like the one shown in Figure 5-19.

13. Change the top margin to .5 inches and the left, right, and bottom margins to 1 inch.

14. When you finish creating the letterhead, choose **Save As** from the **File** menu.

15. In the Save in box, change to the MSOffice Templates directory on your hard drive if necessary. Double-click the Letters & Faxes subdirectory.

16. In the File name box, key **Dove Letterhead XXX** (replace the *X*s with your initials).

17. Choose **Save.**

18. Close the file.

FIGURE 5-19
A letterhead makes a useful template.

Creating a Document Using a Template

You can use the template you created as many times as needed. To use a template, choose New from the File menu. In the New dialog box, click the tab that contains the template. An icon with the name of your template will appear along with other existing templates. Select your template icon and click OK to bring up a copy of your template titled *Document1*. After you make changes to this document, choose Save As to save it to your data disk as a regular Word document.

ACTIVITY

Creating a Document Using a Letterhead Template

1. Choose **New** from the **File** menu. The New dialog box appears.

2. In the New dialog box, click the Letters & Faxes tab.

3. Click the **Dove Letterhead** icon and choose **OK.** A copy of the template named *Document1* appears.

4. Key the letter in Figure 5-20.

FIGURE 5-20

March 12, 19--

Ms. Martha Jones
9007 Sunnydale Boulevard
San Diego, CA 92190-9007

Ms. Jones:

Thank you for your request for more information on Dove Catering Services. I understand that you are planning a reception for your son's engagement.

Dove Catering Services has been providing quality catering since 1990, and we have catered more than 300 events--including engagement and wedding receptions. We have an excellent reputation for quality, reliability, and service.

I've enclosed a brochure that describes our catering services. Please contact me for more information. I would like to be of further service to you.

Again, thank you for your interest in Dove Catering Services.

Sincerely,

Anna Dove
Owner

Enclosures

---

5. Save the document on your data disk as *Dove Letter*.

6. Print and close the document.

Using Template Wizards

A *template wizard* is similar to a template, but it asks you questions and creates a document based on your answers. The word processing template wizards available to you include Memos, Letters & Faxes, and Reports. To start a wizard, choose New from the File menu. In the New dialog box, click the document category, such as Memos. Then, click the wizard icon and choose OK. The wizard dialog box shows a sample of what your document will look like. The wizard will begin by asking you a question or asking you to key information. Sometimes you must choose between two or more alternatives. You can click on each choice and an example is shown in the dialog box. Click Next to go to the next step; click Back to go to the previous step. Click Finish at the end, and the wizard will create the document for you. Once you have created the document, you can add specific text and modify existing text in your document.

ACTIVITY

Using a Wizard Template

1. Choose **New** from the **File** menu. The New dialog box appears.

2. Click the **Letters & Faxes** tab.

3. Click the **Fax Wizard** icon and choose **OK.** The Fax Wizard dialog box appears.

4. Click the Portrait button if it's not chosen already.

5. Click **Next>.**

6. Click **Modern.** The sample changes to Modern style.

7. Click **Jazzy.** The sample changes to Jazzy style.

8. Click **Next>.**

9. In the Type your na<u>m</u>e box, key your name.

10. In the Type your <u>c</u>ompany's name box, key **ABC Success**.

11. In the mailing address box, key

**2288 Uptown Boulevard
Suite 12
Sioux Falls, SD 57187-2288**

12. Click **Next>.**

13. Beside <u>P</u>hone, key **605-555-2890**.

14. Beside Fa<u>x</u>, key **605-555-2892**.

15. Click **Next>.**

16. In the Type recipient's na*m*e box, key **Mitchell Swansen**.

17. In the Type recipient's *c*ompany's name box, key **Swansen Awards**.

18. In the Type recipient's mailing *a*ddress box, key

> **1600 Dakota Road**
> **Suite 209**
> **Sioux Falls, SD 57188-1600**

19. Click **Next>.**

20. In the Recipient's *P*hone box, key **605-555-4530**.

21. In the Recipient's Fa*x* box, key **605-555-4950**.

22. Click **Next>.**

23. Click **Finish.** The Wizard creates the document.

24. Go to the top right of the document. Beside the Number of pages including cover sheet box, key **2**.

25. Beside REMARKS:, click the box beside **Urgent.**

26. Click below the dotted line under REMARKS and key **Please make the attached changes to the Excellence Award.**

27. Save as *Fax Sheet*.

28. Print and close the document.

29. Delete your templates from the Templates folder of MSOffice:
   a. Open **Explorer** from the **Programs** menu.
   b. In the All Folders box, click the plus (+) box beside the hard drive icon (probably C:).
   c. Click the plus box beside the MSOffice folder.
   d. Click the plus box beside the Templates folder.
   e. Double-click the Letters & Faxes folder.
   f. On the right side of the screen under Contents of 'Letters & Faxes,' click **Dove Letterhead XXX.**
   g. Choose **Delete** from the **File** menu. Click **Yes.** The template file is deleted.
   h. Choose **Close** from the **File** menu.

Summary

- You can create documents with multiple columns. The entire document, except for headers and footers, will be made into columns.

- Graphics can enhance documents by illustrating text, or making the page more attractive or functional. Word allows you to add graphics to word processor documents. Or, you can insert clip art using the Microsoft Clip-Art Gallery.

- Graphics created in Word are made up of one or more objects. Word provides a drawing toolbar with tools that let you draw lines, rectangles, ovals, and more. There also are many options for working with graphic objects.

- Borders and shading add interest and emphasis to text. Templates allow you to save the format, font choices, and text of commonly produced documents. Template wizards are similar to templates, but they ask you questions and create the document based on your answers.

▼REVIEW ACTIVITIES

TRUE/FALSE

Circle T or F to show whether the statement is true or false.

T F   **1.** Columns appear only in Page Layout view and Print Preview.

T F   **2.** The Select Drawing Objects tool allows you to select and manipulate objects.

T F   **3.** Selection boxes are small squares that appear around a selected object.

T F   **4.** Grid snap causes objects to align to the nearest object.

T F   **5.** When you draw, you create objects in layers.

T F   **6.** The Rotate Right tool rotates graphics to the right in 90-degree increments.

T F   **7.** Resizing clip art using the handles maintains proportion.

T F   **8.** Clip art is inserted through the Picture dialog box.

T F   **9.** Word contains templates you can use to create documents.

T F   **10.** You can use a template as many times as needed.

COMPLETION

Write the correct answer in the space provided.

1. Give an example of a document that often has two or more columns.

_____

_____

2. How do you resize an object using the handles?

_____

_____

3. Which command makes several objects work together as one?

_____

4. How can you force the Rectangle tool to draw a perfect square?

_____

5. Which two buttons on the drawing toolbar allow you to add color to your document?

_____

6. Explain how you scale an object.

_____

7. Explain how you use Shift-clicking to select more than one object.

_____

_____

8. What is clip art?

_____

_____

9. Why should you use only light shades on entire paragraphs?

_____

10. What is a template wizard?

_____

_____

REINFORCEMENT APPLICATIONS

application 5-1

Refer to Figure 5-21 and write the letter of the drawing toolbar part next to the correct name of the item given below.

FIGURE 5-21

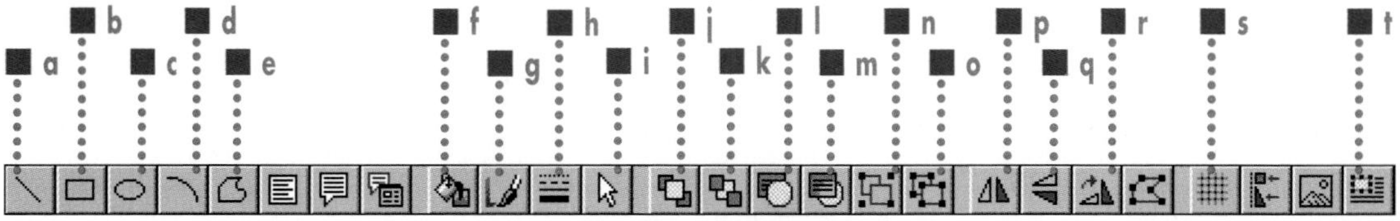

___ 1. Arc tool

___ 2. Line Color tool

___ 3. Select Drawing Objects

___ 4. Send Behind Text

___ 5. Freeform tool

___ 6. Rotate Right

___ 7. Rectangle tool

___ 8. Snap to Grid

___ 9. Line tool

___10. Insert Frame

___11. Ellipse tool

___12. Flip Horizontal

___13. Bring in Front of Text

___14. Fill Color tool

___15. Group

___16. Bring to Front

___17. Flip Vertical

___18. Send to Back

___19. Ungroup

___20. Line Style

application 5-2

1. Create the poster in Figure 5-22 using what you've learned in this chapter. Follow the instructions on the figure.
2. Save the file to your data disk as *For Sale.*
3. Print and close the document.

FIGURE 5-22

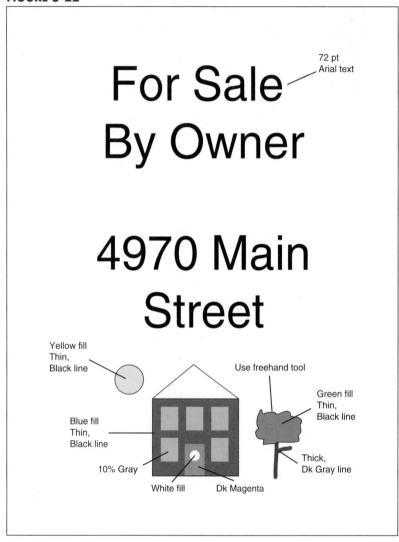

application 5 - 3

1. Create the letterhead template shown in Figure 5-23 using what you learned in this chapter. Follow the instructions on the figure.

2. Save the letterhead as a template with the name *Color Brick Letterhead XXX* (replace the *X*s with your initials).

3. Print and close the letterhead.

FIGURE 5-23

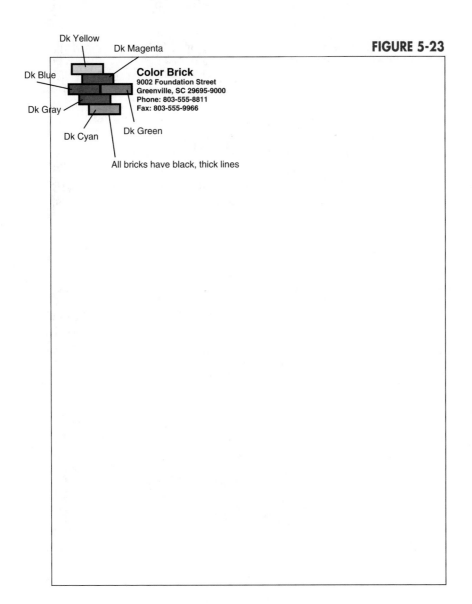

a p p l i c a t i o n 5 - 4

1. Open *Application 5-4* from your template disk.

2. Select all text and change the font size to 10 point.

3. Change all margins to .5 inches.

4. Format the document into 3 columns with lines between columns.

5. Switch to Page Layout view.

6. Position the insertion point in the blank line before the heading, *Using Your Checking Account*.

7. Insert the clip art picture of the bag of money with the Description: *Reward Accounting* from the Currency category of the Microsoft ClipArt Gallery.

8. Scale the height and width of the graphic to 30%. The Width in the Size box should be 1.2 inches and Height should be 1.06 inches.

9. Center the graphic.

10. Insert a blank line before and after the graphic.

11. Save the document as *Checking Account.*

12. Change the font size of the title to 14 point.

13. Draw a rectangle around the title. Fill the rectangle with the color 15% Gray.

14. Change the line color of the rectangle to 15% Gray.

15. Send the object behind the text.

16. Highlight the National Bank mailing address in the second column before the heading, *Managing Your Account.* Create a 20% green shade and a blue shadow box border using a 2¼-point single line.

17. Place the insertion point in the second column on the blank line before the paragraph that begins, *Knowing the amount …*

18. Insert the clip art picture of the stack of coins with the Description: *Reward Accounting* from the Currency category of the Microsoft ClipArt Gallery.

19. Scale the height and width of the graphic to 30%. In the Size box, the width should be 1.2 inches and the height should be 1.15 inches.

20. Center the graphic.

21. Insert a blank line before and after the graphic.

22. Position the insertion point in the blank line before the paragraph that begins, *When you write …*

23. Insert the check mark graphic with the Description: *Performance* from the Shapes category of the Microsoft ClipArt Gallery.

24. Scale the height and width of the graphic to 30%. In the Size box, the width should be .82 inches and the height should be 1.2 inches.

25. Center the graphic. Insert a blank line before and after it.

26. Save the file.

27. Print and close the document.

a p p l i c a t i o n   5 - 5

1. Open *Color Brick Letterhead XXX* by selecting New from the File menu and locating the file in the New dialog box.

2. Key the following letter in Figure 5-24:

FIGURE 5-24

May 4, 19--

Mr. Joe Nunez
6501 Jasper Street
Greenville, SC 29695-6500

Mr. Nunez:

The possibilities are endless! The revolutionary new brick colors you've heard about will be shown at the Home Expo this year. And you're invited to join me for a peek at these amazing products!

I can't wait to show you the beautiful new brick colors and the unique ways you can use them. And, of course, the quality and durability are super. I want to show you examples of these bricks in use. Our purchasing options make it possible to use these bricks for wonderful accents and designs on commercial and residential buildings!

The show will be May 20–23. If you have a free moment, call me before the show, and I'll schedule a time when we can meet. But even if you can't schedule the time in advance, please visit Booth 2112. You'll see what all the excitement in building is about!

Sincerely,

Perry Pratt
Salesperson

3. Save on your data disk as *Nunez Letter.*

4. Print and close the document.

5. Open Windows Explorer.

6. Delete *Color Brick Letterhead XXX* from the MSOffice Templates folder on the hard drive of your computer.

a p p l i c a t i o n 5 - 6

1. Create a portrait layout, modern fax cover sheet using the fax wizard.

2. Key the person sending the fax:

   Yolanda Berry
   Berry Investments
   5994 Cash Street
   Dallas, TX 75298-5999
   Phone: 214-555-6865
   Fax: 214-555-2500

3. Key the person to whom she is sending the fax:

   Heath West
   Cowboy Wear
   4663 Merchant Boulevard
   Space 10
   Fort Worth, TX 76190-4446
   Phone: 817-555-4329
   Fax: 817-555-4532

4. The number of pages is 2.

5. Key her message for his review:

   Please consider the following investments for next year. Call me next week and let me know what you think.

6. Save on your data disk as *Berry Fax*.

7. Print and close the document.

ADVANCED FORMATTING AND EDITING

CHAPTER

6

OBJECTIVES
When you complete this chapter, you will be able to:

1. Switch between, and copy and paste between, multiple documents.

2. Work with multipage documents.

3. Check the spelling of a document.

4. Use the Thesaurus.

5. Find specific text and replace it with other text.

6. Create footnotes and endnotes.

7. Print in landscape orientation.

Working with Multiple Documents

Word allows you to have more than one document open at a time. This is useful when you want to move or copy text between two documents.

In Chapter 3, you learned the two ways to switch between documents. The quickest way to activate a document is to click in the window or on the title bar of the document you want to become active. The other way to switch is to use the Window menu. At the bottom of the Window menu are the names of the documents that are currently open. Choosing one of these documents from the Window menu will make that document active and bring it to the front.

Switching Between Documents

1. Choose **Open** from the **File** menu. The Open dialog box appears.

2. Choose *Activity 6-1* and click **Open.** The *Activity 6-1* document appears.

3. Now open *Activity 6-2*. The *Activity 6-2* document appears in front of the *Activity 6-1* document, as shown in Figure 6-1. You can see that *Activity 6-2* is the active document because the title bar is darkened and it appears in front of the *Activity 6-1* document. If you can't see *Activity 6-1* behind

Activity 6-2, your windows may be maximized. Click the Restore button if necessary.

4. Click the title bar of the *Activity 6-1* document. The window is brought to the front and becomes the active window.

5. Choose **2 Activity 6-2** from the **Window** menu. The document again moves to the front and becomes active.

6. Leave the documents open for the next activity.

FIGURE 6-1
In Word, two documents can be open at the same time.

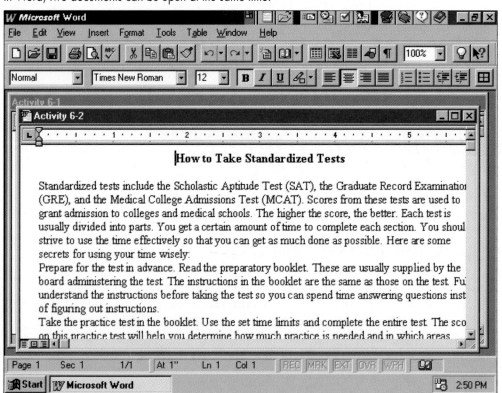

Copying and Pasting Text Between Documents

Just as you can copy or move text within a document, you can copy or move data from one document to another. For example, you might copy a paragraph from one document to another, or you might move a whole section from one report to another.

ACTIVITY

Copying and Pasting Text Between Documents

1. Click anywhere in *Activity 6-1* to make it the active window.

2. Choose **Select All** from the **Edit** menu. The text in the document is highlighted.

3. Click the **Copy** button on the toolbar. The text is placed on the Clipboard.

4. Bring *Activity 6-2* to the front to be the active window.

5. Move the insertion point to the end of the document. Press **Enter** three times to create two blank lines.

6. Click the **Paste** button on the toolbar. The text you copied from *Activity 6-1* is placed in *Activity 6-2*.

7. Click anywhere in the *Activity 6-1* window.

8. Choose **Close** from the **File** menu. *Activity 6-1* closes, leaving *Activity 6-2* on the screen.

9. If the pasted text appears in a different font, select it and change it to the same font and size as the first part of the document.

10. Highlight the title *OVERCOMING TEST ANXIETY*.

11. Change the case to Title Case.

12. Save the document to your data disk as *Test Taking Hints*. Leave the document open for the next activity.

Copying Format and Style

Often you will spend time formatting a paragraph with indents, tabs or styles, such as bold and italic, then find that you need the same format in another part of the document. The Format Painter button on the toolbar allows you to copy the format and style of a block of text, rather than the text itself. You can use the command to quickly apply a complicated format and style to text. To use the Format Painter command, highlight the formatted text you want to copy. Then, click the Format Painter button and highlight the text you want to format. The text changes to the copied format.

ACTIVITY

6-3 Copying Format and Style

1. Move the insertion point to the top of the document.

2. Highlight the title, *How to Take Standardized Tests.* Change the point size to 14.

3. With the title still highlighted, click the **Format Painter** button on the toolbar. The pointer changes to a paintbrush and I-beam.

4. Highlight the title, *Overcoming Test Anxiety.* The center, boldface, and font size formatting from the copied format are applied.

5. Highlight the text under the *How to Take Standardized Tests* heading from the paragraph that begins *Prepare for the test in advance . . .* through *Don't panic.*

6. Click the AutoFormats **Bullets** button.

7. Boldface all the headings under *Overcoming Test Anxiety.*

8. Highlight the three lines of text under *Prepare.*

9. Click the AutoFormats **Bullets** button on the toolbar.

10. Change the text under all of the remaining headings to bullets.

11. Move the insertion point to the top of the document.

12. Save and leave the document open for the next activity.

Working with Multipage Documents

When a document is only one page long, it isn't hard to edit or format the text. These tasks become more challenging in multipage documents because you cannot see the whole document on your screen at once. Word provides several tools that are useful for formatting and editing long documents.

Splitting Windows

Word lets you view two parts of your document at once by using the Split command from the Window menu. Suppose you want to edit text at the beginning and end of a document at the same time. By splitting your document, you can see both parts. Each area of the document, called a ***pane,*** contains separate scroll bars to allow you to move through that part of the document.

ACTIVITY

6-4 Splitting Windows

1. Your insertion point should be at the beginning of the document.

2. Choose **Split** from the **Window** menu. A horizontal bar appears with the mouse pointer as a positioning marker.

3. Position the bar so that the document window is divided into two equal parts.

4. Click the left mouse button. The document window splits into two separate panes, each with independent scroll bars and rulers, as shown in Figure 6-2.

5. Press the down scroll arrow in the bottom pane of the split window. Notice that the document scrolls down while the text in the upper pane remains still.

FIGURE 6-2

The Split command divides the document window into two panes, each with an independent set of scroll bars and rulers.

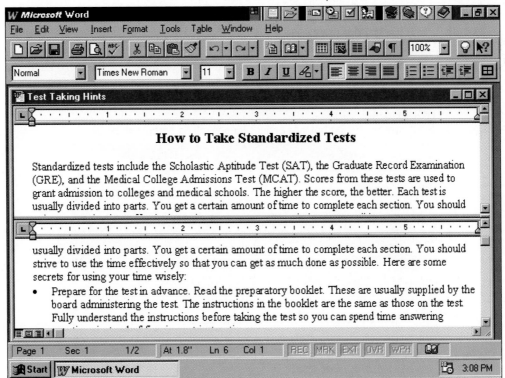

6. Choose **Remove Split** from the **Window** menu. The window returns to one page.

7. Leave the file open for the next activity.

Using the Go To Command

One of the quickest ways to move through a document is to use the Go To command. Go To allows you to skip to a specific part of a document. To skip to a specific page, choose Go To from the Edit menu. The Go To dialog box appears, as shown in Figure 6-3. Page is the default setting in the Go To What box, so key the page number where you want to move in the Enter Page Number box. After you click Go To, Word will move the insertion point to the beginning of the page you specified.

FIGURE 6-3
The Go To command lets you skip quickly to the part of the document you specify.

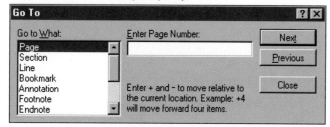

Controlling Paragraph Breaks

Sometimes you may not want page breaks to split a paragraph or separate certain paragraphs. For example, you would not want a table split across two pages or a paragraph heading separated from the text following it. The Text Flow section of the Paragraph dialog box, shown in Figure 6-4, allows you to control how paragraphs break during pagination. The *Widow/Orphan Control* keeps Word from printing an **orphan,** the first line of a paragraph at the end of a page, or a **widow,** the last line of a paragraph at the beginning of a page. To keep

FIGURE 6-4
The Paragraph dialog box has options for controlling paragraph breaks.

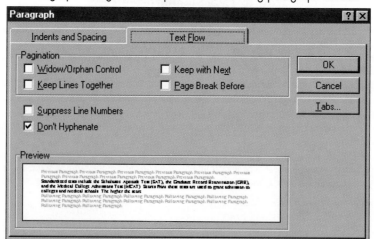

lines of text in a paragraph together, choose the *Keep Lines Together* option. If the *Page Break Before* option is checked, an automatic page break will be inserted before, rather than in the middle of, the paragraph. If the *Keep with Next* option is checked, the current paragraph and the one following it will appear on the same page. To use these options, place the insertion point in the paragraph you want to affect and choose Paragraph from the Format menu. Click the Text Flow tab to access that section of the Paragraph dialog box.

ACTIVITY
6-5 Using Go To and Changing Paragraph Breaks

1. Choose **Go To** from the **Edit** menu. The Go To dialog box appears, as shown in Figure 6-3.

2. In the Enter Page Number box, key **2** and choose **Go To.** The insertion point moves to the beginning of page 2.

3. Choose **Close.** The Go To dialog box disappears.

4. Notice how the automatic page break is located just after the heading, *While Taking the Test.* To keep the heading on the same page with the text below it, place the inser-

tion point in the heading and choose **Paragraph** from the **Format** menu. The Paragraph dialog box appears, as shown in Figure 6-4.

5. Click the **Text Flow** tab.

6. In the Pagination box, click the box beside *Keep with Next* to insert a check mark.

7. Choose **OK.** The automatic page break is moved before the heading.

8. Save the document and leave it open for use in the next activity.

Viewing Hidden Characters

The Show/Hide ¶ button on the toolbar allows you to view hidden formatting characters. These are characters such as paragraph returns or end-of-line marks. Seeing these hidden characters can help you edit your text.

Using the Word Count Command

Sometimes you may want to know how many words the document you're working on contains. The Word Count command quickly counts the pages, words, characters, paragraphs, and lines in your document. The insertion point can be located anywhere in the document when you use Word Count. You can count the words in a specific section of text by first highlighting the text, then using Word Count. To use Word Count, choose Word Count from the Tools menu. A dialog box appears listing Word Count's findings.

ACTIVITY 6-6

Viewing Hidden Characters and Using Word Count

1. Click the **Show/Hide ¶** button on the toolbar. Word makes the paragraph returns and spacebar characters visible, as shown in Figure 6-5.

2. Scroll through the document to observe the different characters.

3. Make sure nothing is highlighted. Choose **Word Count** from the **Tools** menu. The Word Count dialog box appears, as shown in Figure 6-6.

4. Choose **Close.**

5. Click the **Show/Hide ¶** button. The characters are hidden.

6. Save the document.

7. Print and close the document.

FIGURE 6-5
Clicking the Show/Hide ¶ button makes hidden formatting characters appear.

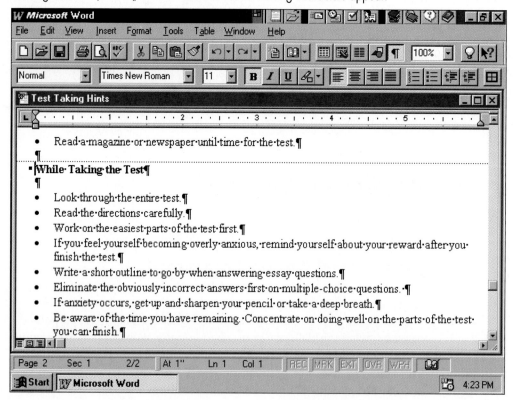

FIGURE 6-6

FIGURE 6-6
The Word Count dialog box lists the number of
pages, words, characters, paragraphs, and
lines in a document.

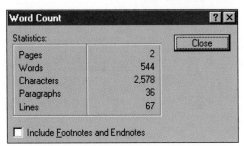

Using the Spelling Checker

As you learned in Chapter 3, Word can automatically check your
spelling as you type, makes some corrections automatically, and underline in
red those words that it doesn't find in its dictionary. However, the Spelling
Checker provides many options the Automatic Spell Checker doesn't. You can
check an entire document or portions of a document by clicking the Spelling
button on the toolbar or by choosing the Spelling command from the Tools
menu.

The Spelling dialog box shown in Figure 6-7 contains options that allow
you to check the spelling of words, ignore words, change misspelled words, or
add words to your own custom dictionary. Table 6-1 explains each of the available options. The dictionary checks spelling only. It will not find grammatical
errors.

FIGURE 6-7
The Spelling dialog box contains several options
for checking the spelling of a document.

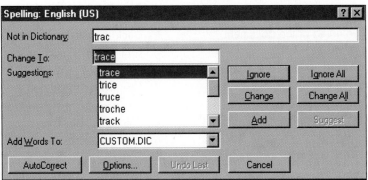

TABLE 6-1
Spelling dialog box options.

OPERATION	ACTION
Ignore	Ignores only the highlighted word
Ignore All	Ignores all instances of the same word
Change	Changes only the highlighted word
Change All	Changes all instances of the same word
Add	Adds the highlighted word to the custom dictionary
Suggest	Displays a list of proposed spellings
AutoCorrect	Adds a word to your AutoCorrect list
Options	Allows you to change default spelling check settings
Undo Last	Reverses your last spelling change
Cancel/Close	Before you make a spelling change, Cancel stops the spelling check. At the end of a spell check, Close stops the spelling check and saves all the changes you have made. After your first spelling change, the button name *Cancel* changes to *Close*.

ACTIVITY

Checking a Document's Spelling

1. Open *Activity 6-7*.

2. Press **Ctrl+Home** to move the insertion point to the beginning of the document.

3. Click the **Spelling** button on the toolbar.

4. The word *trac* is highlighted in the text and the Spelling dialog box appears. Note that a suggested word appears in the Change To box and other alternatives are in the Suggestions box.

5. Click the word *track*. It appears in the Change To box.

6. Click **Change.** Word replaces the misspelled word and continues checking.

7. The word *infomation* is highlighted. *Information* is in the Change To box.

8. Click **Change.**

9. The word *dairey* is highlighted. The word *dairy* and two other words are suggested.

Click **Change.** Word replaces the mis-spelled word and continues checking.

10. The word *americans* is highlighted. The word *Americans*, along with other words, are suggested. Click **Change All.** Word replaces the error each time it occurs in the document, and continues checking.

11. The word *Theye* is highlighted. Click **Change.** Word replaces the error and con-tinues checking.

12. The message, *The spelling check is com-plete,* appears.

13. Click **OK.** The insertion point returns to the beginning of the document.

14. Save the document as *American Diet.* Leave the file open for the next activity.

Using the Thesaurus

The ***Thesaurus*** is a useful feature for finding a synonym, a word with a similar meaning, for a word in your document. For some words, the Thesaurus also lists antonyms, or words with opposite meanings. Use the Thesaurus to find the exact word to express your message or to avoid using the same word re-peatedly in a document. To use the Thesaurus, highlight the word you want to look up and choose Thesaurus from the Tools menu, which brings up the The-saurus dialog box, as shown in Figure 6-8. In the Meanings box, click the word that best describes what you want to say. Then choose from the words listed in the Replace with Synonym box and click Replace. Table 6-2 describes the op-tions in the Thesaurus dialog box.

FIGURE 6-8
The Thesaurus dialog box contains a list of meanings and synonyms for a selected word.

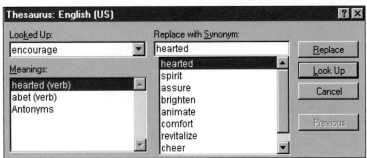

TABLE 6-2
Thesaurus dialog box options.

OPERATION	ACTION
Replace	Click to replace the original word with the word in the Replace with Synonym box
Look Up	Shows a listing of possible synonyms and meanings
Cancel	Click to close the dialog box
Previous	Click to show the last word you looked up in the current Thesaurus session. Does not show words from a previous dialog box.

Using the Thesaurus

1. Highlight the word *encourage* in the second paragraph.

2. Choose **Thesaurus** from the **Tools** menu. The Thesaurus dialog box appears, as in Figure 6-8. The box under Meanings contains a list of the meanings of *encourage* and Antonyms. The box under Replace with Synonym contains a list of synonyms for *encourage* using the *hearted* meaning.

3. In the Meanings box, click **abet (verb).** A new list of synonyms with the new meaning

is shown in the Replace with Synonym box.

4. Click **advocate** and choose **Replace.** Word replaces the word *encourage* with *advocate*.

5. Save the document.

6. Leave the document open for use in the next activity.

Using Find and Replace

Find and Replace are useful editing commands that let you find specific words in a document quickly and, if you wish, replace them instantly with new words. First you will learn about Find, then about Replace.

The Find Command

Using the Find command, you can quickly search a document for every occurrence of a specific word or phrase you key in the Find What box. The Find command moves the insertion point from its present position to the next occurrence of the word or phrase for which you are searching.

Find can locate whole or partial words. For example, Word can find the word *all* or any word with *all* in it, such as *fall, horizontally,* or *alloy*. However, you can choose options in the Find dialog box, explained in Table 6-3, to narrow your search criteria.

TABLE 6-3
Find dialog box options.

OPERATION	ACTION
Search	Lets you search from the location of the insertion point up, from the location of the insertion point down, or all (the entire document)
Match Case	Searches for words with the same case as that keyed in the Find What box
Find Whole Words Only	Finds only the word *all*—not words with *all* in them
Use Pattern Matching	Makes it possible to search for words using a question mark or asterisk, called a special search operator or wildcard, along with a word or characters in the Find dialog box. Each question mark represents a single character in the same position in a word. Each asterisk represents two or more characters (see Table 6-4).
Sounds Like	Locates words that sound alike but are spelled differently. For example, if you key the word *so*, Word would also find the word *sew*.
Find All Word Forms	Lets you find different forms of words. For example, if you search for the word *run*, Word would also find *ran, runs,* and *running*.
Find Next	Goes to the next occurrence of the word
Cancel	Stops the search and closes the dialog box
Format	Lets you search for formatting, such as bold, instead of searching for a specific word. It also allows you to search for words with specific formatting, such as the word *computer* in bold.
Special	Lets you search for special characters that may be hidden, such as a paragraph mark, or special characters that are not hidden, such as an em dash (—)
Replace	Changes the Find dialog box to the Replace dialog box, which is explained in the next section

TABLE 6-4
Using special search operators in the word processor.

TO FIND	KEY
Both *Caleb* and *Kaleb*	?aleb
Any five-letter word beginning with *a* and ending with *n*	a???n
June and *July*	Ju*
Kindness, tenderness, selfishness	*ness

Finding Text

1. Place the insertion point at the beginning of the document.

2. Choose **Find** from the **Edit** menu. The Find dialog box appears as shown in Figure 6-9.

3. In the Find What box, key **Di***.

4. Click the **Use Pattern Matching** option.

5. Choose **Find Next.** Word highlights and stops on the word *Diet* in the title. (You may have to move the Find dialog box down to see the highlighted word behind it.)

6. Choose **Find Next.** Word stops on the word *Dietary.*

7. Click **Cancel.**

FIGURE 6-9
The Find dialog box is used to find a specific word or phrase in a document.

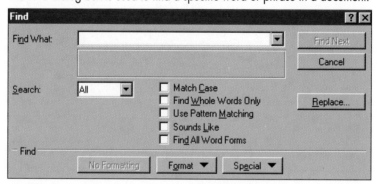

8. Move the insertion point to the beginning of the document.

9. Choose **Find** from the **Edit** menu.

10. Key **cautions** in the Find What box.

11. Click the **Use Pattern Matching** option to remove the check mark.

12. Click the **Find Whole Words Only** option.

13. In the Search box, choose **All.**

14. Click **Find Next.** The insertion point moves to the word *cautions*.

15. Click **Find Next** again. The message, *Word has finished searching the document,* appears. Click **OK.**

16. Click **Cancel.**

17. Save and leave the document open for the next activity.

The Replace Command

The Replace command is an extended version of Find, with all of Find's features. In addition, the Replace dialog box, shown in Figure 6-10, allows you to replace a word or phrase in the Find What box with another word or phrase you key in the Replace With box. The replacements can be made individually using the Replace button, or all occurrences can be replaced at once using the Replace All button.

FIGURE 6-10
The Replace dialog box lets you replace words individually or all at once.

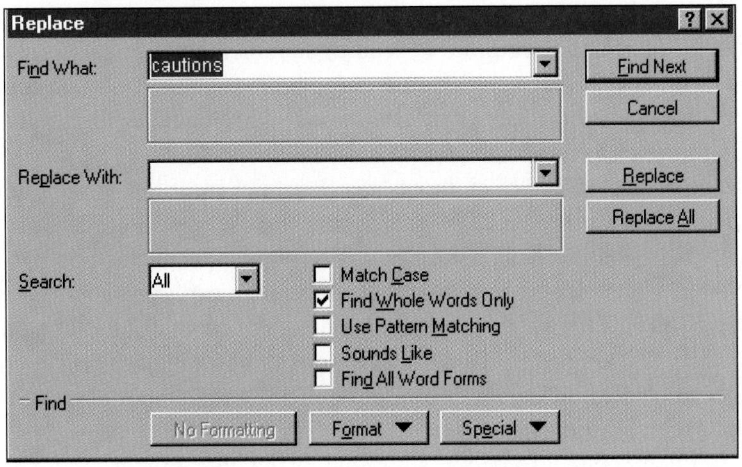

1. Press **Ctrl+Home** to move the insertion point to the beginning of the document.

2. Choose **Replace** from the **Edit** menu. The Replace dialog box appears with the word *cautions* in the Find What box, as shown in Figure 6-10.

3. Place the insertion point in the Replace With box. Key **warnings**.

4. Click **Replace All.** The following message appears: *Word has finished searching the document. 1 replacement was made.*

5. Click **OK.**

6. Click **Close** to close the Replace dialog box.

7. Save the document and leave it open for the next activity.

Creating Footnotes and Endnotes

A *footnote* or *endnote* is used to document quotations, figures, summaries, or other text that you do not want to include in the body of your document. Footnotes are printed at the bottom of each page, while endnotes are printed at the end of the document.

To insert a footnote or endnote, position your insertion point at the place in the document where you need a reference and choose Footnote from the Insert menu. The Footnote and Endnote dialog box appears, as shown in Figure 6-11. Specify in the Insert box whether you want an endnote or footnote. In the Numbering box, choose to reference your endnote or footnote with Auto-Number or a Custom Mark. Click the Options button to choose different types of AutoNumbers, such as 1, 2, 3 or i, ii, iii. Click the Symbol button to choose a symbol, such as ♥ or ♦.

After you create a footnote, a number or the custom mark you chose will appear in the document. The corresponding footnote will print at the end of the page or the endnote will print at the end of the document.

ACTIVITY 6-11 Creating Footnotes and Endnotes

1. Place the insertion point in the first paragraph at the end of the fourth sentence, after the quotation mark.

2. Choose **Footnote** from the **Insert** menu. The Footnote and Endnote dialog box appears, as shown in Figure 6-11. AutoNumber is chosen in the Numbering box. This indicates that your footnotes will be numbered.

FIGURE 6-11
You can represent footnotes in the text with numbers or symbols.

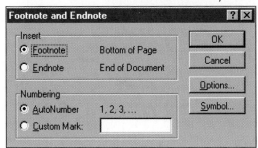

3. Click **OK.** The Footnote pane appears at the bottom of the document window with the insertion point blinking after the number *1*, as in Figure 6-12.

4. Key **"How America Eats,"** *Good House-keeping*, **November 1991, p. 180.** (Key the period.)

5. Click **Close** in the Footnote pane.

6. Place the insertion point at the end of the second paragraph, after the quotation mark.

7. Choose **Footnote** from the **Insert** menu. Click **OK.**

8. Key **U.S. Department of Agriculture and U.S. Department of Health and Human Services, "Nutrition and Your Health: Dietary Guidelines for Americans," Home and Garden Bulletin No. 232, 3d edition, 1990, p. 3.** (Key the period.)

9. Highlight all text in the footnote pane. Change the font to Times New Roman 10 point.

10. Click **Close.**

11. Save, print, and close the document.

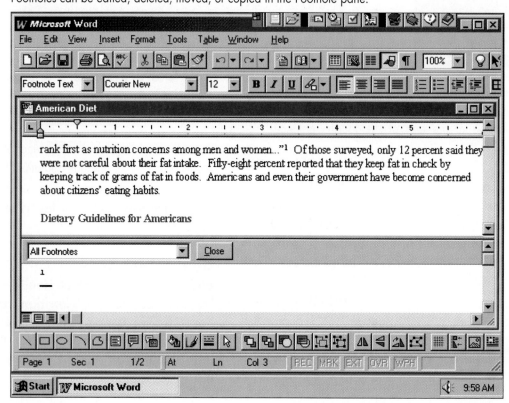

Printing in Portrait and Landscape Orientation

Documents printed in portrait orientation, as seen in Figure 6-13, are longer than they are wide. By default, Word is set to print pages in portrait orientation. In contrast, documents printed in landscape orientation, as seen in Figure 6-14, are wider than they are long. Most documents are printed in portrait orientation. Some documents, however, such as those with graphics or numerical information, look better when printed in landscape orientation.

To print a document in landscape orientation, access the Page Setup dialog box. Click the Paper Size tab and choose the Landscape option in the Orientation box.

FIGURE 6-13

Document pages printed in portrait orientation
are longer than they are wide.

The Monarch Theatre
will be casting actors and actresses
for its production of
Macbeth
on
Saturday, April 2, 19—
at 8 a.m.
Call Shelley Reynolds at
409-555-0993 for more information

FIGURE 6-14

Document pages printed in landscape orientation
are wider than they are long.

Come to Casino Night!

February 3, 7-12 p.m.
Stillwell Club
All Proceeds benefit the Stillwell Arts Foundation

Printing in Landscape Orientation

1. Open *Activity 6-12* from your template disk. Use Print Preview to view the document before you make any changes.

2. Choose **Page Setup** from the **File** menu. The Page Setup dialog box appears.

3. Click the **Paper Size** tab.

4. In the Orientation box, choose the **Landscape** option.

5. Click the **Margins** tab and change all the margins to .5 inches. Click **OK.**

6. Place the insertion point at the beginning of the second line of the document. Press **Backspace.** The line moves to the end of the top line. Insert a space between words.

7. Preview the document.

8. Save the document to your data disk as *Free Seminar.*

9. Print and close the document.

Summary

■ The quickest way to switch between documents is to click in the window or on the title bar of the document you want to become active. The other way to switch is to use the Window menu.

■ The Format Painter command on the toolbar allows you to copy the format or style of a block of text, rather than the text itself. By splitting your document, you can see both parts of the document. Each area of the document is called a pane. Go To allows you to skip to a specific page in a document.

■ Hidden formatting characters include spaces, paragraph returns, and end-of-line marks. The Word Count command quickly counts the pages, words, characters, paragraphs, and lines in your document.

■ The Spelling Checker contains options that allow you to check the spelling of words, ignore words, change misspelled words, or add words to your own custom dictionary.

■ The Thesaurus is a useful feature for finding a synonym (a word with a similar meaning) for a word in your document. For some words, the Thesaurus also lists antonyms, or words with opposite meanings.

■ The Find command moves the insertion point from its present position to the next occurrence of the word or phrase for which you are searching. Replace has all the features of Find. In addition, it allows you to replace a word or phrase in the Find What box with another word or phrase you key in the Replace With box.

■ A footnote or endnote is used to document quotations, figures, summaries, or other text that you do not want to include in the body of your document. Footnotes are printed at the bottom of each page, and endnotes are printed at the end of the document.

■ Documents printed in landscape orientation are wider than they are long.

● ● ● ● ● ● ● ● ● ● ● ● ● ●

REVIEW ACTIVITIES

TRUE/FALSE

Circle T or F to show whether the statement is true or false.

T   F   **1.** Having more than one document open at a time is useful when spell checking.

T   F   **2.** The Window menu allows you to switch between open documents.

T   F   **3.** The Format Painter button allows you to copy text from one document to another.

T   F   **4.** A pane is a part of a split window that contains its own scroll bars and ruler.

T   F   **5.** The Keep with Next option keeps a paragraph on the same page as the paragraph following it.

T   F   **6.** You can use Word Count to count only one paragraph.

T   F   **7.** The spelling checker can find grammatical errors.

T   F   **8.** The Thesaurus finds synonyms and antonyms for words.

T   F   **9.** The Find command will find and replace a word.

T   F   **10.** You can use only numbers for footnotes.

COMPLETION

Write the correct answer in the space provided.

1. Which menu is used to view the documents that are open?

_____

2. What does the Split command do?

_____

_____

3. To copy the indents or tabs from one paragraph to another, which button must be chosen from the toolbar?

_____

4. Why are hidden characters useful?

_____

5. Which command can quickly move the insertion point to a specific page?

_____

6. Which characters are used as wildcards in the Find and Replace dialog boxes?

_____

7. How is the Spelling Checker different from the Automatic Spell Checker?

_____

_____

8. In what menu is the Thesaurus command?

_____

9. What is the difference between an endnote and a footnote?

_____

10. What is the difference between landscape orientation and portrait orientation?

_____

_____

REINFORCEMENT APPLICATIONS

application 6-1

1. Open *Application 6-1a* from the template disk.
2. Open *Application 6-1b* from the template disk.
3. Copy the paragraph in *Application 6-1b* to *Application 6-1a* as the second paragraph of the letter. Adjust spacing between paragraphs as needed.
4. Save *Application 6-1a* as *Consent Letter*.
5. Close *Application 6-1b* without saving.
6. Spell check the document.
7. Find the word *Student* and replace it with *Chris* in all occurrences.
8. Save, print, and close the document.

application 6-2

1. Open *Application 6-2* from the template disk.
2. Replace the word *perfect* in the third paragraph with a synonym that makes sense in context.
3. Replace the word *excellent* in the third paragraph of text with a synonym that makes sense in context.
4. Highlight the first heading, *In the Market for a New Home?*
5. Change the font to Brush Script MT 18 point and remove the boldface.
6. Copy this format to the remaining headings.
7. Save as *Properties*.
8. Spell check the document.
9. Print the document in landscape orientation.
10. Save and close the document.

1. Open *American Diet.*

2. Place the insertion point after the quotation mark at the end of the paragraph that is indented on both sides (after the words, *should eat*).

3. Insert the following numbered footnote: **"Dietary Guidelines for Americans: No-nonsense Advice for Healthy Eating,"** *FDA Consumer,* **November 1985, p. 14.** (Key the period.)

4. Save the document as *Fat in the American Diet.*

5. Place the insertion point after the word *moderation* in the last item of the bulleted list.

6. Insert the following footnote: **"Nutrition and Your Health," p. 4.** (Key the period.)

7. Place the insertion point after the quotation mark after the word *cancer* in the fifth sentence under the heading, *Fat in the American Diet.*

8. Insert the following footnote: **"Nutrition and Your Health," p. 3.** (Key the period.)

9. Place the insertion point after the quotation mark at the end of the first sentence of the *Losing Weight Sensibly* paragraph.

10. Insert the following footnote: **"Nutrition and Your Health," p. 8.** (Key the period.)

11. Place the insertion point after the quotation mark at the end of the last sentence of the *Losing Weight Sensibly* paragraph.

12. Insert the following footnote: **"Nutrition and Your Health," p. 10.** (Key the period.)

13. Place the insertion point after the quotation mark at the end of the first paragraph after *Eating for Future Health.*

14. Insert the following footnote: **"Nutrition and Your Health," p. 16.** Change all the footnotes you keyed to Times New Roman 10 point.

15. Save the document.

16. Select all text in the document.

17. Turn on the Widow/Orphan Control in the Paragraph dialog box.

18. Save, print, and close the document.

INTRODUCTION TO INTEGRATION BASICS

As you have already learned, Office 95 is an integrated program. ***Integration*** means combining more than one Office 95 application to complete a project. For example, you can add a chart from an Excel worksheet to a Power-Point presentation. Or you can use information from an Access database to create form letters in Word. Tables from Word documents can become Excel data. It is just as easy to transfer data from a database to a worksheet as it is to transfer it to another database.

The value of an integrated program like Office 95 is that sharing data among applications is easy. Throughout this book, you will explore several ways to share data among the Office applications. The easiest approach is simply to cut, copy, and paste to move data between applications. Other ways to integrate data are by embedding it, linking it, creating form letters, and creating mailing labels.

Moving Data Between Applications

When you are moving data between applications, the file you are moving data *from* is called the ***source file*** and the file you are moving the data *to* is called the ***destination file.***

The process of moving data among different applications varies, depending on what applications are involved. Word, Excel, and Access documents have unique formats. For example, data from an Excel worksheet is arranged in cells, information in an Access database is collected in fields, and text in a Word document does not follow any particular format. When you move data among applications by cutting or copying and pasting, Office 95 changes the format of the information you are moving so that it may be used in the destination file. For example, information copied from fields in an Access database will be pasted in an Excel worksheet in columns and rows.

After completing each unit, you will be able to practice integrating the applications you have already learned. When you finish the Excel unit, you will have the opportunity to link worksheet data with a Word document. At the end of the Access unit, you will create form letters and mailing labels using database information in a Word document. After learning about PowerPoint, you will practice embedding a Word table in a presentation.

Summary

- Integration refers to using more than one of the Office 95 applications to create a document. Data can be copied and pasted among documents, embedded, or linked to ensure that data is up to date.

- Data is moved from a source file to a destination file. When data is moved between applications, Office 95 changes the format so the information fits the destination file.

• • • • • • • • • • • • • •

▼ REVIEW ACTIVITIES

TRUE/FALSE

Circle T or F to show whether the statement is true or false.

T   F   1. Copying worksheet data into a Word document is one example of integration.

T   F   2. The value of an integrated program like Office 95 is that sharing data among the applications is easy.

T   F   3. When you are moving data between applications, Office 95 does not change the format of data copied and pasted.

COMPLETION

Write the correct answer in the space provided.

1. What is the term for the file you are moving data from when copying information between applications?

_____

2. Give an example of a document that could be created using integration.

_____

_____

▼ INTEGRATION PROJECTS

Home Again Real Estate

In this section, you will create documents in Word that will be used to integrate data in future sections. You are a real estate broker at Home Again Real Estate, and you often use Office 95 to integrate files and complete your work more quickly and efficiently.

PROJECT A

Using Word, create a letterhead that you can use when writing to established and prospective clients. Include the address, telephone number, and fax number of Home Again Real Estate, as well as your name, extension number, and e-mail address. You can use Office 95 clip art, draw a graphic, or use text only. Be creative. Save the file as *Letterhead* and close.

PROJECT B

You want to keep track of the houses you sell each month. Create a table in Word where you can record the address and important features of each house. In the far left column, place the addresses of each of the three houses you sold last month. In the top row, place the features of the house as headings, including the number of bedrooms, bathrooms, and garages; total square footage; type of exterior; age of house; and selling price. Complete the table with information about each house. Get the information from a local newspaper or real estate guide, or make it up. Save the table as *House Table* and close.

PROJECT C

In the past, you have called prospective home buyers to let them know each time there is an upcoming open house. You decide it would be much easier to send letters instead. Open *Letterhead* and compose a letter on it to be sent out to prospective home buyers. The first paragraph should let them know that you are glad to help them search for a new home. Then give information about an open house on 287 Carlisle Lane which Home Again Real Estate is hosting at the end of the month. Include facts about the house that would interest a potential buyer. The last paragraph of the letter should say that you hope to see them there. Do not include name or address information. You will add this later from Access. Save the letter as *Open House Letter* and close.

▼ INTEGRATION SIMULATION

Java Internet Café

NOTE: *Before beginning these activities, make sure you have a Simulation template disk that contains all Simulation template files only. You will save new Simulation files to this disk.*

You work at the Java Internet Café, which has been open a short time. The café serves coffee, other beverages, and pastries, and offers Internet access. Seven computers are set up on tables along the north side of the store. Customers can come in and have a cup of coffee and a Danish while they explore the World Wide Web.

Because of your Office 95 experience, your manager asks you to create and revise many of the business's documents.

MARCH 4

Many customers ask questions about terms they come across while on the Internet. Your manager asks you to create a sign with definitions of the most common terms. The sign will be posted near each computer.

1. Open a new Word document.
2. Create the poster shown in Figure I-1. Follow the instructions in the margins.
3. Save as *Terminology Poster* on your Simulation template disk.
4. Print and close.

MARCH 5

Many customers become curious when they see computers through the windows of the coffee shop. The café servers are often too busy to explain the concept when the customer enters the store. Your manager asks you to revise the menu to include a short description of the café. These menus will be printed and placed near the entrance.

1. Open the file *Java Logo* from the Simulation template disk.
2. Key the text below.

> **The Java Internet Café is a coffee shop with a twist. As you can see, there are seven computers on tables at the north side of the café. These computers provide high-speed Internet access to our customers. Whether you're a regular on the Net or a novice, our system is designed to allow you easy exploration of the World Wide Web. You've heard about it; now give it a try. Ask your server to help you get started.**

FIGURE I-1

Top & Bottom Margins – 1"
Left & Right Margins – 1.25"

Arial Bold 26pt.
Dk. Blue

Internet Terminology

Terms: Bold
Dk. Blue

Browser: A program used on a computer connected to the Internet that provides access to the World Wide Web (WWW). There are two kinds of Web browsers: text-only and graphical. Graphical browsers are best because they allow you to see images and document layouts.

Text:
Arial
Narrow
16pt.

Download: To transfer a file from a remote computer to your computer through a modem and a telephone line.

E-mail (electronic mail): The use of a computer network to send and receive messages. With an Internet connection, you can compose messages and send them in seconds to a friend with an Internet connection in your city or in another country.

FAQ (Frequently Asked Questions): In USENET, a document posted to a newsgroup at regular intervals. It contains a list of the most common questions and answers for assisting new users.

Internet: A world-wide system of linked computer networks that eases data communication such as file transfer, e-mail, and newsgroups.

Newsgroup: In a bulletin board system (BBS), a discussion group that's devoted to a single topic. Members post e-mail messages to the group, and those reading the group messages send reply e-mail messages to the author or to the group.

USENET: The leading distributed bulletin board linked through the Internet, which offers more than 1,500 newsgroups.

World Wide Web (WWW): A global system that uses the Internet as its carrier. You navigate from "page" to page by clicking underlined links, which display other documents (containing their own links).

¾ pt. dotted line
box, Dk. Blue,
6pt. from text

3. Save as *Java Menu* on the Simulation template disk.

4. Change the left and right margins to 1 inch.

5. Change the font of the paragraph you just keyed to Arial 11 pt. if it's not already.

6. Insert one blank line after the paragraph and key the title **Menu** and center it.

7. Change the font of *Menu* to Arial Narrow 18 pt. bold. If you don't have this font, substitute another one. You'll paste the menu information from Excel later.

8. Insert and center the following footer.

   Sit back, sip your coffee, and surf the net.

9. Change the font to Arial Narrow 14 pt. bold.

10. Save, print, and close the document.

U N I T 3

MICROSOFT EXCEL

SPREADSHEET BASICS

OBJECTIVES
When you complete this chapter, you will be able to:

1. Understand the role of Excel in Office 95.
2. Define the terms *spreadsheet* and *worksheet*.
3. Identify the parts of the worksheet.
4. Move the highlight in the worksheet.
5. Select cells and enter data in the worksheet.
6. Change column width and edit cells.
7. Change the appearance of a cell.
8. Save and print a worksheet.

What Is Excel?

Excel is the spreadsheet application of the Office 95 programs. A *spreadsheet* is a grid of rows and columns containing numbers, text, and formulas. The purpose of a spreadsheet is to solve problems that involve numbers. Before computers, spreadsheets were created with pencils on ruled paper. Calculators were used to solve complicated mathematical operations (see Figure 7-1). Computer spreadsheets also contain rows and columns, but they perform calculations much faster and more accurately than worksheets created with pencil, paper, and calculator.

Spreadsheets are used in many ways. For example, a spreadsheet can be used to prepare a budget for the next few months or determine payments to be made on a loan. The primary advantage of the spreadsheet is the ability to complete complex and repetitious calculations accurately, quickly, and easily. For

FIGURE 7-1
Computer spreadsheets automate calculations and are replacing spreadsheets prepared with paper, pencil, and calculator.

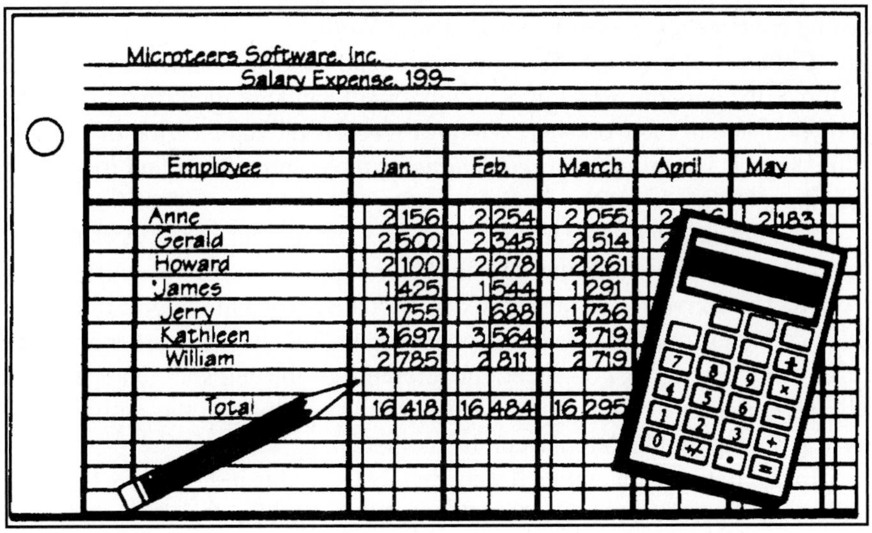

example, you might use a spreadsheet to calculate your grade in a class; your instructor may use a spreadsheet to calculate grades for the entire class.

Besides calculating rapidly and accurately, spreadsheets are flexible. Making changes to an existing spreadsheet is usually as easy as pointing and clicking with the mouse. Suppose, for example, you have prepared a budget on a spreadsheet and have overestimated the amount of money you will need to spend on books. You may change a single entry in your spreadsheet and watch the entire spreadsheet recalculate the new budgeted amount. You can imagine the work this change would require if you were calculating the budget with pencil and paper.

Excel uses the term *worksheet* to refer to computerized spreadsheets. Sometimes you may want to use several worksheets that relate to each other. A collection of related worksheets is referred to as a *workbook.*

Parts of a Worksheet

You can open a new Excel worksheet by clicking Microsoft Excel from the Windows 95 Programs menu. Or, you can choose Start a New Document from the Shortcut Bar, or New Office Document from the Start menu and then choose Blank Workbook from the New dialog box.

When the worksheet appears on the screen, you will see some of the basic features that you learned while using Word: the title bar, menu bar, and the toolbar. However, as shown in Figure 7-2, the formatting bar has several new buttons. Other parts of the worksheet, such as the formula bar and the grid of cells created by columns and rows, do not appear in Word.

Columns of the worksheet appear vertically and are identified by letters at the top of the window. *Rows* appear horizontally and are identified by numbers on the left side of the worksheet window. A *cell* is the intersection of a row and column and is identified by a *cell reference,* the column letter and row number (for example, C4, A1, B2).

The *formula bar* appears directly below the toolbar in the worksheet. On the far left side of the formula bar is the cell reference area that identifies the *active cell.* The active cell is the cell ready for data entry. On the grid of cells, the active cell is surrounded by a dark border. Figure 7-2 shows a border around the active cell (A1) on the worksheet; the reference of the cell should appear in the cell reference area of the formula bar. You may change the active cell by moving the highlight from one cell to another.

In Word, the point at which a character is keyed is indicated by the cursor. In the worksheet the entry point is indicated by a *highlight.*

FIGURE 7-2
Some parts of the worksheet are similar to the word processor screen in Word. The worksheet, however, has additional parts used with numerical data.

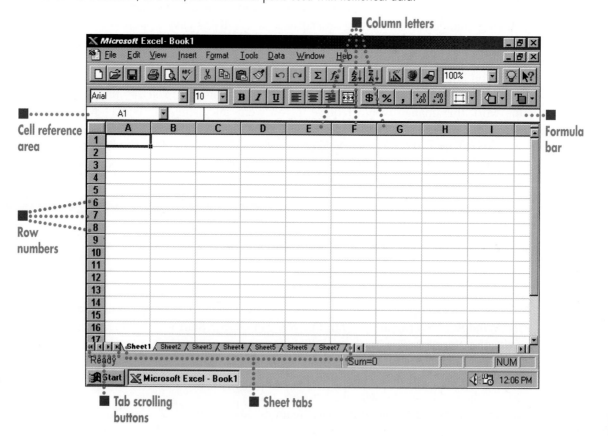

Opening an Existing Worksheet

When you begin Excel, the program displays a new worksheet temporarily titled *Book1*. This worksheet will be eliminated if you open another file.

ACTIVITY

Opening an Existing Worksheet

• •

1. If you have not started Excel already, do so by clicking the Microsoft Excel button on the Windows 95 Programs menu. An empty worksheet titled *Book1* appears on the screen.

2. Choose **Open** from the **File** menu. The Open dialog box appears.

3. In the Look in selection box, click the down arrow to show your computer's drives.

4. Click the drive containing your template disk. The files on the disk appear in the display window.

5. Double-click the filename *Activity 7-1*. The worksheet appears on the screen.

6. Maximize the document window. Your screen should appear similar to Figure 7-3.

7. Leave *Activity 7-1* on the screen for the next activity.

FIGURE 7-3

The worksheet is ideal for solving numerical problems, such as preparing a summer budget.

	A	B	C	D	E	F	G	H	I
1	Summer Budget								
2		June	July	August					
3	Income								
4	Summer Job	1500	1500	1500					
5	Recycling Cans	50	50	50					
6	Total Income	1550	1550	1550					
7									
8	Expenses								
9	Tuition Payment	0	0	2000					
10	Car Payment	350	350	350					
11	Clothing	200	100	150					
12	Eating Out	50	50	50					
13	Toiletries/Cosmet	25	25	25					
14									
15	Entertainment	15	15	15					
16	Total Expenses	640	540	2590					
17									

Moving the Highlight in a Worksheet

When working with a large worksheet, you may not be able to view the entire worksheet on the screen. You can use the mouse to scroll throughout the worksheet by dragging the scroll box in the scroll bar to the desired position. You can also move the highlight to different parts of the worksheet using direction keys or the Go To command in the Edit menu.

Using Keys to Move the Highlight

You can move the highlight by pressing certain keys or key combinations. Table 7-1 illustrates the use of these keys. You will see that many of these keys and key combinations are familiar to you from Word.

TABLE 7-1
You may move the highlight in the worksheet by pressing direction keys.

TO MOVE	PRESS
Left one column	Left arrow
Right one column	Right arrow
Up one row	Up arrow
Down one row	Down arrow
To the first cell of a row	Home
To cell A1	Ctrl+Home
To the last cell containing data	Ctrl+End
Up one window	Page Up
Down one window	Page Down
To the previous worksheet in a workbook	Ctrl+Page Up
To the next worksheet in a workbook	Ctrl+Page Down

NOTE: *When an arrow key is held down, the movement of the highlight will repeat and move quickly.*

Using the Go To Command to Move in the Worksheet

You may want to move the highlight to a cell that does not appear on the screen. The fastest way do this is by using the Go To command in the Edit menu, then designating the cell reference of the cell in which you want the highlight to appear. The F5 key may be used as a shortcut to access the Go To command.

ACTIVITY 7-2
Moving the Highlight in the Worksheet

1. Move to the last cell in the worksheet that contains data by pressing **Ctrl+End.** The highlight moves to cell D19 in the lower right side of the worksheet.

2. Move to the first cell of the row by pressing **Home.** The highlight appears in a cell containing the words *Cumulative Surplus.*

3. Move up one cell by pressing the up arrow key. The highlight appears in a cell containing the word *Surplus.*

4. Move to B4 by using the Go To command:
   a. Press **F5.** The Go To dialog box appears.
   b. Key **B4**.
   c. Click **OK.** The highlight should move to B4.

5. Leave *Activity 7-1* on the screen for the next activity.

Selecting a Group of Cells

In later chapters, you will perform operations on more than one cell at a time. A selected group of cells is referred to as a ***range.*** In a range, all cells touch each other and form a rectangle. The range is identified by the cell in the upper left corner and the cell in the lower right corner, separated by a colon (for example, A3:C5). To select a range of cells, place the highlight in one corner of the range of cells and drag the highlight to the cell in the opposite corner. As you drag the highlight, the range of selected cells will become shaded (except for the cell you originally selected), as in Figure 7-4.

FIGURE 7-4
A range is selected by dragging the highlight from one corner of a range to the opposite corner.

	A	B	C	D	E	F	G	H	I
1	Summer Budget								
2		June	July	August					
3	Income								
4	Summer Job	1500	1500	1500					
5	Recycling Cans	50	50	50					
6	Total Income	1550	1550	1550					
7									
8	Expenses								
9	Tuition Payment	0	0	2000					
10	Car Payment	350	350	350					
11	Clothing	200	100	150					
12	Eating Out	50	50	50					
13	Toiletries/Cosmet	25	25	25					
14									
15	Entertainment	15	15	15					
16	Total Expenses	640	540	2590					
17									

Cell reference: B4 — 1500

ACTIVITY 7-3

Selecting a Range of Cells

1. Select the range B4:D4.
   a. Move the pointer to cell B4 if necessary.
   b. Hold down the mouse button and drag to the right until D4 is highlighted.
   c. Release the mouse button. Cells C4 and D4 become shaded.

2. Select the range B2:D17. (You may need to scroll up to view cell B2.)

   a. Move the pointer to cell B2.
   b. Hold down the mouse button and drag down and to the right until D17 is highlighted.
   c. Release the mouse button.

3. Leave *Activity 7-1* on the screen for the next activity.

Entering Data into a Cell

Worksheet cells may contain data in the form of text, numbers, formulas, or functions. Text consists of alphabetical characters and is usually in the form of headings, labels, or explanatory notes. Numbers can be in the form of values, dates, or times. Formulas are equations that calculate a value stored in a cell. Functions are special formulas that place either values or characters in cells. (Formulas and functions are discussed in later chapters.)

You enter data by keying it, then either clicking the Enter button on the formula bar (indicated by a check mark) or pressing Enter on the keyboard. If you choose not to enter the data you have keyed, simply click the Cancel button in the formula bar (indicated by an *X*) and the keyed data will be deleted. If you make a mistake, the Undo command in the Edit menu can reverse your most recent change. Functions may be placed in the cell by clicking the Function Wizard button (indicated by an f_x).

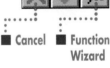

■ Enter

■ Cancel ■ Function Wizard

ACTIVITY

7-4 Entering Text and Numbers in Cells

Notice that row 14 does not contain data. Suppose you would like to change the budget to include expenses of $25 a month for compact discs.

1. Move the highlight to A14 and key **Compact Discs**. As you key, the letters appear both in the cell and in the formula bar.

2. Click the **Enter** button (indicated by a check mark) in the formula bar or press the **Enter** key.

3. Move to B14 and key **25**. Before entering the data by clicking the Enter button, notice the total expenses for June are 640.

4. Click the **Enter** button. The amount of total expenses for June, shown in cell B16, changes from 640 to 665. You can now appreciate the value of the worksheet in making quick calculations when budget data changes.

5. Enter **25** into C14 and D14. Notice how the worksheet recalculates the amounts each time you make a change. Your screen should appear similar to Figure 7-5.

6. Leave *Activity 7-1* on the screen for the next activity.

FIGURE 7-5
Both text and numbers may be entered into worksheet cells.

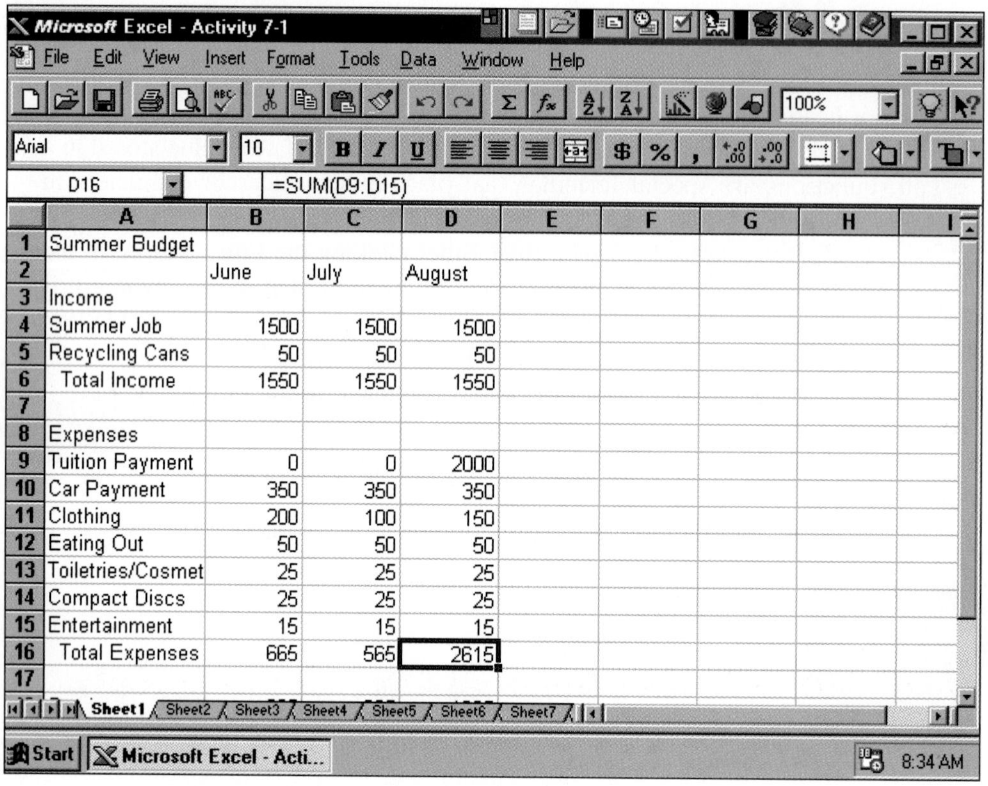
Microsoft Excel - Activity 7-1
File Edit View Insert Format Tools Data Window Help
100%
Arial
10
D16
=SUM(D9:D15)
A B C D E F G H I
1 Summer Budget
2 June July August
3 Income
4 Summer Job 1500 1500 1500
5 Recycling Cans 50 50 50
6 Total Income 1550 1550 1550
7
8 Expenses
9 Tuition Payment 0 0 2000
10 Car Payment 350 350 350
11 Clothing 200 100 150
12 Eating Out 50 50 50
13 Toiletries/Cosmet 25 25 25
14 Compact Discs 25 25 25
15 Entertainment 15 15 15
16 Total Expenses 665 565 2615
17
Sheet1 Sheet2 Sheet3 Sheet4 Sheet5 Sheet6 Sheet7
Start
Microsoft Excel - Acti...
8:34 AM

Changing Cell Width and Height

Sometimes the data you key will not fit in the column. When data is wider than the column, Excel will respond in one of the following ways:

- Displaying a series of number signs (######) in the cell.
- Truncating the data (the right-hand portion of the data will not be displayed).
- Letting the data run outside the column.
- Converting the data to a different numerical form (for example, changing long numbers to exponential form).

You may widen the column by placing the mouse pointer on the boundary of the right edge of the column heading. The pointer then changes into a double-headed arrow. To widen the column, drag to the right until the column is the desired size.

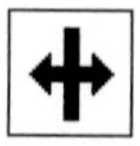

You can also change the height of a row by dragging the bottom edge of the row heading. Right now you may see no reason to change the height of a row, but later in this chapter you will learn how to change the font size of data in cells. A larger font size may require a taller cell.

Widening a Column

1. Key **September** into E2 and press **Enter.** The data appears partially in column F.

2. Place the mouse pointer to the right of the heading for column E. The pointer should turn into a double-headed arrow.

3. Drag the double-headed arrow to the right and release. The entire word *September*

should appear within column E. If it does not, you may need to drag the double-headed arrow farther.

4. Leave *Activity 7-1* on the screen for the next activity.

Letting Excel Find the Best Fit

Suppose you have a column full of data of varying widths. You want the column to be wide enough to display the longest entry, but no wider than necessary. Excel will determine the optimal width of the cell when you double-click the double-arrow symbol.

Finding the Best Fit

As you worked on previous activities, you may have noticed that the data in cell A13 exceeds the width of column A. In this activity, Excel will determine the optimal width of column A.

1. Place the mouse cursor to the right of the heading for column A. The pointer turns into

a double-headed arrow.

2. Double-click the mouse button. Column A widens to show all the data in cell A13.

3. Leave *Activity 7-1* on the screen for the next activity.

Determining a Specific Column Width

You may want to create a column that has a specific character width. For example, if you know that all the data to be entered into a particular column will be numbers less than 100, you may want to specify that the column be four characters wide (adding an extra character to keep the data from being too close to the next column).

FIGURE 7-6
The Column Width dialog box allows you to determine a specific character width for a column.

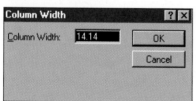

The Column Width dialog box, shown in Figure 7-6, allows you to key the desired number of characters for a column width. To specify the column width, place the highlight in the column you would like to change, point to the Column command in the Format menu, and click Width. If you would like to change the column width of several columns at once, select a range of cells within those columns, or select all the columns by dragging across the column headings, and specify the width in the Column Width dialog box.

Text Wrap

Text that is too long for a cell will spill over into the next cell, if the next cell is empty. If the next cell is not empty, the text that does not fit into the cell will not display. You can choose to have text wrap within a cell in the same way text wraps within a Word word processor document. The row height will automatically adjust to show all the lines of text.

To turn on the text wrap option, select the cells in which you intend to wrap text. Then choose Cells from the Format menu and click the Alignment tab. A dialog box similar to Figure 7-7 will appear. Click the Wrap Text check box to turn on the text wrap option.

FIGURE 7-7
The Wrap Text check box is located on the Alignment tab of the Format Cells dialog box.

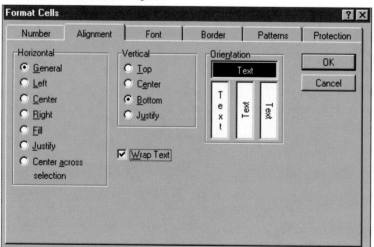

ACTIVITY

Specifying Column Width and Wrapping Text

1. Move the highlight to cell A1.

2. Key **Personal Budget for the Summer**. Press **Enter.** The text spills into the next cell.

3. Return the highlight to cell A1.

4. Choose **Cells** from the **Format** menu.

5. Click the **Alignment** tab.

6. Click the **Wrap Text** check box until a check mark appears.

7. Click **OK.** The text wraps in the cell and the cell height adjusts automatically.

8. Drag column headings B through E. All the columns become shaded.

9. Choose **Column** from the **Format** menu, then choose **Width** from the pop-out menu. The Column Width dialog box appears.

10. Enter **10** in the Column Width box.

11. Click **OK.** Your screen should appear similar to Figure 7-8. The selected columns have been widened to 10-character widths.

12. Leave *Activity 7-1* on the screen for the next activity.

FIGURE 7-8
With the Wrap Text option, a cell can contain more than one line of text.

```
X Microsoft Excel - Activity 7-1                                      _ □ ×
File   Edit   View   Insert   Format   Tools   Data   Window   Help    _ 8 ×

Arial            10    B  I  U   ≡ ≡ ≡ 国   $ % , ...
                 B1

        A              B         C         D         E       F    G    H
    Personal Budget for
 1  the Summer
 2                    June      July      August    September
 3  Income
 4  Summer Job        1500      1500      1500
 5  Recycling Cans      50        50        50
 6    Total Income    1550      1550      1550
 7
 8  Expenses
 9  Tuition Payment      0         0      2000
10  Car Payment        350       350       350
11  Clothing           200       100       150
12  Eating Out          50        50        50
13  Toiletries/Cosmetics 25       25        25
14  Compact Discs       25        25        25
15  Entertainment       15        15        15
16    Total Expenses   665       565      2615

Sheet1 / Sheet2 / Sheet3 / Sheet4 / Sheet5 / Sheet6 / Sheet7

Start   X Microsoft Excel - Acti...                              8:37 AM
```

Changing Data in a Cell

As you work with the worksheet, you may change your mind about data or make a mistake. If so, you may edit, replace, or clear existing data in the worksheet's cells.

Editing Data

Edit data when only minor changes to cell data are necessary. Data in a cell may be edited in the formula bar by using the Edit key—F2 on your keyboard. To edit data in a cell, select the cell by placing the highlight in the cell and pressing F2. A cursor similar to the one in the word processor will appear in the cell. You may use the cursor to change the data in the cell. Press Enter to reenter the data.

You may prefer to use the mouse to edit a cell. First, click the cell you want to edit; then click in the formula bar at the place you want to change the data. After you have made your changes, click the Enter button.

Replacing Data

Cell contents are usually replaced when you must make significant changes to cell data. To replace cell contents, select the cell, key the new data, and enter the data by clicking the Enter button or by pressing the Enter key.

Clearing Data

Clearing a cell will empty the cell of all its contents. To clear an active cell, you may either press the Delete key or choose the Clear command in the Edit menu. Clicking the Clear command gives you a pop-out menu that allows you to delete the format of the cell, the contents of the cell, or a note with the cell.

ACTIVITY

Changing Data in a Cell

1. Cell A18 contains the word *Surplus*. Edit the cell so that it contains the words *Cash Surplus*.
   a. Move the highlight to **A18.**
   b. Press **F2.** A cursor should appear in the cell.
   c. Move the cursor between the left edge of the cell and the *S* by pressing the left arrow key.
   d. Key **Cash** and a space.

   e. Press **Enter.** The edited contents should appear in the cell.

2. Cell A3 now contains the word *Income*. Replace this word with the word *Revenue*.
   a. Move the highlight to **A3.**
   b. Key **Revenue**.
   c. Click the **Enter** button on the formula bar.

3. In the previous activity, you entered the word *September* into E2. Suppose you change your mind and now want to delete that entry.
   a. Move the highlight to **E2.**
   b. Press the **Delete** key. The contents should be cleared from the cell. Your screen should appear similar to Figure 7-9.

4. Leave *Activity 7-1* on the screen for the next activity.

FIGURE 7-9

Changes may be made to a cell in a worksheet by editing or replacing data.

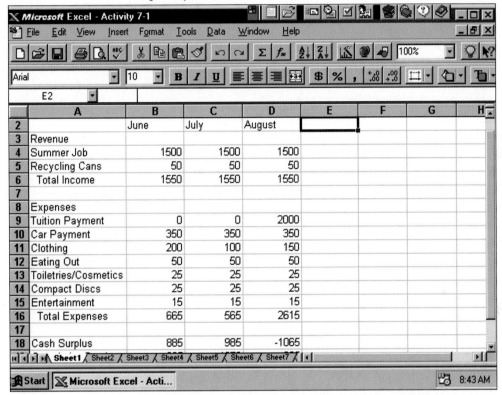

Changing Cell Appearance

You can change the appearance of a cell's contents to make it easier to read. In this section, you will learn to alter the appearance of cell contents by changing the font, font size, style, alignment, format, and borders. Examples of alternative appearances are shown in Figure 7-10. Most of the changes use the toolbar, which provides shortcuts to many worksheet commands.

Fonts and Font Sizes

The font and font size may significantly affect the readability of the worksheet if you decide to print it. The number and types of fonts available are deter-

FIGURE 7-10

The appearance of cell contents may be changed in style, alignment, and format.

	A	B	C	D	E	F
1	**CHANGING TEXT APPEARANCE**					
2	**Bolded Text**					
3	*Italicized Text*					
4	Underlined Text					
5	Left Aligned					
6	Centered					
7	Right Aligned					
8	**CHANGING NUMBER APPEARANCE**					
9	General	1000				
10	Number	1000.00				
11	Currency	$1,000.00				
12	Percent	35.2%				
13	Comma	1,000.00				
14	Scientific	1.00E+03				
15	Fraction	35 7/8				

mined by the printer you are using. You can choose different fonts for different parts of a worksheet. For example, you may want your numbers displayed in a 12-point serif font, and the worksheet's title in an 18-point sans serif font.

Changing fonts in a worksheet is similar to changing fonts in Word. Highlight the cells you want the change to affect and choose the font and size you desire. You can use the toolbar, or choose the Cells command on the Format menu and click the Font tab.

Style

Bolding, italicizing, or underlining can add emphasis to the contents of a cell. Highlight the cell or cells you want to change and click the appropriate style button in the toolbar. To return the contents of the cell to a normal style, simply click the button again.

In addition to the styles available on the toolbar, you can add shading, color, or colored text to the cells to add emphasis. Choose the Cells command in the Format menu, then click the Patterns tab. Choose a pattern and color from the dialog box.

To add color to the cell or cell text, you can also click the Color button or Font Color button on the toolbar and choose a color.

■ Color   ■ Font Color

Cell Alignment

You may align the contents of a cell or cells in four ways: against the left margin of the cell, in the center of the cell, against the right margin of the cell, or centered across several columns. Excel automatically aligns all text entries with the left side of the cell. All numbers are aligned on the right side of the cell unless a different alignment is specified.

To change the alignment of the cell, place the highlight in the cell and click the alignment button you prefer. To access alignment options not present on the toolbar, choose Cells from the Format menu, then click the Alignment tab.

■ Center Across Columns

Formats

Several cell formats are available for the worksheet. The default format is called *general format,* which accommodates both text and numerical data. However, you can use several other formats (see Table 7-2). You may format a cell by highlighting the cell or range and choosing Cells from the Format menu. Then click the Number tab and select a format (see Figure 7-11). You can also access some of these formats from the toolbar.

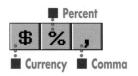

■ Percent

■ Currency ■ Comma

TABLE 7-2
Cells of a worksheet may be formatted in several ways.

FORMAT NAME	DISPLAY DESCRIPTION
General	The default format; displays both text and numerical data as keyed
Number	Displays numerical data with a fixed number of places to the right of the decimal point
Currency	Displays numerical data preceded by a dollar sign
Accounting	Displays numerical data in a currency format that lines up the dollar sign and decimal point vertically within a column
Date	Displays text and numerical data as dates
Time	Displays text and numerical data as times
Percentage	Displays numerical data followed by a percent sign
Fraction	Displays numerical data as fractional values
Scientific	Displays numerical data in exponential notation
Text	Displays numerical data that will not be used for calculation, such as serial numbers containing hyphens
Special	Displays numerical data in specific formats such as ZIP codes, phone numbers, and social security numbers
Custom	Displays a variety of formats that may be selected or designed (for example, numerical formats with commas or leading zeros may be selected)

FIGURE 7-11
Cell formats are selected by clicking the Number
tab in the Format Cells dialog box.

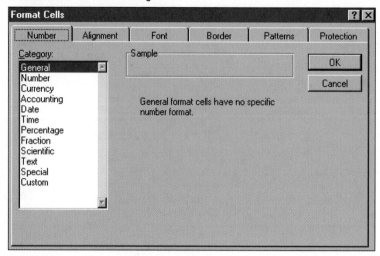

Borders

Emphasis may be added to a cell by placing a border around its edges. You may place the border around the entire cell, or only on certain sides of the cell. Borders may be placed in two ways. First, choose the Cells command in the Format menu, then click the Border tab. Select the desired border style.

FIGURE 7-12
Choose an option from the grid to add a border line.

The second way to place a border is to click the Borders button on the formatting bar. When you click the down arrow of the Borders button, a grid of border choices appears, as shown in Figure 7-12. Choose an option from the grid to set a border line.

ACTIVITY

Changing the Appearance of Cells in the Worksheet

1. Bold the following cells for emphasis:
   a. Move the highlight to **A1.**
   b. Click the **Bold** button on the toolbar. The words in cell A1 should become bold.
   c. Drag the mouse pointer from **B2** and release in **D2** to define the range B2:D2. The group of cells becomes shaded. (B2 will not be shaded.)
   d. Click the **Bold** button in the toolbar. All of the month names in the cells should become bold.
   e. Bold the following cells using the same procedure: **A3, A6, A8, A16, A18,** and **A19.** If necessary, widen column A to accommodate the data in cell A19.

2. Underline the names of the months to show they are column headings:
   a. Select the range **B2:D2.**
   b. Click the **Underline** button on the toolbar.

3. Align the names of the months in the centers of the columns:
   a. Make sure **B2** through **D2** are still selected.
   b. Click the **Center** button on the toolbar.

4. Format the following cells in currency format by selecting with the highlight and clicking the Currency button on the toolbar: **B4, C4, D4, B19, C19,** and **D19.**

5. Format the cell range from B5 through D18 in Currency format that excludes the dollar sign:
   a. Select the range **B5:D18.**
   b. Choose **Cells** from the **Format** menu.
   c. Click the **Number** tab.
   d. Click **Currency** in the **Category** list.
   e. Enter **2** in the **Decimal Places** box if it does not appear already.
   f. Click the **Use $** check box until the check disappears.
   g. Click **OK.** The selected group should change to a currency format, without the dollar sign, and with two decimals to the right of the decimal point.

6. Italicize the account names:
   a. Select **A4** and **A5.**
   b. Click the **Italic** button on the toolbar.
   c. Select **A9** through **A15.**
   d. Click the **Italic** button.

7. Place a border around the worksheet title, *Personal Budget for the Summer*:
   a. Highlight **A1.**
   b. Choose **Cells** from the **Format** menu.
   c. Click the **Border** tab.

d. Click a dark, solid line in the **Style** list.
e. Click the **Outline** box in the **Border** list until a line appears in the box.
f. Click **OK.** When the highlight is moved from A1, a border will appear on all sides of the cell.

8. Shade the cell containing the worksheet title.
   a. Highlight **A1.**
   b. Choose **Cells** from the **Format** menu.
   c. Click the **Patterns** tab.
   d. Click the down arrow in the **Pattern** box. A grid of shades, patterns and colors will appear, as shown in Figure 7-13.
   e. Click a pattern from the top part of the grid. The dialog box disappears and your selected pattern will appear in the Sample box.
   f. Click a color from the **Color** list.
   g. Click **OK.** The title will be shaded with the color you selected. If the title is difficult to see, select a thinner pattern or lighter color. When the highlight is moved from A1, your screen should appear similar to Figure 7-14.

9. Leave *Activity 7-1* on the screen for the next activity.

FIGURE 7-13
The grid in the Pattern tab of the Format Cells dialog box may be used to determine cell colors and shading patterns.

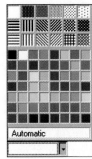

FIGURE 7-14
The appearance of cell contents may be changed by bolding, underlining, and centering.

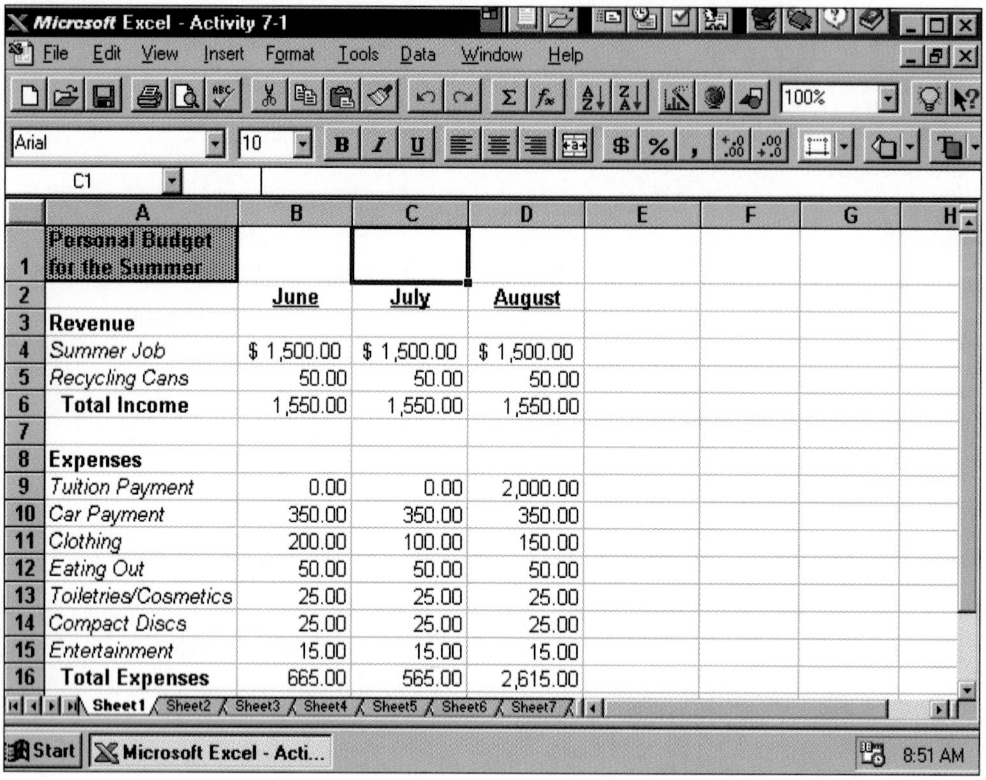

	A	B	C	D
1	Personal Budget for the Summer			
2		June	July	August
3	Revenue			
4	Summer Job	$ 1,500.00	$ 1,500.00	$ 1,500.00
5	Recycling Cans	50.00	50.00	50.00
6	Total Income	1,550.00	1,550.00	1,550.00
7				
8	Expenses			
9	Tuition Payment	0.00	0.00	2,000.00
10	Car Payment	350.00	350.00	350.00
11	Clothing	200.00	100.00	150.00
12	Eating Out	50.00	50.00	50.00
13	Toiletries/Cosmetics	25.00	25.00	25.00
14	Compact Discs	25.00	25.00	25.00
15	Entertainment	15.00	15.00	15.00
16	Total Expenses	665.00	565.00	2,615.00

Saving a Worksheet

You can save worksheets using the same process you learned for Word documents. The first time you save a worksheet, you will see the Save As dialog box asking you to name the worksheet. Once a worksheet has been saved, the Save command will update the latest version on disk.

ACTIVITY 7-10 Saving a Worksheet

1. Choose **Save As** from the **File** menu. The Save As dialog box appears.
2. Click the Save in box and specify the drive of your data disk.

3. Key **Summer Budget** in the File name box.

4. Click **Save.** The document is saved as

Summer Budget on your data disk. Leave the document open for the next activity.

Basics of Printing a Worksheet

Printing a worksheet is similar to printing a Word document. There are options available to print part of a worksheet or to change the way your worksheet prints. You will learn more about these options in the next chapter. For now, you will print the entire worksheet using what you learned in Word.

ACTIVITY

7-11 Printing a Worksheet

1. Choose **Print** from the **File** menu. The Print dialog box appears. This worksheet has only one page and you want only one copy, so you will not need to make any changes in the default settings.

2. Click **OK.** The worksheet should begin printing.

3. Choose **Close** from the **File** menu. If you are asked to save changes, click **Yes.** The worksheet closes.

Summary

■ The purpose of a worksheet is to solve problems involving numbers. The primary advantage of the worksheet is to complete complex and repetitious calculations quickly and easily.

■ The worksheet consists of columns and rows intersecting to form cells. Each cell is identified by a cell reference, which is the letter of the column and number of the row. You may move to different cells of the worksheet by using a series of keystrokes or by scrolling with the mouse. Both text and numerical data may be entered into the worksheet. Data may be altered by editing, replacing, or deleting.

■ The appearance of cell data may be changed to make the worksheet easier to understand. Font and font size may be changed for the entire worksheet. Style (bold, italic, and underline) and alignment (left, center, and right justification) of individual cells may be changed and borders may be added. In addition, the appearance of the cell may be changed to accommodate data in a variety of numerical formats.

• • • • • • • • • • • • • •

REVIEW ACTIVITIES

TRUE/FALSE

Circle T or F to show whether the statement is true or false.

T F 1. The primary advantage of a worksheet is to summarize text documents.

T F 2. A cell is the intersection of a row and column.

T F 3. The active cell reference will appear in the toolbar.

T F 4. The Go To command saves a file and exits Excel.

T F 5. To select a group of cells, click each cell individually until all cells in the range have been selected.

T F 6. The Clear command in the Edit menu can be used to remove the contents of a cell.

T F 7. The best way to make minor changes to existing data in a cell is to key new data and press the Enter key.

T F 8. To change the cell to exponential format, choose the Cells command from the Format menu and click the Number tab.

T F 9. Border formats define the portion of the worksheet that will be saved when the Save command is selected.

T F 10. Saving a worksheet file differs significantly from saving a Microsoft Word file.

COMPLETION

Write the correct answer in the space provided.

1. What term describes a cell that is ready for data entry?

2. How are columns identified in a worksheet?

3. What indicates that a cell is ready to accept data?

4. Which keys should be pressed to move the highlight to the last cell of the worksheet that contains data?

5. Which default cell format accommodates both textual and numerical data?

6. How will Excel respond when data is too wide for the column in which it has been entered?

_____

_____

7. Which key is pressed to edit data in an active cell?

_____

8. Which key is pressed to clear data from an active cell?

_____

9. Which part of the worksheet provides shortcuts for the most frequently used commands?

_____

10. What forms of cell alignment are available in the worksheet?

_____

application 7-1

In the blank space, write the letter of the keystroke that matches the highlight movement.

___ 1. Left one column

___ 2. Right one column

___ 3. Up one row

___ 4. Down one row

___ 5. To the first cell of a row

___ 6. To cell A1

___ 7. To the last cell containing data

___ 8. Up one window

___ 9. Down one window

___10. To the previous worksheet in a workbook

___11. To the next worksheet in a workbook

a. Ctrl+Home

b. Page Up

c. Right arrow

d. Home

e. Ctrl+Page Up

f. Left arrow

g. Ctrl+End

h. Up arrow

i. Ctrl+Page Down

j. Down arrow

k. Page Down

application 7-2

In the blank space, write the letter of the key or mouse procedure that matches the worksheet operation. You may use the items in the right column more than once if necessary. For some questions, more than one answer may be correct; however, you are required to identify only one of the correct answers.

___ 1. Open an existing worksheet file

___ 2. Move to a specific cell

___ 3. Edit data in a cell

___ 4. Widen a worksheet column

___ 5. Clear data in a cell

___ 6. Change the style of a cell to italics

___ 7. Change the format of a cell to exponential

___ 8. Change the alignment of a cell

___ 9. Add borders to a cell

___10. Save a worksheet file

___11. Exit Excel

a. Choose a command in the File menu

b. Choose a command in the Format menu

c. Choose a command in the Edit menu

d. Click a button on the toolbar

e. Click a button on the formatting bar

f. Press the Delete key

g. Press the F2 key

h. Press the F5 key

i. Drag a double-headed arrow

application 7-3

In the blank space, write the letter that matches the worksheet format described.

___ 1. Displays both text and numerical data as keyed

___ 2. Displays numerical data with a fixed amount of places to the right of the decimal point

___ 3. Displays numerical data preceded by a dollar sign; however, dollar signs and decimal points do not necessarily line up vertically within the column

___ 4. Displays numerical data in a currency format that lines up the dollar sign and decimal point vertically within a column

___ 5. Displays text and numerical data as dates

___ 6. Displays text and numerical data as times

___ 7. Displays numerical data followed by a percent sign

___ 8. Displays the value of .5 as ½

___ 9. Displays numerical data in exponential notation

___10. Displays numerical data that will not be used for calculation, such as serial numbers containing hyphens

___11. Displays ZIP codes, phone numbers, and social security numbers

___12. Displays a variety of formats that may be selected or designed

a.	Special
b.	Accounting
c.	Time
d.	Scientific
e.	Fraction
f.	Text
g.	General
h.	Date
i.	Number
j.	Percentage
k.	Custom
l.	Currency

application 7-4

As a volunteer for a local environmental awareness group, you have agreed to conduct a census of species of birds in a particular area. To help with your census calculations, you have prepared the worksheet *Application 7-4* to account for each species of bird. Complete the worksheet by performing the following steps:

1. Open the file *Application 7-4* from the template disk.

2. Enter the following number of birds that were sighted during Week 4. The totals for each category should change as you enter the data.

Boat-Tailed Grackles	15
Goldfinches	5

Black-Capped Chickadees	**20**
Red-Headed Woodpeckers	**4**
Eastern Bluebirds	**10**
English Sparrows	**16**

3. In addition to the species listed, you sighted a blue heron. Enter a new category in cell A11 called Blue Heron. Then enter the number 1 in cell E11.

4. You made a mistake when entering data for Week 4. Edit the cell for English Sparrows to show 18 rather than 16.

5. Save the file as *Bird Census* to your data disk and leave the file open for the next application.

a p p l i c a t i o n   7 - 5

In Application 7-4, you updated a worksheet by entering new data. In this application, you will improve the appearance of the worksheet file *Bird Census* so that you may present your results. Complete the following steps in the worksheet:

1. Change the appearance of the following cells and cell ranges in the style indicated:
   a. Change cell A1 to bold.
   b. Change range A3:F3 to bold.
   c. Change range B3:F3 to underline.
   d. Change range A13:F13 to bold.
   e. Change range F5:F11 to bold.
   f. Change range B11:F11 to have a border on the bottom.
   g. Widen column F to fit the data in F3 entirely within the column.
   h. Center the data in cells B3 through F3.

2. Center the data in A1 by the following steps:
   a. Select **A1:F1.**
   b. Click the Center Across Columns button on the formatting bar.

3. Save the file.

4. Print and close the file.

The file *Application 7-6* is a worksheet containing the inventory of the Pager Shop. The headings and numerical data have already been keyed in the worksheet. You are to make the spreadsheet easier to read and more attractive. There are many ways to change the appearance of a spreadsheet to make it more useful. Your answer to this application may be different from those of other students in the class.

1. Open the file *Application 7-6* from the template disk.

2. Change the appearance of the worksheet by:
   a. Adding underlining, bold, italics, shading, or color to cells you believe need emphasis.
   b. Adjusting the alignment of data in cells if needed.
   c. Formatting appropriate cells to have dollar signs.
   d. Formatting all cost data to have two places to the right of the decimal.
   e. Adjusting column width if necessary.

3. Print the worksheet.

4. Save the file as *Pager Inventory* to your data disk.

STRENGTHENING SPREADSHEET SKILLS

CHAPTER

8

OBJECTIVES
When you complete this chapter, you will be able to:

1. Copy data to other cells.

2. Move data to other cells.

3. Insert and delete columns and rows.

4. Freeze headings.

5. Protect a worksheet.

6. Insert a note in the worksheet.

7. Use print options when printing a worksheet.

Copying Data

When creating or enlarging a worksheet, you may want to use the same text or numbers in another portion of the worksheet. Rather than key the same data over again, the data may be copied. There are several ways to copy data in a worksheet. In this chapter, you will learn to copy and paste, use the drag-and-drop method, and fill cells. These operations can significantly decrease the amount of time you need to prepare a worksheet.

NOTE: *Although copying data can increase the efficiency of creating a spreadsheet, there is one danger. Data copied into a cell will replace data already in that cell. Check your destination cells for existing data before copying.*

Copy and Paste

Choosing the Copy command in the Edit menu or clicking the Copy button in the toolbar duplicates the contents of a cell or cells on the Clipboard so that you can enter the data in another part of the worksheet, as seen in Figure 8-1. The Copy command, however, will not affect the data in the original cell(s).

After placing the highlight in the part of the worksheet where the data is to be copied, choose the Paste command in the Edit menu or click the Paste button in the toolbar to enter the stored data into the cell or cells. It is not necessary to select the entire range of cells; you need only highlight the upper left corner of the range into which data will be copied.

The data stored on the Clipboard will remain until it is replaced with new data. If you would like to make multiple copies, simply choose the Paste command once more.

FIGURE 8-1
Data in one part of the worksheet may be duplicated in another
part of the worksheet by using the Copy and Paste commands.

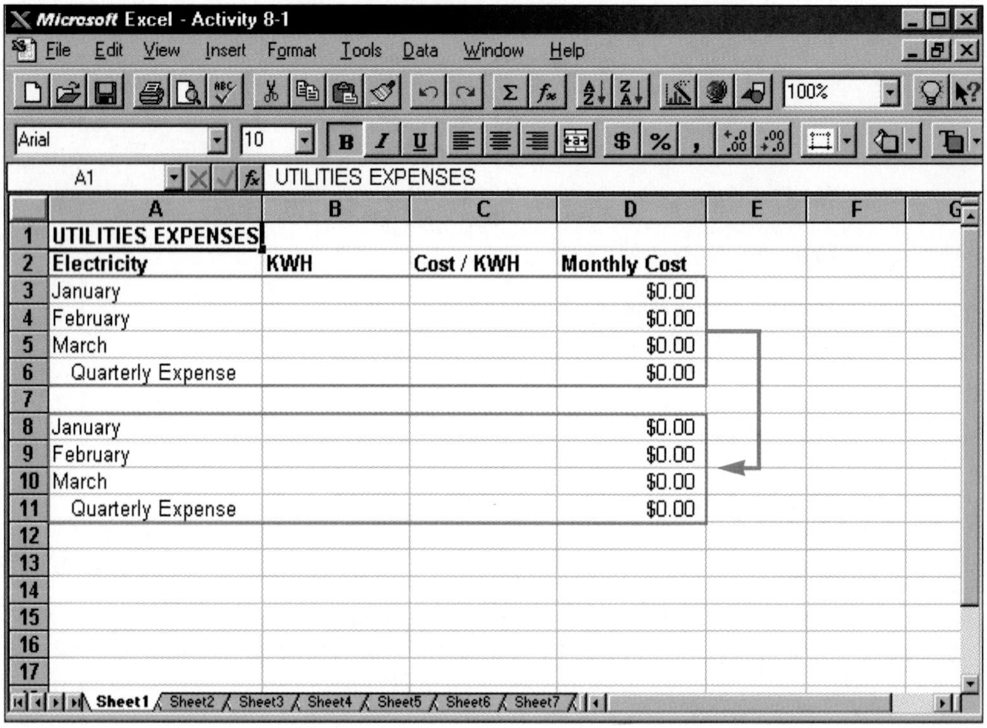

ACTIVITY

8-1 Copying and Pasting

• •

Activity 8-1 is a worksheet intended to track electric utility costs. The worksheet will be expanded to accommodate natural gas and water costs.

1. Open the file *Activity 8-1* from your template disk. The worksheet contains columns for the number of kilowatt hours, the cost per kilowatt hour, and the monthly electric bill.

2. Maximize the document window.

3. Expand the worksheet to calculate the monthly costs of natural gas:
   a. Select range **A3:D6.**
   b. Choose **Copy** from the **Edit** menu. The range will be surrounded by a border that seems to be revolving clockwise.

   c. Highlight **A8.**
   d. Choose **Paste** from the **Edit** menu. The range of cells should be copied from A3:D6 to A8:D11.

4. Key **Natural Gas** into A7.

5. Key **100 cf** into B7 to indicate the amount of cubic feet in hundreds.

6. Key **Cost/100 cf** into C7 to indicate the cost per hundred cubic feet.

7. Key **Monthly Cost** into D7.

8. Leave *Activity 8-1* on the screen for the next activity.

Using the Drag-and-Drop Method

Similar to Word, Excel allows you to quickly copy data using the drag-and-drop method. First highlight the cells you want to copy. Then move the pointer to the top border of the highlighted cells. The cross turns into a pointer. While holding down the Ctrl key, drag the cells to a new location and release the mouse button. As you press the Ctrl key, a small plus sign (+) appears below the mouse pointer.

Copying with Drag-and-Drop

1. Expand the worksheet to calculate monthly costs for water use.

2. Select range **A8:D11.**

3. Move the pointer to the top edge of cell A8. When you have the pointer in the correct position, the cross turns into an arrow.

4. While holding down the **Ctrl** key, drag down until the pointer is in cell A13. Release the mouse button, then the Ctrl key. The data will be copied from A8:D11 to A13:D16.

5. Key **Water** into **A12.**

6. Key **1000 gallons** into **B12.**

7. Key **Cost/1000 gal** into **C12** to indicate the cost per 1,000 gallons of water.

8. Key **Monthly Cost** into **D12.**

9. Bold the contents of cells **A7:D7** and **A12:D12.**

10. Save the file as *Utilities* and compare your screen to Figure 8-2.

11. Leave *Utilities* on the screen for the next activity.

FIGURE 8-2
Copying and pasting speed the process of creating a worksheet.

	A	B	C	D	E	F	G
1	**UTILITIES EXPENSES**						
2	**Electricity**	**KWH**	**Cost / KWH**	**Monthly Cost**			
3	January			$0.00			
4	February			$0.00			
5	March			$0.00			
6	Quarterly Expense			$0.00			
7	**Natural Gas**	**100 cf**	**Cost / 100 cf**	**Monthly Cost**			
8	January			$0.00			
9	February			$0.00			
10	March			$0.00			
11	Quarterly Expense			$0.00			
12	**Water**	**1000 gallons**	**Cost / 1000 gal**	**Monthly Cost**			
13	January			$0.00			
14	February			$0.00			
15	March			$0.00			
16	Quarterly Expense			$0.00			
17							

The Fill Command

Filling copies data into the cell(s) adjacent to the original. As shown in Figure 8-3, the Fill command in the Edit menu contains several selections on the pop-out menu, such as Down, Right, Up, and Left. The Down selection copies data into the cell(s) directly below the original cell, as shown in Figure 8-4. The Up selection copies data into the cell(s) directly above the original cell.

FIGURE 8-3

The Fill command on the Edit menu copies data to adjacent cells.

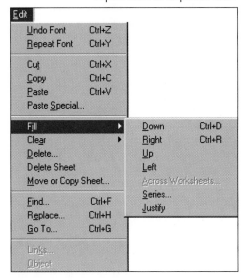

The Right and Left selections will copy data into the cell(s) to the right or left of the original cell, as shown in Figure 8-5. All selections make multiple copies if more than one destination cell is selected. For example, the Down selection can copy data into the next several cells below the original cell. The Fill selections are somewhat faster than copying and pasting because filling requires choosing only one command. However, filling can be used only when the destination cells are adjacent to the original cell.

FIGURE 8-4

The Down selection in the Fill command copies data to adjacent cells below the original cell. The Up selection copies data to adjacent cells above the original cell.

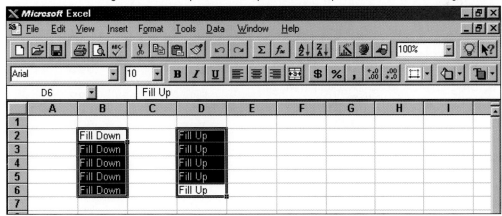

FIGURE 8-5
The Right and Left selections of the Fill command copy data to cells adjacent to the original cell.

	A	B	C	D	E	F	G	H	I
1									
2		Fill Right	Fill Right	Fill Right	Fill Right				
3									
4		Fill Left	Fill Left	Fill Left	Fill Left				
5									
6									
7									

(Cell reference box: E4, showing "Fill Left")

ACTIVITY

Using the Fill Down Command

Follow the steps below to enter utilities expenses for three months into the worksheet:

1. The cost of electricity for all three months is $0.086 per kilowatt hour. Enter the amount in range C3:C5 by following these steps:
   a. Enter **.086** in C3.
   b. Drag from C3 to C5 to select the range to be filled.
   c. Choose **Fill** from the **Edit** menu, then choose **Down** from the pop-out menu. The contents of C3 will be copied to cells C4 and C5.

2. Use the same procedure to enter the costs for natural gas and water.
   a. Enter **.512** in C8 to record the cost per 100 cubic feet of natural gas.
   b. Use the Fill command to copy the data from C8 to C9 and C10.
   c. Enter **.69** in C13 to record the cost per 1000 gallons of water.

d. Use the Fill command to copy the data from C13 to C14 and C15.

3. Enter the utility usage data into the worksheet.

Electricity	KWH
January	548
February	522
March	508
Natural Gas	100 cf
January	94
February	56
March	50
Water	1000 gallons
January	9
February	10
March	12

4. After completing the worksheet you may notice that the monthly costs have been calculated based on the data entered. Compare your screen to Figure 8-6.

5. Leave *Utilities* on your screen for the next activity.

FIGURE 8-6

In this worksheet, the Fill Down command was used to copy the cost data.

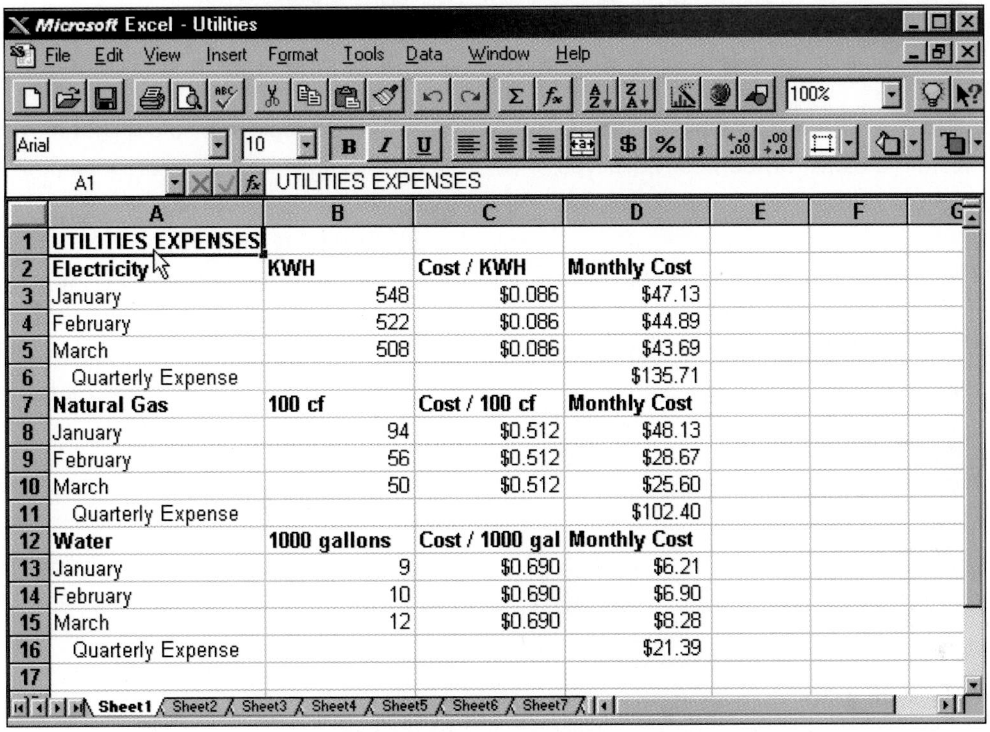

	A	B	C	D	E	F	G
1	UTILITIES EXPENSES						
2	Electricity	KWH	Cost / KWH	Monthly Cost			
3	January	548	$0.086	$47.13			
4	February	522	$0.086	$44.89			
5	March	508	$0.086	$43.69			
6	Quarterly Expense			$135.71			
7	Natural Gas	100 cf	Cost / 100 cf	Monthly Cost			
8	January	94	$0.512	$48.13			
9	February	56	$0.512	$28.67			
10	March	50	$0.512	$25.60			
11	Quarterly Expense			$102.40			
12	Water	1000 gallons	Cost / 1000 gal	Monthly Cost			
13	January	9	$0.690	$6.21			
14	February	10	$0.690	$6.90			
15	March	12	$0.690	$8.28			
16	Quarterly Expense			$21.39			
17							

Moving Data

Data is sometimes moved in the worksheet to improve its appearance and use. Moving can be performed in two ways. The first method, *cutting and pasting,* is most appropriate when you want to move data to an area of the worksheet that is not currently viewed on the screen. Previously, you learned that the Copy command places data on the Clipboard so that it may be copied into another area of the worksheet. The Cut command also places selected data on the Clipboard; however, it will remove data from its original position in the worksheet. Because cut data is stored on the Clipboard, you may restore the data at any time by simply choosing the Paste command.

The drag-and-drop method can also be used to move data in the worksheet. The procedure is the same as you learned earlier in this chapter, except you do not hold down the Ctrl key. This actually makes the drag-and-drop method the easiest way to move data in a worksheet because you can do it without touching a key or using a menu.

ACTIVITY

8-4 Moving Data in a Worksheet

• •

You decide that the worksheet may be easier to read if there is a blank row between each type of utility.

1. Move the data for water down two rows:
   a. Select range **A12:D16.**
   b. Click the **Cut** button on the toolbar. The data in the range is surrounded by a border that seems to revolve clockwise.
   c. Highlight **A14.**
   d. Click the **Paste** button on the toolbar. The data appears in the range A14:D18.

2. Move the data for natural gas down one row using the drag-and-drop method:
   a. Select range **A7:D11.**
   b. Move the cross to the top edge of cell A7. When you have the cross in the correct position, it turns into an arrow.
   c. Using the mouse, drag down until the pointer is in cell A8. Release the mouse button. The data appears in the range A8:D12. Your screen should be similar to Figure 8-7.

3. Leave *Utilities* on the screen for the next activity.

FIGURE 8-7
The Cut command moves data to another part of the worksheet.

	A	B	C	D	E	F	G
3	January	548	$0.086	$47.13			
4	February	522	$0.086	$44.89			
5	March	508	$0.086	$43.69			
6	Quarterly Expense			$135.71			
7							
8	**Natural Gas**	**100 cf**	**Cost / 100 cf**	**Monthly Cost**			
9	January	94	$0.512	$48.13			
10	February	56	$0.512	$28.67			
11	March	50	$0.512	$25.60			
12	Quarterly Expense			$102.40			
13							
14	**Water**	**1000 gallons**	**Cost / 1000 gal**	**Monthly Cost**			
15	January	9	$0.690	$6.21			
16	February	10	$0.690	$6.90			
17	March	12	$0.690	$8.28			
18	Quarterly Expense			$21.39			
19							

Inserting and Deleting Rows and Columns

The appearance of the worksheet may also be changed by adding and removing rows and columns of the worksheet. In fact, in the previous activity you could have inserted rows between the types of utilities rather than move existing data.

Inserting adds rows or columns to the worksheet. If you choose the Rows command in the Insert menu, rows will be added above the highlight. If you choose Columns from the Insert menu, columns will be added to the left of the highlight.

Deleting removes the row or column in which the highlight appears. When the Delete command is chosen from the Edit menu, the Delete dialog box appears. (See Figure 8-8.) After an option is selected, the appropriate part of the worksheet is deleted.

The Delete command is potentially dangerous because it erases the data contained in the row or column. If you accidentally delete the wrong column or row, the data in the column or row will be erased. The data may be restored only by selecting the Undo command in the Edit menu.

FIGURE 8-8
You may choose whether a row or column is to be removed from the worksheet in the Delete dialog box.

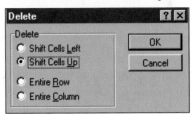

ACTIVITY 8-5 Inserting and Deleting Rows and Columns

1. Insert a row near the top of the worksheet:
   a. Highlight any cell in row 2.
   b. Choose **Rows** from the **Insert** menu. Row 2 will be blank. The original row 2 becomes row 3.

2. Suppose you want to include a column in the worksheet for the date the bill was paid. Insert a column between columns A and B:
   a. Highlight any cell in column B.
   b. Choose **Columns** from the **Insert** menu. A blank column will appear as column B. The original column B becomes column C.

   c. Key **Date Paid** in B3.
   d. Press **Enter.**

3. Suppose you change your mind about the date column. Delete column B.
   a. Highlight any cell in column B.
   b. Choose **Delete** from the **Edit** menu. The Delete dialog box appears.
   c. Click **Entire Column.**

4. Leave *Utilities* on the screen for the next activity.

Freezing Titles

Often a worksheet can become so large that it is difficult to view the entire worksheet on the screen. As you scroll to lower parts of the worksheet column, titles at the top or side of the worksheet may disappear from the screen, making it difficult to identify the contents of the column. For example, you may have noticed that the worksheet title (*Utilities Expenses*) in previous activities scrolled off the screen when you were working in the lower part of the worksheet and, consequently, rows 1 and 2 cannot be viewed in the screen in Figure 8-7.

Freezing will keep the row or column titles on the screen no matter where you scroll in the worksheet. To freeze titles, select the Freeze Panes command in the Window menu (see Figure 8-9). All rows above the highlight and columns to the left of the highlight will be frozen. Frozen titles are indicated by a darkened gridline that separates the frozen portion of the worksheet from the unfrozen portion. To unfreeze a row or column title, choose the Unfreeze Panes command; the darkened gridline disappears and the titles will be unfrozen.

FIGURE 8-9
The Freeze Panes command in the Window menu will keep a portion of the worksheet on the screen no matter where you scroll in the worksheet.

ACTIVITY

8-6 **Freezing Titles**

1. Enter the following column titles into the designated cells:

Cell	Column Title
B2	**Units Used**
C2	**Unit Cost**
D2	**Billed Amount**

2. Underline and bold the contents of B2, C2, and D2.

3. Highlight **A3.**

4. Choose **Freeze Panes** from the **Window** menu. The title and column headings in

rows 1 and 2 are now frozen. A darkened gridline appears between rows 2 and 3.

5. Scroll to the lower part of the worksheet. You will notice that the column headings remain at the top of the screen no matter where you move.

6. Choose **Unfreeze Panes** from the **Window** menu. The column headings are no longer frozen.

7. Save the file and leave *Utilities* on the screen for the next activity.

Protecting a Worksheet

Protecting a worksheet prevents anyone from making changes to the worksheet inadvertently. In other words, you may not add to, remove, or edit the data until the protection is removed.

To protect a worksheet, choose the Protection command on the Tools menu, then choose Protect Sheet from the pop-out menu. When the Protect Sheet dialog box appears, as shown in Figure 8-10, make sure the Contents check box is checked. If you choose to enter a password, the spreadsheet user will not be able to change the contents of a protected range unless that password is entered. If no password is entered, the contents may be unprotected and changed by anyone.

If you attempt to change the data in the worksheet after it has been protected, Excel displays a message telling you the cells cannot be changed. If you intend to change the worksheet, you must first unprotect it by choosing Unprotect Sheet from the Protection command's pop-out menu.

FIGURE 8-10
When Contents is checked in the Protect Sheet dialog box, the data within the worksheet may not be changed.

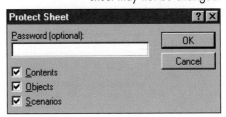

ACTIVITY

8-7 Protecting a Worksheet

1. Choose **Protection** from the **Tools** menu, then choose **Protect Sheet** from the pop-out menu. The Protect Sheet dialog box appears.

2. Check the **Contents** check box if it is not currently checked.

3. Click **OK.** The worksheet is now protected.

4. Check the worksheet protection.
   a. Move the highlight to **B4,** a cell within the protected range.

   b. Enter **550**. Excel should display a message telling you the locked cell cannot be changed.
   c. Click **OK** to close the message.

5. Choose **Unprotect Sheet** from the **Protection** pop-out menu to turn the protection off.

6. Leave *Utilities* on the screen for the next activity.

Inserting a Note in the Spreadsheet

A *cell note* is a message that provides information concerning data in a cell that may be too large to enter into the cell. The note explains, identifies, or comments on information contained in the cell. For example, when abbreviations have been entered into cells, you may use a cell note to spell the words in their entirety. In addition, notes may be used to explain the calculations in cells that contain formulas.

You insert cell notes by choosing the Note command in the Insert menu. When the Cell Note dialog box appears (see Figure 8-11), enter the note in the Text Note box.

FIGURE 8-11
The Cell Note dialog box is used to enter messages that will appear in the spreadsheet.

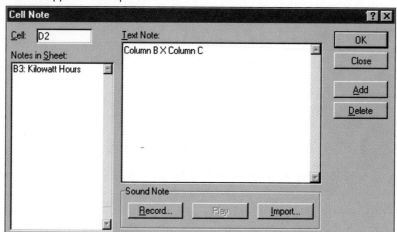

ACTIVITY

Inserting a Cell Note

1. Highlight **B3.**

2. Choose **Note** from the **Insert** menu. The Cell Note dialog box appears with B3 in the Cell box.

3. Enter **Kilowatt hours** in the Text Note box.

4. Click **OK.** A small red dot appears in the upper right portion of the cell, indicating that the cell contains a note.

5. Place the highlight cross on cell B3. The note you entered appears on the screen, similar to Figure 8-12.

6. Enter the following notes in the designated cells:

Cell	Note
B9	**One hundred cubic feet**
B15	**One thousand gallons**
C3	**Cost per kilowatt hour**
C9	**Cost per one hundred cubic feet**
C15	**Cost per one thousand gallons**
D2	**Units used times the unit cost**

7. Leave *Utilities* on the screen for the next activity.

FIGURE 8-12
Cell notes can be used to spell out cell contents that have been abbreviated.

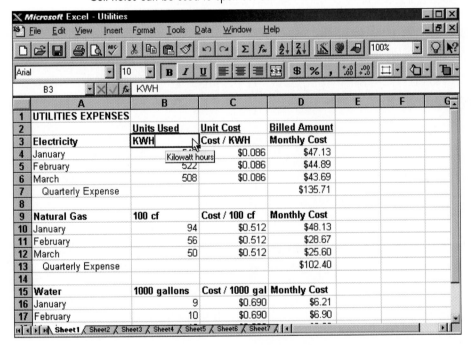

Using Print Options When Printing a Spreadsheet

In Chapter 7 you printed a spreadsheet using the default settings. There are, however, commands to help you control the way your spreadsheet prints.

Setting the Print Area

You may print the entire worksheet or a portion of the worksheet. The Set Print Area command tells Excel the part of the worksheet you want to print. To designate the area you want to print, select the range to be printed, choose Print Area from the File menu, then choose Set Print Area from the pop-out menu.

Designing the Printed Page

The Page Setup command in the File menu will produce a dialog box that allows you to set page margins, lengths, and widths; designate page numbers; and determine whether column letters, row numbers, and gridlines should be printed. The Page Setup dialog box is divided into four tabbed sections. Figure 8-13 shows the four sections of the Page Setup dialog box. These sections are discussed on the following page.

FIGURE 8-13
The Page Setup dialog box has four tabbed sections for setting options such as margins, page dimensions, and page numbers.

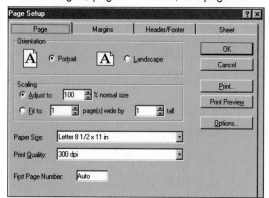

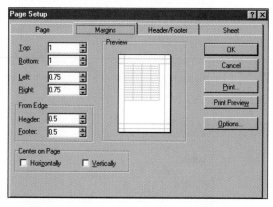

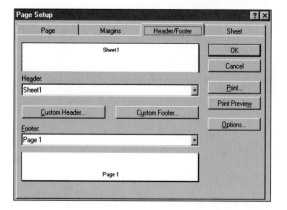

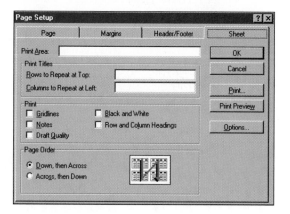

- **Page.** Page orientation (portrait or landscape), scaling, and page size are designated under the Page tab. In addition, you may designate the page number of the first page of the worksheet.

- **Margins.** The Margins section of the dialog box allows you to change the margins of the printed page by entering the desired margin in the appropriate box.

- **Header/Footer.** You may indicate words to be printed at the top and bottom of each page under the Header/Footer tab.

- **Sheet.** Under the Sheet tab, you may set the print area and title the worksheet. You may also determine whether gridlines, column headings, row headings, and cell notes are printed.

ACTIVITY

Changing the Appearance of a Printed Page

1. Choose **Page Setup** from the **File** menu.

2. Change the page orientation to landscape.
   a. Click the **Page** tab.
   b. Click the **Landscape** button.

3. Set the bottom page margin to .5 inch.
   a. Click the **Margins** tab.
   b. Click the down arrow on the Bottom box until **0.5** appears.

4. Change the worksheet header.
   a. Click the **Header/Footer** tab.
   b. Click the down arrow on the Header text box.
   c. Click **Utilities, Page 1.**

5. Click **OK.**

6. Leave *Utilities* on the screen for the next activity.

Previewing a Spreadsheet before Printing

The Print Preview command of the worksheet is exactly the same as in Word. The Print Preview command shows how your printed pages will appear before you actually print them. To access the Print Preview screen (see Figure 8-14), choose the Print Preview command from the File menu or click the Print Preview button on the toolbar. When you have finished previewing the printed pages, you may either return to the worksheet by clicking Close or print the worksheet by clicking Print.

FIGURE 8-14
Use the Print Preview screen to check the worksheet before printing.

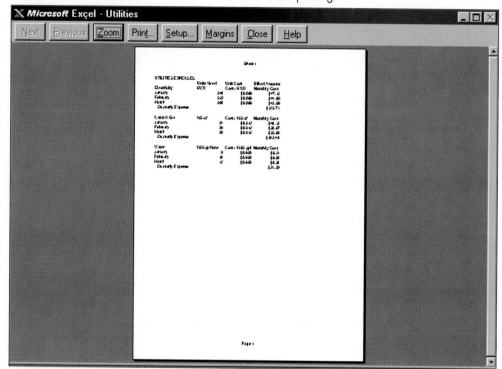

ACTIVITY

8-10 Using Print Options

1. Set the area of the worksheet to be printed:
   a. Select **A1:D19.**
   b. Choose the **Print Area** command from the **File** menu, then choose **Set Print Area** from the pop-out menu.

2. Preview the worksheet to be printed:
   a. Click the **Print Preview** button on the toolbar.
   b. Click the **Zoom** button. A portion of the previewed page becomes larger so that it can be examined in more detail.

3. Click the **Print** button. The Print dialog box appears.

4. Click **OK.** The worksheet should begin printing.

5. Save and close the file.

Summary

- The data in a worksheet can be moved or copied to another location in the worksheet by using the Cut, Copy, Paste, and Fill commands from the Edit menu. These commands can save time by eliminating the need to rekey large quantities of data. The drag-and-drop method can also be used to copy and move data in worksheets.

- The appearance of the worksheet can be changed by inserting or deleting rows and columns. When a worksheet becomes large, the column or row titles will disappear from the screen as you scroll to distant parts of the worksheet. You may keep the titles on the screen at all times by freezing them.

- A worksheet may be protected from accidental change by choosing Protect Sheet from the Protection command in the Tools menu. The protection applies to the entire worksheet. A worksheet may be unprotected if changes are necessary.

- Cell notes provide messages that explain the contents of a cell. Notes appear when the mouse pointer is placed over the cell.

- The Print Area command designates the portion of the worksheet you want to print. The Page Setup command controls the page size and the margins that will be printed. To view the worksheet as it will appear before actually printing it, use the Print Preview command.

• • • • • • • • • • • • • •

REVIEW ACTIVITIES

TRUE/FALSE

Circle T or F to show whether the statement is true or false.

T F 1. If you copy into cells already containing data, the data will be replaced by the copied data.

T F 2. The Fill Down and Fill Right commands are available only if you plan to copy to cells adjacent to the original cell.

T F 3. The Paste command is used for both copying and moving.

T F 4. Deleting a row or column will erase the data contained in the row or column.

T F 5. The Insert Column command is in the Format menu.

T F 6. When using the Delete Row command, the row above the highlight will be deleted.

T F 7. The Freeze Panes command will freeze rows above and columns to the right of the highlight.

T F 8. A message will appear if you attempt to edit a cell in a worksheet that has been protected.

T F 9. Notes cannot be seen unless the mouse pointer is placed in the cell.

T F 10. A worksheet may be previewed before printing by clicking the Print Preview button on the toolbar or by choosing the Print Preview command in the File menu.

COMPLETION

Write the correct answer in the space provided.

1. Which command is used in conjunction with the Copy command to duplicate data and the Cut command to move data?

_____

2. Identify at least three ways that data may be copied in the worksheet.

_____

_____

_____

3. In which menu are the commands used for copying data located?

_____

4. Cutting and pasting is used in Excel to perform what process?

_____

5. What should you do if you accidentally delete a column or row?

_____

6. Which command keeps the titles of a worksheet on the screen no matter where the highlight is moved?

_____

7. The Protection command is contained in which menu?

_____

8. What is the purpose of a cell note?

_____

9. Identify at least four examples of printing characteristics that may be designated in the Page Setup dialog box.

_____

_____

10. Where is the orientation of a printed page determined?

_____

REINFORCEMENT APPLICATIONS

application 8-1

In the blank space, write the letter of the worksheet command that will solve the problem.

___ 1. You are tired of keying repetitive data.

___ 2. A portion of the worksheet would be more useful in another area of the worksheet.

___ 3. You forgot to key a row of data in the middle of the worksheet.

___ 4. You no longer need a certain column in the worksheet.

___ 5. Column headings cannot be viewed on the screen when you are working in the lower part of the worksheet.

___ 6. You want to prevent others from entering data in a worksheet.

___ 7. Information you have entered into a cell requires an explanation that is too long to fit into the cell.

___ 8. Your boss would rather not view your worksheet on the screen and has requested a copy on paper.

___ 9. You want to print only a portion of the worksheet.

> a. Print command or Print button on the toolbar
>
> b. Fill command or Copy command
>
> c. Rows or Columns command
>
> d. Protection command
>
> e. Cut command, Paste command
>
> f. Print Area command
>
> g. Delete command
>
> h. Freeze Panes command
>
> i. Note command

application 8-2

The file *Application 8-2* is a spreadsheet used to account for inventory purchases of a small office supply store. The worksheet is not currently organized by suppliers of the inventory.

1. Open *Application 8-2*. Organize the worksheet following the format given in the table below. The new worksheet should have inventory items organized by supplier, with proper headings.

HINTS:

a. *Use the Cut and Paste commands or drag-and-drop to move some of the data.*
b. *Some of the data is out of order. Use cut and paste to move the data.*
c. *Remember to bold appropriate data.*

Item	Ordering Code	Quantity
Mega Computer Manufacturers		
Mega X-39 Computers	X-39-25879	20
Mega X-40 Computers	X-40-25880	24
Mega X-41 Computers	X-41-25881	28

Xenon Paper Source

Xenon Letter Size White Paper	LT-W-45822	70
Xenon Letter Size Color Paper	LT-C-45823	10
Xenon Legal Size White Paper	LG-W-45824	40
Xenon Legal Size Color Paper	LG-C-45825	5

MarkMaker Pen Co.

MarkMaker Blue Ball Point Pens	MM-Bl-43677	120
MarkMaker Black Ball Point Pens	MM-Bk-43678	100
MarkMaker Red Ball Point Pens	MM-R-43679	30

2. The following inventory item has been accidentally excluded from the worksheet. Add the item by using the Fill Down command and then editing the copied data.

Item	Ordering Code	Quantity
MarkMaker Green Ball Point Pens	**MM-G-43680**	**30**

3. Print the worksheet.

4. Save the worksheet to your data disk as *Inventory Purchases* and close the file.

a p p l i c a t i o n   8 - 3

You are a member of the Booster Club, an organization that raises money to purchase sports equipment for the local high school. You have been allocated $1,210 to purchase sports equipment for the school. You decide to prepare a worksheet to help you calculate the cost of various purchases. Open the file *Application 8-3* from your template disk and make the following adjustments to the worksheet:

1. Bold and center the column headings appearing in row 2.

2. Insert a row above row 3.

3. Freeze the column headings in row 2.

> **H I N T:** *The highlight should be placed in A3.*

4. Insert a row above row 8 and key **Bats** into column A of the new row.

5. Use the Fill Down command to copy the formula in E4 to E5:E11. Do not copy the formula into E12.

6. Format the Cost (D4:D11) and Total (E4:E12) columns for currency with two places to the right of the decimal.

7. Key the data for Sport and Cost, as given in the table that follows. Use the Fill Down command as needed to copy repetitive data. Widen the columns if necessary.

Item	Sport	Cost
Basketballs	**Basketball**	28
Hoops	**Basketball**	40
Backboards	**Basketball**	115
Softballs	**Softball**	5
Bats	**Softball**	30
Masks	**Softball**	35
Volleyballs	**Volleyball**	25
Nets	**Volleyball**	125

8. The organization has requested you to purchase the items listed below. Any remaining cash should be used to purchase as many basketballs as possible.

Basketballs	**5**
Hoops	**2**
Backboards	**2**
Softballs	**20**
Bats	**5**
Masks	**1**
Volleyballs	**7**
Nets	**1**

> **HINT:** *Increase the number of basketballs and watch the dollar amount in the total. You should use $1,203 and have $7 left over.*

9. Print the worksheet.

10. Save the worksheet to your data disk as *Sports Equipment* and close the file.

application 8-4

The file *Application 8-4* contains the grades of several students taking Biology 101 during the spring semester. The instructor has asked that you, the student assistant, help maintain the grade records of the class. Perform the following spreadsheet operations to make the worksheet more useful:

1. The word *Homework* has been abbreviated in cells B3 through D3. Enter notes into the following cells to clarify the contents of the column:

Cell	Cell Note
B3	**Homework Number 1**
C3	**Homework Number 2**
D3	**Homework Number 3**

2. Column A contains the last names of students in the class.
   a. Add a column between the current columns A and B to hold the first names of the students.
   b. Enter **First Name** in B3 of the new column.
   c. Enter the following names in the new column you created:

Row	Entry
4	**Allen**
5	**Kevin**
6	**Cindy**
7	**Raul**
8	**Sally**
9	**Samuel**

3. Several grades were recorded as zero because the student did not turn in the homework or take the examination. Add notes to the following cells:

Cell	Cell Note
C5	**Claimed homework was stolen**
D5	**Claimed dog ate homework**
H5	**Did not attend exam**
H8	**Absent due to illness**

4. Freeze the titles in the spreadsheet to keep the student names and assignment titles on the screen at all times.

   HINT: *Your highlight should be in cell C4 when the Freeze Panes command is chosen.*

5. Protect the worksheet to prevent inadvertent changes.

6. Print the worksheet.

7. Save the worksheet to your data disk as *Spring Grades* and close the file.

ADVANCED SPREADSHEET OPERATIONS

CHAPTER

9

OBJECTIVES

When you complete this chapter, you will be able to:

1. Use the worksheet as a calculator.

2. Enter and edit worksheet formulas.

3. Distinguish between relative and absolute cell references.

4. Use the AutoSum button.

5. Display formulas in the worksheet.

6. Perform immediate and delayed calculations.

7. Use function formulas.

Using the Spreadsheet as a Calculator

A primary advantage of the spreadsheet is the power of rapid calculation. In fact, the spreadsheet will perform the same functions as a hand or desk calculator.

ACTIVITY
9-1 Using the Worksheet as a Calculator

1. Open the file *Activity 9-1* from your template disk. This worksheet contains headings for the four primary mathematical functions of addition, subtraction, multiplication, and division.

2. Key **10** in B4 and **24** in D4. The value in F4 should display 34, which is the sum of 10 and 24.

3. Highlight **F4.** Notice that the formula bar at the top of the screen displays the formula =B4+D4. The formula indicates that F4 contains the sum of the values in B4 and D4.

4. Key **48** in B13 and **8** in D13. The value in F13 should display 6, which is the result of 48 divided by 8.

5. Highlight **F13.** Notice that the formula bar at the top of the screen displays the formula =B13/D13. The formula indicates that F13 contains the result of the value in B13 divided by the value in D13.

6. Experiment by entering numbers into other cells of the worksheet. Calculations will take place as soon as you press the Enter key or click the Enter box.

7. Close *Activity 9-1* without saving.

What Are Formulas?

Spreadsheets can use numbers entered in certain cells to calculate values in other cells. The equations used to calculate values in a cell are known as *formulas.* Excel recognizes the contents of a cell as a formula when an equal sign (=) is the first character in the cell. For example, if the formula =8+6 were entered into cell B3, the value of 14 would be displayed in the worksheet. The formula bar displays the formula =8+6, as shown in Figure 9-1.

Structure of a Formula

A worksheet formula is composed of two types of characters: operands and operators. An *operand* is a number or cell reference used in formulas. An *operator* tells Excel what to do with the operands. For example, in the formula =B3+5, B3 and 5 are operands. The plus sign (+) is an operator that tells Excel to add the value contained in cell B3 to the number 5. The operators used in formulas are shown in Table 9-1.

FIGURE 9-1

Excel recognizes an entry as a formula when an equal sign is the first character in the cell.

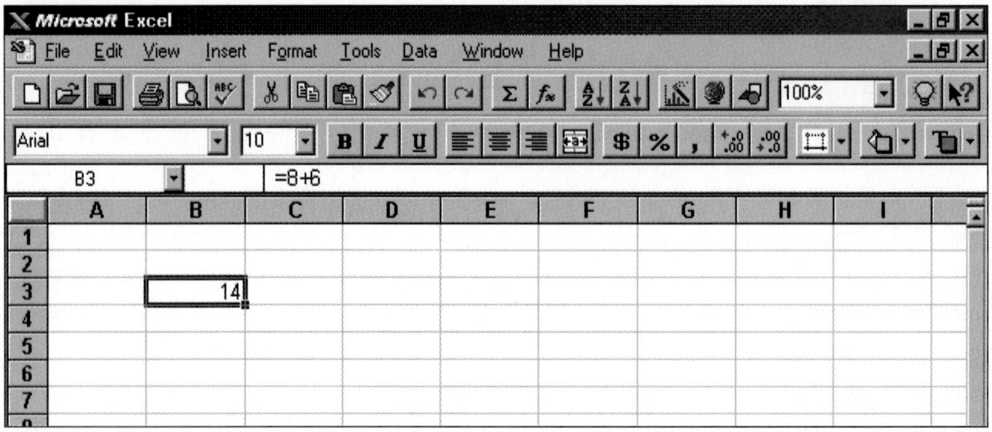

B3	=8+6

Cell B3 contains: 14

TABLE 9-1

Operators tell Excel what to do with operands.

OPERATOR	OPERATION	EXAMPLE	MEANING
+	Addition	B5+C5	Adds the values in B5 and C5
-	Subtraction	C8-232	Subtracts 232 from the value in C8
*	Multiplication	D4*D5	Multiplies the value in D4 by the value in D5
/	Division	E6/4	Divides the value in E6 by 4
^	Exponentiation	B3^3	Raises the value in B3 to the third power

Order of Evaluation

Formulas containing more than one operator are called **complex formulas.** For example, the formula =C3*C4+5 will perform both multiplication and addition to calculate the value in the cell. The sequence used to calculate the value of a formula is called the **order of evaluation.**

Formulas are evaluated in the following order:

1. Contents within parentheses are evaluated first. You may use as many pairs of parentheses as you desire. Excel will evaluate the innermost set first.

2. Mathematical operators are evaluated in order of priority, as shown in Table 9-2.

3. Equations are evaluated from left to right if two or more operators have the same order of evaluation. For example, in the formula =20-15-2, 15 would be subtracted from 20, then 2 would be subtracted from the difference (5).

TABLE 9-2
The sequence of calculations in a formula is determined by the order of evaluation.

ORDER OF EVALUATION	OPERATOR	SYMBOL
First	Exponentiation	^
Second	Positive or negative	+ or –
Third	Multiplication or division	* or /
Fourth	Addition or subtraction	+ or –

Editing Formulas

If you key a formula incorrectly, Excel will not let you enter it and a message explaining the error appears. For example, if you attempt to enter a formula with an open parenthesis, but no closing one, a message stating "Parentheses do not match" will appear. You may then correct the formula by editing in the formula bar.

You may also edit formulas already entered in the worksheet. After highlighting the cell, press the Edit key (F2) or click in the formula bar and add or delete data as necessary.

ACTIVITY

9-2 **Entering Formulas into a Worksheet**

● ●

1. Open the file *Activity 9-2* from your template disk.

2. Enter the formulas given in the cells. Remember to precede each formula with an

equal sign. After you enter a formula, the formula result appears in the cell. You may check your results by comparing them to the screen shown in Figure 9-2.

Cell	Formula
C3	=A3+B3
C4	=A4-B4
C5	=A5*B5
C6	=A6/B6

3. Enter a complex formula in D3 that will add the values in cells A3 and B3, then multiply the result by 20.
   a. Move the highlight to **D3.**
   b. Key **=(A3+B3)*20.**
   c. Press **Enter.** The resulting value should be 7600.

4. You can see the importance of the parentheses in the order of evaluation by creating an identical formula without the parentheses.
   a. Move the highlight to **E3.**
   b. Key **=A3+B3*20**, the same formula as in D3 but without the parentheses.
   c. Press **Enter.** The resulting value in E3 should be 4921. This value differs from the value in D3 because Excel multiplied the value in B3 by 20 before adding A3. In D3, the values in A3 and B3 were added together and the sum multiplied by 20.

5. Save the file to your data disk as *Calculation* and leave the file on the screen for the next activity.

FIGURE 9-2
Formulas may be used to determine values in the cells of a worksheet.

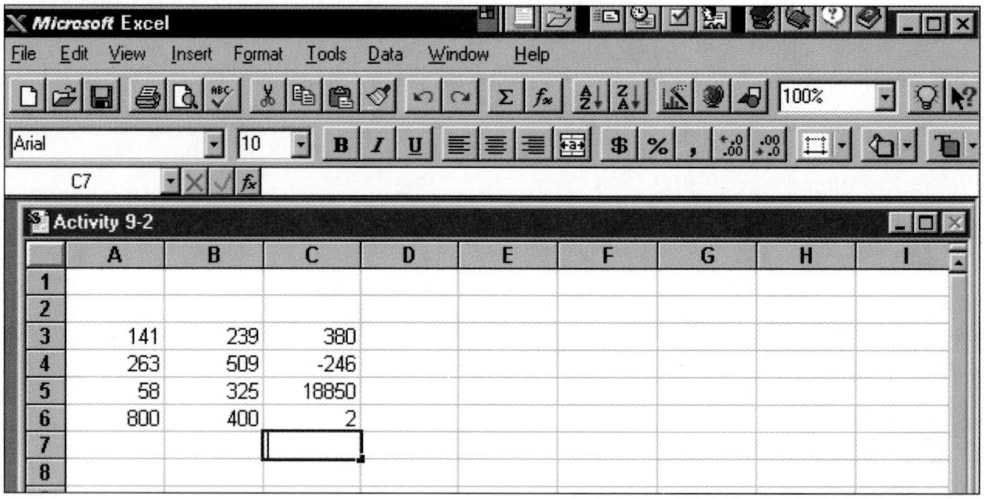

Relative, Absolute, and Mixed Cell References

Three types of cell references are used to create formulas: relative, absolute, and mixed. A ***relative cell reference*** adjusts to its new location when copied or moved. For example, in Figure 9-3, if the formula =B2+A3 is copied or moved from B3 to C4, the formula will be changed to =C3+B4. In other words, this particular formula is instructing Excel to add the cell directly above to the cell directly to the right. When the formula is copied or moved, the cell references change, but the instructions remain the same.

Absolute cell references contain row numbers and column letters preceded by a dollar sign ($). They do not adjust to the new cell location when copied or moved. For example, in Figure 9-3, if the formula =$A$8+$B$7 is copied from B8 to C9, the formula remains the same in the new location.

Cell references containing both relative and absolute references are called ***mixed cell references.*** When formulas with mixed cell references are copied or moved, the row or column references preceded by a dollar sign will not change;

FIGURE 9-3

When cell B3 is copied to cell C4, the relative cell reference will change.
When cell B8 is copied to cell C9, the absolute cell reference will not change.

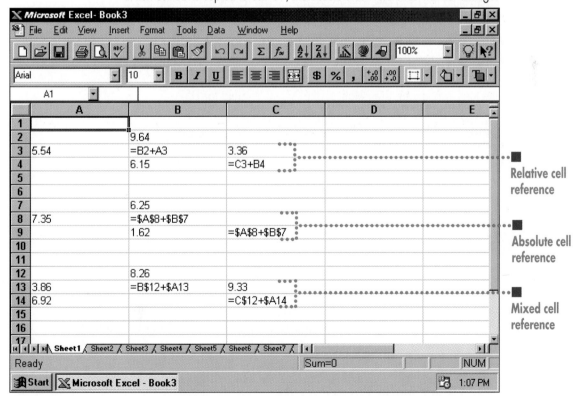

the row or column references not preceded by a dollar sign will adjust relative to the cell to which they are moved. For example, if the formula =B$12+$A13 is copied from B13 to C14, the formula will change to =C$12+$A14.

The use of relative and absolute cell references is important only when you are copying and moving data in a worksheet. If you want a moved or copied cell formula to use values in a specific part of the worksheet, you should use absolute cell references. If you want a moved or copied cell formula to use values that correspond to the new location of the data, you should use relative cell references.

ACTIVITY 9-3 Relative and Absolute Cell References

1. Place the highlight in **D3.** All cell references in the formula =(A3+B3)*20 (shown in the formula bar) are relative because neither the rows nor the columns are preceded by a dollar sign.

2. Copy the formula in **D3** to **D4.** The value in D4 should be 15440, and the formula in the formula bar should be =(A4+B4)*20. The operators in the formula remain the same as the formula in D3. However, because the cell references are relative, the row references in the operands changed down one row to reflect a change in the location of the formula.

3. Key **=$A$3*($B$3-200)** in D5. The value in D5 should be 5499. The formula in the formula bar contains absolute cell references, indicated by the dollar signs that precede row and column references.

4. Copy the formula in **D5** to **D6.** The value in D6 should be 5499, the same as in D5. Because the formula in D5 contains absolute cell references, the formula appearing in the formula bar should be the same as the formula for D5.

5. Save and close the file.

Creating Formulas Quickly

You have already learned how to create formulas by keying the formula or editing existing formulas. In this section, you will learn ways to create formulas quickly by using the Point and Click method or clicking the AutoSum button.

Point and Click Method

Previously you constructed formulas by keying the entire formula in the cell of the worksheet. You may include cell references in a formula more quickly by clicking on the cell rather than keying the reference. This is known as the *Point and Click method.* The Point and Click method is particularly helpful when you must enter long formulas that contain several cell references.

To enter the formula =A3+B3 in a cell, you would:

1. Highlight the cell that will contain the formula.
2. Press =.
3. Click **A3.**
4. Press +.
5. Click **B3.**
6. Press **Enter.**

ACTIVITY

Pointing and Clicking to Create Formulas

In this activity, you will create formulas using the Point and Click method. The file *Activity 9-4* is a worksheet that records the sales of juice and soda at the Fruit and Fizz Shop during the week. Prices of individual servings are as follows:

	Large	**Small**
Juice	$1.50	$ .90
Soda	$ .80	$ .50

Create formulas to calculate the total sales of juice and soda during the week by completing the following steps:

1. Open the worksheet file *Activity 9-4* from your template disk.

2. Enter a formula in D6 to calculate the weekly sales of juices:
   a. Highlight **D6.**
   b. Key **=(1.5*.**
   c. Click **B6.**
   d. Key **)+(.9*.**
   e. Click **C6.**
   f. Key **).**
   g. Press **Enter.** The amount 567 will appear in the cell.

3. Use the Fill Down command to copy the formula in D6 to D7:D8.

4. Enter a formula in D9 to calculate the total sales of sodas:
   a. Highlight **D9.**
   b. Key **=(.8*.**
   c. Click **B9.**
   d. Key **)+(.5*.**
   e. Click **C9.**
   f. Key **).**
   g. Press **Enter.**

5. Use the Fill Down command to copy the formula in D9 to D10:D11.

6. Remove dollar signs from cells **D7:D11.** (Click to remove the check mark beside *Use$* in the Format Cells dialog box.)

7. Compare your screen to the one in Figure 9-4.

8. Save the file as *Drink Sales* on your data disk and leave the file on your screen for the next activity.

FIGURE 9-4
Worksheet formulas may be created quickly using the mouse.

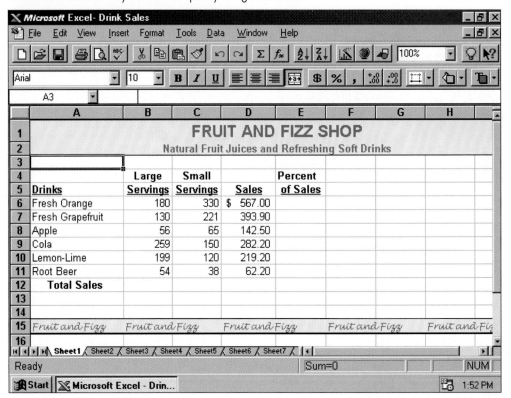

The AutoSum Button

Spreadsheet users frequently need to sum long columns of numbers. Excel has a button on the toolbar, the AutoSum button, that makes the process of summing a simple operation. The AutoSum button has the Greek letter *sigma* on it. When you click the AutoSum button, Excel scans the worksheet to determine the most logical column of numbers to sum in the cell and highlights the range of cells to be summed. This range is displayed in the cell where you want the sum to appear. If you prefer a range other than the one Excel selects, choose an alternate range by highlighting those cells. Click Enter to display the sum in the cell.

The sum of a range is indicated by a special formula in the formula bar called a **function formula.** For example, if the sum of the range D5:D17 is entered in a cell, the function formula in the formula bar will be =SUM(D5:D17). The SUM function is the most frequently used type of function formula. Function formulas will be discussed in detail later in this chapter.

ACTIVITY 9-5 Using the AutoSum Button

The manager of the Fruit and Fizz Shop would like to determine the total sales of juice and soda during the month, plus what percentage each type of juice and soda is of the total items sold.

1. Determine the total sales of juice and soda sold this month by summing D6:D11.
   a. Highlight **D12.**
   b. Click the **AutoSum** button. The range D6:D11 should be highlighted. Excel has correctly selected the range of cells you would like to sum.
   c. Press **Enter.** The formula =SUM(D6:D11) should appear in the formula bar. Cell D12 should display $1,667.00 the sum of the numbers in column D.

2. Format E6:E11 for percent with one place to the right of the decimal.

3. Determine the percent of total sales for each type of juice and soda.
   a. Highlight **E6.**
   b. Press **=.**
   c. Click **D6.**
   d. Press **/.**
   e. Key **$D$12.**
   f. Press **Enter.** The cell should display 34.0%.

4. Copy the formula in **E6** to **E7:E12** using the Fill Down command. All of the drink sales should be expressed as a percentage of the total drink sales. E12 should show 100.0%.

5. Compare your screen to the one shown in Figure 9-5.

6. Leave *Drink Sales* on your screen for the next activity.

FIGURE 9-5
The AutoSum button adds a column of numbers quickly.

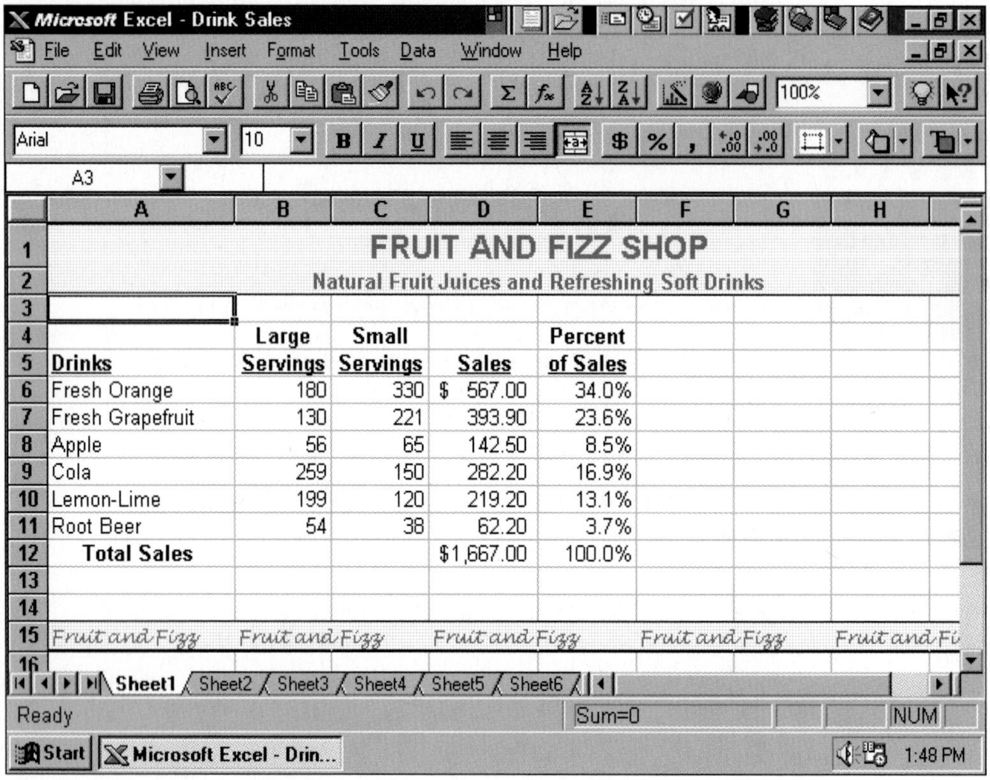

Formula Helpers

The Options dialog box, which you display by clicking Options on the Tools menu, contains several tabbed sections that define features in the worksheet. For example, the Formulas check box under the View tab will replace the values in the worksheet's cells with the formulas that created them. The Manual radio button under the Calculation tab will prevent worksheet formulas from calculating until you press the F9 key.

Showing Formulas on the Worksheet

In previous activities, you were able to view formulas only in the formula bar. Cells of the worksheet contained the values created by formulas rather than the formulas themselves. When creating a worksheet containing many formulas, you may find it easier to organize formulas and detect formula errors when you can view all formulas simultaneously.

When the Formulas check box under the View tab of the Options dialog box is checked (see Figure 9-6), Excel displays formulas rather than values in the

FIGURE 9-6
The View tab in the Options dialog box defines the
way that the worksheet will appear on the screen.

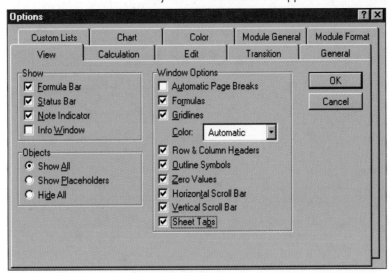

cells of the worksheets that contain formulas. If a cell does not contain a formula, Excel displays the data entered in the cell. To display values determined by the formulas again, remove the check from the Formulas checkbox. You may also switch between viewing formulas and formula results by pressing Ctrl+` (the ` is located in the upper left of most keyboards).

Delayed Calculations

Values in the worksheet are usually calculated as each new value is entered in the worksheet, but you can also calculate in the worksheet at a specific moment. Delayed calculation can be useful when you are working with a large worksheet that will take longer than usual to calculate; or you may want to view the difference in a particular cell after you have made changes throughout the worksheet.

To delay calculation, click the Manual button in the Calculation tab of the Options dialog box (see Figure 9-7). No calculation will occur until you press the F9 key. To return to automatic calculation, click the Automatic button under the Calculation tab.

FIGURE 9-7

The Calculation tab in the Options dialog box determines when the values of the formulas will be calculated.

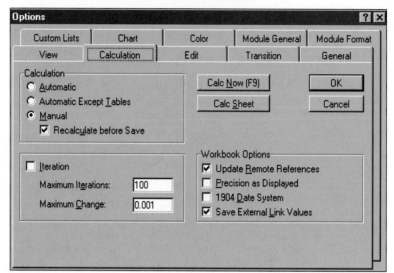

Showing Formulas and Delaying Calculation

1. View all the formulas in the worksheet simultaneously.
   a. Choose **Options** from the **Tools** menu.
   b. Click the **View** tab.
   c. Click the **Formulas** check box until a check appears.
   d. Click **OK.**
   e. Scroll to the right so that columns D and E appear on the screen. Each value in the worksheet created by a formula has been replaced by the formula creating the value.

2. Press **Ctrl+`.** Cells with formulas now appear with formula results.

3. Delay calculation in the worksheet.
   a. Choose **Options** from the **Tools** menu.

   b. Click the **Calculation** tab.
   c. Click the **Manual** button in the **Calculation** box.
   d. Click **OK.**

4. Change the following values in the worksheet:
   a. Key **182** in B6.
   b. Key **220** in C7.
   c. Key **125** in C10.

5. Press **F9** while watching the screen. Calculations occur as you press the key. The total sales in cell D12 should be $1,671.60.

6. Save and close the file.

Function Formulas

Function formulas, as you learned earlier in this chapter, are special formulas that do not use operators to calculate a result. They perform complex calculations in specialized areas of mathematics, statistics, logic, trigonometry, accounting, and finance. Function formulas also are used to convert worksheet values to dates and times. There are over 200 function formulas in Excel. In this section, you will learn the more frequently used function formulas.

Parts of Function Formulas

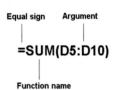

A function formula contains three components: the equal sign, a function name, and an argument.

- The *equal sign* tells Excel a function formula will be entered into the cell.

- The *function name* identifies the operation to be performed.

- The *argument* is a value, cell reference, range, or text that acts as an operand in a function formula. The argument is enclosed in parentheses after the function name. If a function formula contains more than one argument, the arguments are separated by commas. The range of cells that make up the argument is separated by a colon.

You have already created a function formula in a previous activity by using the AutoSum button. When pressed, the AutoSum button inserted an equal sign followed by the word *SUM*. The range of cells to be summed was designated within parentheses; for example, =SUM(D5:D10). In this function formula, the word *SUM* is the function name that identifies the operation. The argument is the range of cells that will be added together.

Function formulas may be entered into the worksheet in two ways. First, the function formula may be entered directly into the cell by keying an equal sign, the function name, and the argument.

Function formulas may also be entered through dialog boxes by choosing Function from the Insert menu or by clicking the Function Wizard button in the toolbar. The Function Wizard dialog boxes guide you through the insertion of a function in a cell (see Figure 9-8). The first dialog box makes it easy to browse through all of the available functions to select the one you want. The dialog box also provides a brief explanation of any function you choose. The function classifications may be selected by clicking in the Function Category box. Individual function formulas within the category appear in the Function Name box. A description of the function formula appears near the bottom of the dialog box.

You select the function formula argument in the second step. In a new dialog box, you may select a cell or range to appear in the argument. The function you choose while in the dialog box will then be inserted in the highlighted cell.

FIGURE 9-8
The Function Wizard dialog boxes allow you to
browse through all of the available functions.

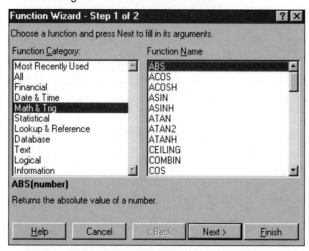

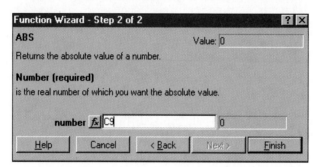

Mathematical and Trigonometric Functions

Mathematical and trigonometric functions manipulate quantitative data
in the worksheet. Some mathematical operations, such as addition, subtraction,
multiplication, and division, do not require function formulas. However, mathematical and trigonometric functions are particularly useful when you need to
determine values such as logarithms, factorials, sines, cosines, tangents, and absolute values.

You have already learned to use one of the mathematical and trigonometric functions when you used the AutoSum button to create SUM functions.
Two other mathematical functions, the square root and rounding functions, are
described in Table 9-3. Notice that two arguments are required to perform the
rounding operation.

TABLE 9-3
Mathematical functions manipulate quantitative data in the worksheet.

FUNCTION	OPERATION
SQRT(number)	Displays the square root of the number identified in the argument. For example, =SQRT(C4) will display the square root of the value in C4.
ROUND(number,num_digits)	Displays the rounded value of a number to the number of places designated by the second argument. For example, =ROUND(14.23433,2) will display 14.23. If the second argument is a negative number, the first argument will be rounded to the left of the decimal point.

ACTIVITY

9-7 Mathematical Functions

1. Open the file *Activity 9-7* from your template disk.

2. Determine the sum of the numbers in column B using the SUM function.
   a. Highlight **B8.**
   b. Enter **=SUM(B3:B7)**. (The same operation could have been performed using the AutoSum button on the toolbar.)

3. Determine the square root of the sum determined in B8 using the SQRT function.
   a. Highlight **B9.**
   b. Choose **Function** from the **Insert** menu. The Function Wizard dialog box appears.
   c. Click **Math & Trig** in the **Function Category** box.
   d. Click **SQRT** in the **Function Name** box. (You may need to scroll downward.)

e. Click **Next>.**
f. Enter **B8** in the **number** box. (Alternatively, you may click B8 if it is visible in the worksheet.) You will notice the value in B8, 2466, appears to the right of the number box. The value that will appear in B9, 49.65883607, appears in the upper right of the dialog box.
g. Click **Finish.**

4. Round the square root determined in B9 to the tenths place using the ROUND function.
   a. Highlight **B10.**
   b. Click the **Function Wizard** button on the toolbar. The Function Wizard dialog box will appear.
   c. Click **Math & Trig** in the **Function Category** box if it has not already been selected.

d. Click **ROUND** in the **Function Name** box.

e. Click **Next>.**

f. Enter **B9** in the **number** box.

g. Enter **2** in the **num_digits** box.

h. Click **Finish.**

5. Compare your results to the screen shown in Figure 9-9. Save the file as *Functions* on your data disk and leave the file on your screen for the next activity.

FIGURE 9-9

Mathematical and trigonometric functions perform calculations such as summing, determining square roots, and rounding on worksheet data.

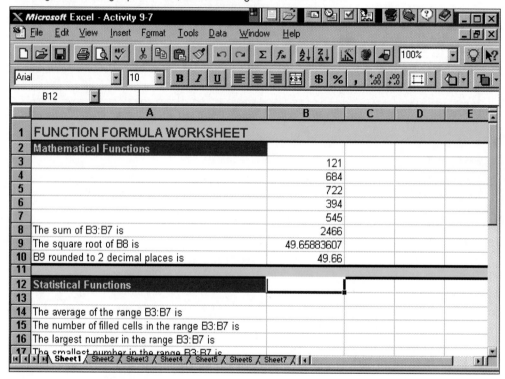

Statistical Functions

Statistical functions are used to describe large quantities of data. For example, function formulas can determine the average, standard deviation, or variance of a range of data. Statistical functions can also be used to determine the number of values in a range, the largest value in a range, and the smallest value in a range. Table 9-4 shows some of the statistical functions available in Excel. Notice that all the statistical functions contain a range for the argument. The range is the body of numbers the statistics will describe.

TABLE 9-4
Statistical functions are used to analyze large amounts of numbers.

FUNCTION	OPERATION
AVERAGE(number1,number2...)	Displays the average of the list identified in the argument. For example, =AVERAGE(E4:E9) displays the average of the numbers contained in the range E4:E9.
COUNT(value1,value2...)	Displays the number of filled cells in the range identified in the argument. For example, =COUNT(D6:D21) displays 16 if all the cells in the range are filled.
MAX(number1,number2...)	Displays the largest number contained in the range identified in the argument
MIN(number1,number2...)	Displays the smallest number contained in the range identified in the argument
STDEV(number1,number2...)	Displays the standard deviation of the numbers contained in the range of the argument
VAR(number1,number2...)	Displays the variance for the numbers contained in the range of the argument

ACTIVITY

9-8 **Statistical Functions**

● ●

1. Determine the average of the values in the range B3:B7.
   a. Highlight **B14.**
   b. Click the **Function Wizard** button on the toolbar. The Function Wizard dialog box appears.
   c. Click **Statistical** in the **Function Category.**
   d. Click **AVERAGE** in the **Function Name** box.
   e. Click **Next>.**
   f. Enter **B3:B7** in the **number1** box.
   g. Click **Finish.**

2. Determine the number of filled cells in the range B3:B7.
   a. Highlight **B15.**
   b. Click the **Function Wizard** button on the toolbar. The Function Wizard dialog box appears.
   c. Click **Statistical** in the **Function Category.**
   d. Click **COUNT** in the **Function Name** box.
   e. Click **Next>.**
   f. Enter **B3:B7** in the **value1** box.
   g. Click **Finish.**

3. Determine the largest number in the range B3:B7.
   a. Highlight **B16.**
   b. Enter **=MAX(B3:B7)**.

4. Determine the smallest number in the range B3:B7.
   a. Highlight **B17.**
   b. Enter **=MIN(B3:B7)**.

5. Determine the standard deviation of the range B3:B7.
   a. Highlight **B18.**

   b. Enter **=STDEV(B3:B7)**. (Your rounded amount may vary depending on your column width.)

6. Determine the variance of the range B3:B7.
   a. Highlight **B19.**
   b. Enter **=VAR(B3:B7)**. The value 59952.7 should appear in the cell.

7. Compare your results to the screen shown in Figure 9-10. Leave *Functions* on the screen for the next activity.

FIGURE 9-10
Statistical functions perform various operations, such as finding the average, maximum, minimum, standard deviation, and variance.

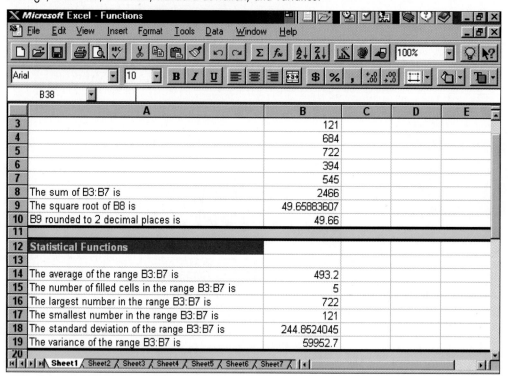

Financial Functions

Financial functions are used to analyze loans and investments. The primary financial functions are future value, present value, and payment, which are described in Table 9-5.

TABLE 9-5

Financial functions are used to analyze loans and investments.

FUNCTION	OPERATION
FV(rate,nper,pmt,pv,type)	Displays the future value of a series of equal payments (third argument), at a fixed rate (first argument), for a specified number of periods (second argument). (The fourth and fifth arguments are optional.) For example, =FV(.08,5,100) determines the future value of five $100 payments at the end of five years if you earn a rate of 8%.
PV(rate,nper,pmt,fv,type)	Displays the present value of a series of equal payments (third argument), at a fixed rate (first argument), for a specified number of payments (second argument). (The fourth and fifth arguments are optional.) For example, =PV(.1,5,500) displays the current value of five payments of $500 at a 10% rate.
PMT(rate,nper,pv,fv,type)	Displays the payment per period needed to repay a loan (third argument), at a specified interest (first argument), for a specified number of periods (second argument). (The fourth and fifth arguments are optional.) For example, =PMT(.01,36,10000) displays the monthly payment needed to repay a $10,000 loan at a 12% annual rate (.01 times 12 months) for three years (36 months divided by 12*).

*NOTE: Rate and term functions should be compatible. In other words, if payments are monthly, the annual rate should be divided by 12 to determine the monthly rate.

1. Scenario 1: You plan to make six yearly payments of $150 into a savings account that earns 9.5% annually. Use the FV function to determine the value of the account at the end of six years.
   a. Enter **.095** in B24.
   b. Enter **6** in B25.
   c. Enter **-150** in B26. (A negative is entered to indicate that the payment is outgoing.)
   d. Click in cell B27. Click the **Function Wizard** button on the toolbar.
   e. Click **Financial** in the **Function Category.**
   f. Click **FV** in the **Function Name** box.
   g. Click **Next>.**
   h. Enter **B24** in the **rate** box.
   i. Enter **B25** in the **nper** box.
   j. Enter **B26** in the **pmt** box.
   k. Click **Finish.** The savings account will have grown to the amount shown in B27 after six years.

2. Scenario 2: You have a choice of receiving $1,200 now or eight annual payments of $210. A typical rate for a savings account in your local bank is 6%. Use the PV function to determine which is the most profitable alternative.
   a. Enter **.06** in B29.
   b. Enter **8** in B30.
   c. Enter **-210** in B31. (A negative number is entered to indicate that the money would not be received if the other alternative was selected.)

   d. Enter **=PV(B29,B30,B31)** in B32. The best decision is to take the delayed payments because the present value, $1,304.06, is greater than $1,200.

3. Scenario 3: You need to borrow $5,000. Your banker has offered you an annual rate of 12% interest for a five-year loan. Use the PMT function to determine your monthly payments.
   a. Enter **.01** in B34. (A 1% monthly rate [12% divided by 12 months] is used because the problem specifies monthly, rather than annual, payments.)
   b. Enter **60** in B35. (A period of 60 months [5 years times 12 months] is used because the problem specifies monthly, rather than annual, payments.)
   c. Enter **5000** in B36.
   d. Enter **=PMT(B34,B35,B36)** in B37. The value ($111.22) will be in the cell. The number is negative because you must make a payment. Under the conditions of this loan, you will pay a total of $1,673.20 [($111.22 * 60 months) - $5,000 principal] in interest over the life of the loan.

4. Compare your results to the screen shown in Figure 9-11.

5. Print the file and save it to your data disk. Close the file.

FIGURE 9-11

Financial functions perform various operations, such as finding present and future values.

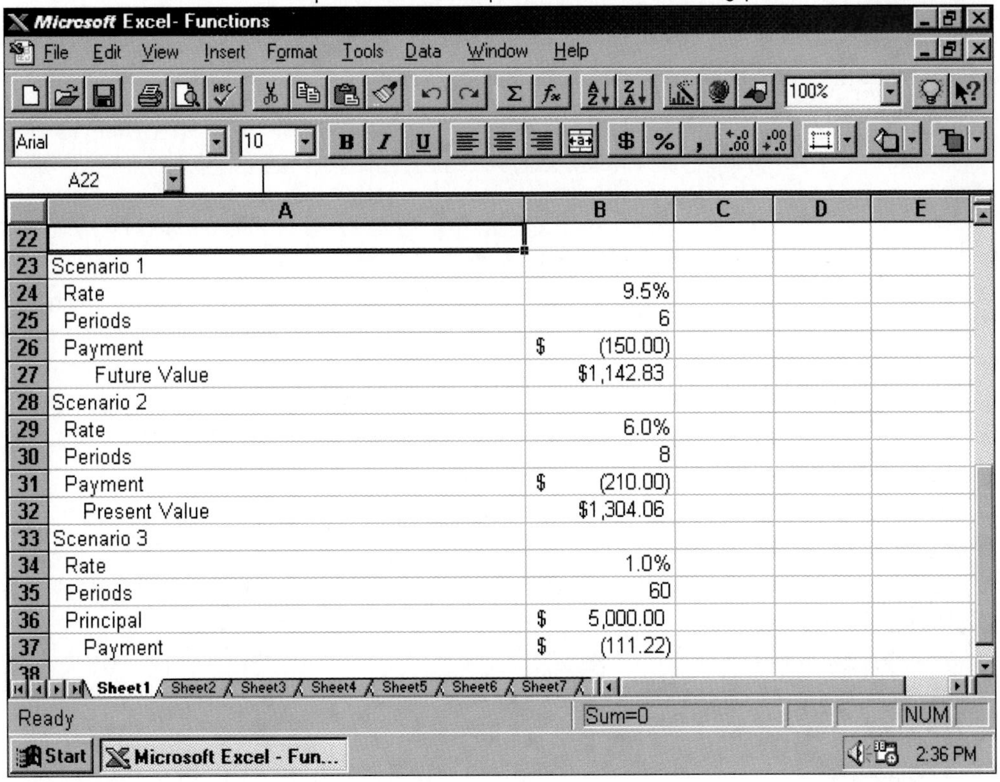

Date, Time, and Text Functions

Functions may also be used to insert dates and certain kinds of text into a spreadsheet (see Table 9-6). For example, date and time functions may be used to convert serial numbers to a month, day, or year. A date function may also be used to insert the current date or time.

A text function can be used to convert text in a cell to all uppercase or lowercase letters. Text functions can also be used to repeat data contained in another cell.

TABLE 9-6
Date and time functions are used to convert serial numbers to a date or time.
Text functions convert numbers to text, or format text.

FUNCTION	OPERATION
DATE(year,month,day)	Displays the serial number of a date. For example, =DATE(1998,12,17) inserts the serial number 36146. If the cell is formatted for a particular date format, it may be displayed as *12/17/98* or *December 17, 1998*, as well as other date formats.
NOW()	Displays the serial number of the current date or time. For example, =NOW() in a cell formatted for time will display the current time, such as *10:05PM*.
UPPER(text)	Displays the text in the argument in uppercase letters. For example, =UPPER(A5) displays the text in cell A5 in all uppercase letters.
LOWER(text)	Displays the text in the argument in lowercase letters. For example, =LOWER(BOSTON) displays *boston*.
REPT(text,number_times)	Displays the text (first argument) a specified number of times (second argument). For example, REPT(B6,3) will repeat the text in cell B6 three times.

ACTIVITY

Inserting Dates and Text

In this activity, you will insert a function using the Insert Function dialog box.

1. Open the file *Activity 9-10* from your template disk.

2. Replace the words *NEXT YEAR* with the number for next year.

3. Insert today's date in B13.
   a. Choose **Function** from the **Insert** menu. The Function Wirard dialog box appears.
   b. Click **Date & Time** in the **Function Category** box.
   c. Click **NOW** in the **Function Name** box.

   d. Click **Next>.**
   e. Click **Finish.** The function formula =NOW() appears in the formula bar. A date and time appear in the cell.

4. Format the date.
   a. Choose **Cells** from the **Format** menu.
   b. Click the **Number** tab if it is not already tabbed.
   c. Click **Date** in the Category box.
   d. Choose the ninth option, which displays the month in text form, followed by the date and year in numerical form.
   e. Click **OK.**

5. Insert the current time in C13.
   a. Copy the contents of **B13** to **C13.**
   b. Highlight **C13.**
   c. Choose **Cells** from the **Format** menu.
   d. Click the **Number** tab if it is not already tabbed.
   e. Click **Time** in the Category box.
   f. Choose the second option, which displays the time in numerical form followed by either AM or PM.
   g. Click **OK.**

6. Repeat the text in A1 in B14 using the following steps:
   a. Highlight **B14.**
   b. Click the **Function Wizard** button in the toolbar.
   c. Click **Text** in the **Function Category** box.
   d. Click **REPT** in the **Function Name** box.
   e. Click **Next>.**
   f. Enter **A1** in the **text** box.
   g. Enter **1** in **number_times**.
   h. Click **Finish.** The title will be repeated in B14.

7. Save the file under the name that appears in B14.

8. Print and close the file.

Summary

- The spreadsheet has the power to perform rapid calculations. Worksheet formulas perform calculations on values referenced in other cells of the worksheet.

- Cell references in formulas may be relative or absolute. Relative cell references adjust to a different location when copied or moved. Absolute cell references describe the same cell location in the worksheet regardless of where it is copied or moved. Mixed cell references contain both relative and absolute cell references.

- Formulas may be created quickly by using the Point and Click method. This method inserts cell references by clicking the cell with the mouse rather than keying its column letter and row number.

- A group of cells may be summed quickly by using the AutoSum button on the toolbar. Excel will insert the SUM formula function and determine the most likely range to be summed.

- Function formulas are special formulas that do not require operators. Excel has over 200 function formulas that may be used to perform mathematical, statistical, financial, and other operations.

REVIEW ACTIVITIES

TRUE/FALSE

Circle T or F to show whether the statement is true or false.

T   F   **1.** A worksheet can be used to perform the same functions as a calculator.

T   F   **2.** An operator is a number or cell reference used in formulas.

T   F   **3.** In a complex formula, subtraction will be performed before multiplication.

T   F   **4.** Operations within parentheses will be performed before operations outside parentheses in a formula.

T   F   **5.** An absolute cell reference will change if the formula is copied or moved.

T   F   **6.** The AutoSum button creates the function formula =SUM in the highlighted cell.

T   F   **7.** The Formulas command will display formulas rather than values in the worksheet.

T   F   **8.** Manual calculation is performed by pressing the F2 key.

T   F   **9.** Statistical function formulas are used to analyze loans and investments.

T   F   **10.** Function formulas do not have operators.

COMPLETION

Write your answer in the blank space.

1. Which operator has the highest priority in the order of evaluation in a worksheet formula?

_____

2. What type of cell reference adjusts to its new location when it is copied or moved?

_____

3. What type of cell reference will remain the same when it is copied or moved?

_____

4. Which technique inserts cell references in a formula by clicking the mouse?

_____

5. Which function formula is inserted in a cell by clicking the AutoSum button?

_____

6. Which toolbar button is used to create a function formula that adds numbers in a column?

_____

7. Which keystrokes will display formulas in the worksheet?

_____

8. Which command delays calculation until the F9 key is pressed?

_____

9. What is the name of the item enclosed in parentheses in a function formula?

_____

10. Which dialog box allows you to browse through worksheet functions?

_____

REINFORCEMENT APPLICATIONS

application 9 - 1

Match the letter of the worksheet formula to the description of the worksheet operation performed by the formula.

___ 1. Adds the values in A3 and A4

___ 2. Subtracts the value in A4 from the value in A3

___ 3. Multiplies the value in A3 by 27

___ 4. Divides the value in A3 by 27

___ 5. Raises the value in A3 to the 27th power

___ 6. Divides the value in A3 by 27, then adds the value in A4

___ 7. Divides the value in A3 by the result of 27 plus the value in A4

___ 8. Multiplies the value in A3 by 27, then divides the product by the value in A4

___ 9. Divides 27 by the value in A4, then multiplies the result by the value in A3

___10. Raises the value in A3 to the 27th power, then divides the result by the value in A4

a.	=A3/(27+A4)
b.	=A3^27
c.	=A3^27/A4
d.	=A3+A4
e.	=A3/27
f.	=A3/27+A4
g.	=(A3*27)/A4
h.	=A3-A4
i.	=A3*(27/A4)
j.	=A3*27

application 9 - 2

The file *Application 9-2* is a worksheet containing several values. Enter formulas in the specified cells that will perform the requested operations. After you enter each formula, write the resulting value in the space provided. When you have completed the application, save the file to your data disk as *Formulas* and close it.

Resulting Value		Cell	Operation
_____	1.	C3	Add the values in A3 and B3.
_____	2.	C4	Subtract the value in B4 from the value in A4.
_____	3.	C5	Multiply the value in A5 by the value in B5.
_____	4.	C6	Divide the value in A6 by the value in B6.
_____	5.	B7	Sum the values in the range B3:B6.
_____	6.	D3	Add the values in A3 and A4, then multiply the sum by 3.
_____	7.	D4	Add the values in A3 and A4, then multiply the sum by B3.

_____ 8. D5 Raise the value in A5 to the 3rd power.

_____ 9. D6 Subtract the value in B6 from the value in A6, then divide by 2.

_____10. D7 Divide the value in A6 by 2, then subtract the value in B6.

a p p l i c a t i o n   9 - 3

You are a fund raiser for Zoo America. Because winter is typically a slow time for the zoo, you have decided to have a special fundraiser during the holiday. Zoo employees will set up booths at holiday events to sell T-shirts, sweatshirts, and coffee mugs. You have been asked to create a worksheet that will calculate the bills of individuals who purchase these items. You will be required to charge a sales tax of 5% on each sale. The file *Application 9-3* is a worksheet lacking the formulas required to calculate the bills. Complete the worksheet following these steps:

1. Open the file *Application 9-3*.

2. Enter formulas in D6, D7, D8, and D9 to calculate the cost of each item when quantities are entered in column C.

3. Enter a formula in D10 to sum the totals in D6:D9.

4. Enter a formula in D11 to calculate a sales tax equal to 5% of the subtotal in D10.

5. Enter a formula in D12 to add the subtotal and sales tax.

6. Change the worksheet for manual calculation.

7. Format D6:D12 for currency.

8. Save the file to your data disk as *Bill Form*. The saved data applies to all customers. The worksheet is now ready to accept data unique to the individual customer.

9. A customer purchases two tiger T-shirts, three dolphin T-shirts, one sweatshirt, and four coffee mugs. Enter the quantities in column C and press **F9** to calculate.

10. Check the calculations made by the formulas by hand to make sure that you have entered the formulas correctly. If any of the formulas are incorrect, edit them and recalculate the worksheet.

11. When you are confident that the worksheet is calculating as you intended, print the customer's bill.

12. Close the file without saving the most recent changes.

a p p l i c a t i o n   9 - 4

Write the appropriate function formula to perform each of the described operations. You may refer to Tables 9-3 through 9-5 to help you prepare the function formulas.

_____ 1. Determine the smallest value in A4:A90.

_____ 2. Determine the standard deviation of the values in K6:K35.

_____ 3. Determine the average of the values in B9:B45.

_____ 4. Determine the yearly payments on a $5,000 loan at 8% for 10 years.

_____ 5. Determine the value of a savings account at the end of 5 years after making $400 yearly payments; the account earns 8%.

_____ 6. Round the value in C3 to the tenths place.

_____ 7. Determine the present value of a pension plan that will pay you 20 yearly payments of $4,000; the current rate of return is 7.5%.

_____ 8. Determine the square root of 225.

_____ 9. Determine the variance of the values in F9:F35.

_____ 10. Add all the values in D4:D19.

_____ 11. Determine how many cells in H7:H21 are filled with data.

_____ 12. Determine the largest value in E45:E92.

a p p l i c a t i o n   9 - 5

The file *Application 9-5* contains a worksheet of student grades for one examination. Calculate statistics on these grades by following these steps:

1. Open the file *Application 9-5* from your template disk.

2. Determine the number of students taking the examination by entering a function formula in B26.

3. Determine the average exam grade by entering a function formula in B27.

4. Determine the highest exam grade by entering a function formula in B28.

5. Determine the lowest exam grade by entering a function formula in B29.

6. Determine the standard deviation of the exam grades by entering a function formula in B30.

7. Save the file to your data disk as *Grades Statistics* and print it. Close the file.

a p p l i c a t i o n   9 - 6

Generic National Bank makes a profit by taking money deposited by customers and lending it to others at a higher rate. In order to encourage depositing and borrowing, you have helped the bank develop a worksheet that will inform depositors about the future value of their investments. Another portion of the worksheet informs borrowers of the yearly payments they must make on their loans. The incomplete worksheet is in file *Application 9-6*. Complete the worksheet by following these steps:

1. Open *Application 9-6* from your template disk.

2. Enter a function formula in B11 that will inform borrowers of the yearly payment. Assume that the loan principal (or present value) will be entered in B5, the lending rate will be entered

in B7, and the term of the loan will be entered in B9. (#DIV/0!, indicating an error due to division by zero, will appear in the cell because no data is in the argument cell references yet.)

3. A potential borrower inquires about the payments on a $5,500 loan for four years. The current lending rate is 11%. Determine the yearly payment on the loan. (The amount in B11 will appear as a negative because it is an amount that must be paid.)

4. Print the portion of the worksheet that pertains to the loan (A1:B12) so that it may be given to the potential borrower.

5. Enter a function formula in B24 informing depositors of the future value of periodic payments. Assume the yearly payments will be entered in B18, the term of the payments will be entered in B20, and the interest rate will be entered in B22. ($0.00 will appear because no data is in the argument cell references yet.)

6. A potential depositor is starting a college fund for her son. She inquires about the value of yearly deposits of $450 at the end of 15 years. The current interest rate is 7.5%. Determine the future value of the deposits. (Remember to enter the deposit as a negative because it is an amount that must be paid.)

7. Print the portion of the worksheet that applies to the deposits (A14:B25) so that it may be given to the potential depositor.

8. Save the file to your data disk as *Payment and Interest* and close it.

a p p l i c a t i o n   9 - 7

Part 1

Alice Grant has been saving and investing part of her salary for several years. She decides to keep track of her investments on a spreadsheet. The file *Application 9-7* contains Alice Grant's investments. She owns several types:

- **Money Market Account**—a bank savings account that does not require notification before money is withdrawn.

- **Stocks**—shares of ownership in a corporation.

- **Mutual Fund**—collection of several stocks and/or bonds (borrowings) of corporations that are combined to form a single investment.

Alice's stock and mutual fund shares are sold on a major exchange and the value of the shares may be looked up in the newspaper after any business day.

1. Calculate the values of the stocks in column D by entering formulas in D6 through D8. The formulas should multiply the number of shares in column B by the price of the shares in column C.

2. Calculate the values of the mutual funds in column D by entering formulas in D10 through D11. Similar to the stocks, the formulas should multiply the number of shares in column B by the price of the shares in column C.

3. Enter a formula in D12 that sums the values in D4 through D11.

> **HINT:** *You may either use a function formula from the Insert menu or use the AutoSum key in the toolbar.*

4. Alice would like to know what percentage each investment is with respect to her total investments. Enter the formula **=D4/$D$12** in E4.

> **HINT:** *The value 16% should appear in the cell.*

5. You may have noticed that the formula you entered in E4 contains an absolute cell reference. If this formula is copied into other cells, the denominator will remain the value that appears in cell D12. Copy the formula in E4 to cells E6 through E8, and cells E10 through E12.

6. Save the file to your data disk as *Alice's Investments*.

Part 2

After glancing at the newspaper, Alice realizes that the values of her investments have changed significantly. She decides to update the spreadsheet containing her investment records.

1. Convert the spreadsheet to manual calculation.

2. Enter the following updated share price amounts:

Investment	Price
MicroCrunch, Corp.	$16.00
Ocean Electronics, Inc.	$20.25
Photex, Inc.	$14.50
Prosperity Growth Fund	$5.50
Lucrative Mutual Fund	$13.00

3. Perform manual calculation by pressing **F9.**

4. Save the file to your data disk and print it. Close the file.

SPREADSHEET CHARTS

OBJECTIVES
When you complete this chapter, you will be able to:

1. Identify the purpose of charting spreadsheet data.

2. Identify the types of spreadsheet charts.

3. Create and save a chart.

4. Edit a chart.

5. Print a chart.

What Is a Worksheet Chart?

A *chart* is a graphical representation of data contained in a spreadsheet. Charts make the data of a spreadsheet easier to understand. For example, the spreadsheet in Figure 10-1 shows the populations of four major American cities for three years. You may be able to detect the changes in the populations by carefully examining the spreadsheet. However, the increases and decreases in the populations of each city are easier to detect when the contents of the spreadsheet are illustrated in a chart, such as the one shown in Figure 10-2.

Types of Spreadsheet Charts

In this chapter, you will create four of the most commonly used spreadsheet charts: column chart, line chart, pie chart, and scatter chart. These charts, and several other types, are illustrated in Figure 10-3.

FIGURE 10-1
Spreadsheets contain numerical data but do not illustrate relationships among data.

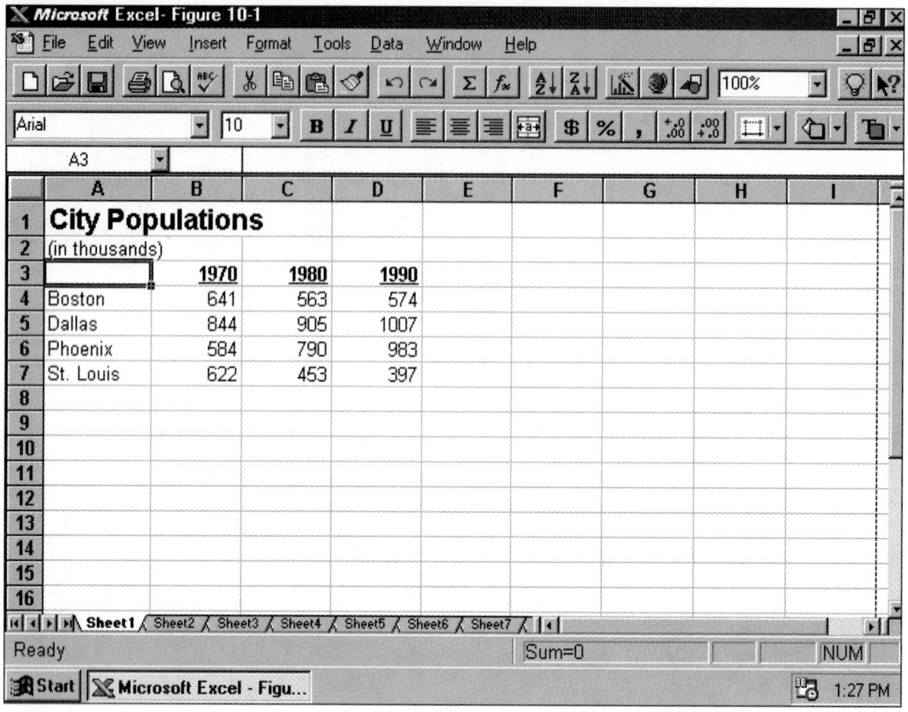

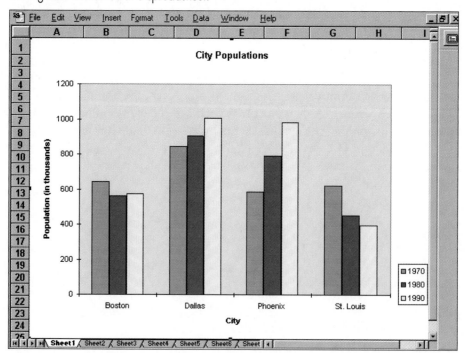

FIGURE 10-2
Spreadsheet charts are ideal for illustrating the relationships among data contained in a spreadsheet.

FIGURE 10-3

Several types of charts are available in Excel.

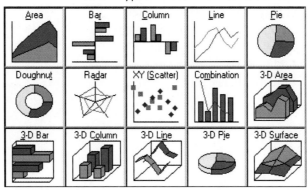

Column Chart

A ***column chart*** uses rectangles of varying heights to illustrate values in a spreadsheet. For example, the column chart in Figure 10-2 has one vertical column to show the population of a city for each year. A column chart is well suited for showing relationships among categories of data. The chart shows how the population of one city compares to those of other cities.

Line Chart

A ***line chart*** is similar to the column chart, except columns are replaced by points connected by a line. The line chart is ideal for illustrating trends over time. For example, Figure 10-4, a line chart printed in landscape orientation, shows the growth of the U. S. federal debt from 1982 to 1992. The vertical axis represents the level of the deficit, and the horizontal axis shows years in chronological order from 1982 to 1992, representing the passage of time. The line chart makes it easy to see how the federal debt has grown over time.

FIGURE 10-4

A line chart is ideal for illustrating trends of data over time.

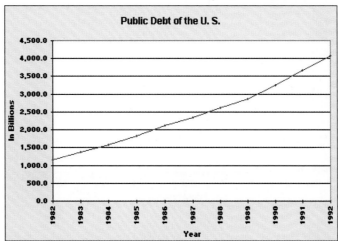

Pie Chart

Pie charts show the relationship of a part to a whole. Each part is presented as a "slice" of the pie. For example, a teacher could create a pie chart of the distribution of grades in a class, as shown in Figure 10-5. Each slice represents the portion of grades given for each letter grade.

Scatter Chart

Scatter charts, sometimes called *XY charts,* show the relationship between two categories of data. One category is represented on the vertical (Y) axis, and the other category is represented on the horizontal (X) axis. The result is a "cloud" of data points that may or may not have a recognizable shape. It is not practical to connect the data points with a line because points on a scatter chart usually do not relate to each other, as they do in a line chart. For example, the scatter chart in Figure 10-6 shows a data point for each of twelve individuals based on their height and weight. In most cases, a tall person tends to be heavier than a short person. However, because some people are tall and skinny, whereas others are short and stocky, the relationship between height and weight cannot be represented by a line.

FIGURE 10-5
Each "slice" of a pie chart represents part of a larger group.

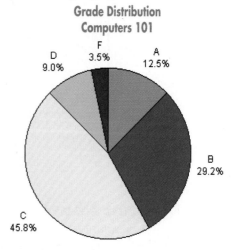

FIGURE 10-6
Scatter charts show the relationship between two categories of data, such as height and weight.

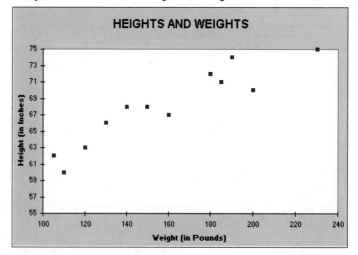

Creating a Chart from a Worksheet

You can create and display charts in two ways: by embedding the chart in the worksheet, or placing it on a chart sheet. An **embedded chart** is created within the worksheet. The primary advantage of an embedded chart is that it may be viewed at the same time as the data from which it is created. You'll learn more about embedded charts later in this chapter.

A **chart sheet** is a separate "tabbed" sheet on which you can create and store a chart. You can name the chart sheet to identify its contents and access it by clicking the tab that appears near the bottom of the screen. A chart sheet is appropriate when it is inconvenient to have the chart and data on the same screen, or when you plan to create more than one chart from the same data.

Creating a Chart on a Chart Sheet

Create a new chart sheet by first selecting the data from the worksheet that is to be included in the chart. Then choose Chart from the Insert menu and As New Sheet from the pop-out menu. The **ChartWizard**, a five-step, on-screen guide that helps you to prepare a chart, appears. The ChartWizard will take you through the following steps:

- In Step 1, you confirm the range of data to be included in the chart. The range should include both numerical data and the data you plan to use as row and column labels in the chart.

- In Step 2, you select a general type of chart, such as column, line, or pie.

- In Step 3, you select a more specific type of chart. For each chart type, you have a number of variations that differ in the way that they display the chart in relation to the axes. They may also differ by including gridlines or data labels. **Gridlines** are lines displayed through a chart that relate the objects (such as columns or data points) in a chart to the axes. **Data labels** print the values depicted by the chart objects directly on the chart. Gridlines and data labels make the chart easier to understand.

- In Step 4, you specify the data series, labels, and legends for the chart. A **data series** is a group of related information in a column or row of a worksheet that will be plotted on a worksheet chart. A **legend** is a list that identifies patterns or symbols used in a worksheet chart.

- In Step 5, you indicate whether the chart should have a legend and enter the titles for the chart and axes of the chart.

After you have completed these steps, a chart appears on screen.

10-1 Creating a Worksheet Chart

1. Open the file *Activity 10-1* from the template disk. Column A contains educational levels and column B contains the median incomes of those with that level of education. You'll prepare a chart to show the relationship of income to education.

2. Select the range **A3:B9.** The highlighted items are the data to be included in the chart that you will create.

3. Choose **Chart** from the **Insert** menu, then choose **As New Sheet** from the pop-out menu. Step 1 of the ChartWizard appears on the screen (similar to Figure 10-7). The dialog box shows an absolute range: $A$3:$B$9. If that range does not appear, correct it by dragging the appropriate range in the worksheet. (You may need to move the dialog box to view the entire range.)

4. Click **Next>.** Step 2 of the ChartWizard, similar to Figure 10-8, appears.

5. Click the **Column** button if it is not already selected. The picture of the column chart darkens to indicate it has been selected.

FIGURE 10-7
Confirm the range of data to be charted
in Step 1 of the ChartWizard.

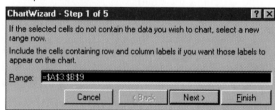

FIGURE 10-8
Designate a general chart type in Step 2 of the ChartWizard.

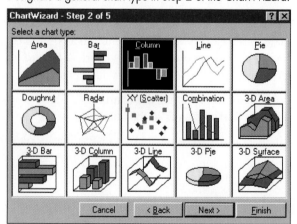

6. Click **Next>.** Step 3 of the ChartWizard, similar to Figure 10-9, appears.

7. Click **Option 8,** a chart of one series of data without gridlines.

8. Click **Next>.** Step 4 of the ChartWizard, similar to Figure 10-10, appears. In this dialog box, Excel has created a chart from the data you have specified. The chart uses the data in the first column of the range as labels for the X axis and displays a legend created from the data in the first row of the range. Excel has created a logical chart from the range of data.

9. Click **Next>.** Step 5 of the ChartWizard, similar to Figure 10-11, appears.
    a. Click **No** to eliminate the legend. This chart use only one series of data and does not need a legend to distinguish between data.
    b. Key **YOUR EDUCATION PAYS** in the Chart Title box.
    c. Key **Education Level** in the Category (X) box.
    d. Key **Median Income** in the Value (Y) box. The titles you created appear in the Sample Chart area of the dialog box.

10. Click **Finish.** Your screen displays a chart sheet with the chart you created. Near the

FIGURE 10-9
Designate a more specific type of chart in Step 3 of the ChartWizard.

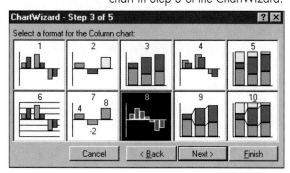

FIGURE 10-10
Specify characteristics of the chart in Step 4 of the ChartWizard.

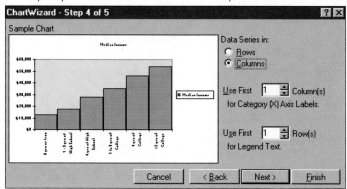

FIGURE 10-11
Enter titles and axes in Step 5 of the ChartWizard.

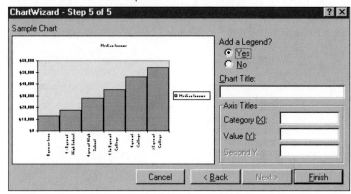

bottom of the page, a tab titled Chart1 appears. A Chart shortcut bar may also appear on top of the chart sheet. You can  close this shortcut bar or drag it out of the way to view the chart.

11. Leave the file open for the next activity.

The chart illustrates the value of education in attaining higher income. Notice that the columns get higher on the right side of the chart, indicating that those who stay in school will be rewarded with higher incomes.

Saving a Chart

A worksheet chart is considered part of a worksheet. When you save the worksheet, you will also save the charts you have created from the worksheet. Save the worksheet and its associated chart(s) by choosing Save from the File menu. The File menu may be accessed from either the worksheet or chart sheet.

ACTIVITY

10-2 Saving a Chart

● ●

1. Choose **Save As** from the **File** menu.

2. Save the chart to your data disk as *Education Pays*.

3. Leave the file open for the next activity.

Switching Between Chart Sheets and Worksheets

A chart sheet is closely related to the worksheet from which it was created. For example, if you change the data in a worksheet, these changes will automatically be made in the chart created from the worksheet.

When you create a chart, it is identified by a name on a tab that appears near the bottom of the screen. The tab of the chart appears directly to the left of the tab of the worksheet from which the chart was created. Excel names the first chart *Chart1*. If additional charts are created from the worksheet, they become *Chart2*, *Chart3*, and so on.

To return to the worksheet from which a chart was created, click the tab of the worksheet. The chart may be accessed once more by clicking the chart tab.

ACTIVITY

Switching to and from the Chart

1. Click the **Sheet1** tab near the bottom of the screen. The worksheet appears.

2. Edit the contents of A4 to A9 to change the abbreviation *yrs* to the word *years*.

3. Click the **Chart1** tab. The chart sheet appears. The labels under the X axis are now unabbreviated.

4. Leave *Education Pays* on the screen for the next activity.

Naming a Chart Sheet

Naming a chart sheet is particularly useful after you have prepared several charts from one worksheet. These charts may become difficult to distinguish by their chart sheet number and are easier to recognize with more descriptive names. Change the name of the chart sheet by choosing the Sheet command from the Format menu, then choosing Rename from the pop-out menu. The Rename Sheet dialog box appears, allowing you to rename the chart sheet.

10-4 Naming a Chart Sheet

1. Choose **Sheet** from the **Format** menu, then select **Rename** from the pop-out menu. The Rename Sheet dialog box appears.

2. Key **Pay Chart** in the Name text box.

3. Click **OK.** The new name should appear on the tab near the bottom of the screen.

4. Leave the *Pay Chart* chart sheet of *Education Pays* on the screen for the next activity.

Editing a Chart

The ChartWizard creates charts in a general way that may be useful to many Excel users. However, you may want to edit the chart in a manner that changes or emphasizes parts of the chart. Your screen currently shows the *Pay Chart* sheet you created from the *Education Pays* worksheet. Figure 10-12

FIGURE 10-12
Charts may be edited by clicking on one of six parts of the chart.

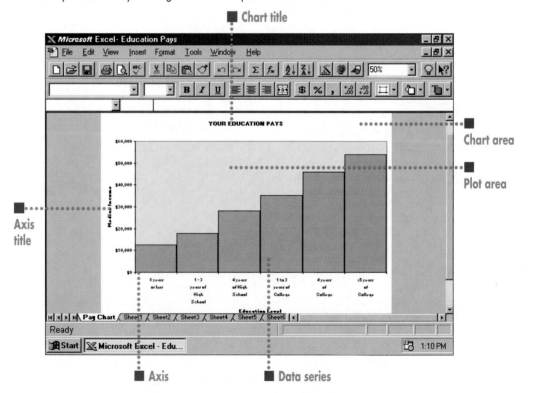

shows six areas of the chart that may be edited. You edit these areas using the mouse in the following ways:

1. Clicking with the left mouse button selects the chart part.
2. Double-clicking with the left mouse button produces one of the dialog boxes identified in Table 10-1. Within the dialog box, you may access tabbed areas to edit specific chart characteristics.
3. Clicking the right mouse button produces an on-screen menu that may be used to clear data, insert data, or change chart types.

TABLE 10-1
Charts may be edited using one of six Format dialog boxes.

FORMAT DIALOG BOX	TABBED AREAS OF THE DIALOG BOX
Format Chart Title	Patterns—designates the border and color of the chart title
	Font—designates the font and font size of characters in the chart title
	Alignment—determines the justification of the chart title
Format Axis Title	Patterns—designates the border and color of the axis title
	Font—designates the font and font size of characters in the axis title
	Alignment—determines the justification of the axis title
Format Axis	Patterns—designates the border and color of the axis
	Scale—designates characteristics of the axis scale, such as the maximum and minimum values and whether the scale is logarithmic or reversed
	Font—designates the font and font size of characters in the axis
	Number—designates the format of numbers in the labels in the axis (for example, currency, text, date)
	Alignment—determines the justification of the labels in the axis
Format Data Series	Patterns—designates the border and color of the data series
	Name and Values—designates the name and Y values to be included in the data series of the chart
	Data Labels—designates the words or values that may appear on the points of a graph
	Axis—designates whether the data is plotted on a primary or secondary axis
	Y Error Bars—designates the treatment of points that extend beyond the scale of the chart
	X Values—designates the cell range of the values in the horizontal axis
Format Plot Area	Patterns—designates the border and color of the plot area
Format Chart Area	Patterns—designates the border and color of the chart background
	Font—designates the font and font size of characters in the chart area

1. Add a subtitle following these steps:
   a. Click **YOUR EDUCATION PAYS,** the chart title. A shaded border with handles surrounds it.
   b. Click to the right of the *S* in the title. A cursor appears.
   c. Press **Enter.** The cursor is centered under the first line of the title.
   d. Key **Stay in School**. The subtitle appears in the chart.

2. Change the font size of the X axis labels following these steps:
   a. Double-click the X axis. The Format Axis dialog box appears.
   b. Click the **Font** tab. The axis labels are currently 10 point size.
   c. Click **12** to change the font size.
   d. Click **OK.** You are returned to the chart sheet. The X axis labels are now larger.

3. Change the color of the chart area following these steps:
   a. Double-click near the outside edge of the chart. The Format Chart Area dialog box appears.
   b. Click the **Patterns** tab.
   c. Click a dark yellow color in the Area box. Dark yellow appears in the Sample box.
   d. Click **OK.** You are returned to the chart sheet. The chart appears with a dark yellow border. Your screen should appear similar to Figure 10-13.

4. Leave the *Pay Chart* chart sheet of *Education Pays* on the screen for the next activity.

Changing the Type of Chart

fter you have created a chart, you may change it to a different type by choosing the Chart Type command in the Format menu (or by clicking the chart area or plot area with the right mouse button, then choosing the Chart Type command). In the Chart Type dialog box (see Figure 10-14), you may select a new type of chart.

WARNING! Not all charts are interchangeable. For example, data that is suitable for a pie chart is often not logical in a scatter chart.

FIGURE 10-13
The appearance of a chart may be changed in Format dialog boxes that are accessed by double-clicking parts of the chart.

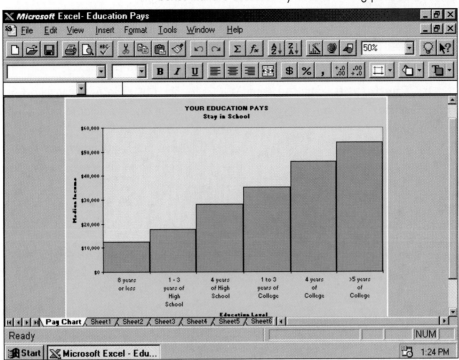

FIGURE 10-14
The type of chart may be changed in the Chart Type dialog box.

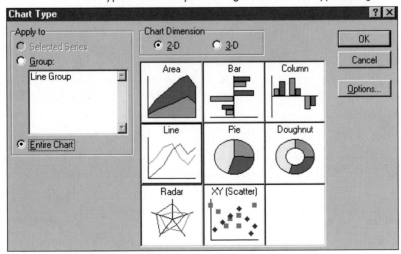

Changing the Type of Chart

1. Choose the **Chart Type** command from the **Format** menu. The Chart Type dialog box appears.

2. Click the **Line** option.

3. Click **OK.** The new line chart appears on screen and is similar to Figure 10-15.

4. Leave the *Pay Chart* chart sheet of *Education Pays* on the screen for the next activity.

FIGURE 10-15
A column chart is easily changed into a line chart.

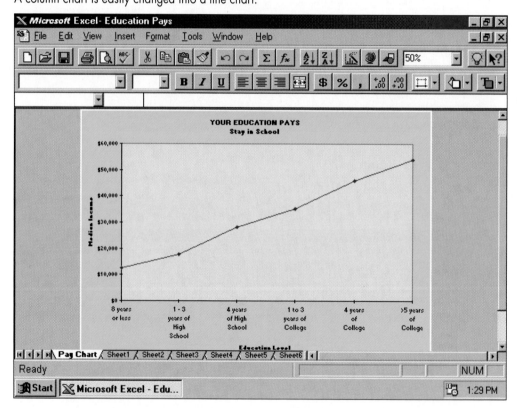

Previewing and Printing a Chart

You preview and print a chart in the same way you do any worksheet. The chart sheet's toolbar has both the Print and Print Preview buttons that work the same as in other Office 95 applications.

ACTIVITY

10-7 Previewing and Printing a Worksheet Chart

1. Click the **Print Preview** button. The chart appears as it will be printed.

2. Click the **Print** button in the Print Preview window.

3. Click **OK.**

4. After printing is complete, save and close the workbook.

Creating an Embedded Chart

As you will recall from earlier in the chapter, an embedded chart is one that is created within the worksheet. To create an embedded chart, choose Chart from the Insert menu, then choose On This Sheet from the pop-out menu. Before the ChartWizard appears, you must select a range of cells in the spreadsheet where the chart will appear.

In the next activity, you will embed a pie chart in a worksheet. Pie charts differ from column or line charts because they use only one set of data. In the column chart you created, you compared the level of education to median incomes. Pie charts compare items within one group to other items within the same group. For example, you can determine how many (or what percent) of pet owners in a group own dogs, cats, or fish. When you prepared a column chart or a line chart, you selected two columns of data. To create a pie chart, select only one column of numerical data before choosing the Chart command in the Insert menu.

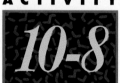
1. Open file *Activity 10-8*.

2. Drag the range **A5:B11.**

3. Choose **Chart** from the **Insert** menu, then select **On This Sheet** from the pop-out menu. The ChartWizard pointer appears. You must now drag the area of the worksheet in which you want the chart to appear.

4. Drag from the upper left corner of cell C3 to the lower right corner of cell H14, to set the area of the chart. When you release, Step 1 of the ChartWizard appears. Confirm that the range $A$5:$B$11 appears in the Range text box.

5. Click **Next>.** Step 2 of the ChartWizard appears.

6. Click the **Pie** option.

7. Click **Next>.** Step 3 of the ChartWizard appears.

8. Click **Option 7,** a pie chart with labels and percentages.

9. Click **Next>.** Step 4 of the ChartWizard appears. The chart you created appears in the dialog box. Excel has correctly used the first column for labels in the chart.

10. Click **Next>.** Step 5 of the ChartWizard appears.

11. Key **HOME ACCIDENT DEATHS** in the Chart Title box.

12. Click **Finish.** The chart sheet on your screen should look similar to Figure 10-16.

13. Save the file as *Home Accidents* and leave the file on your screen for the next activity.

FIGURE 10-16

Pie charts can express parts as a percentage of a whole.

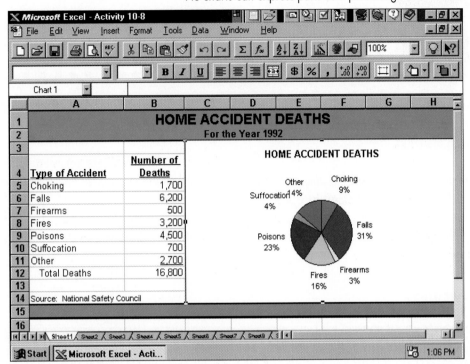

Creating Other Types of Charts

Y ou have already created a column chart, line chart, and pie chart. In the remainder of this chapter, you will learn to create a three-dimensional pie chart and a scatter chart.

Three-Dimensional Charts

Excel allows you to make three-dimensional charts to present data in a more attractive way. Area, Bar, Column, Line, and Pie charts are available in three-dimensional formats.

Creating a 3-D Chart

1. Double-click the chart embedded in the worksheet. A shadowed border appears around the chart.

2. Choose **Chart Type** from the **Format** menu. The Chart Type dialog box appears.

3. Click the **3-D** option in the Chart Dimension box. The 3-D Pie picture in the dialog box should appear darkened. (If it does not, click the 3-D Pie button.)

4. Click **OK.** You are returned to the worksheet. The chart sheet on your screen should look similar to Figure 10-17.

5. Save the file as *Three D Pie* and close it.

FIGURE 10-17
Area, Column, Line, and Pie charts are available in 3-D.

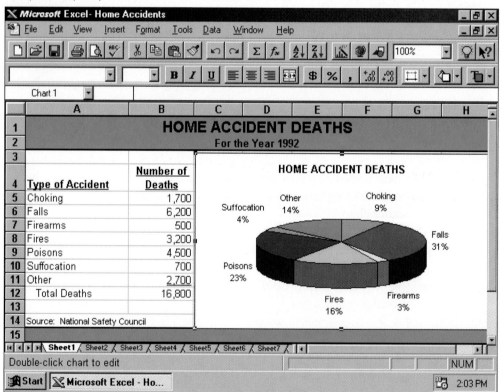

Scatter Charts

Scatter charts are sometimes referred to as *XY charts* because they place data points between an X and Y axis. Scatter charts are usually harder to prepare than the previous charts you created because Excel has difficulty identifying which data should be used as a scale on each axis of the chart.

ACTIVITY
10-10 Creating a Scatter Chart

1. Open the file *Activity 10-10.*

2. Select the range **B3:C15.**

3. Use the ChartWizard following these steps:
   a. Choose **Chart** from the **Insert** menu, then select **As New Sheet.** Step 1 of the ChartWizard appears. Confirm that the range $B$3:$C$15 appears in the Range text box.
   b. Click **Next>.** Step 2 of the ChartWizard appears.
   c. Click the **XY (Scatter)** option.
   d. Click **Next>.** Step 3 of the ChartWizard appears.
   e. Click **Option 1,** a scatter chart that does not contain connecting lines or gridlines.
   f. Click **Next>.** Step 4 of the ChartWizard appears. The chart you have created appears in the dialog box.
   g. Click **Next>.** Step 5 of the ChartWizard appears.
   h. Click **No** to delete the legend in the chart.
   i. Enter **HEIGHTS AND WEIGHTS** in the Chart Title box.
   j. Enter **Weight** in the Category (X) box of Axis Titles.

   k. Enter **Height** in the Value (Y) box of Axis Titles.
   l. Click **Finish.** A scatter chart appears on a chart sheet. Notice that the data points are concentrated in the upper right portion of the chart. You may adjust the scale of the chart to make it more meaningful.

4. Adjust the Y axis downward following these steps:
   a. Double-click the **Y axis.** The Format Axis dialog box appears.
   b. Click the **Scale** tab.
   c. Enter **55** in the Minimum box.
   d. Click **OK.** The portion of the chart that appeared below 55 on the Y axis, which did not have any data points, has been removed from the chart.

5. Adjust the X axis to the left following these steps:
   a. Double-click the **X axis.** The Format Axis dialog box appears.
   b. Click the **Scale** tab.
   c. Enter **100** in the Minimum box.
   d. Click **OK.** The portion of the chart that appeared to the left of 100 has been removed from the chart.

6. Edit the titles and labels of the chart to make them larger. The chart sheet on your screen should look similar to Figure 10-18.

7. Print the chart.

8. Save the file as *Heights and Weights* and close it.

FIGURE 10-18
Scatter charts can show labeled points between two axes.

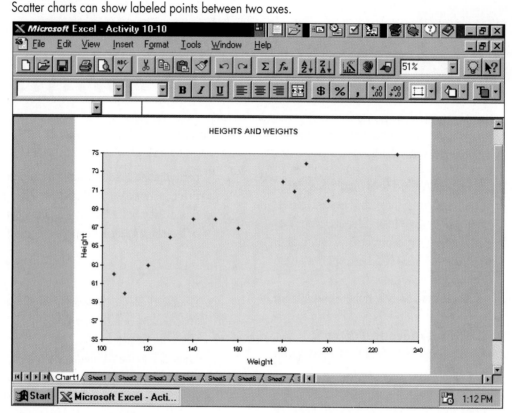

Summary

■ A chart is a graphical representation of worksheet data. You can create several types of worksheet charts, including column charts, line charts, pie charts, and scatter charts. Column, area, surface, bar, line, and pie charts can also be created as three-dimensional charts.

■ Charts may either be embedded in a worksheet or created on a chart sheet. A chart sheet is an area separate from the Excel worksheet in which a chart is created and stored.

■ The ChartWizard is a five-step, on-screen guide that aids in preparing a chart from an Excel worksheet. The ChartWizard is used to prepare a chart whether it is to appear in the worksheet or in a chart sheet.

■ A chart created from a worksheet is considered part of that worksheet. When you save the worksheet, you will also save the charts you have created from the worksheet. You may save the worksheet and its associated charts by choosing Save from the File menu or clicking the Save button on the toolbar.

● ● ● ● ● ● ● ● ● ● ● ● ● ●

REVIEW ACTIVITIES

TRUE/FALSE

Circle T or F to show whether the statement is true or false.

T   F   **1.** Charts are a graphical representation of worksheet data.

T   F   **2.** Column charts are the best way to represent data groups that are part of a whole.

T   F   **3.** Line charts are well suited for representing trends over a period of time.

T   F   **4.** A scatter chart produces a "cloud" of data points not connected by lines.

T   F   **5.** A column chart represents values in the worksheet by varying heights of rectangles.

T   F   **6.** The ChartWizard may only be used to create two-dimensional charts.

T   F   **7.** When the worksheet data changes, charts created from the worksheet also change.

T   F   **8.** A pie chart may be created in either two or three dimensions.

T   F   **9.** The charts of a worksheet file are erased when the worksheet file is closed.

T   F **10.** A chart may be printed from the chart sheet.

COMPLETION

Write the correct answer in the space provided.

1. What type of chart represents values in a worksheet by points connected by a line?

_____

2. What type of chart uses rectangles to represent values in a worksheet?

_____

3. What type of chart is represented by a circle divided into portions?

_____

4. What term refers to the type of chart that is created on the same screen as a worksheet?

_____

5. What term refers to a list that identifies patterns or symbols used in a worksheet chart?

_____

6. What name is shown on the tab of a newly created chart sheet?

   _____

7. Which menu contains the command for renaming a chart sheet?

   _____

8. What procedure is used to switch between a chart sheet and a worksheet?

   _____

   _____

9. What characteristics may be added to a column chart to help in identifying the worksheet value a column represents?

   _____

   _____

10. What toolbar button in the chart sheet allows you to see a printed chart before it is printed?

    _____

REINFORCEMENT APPLICATIONS

application 10-1

The file *Application 10-1* contains the populations of the world's largest cities. In a chart sheet, create a column chart indicating larger populations with a higher column.

1. Open *Application 10-1*.

2. Create a column chart with grids from the data in A5:B12.

   HINT: *Select Option 6 in Step 3 of the ChartWizard.*

The chart should not contain a legend.

3. Title the column chart **The World's Largest Cities**.

4. Title the vertical axis **Population in Millions**.

5. No X axis title is needed.

6. Print the chart.

7. Save the file to your data disk as *Largest Cities* and close it.

application 10-2

You have been running each morning to stay in shape. Over the past ten weeks you have recorded running times along a specified route and entered them in file *Application 10-2*. In a chart sheet, create a line chart indicating the trend in running times over the ten-week period.

1. Open *Application 10-2*.

2. Create a line chart with gridlines in a chart sheet for the data contained in A5:B14.

   HINT: *Select Option 4 in Step 3 of the ChartWizard.*

Do not include a legend in the chart.

3. Title the line chart **Ten-Week Workout Program**.

4. Title the vertical axis **Time in Minutes**.

5. No X axis title is needed.

6. Print the chart.

7. Save the file to your data disk as *Workout Program* and close it.

application 10 - 3

The file *Application 10-3* contains the number of McDonald's hamburger restaurants in different regions of the world. In a chart sheet, create a pie chart in which each slice represents a region in column A of the worksheet.

1. Open *Application 10-3*.

2. Create a pie chart in a chart sheet for the data contained in A4:B8. The pie chart should include percentages next to each slice, but refer to geographical regions in a legend.

   HINT: *Select Option 6 in Step 3 of the ChartWizard.*

3. Title the chart **Worldwide Locations**.

4. Edit the chart to include the following font sizes.

   HINT: *Double-click on the appropriate part of the chart and click the Font tab.*

   a. The chart title should be 18 point.
   b. The slice percentages should be 14 point.
   c. The legend should be 14 point.

5. Title the chart sheet **Pie Chart**.

6. Print the chart.

7. Save the file to your data disk as *Worldwide Locations* and close it.

application 10 - 4

The file *Application 10-4* contains the monthly cash flow of a young family. To better explain their expenses to family members, the head of the household finances decides to create a pie chart in which each slice represents an expense category that contributes to total expenses. The pie chart should be created in a chart sheet.

1. Open *Application 10-4*.

2. Create a three-dimensional pie chart on a separate chart sheet for the data contained in A6:B13. The pie chart should include the cash use labels and the percentages of total cash use for each slice. The chart should not include a legend.

3. Title the pie chart **Where Our Money Goes**.

4. Change the chart title to 18 point.

5. Title the chart sheet **3D Pie Chart**.

6. Print the chart.

7. Save the file to your data disk as *Where Our Money Goes* and close it.

application 10-5

The file *Application 10-5* contains the study time and examination scores for several students. The instructor is attempting to determine if there is a relationship between study time and examination score. Create a scatter chart of the data in the worksheet to indicate the relationship between study time and examination scores.

1. Open *Application 10-5*.

2. Create a scatter chart in a chart sheet for the data in B3:C21. The chart should not contain gridlines or connecting lines.

   HINT: *Select Option 1 in Step 3 of the ChartWizard.*

3. The chart should not contain a legend.

4. Title the scatter chart **Comparison of Exam Grades to Study Time**.

5. Title the vertical (Y) axis **Examination Grades**.

6. Title the horizontal (X) axis **Hours of Study**.

7. Change the size of the chart title to 20 point.

8. Change the size of the axis titles to 14 point

9. Change the size of the axis labels to 12 point.

10. The minimum value of the vertical scale (Y axis) should be 40.

11. Print the chart.

12. Save the worksheet to your data disk as *Study Hours* and close it.

application 10-6

You operate the concession stand at the home baseball games of Mountain College, and have noticed that certain items have decreased in popularity as the season has progressed. The sales for each game have been kept on a spreadsheet. Now you would like to use the spreadsheet to create a chart that illustrates how levels of sales for each product have changed during the season. The chart should be created in a chart sheet.

1. Open *Application 10-6*.

2. Create a chart on a chart sheet with the following characteristics:
   a. It should be a stacked column chart in which the columns are joined by lines that connect the corresponding item in the next column.

   HINT: *Select Option 9 in Step 3 of the ChartWizard.*

   b. The data to be charted is contained in A4:E9.
   c. The data series is contained in the rows of the worksheet.

   HINT: *Click Rows in Step 4.*

   d. The chart title should be **Concession Sales**.

e. The Y axis title should be **Sales in Dollars**.

f. No X axis title is needed.

g. A legend should appear in the chart to identify the types of items sold.

3. Increase the font size of the following items in the chart:

   a. Change the chart title to 18 point.

   b. Change the X axis labels (game labels) to 14 point.

   c. Change the Y axis title to 14 point.

   d. Change the Y axis labels to 12 point.

   e. Change the legend labels to 12 point.

4. Title the chart sheet **Stacked Column Chart**.

5. Print the chart.

6. Save the file to your data disk as *Concession Sales* and close it.

··

LINKING DATA IN EXCEL AND WORD

NOTE: *Before beginning these activities, make sure you have an Integration template disk that contains all Integration template files only. You will save new Integration files to this disk.*

Moving and Copying Data Between Applications

You have already learned how easy it is to move and copy data among documents created in any one of the Office 95 applications using the Cut, Copy, and Paste commands. The process of copying and pasting data between applications is similar to copying and pasting data within an application. Office 95 makes the process easy by adjusting the format of the data being copied to fit the application where it is being pasted.

Word to Excel

Suppose you want to place data from a table in a Word report in an Excel worksheet to make calculations using the data. Office 95 handles pasting into a worksheet from the word processor in one of two ways:

1. If the text from Word is set up as a table with data separated by tabs, Excel will place the text in separate cells in the worksheet.

2. If the text is in a single block, all of the text will be pasted into the currently highlighted cell of the worksheet.

Excel to Word

A common integration operation is to paste numbers from a worksheet into a word processor document. When Excel data is copied to Word, Word automatically places it in a table.

ACTIVITY

II-1 Excel to Word

● ●

1. Open Word; then, open the *Insurance Info* document from your Integration template disk.

2. Open Excel; then, open the *Insurance Rates* Excel worksheet from your Integration template disk.

3. Increase the window size, if necessary, so the whole document is visible. Highlight the data in the worksheet from cell A1 to cell D7.

4. Click the **Copy** button on the toolbar.

5. Click the **Microsoft Word** button on the taskbar to switch to Word and bring the insurance letter to the front.

6. Place the insertion point between the first and second paragraphs.

7. Click the **Paste** button on the toolbar. The data from the worksheet appears in the letter.

8. Save *Insurance Info* on your Integration template disk as *Insurance Letter*.

9. Print *Insurance Letter* and close it.

10. Switch to Excel and save *Insurance Rates* on your Integration template disk as *Term Rates* and close it. Leave Word and Excel open.

Linking Data

There will be times when the data you are inserting may change periodically. Then you can use a process called **linking** to integrate data so that it is automatically updated. Suppose it is your job as treasurer of an organization to file a monthly financial report. Your report is basically the same each month except for the month's cash flow (money received and spent) numbers. You keep the cash flow data up to date in an Excel worksheet. Using the copying and pasting techniques discussed before, you would have to copy the latest worksheet numbers and paste them into your Word document each month.

There is an easier way. Instead of pasting the data manually each time, you can use the Paste Special command to link the two files. When you link data, the information you insert in the destination document is connected to information in the source file. The linked data is not actually part of the destination file, but contains a description of where Word should go to find the data. Then each time changes are saved to the worksheet data in the source document, the changes are reflected in the Word destination document when it is opened.

Figure II-1 shows the Paste Special dialog box that appears when data from an Excel worksheet is pasted into a Word document using the Paste Special command. The Paste Link option places the worksheet data into the document and creates the link to the actual worksheet.

FIGURE II-1
The Paste Special dialog box allows you to link a Word document to Excel data.

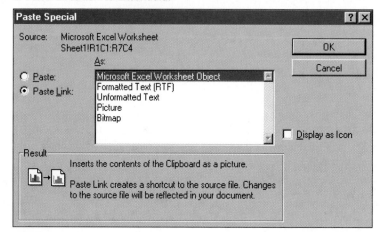

ACTIVITY II-2 Linking Data

1. Open the *Insurance Info* Word document from the Integration template disk.

2. Switch to Excel and open *Term Rates* from your Integration template disk.

3. Highlight cells A1 through D7, if they are not already. Copy the cells and switch back to *Insurance Info*.

4. Place the insertion point between the first and second paragraphs.

5. Choose **Paste Special** from the **Edit** menu. The Paste Special dialog box appears.

6. Click **Paste Link.** In the As box, click *Mi-* *crosoft Excel Worksheet Object.* The Paste Special dialog box should look similar to Figure II-1.

7. Click **OK.** The worksheet data appears in the Word document. The data is linked to *Term Rates.* Any changes made to *Term Rates* will be reflected in *Insurance Info.*

8. Save *Insurance Info* on your Integration template disk as *Insurance Link.*

9. Print *Insurance Link* and close it.

10. Save *Term Rates* and leave it on the screen for the next activity.

When you open *Insurance Link*, the document is updated with the latest worksheet data from *Term Rates*.

ACTIVITY II-3 Updating a Linked Document

1. *Term Rates* should be open on the screen.

2. Change the cost of the annual premium in C3 to $175 for the Annual Renewable Term and $188.50 in C5 for the 10-Year Level Term. The monthly bank draft amounts for those two types of policies will change automatically.

3. Save *Term Rates*.

4. Switch to Word and open *Insurance Link* from your Integration template disk. Notice that the annual premium and monthly bank draft costs (money deducted from a bank account automatically) were updated because the data was linked.

5. Save as *Insurance Link 2* and print.

6. Open *Insurance Letter* from your Integration template disk. Scroll down until the chart is in view. The data was not updated in *Insurance Letter* because the data was not linked.

7. Close both Word files. Switch to Excel and close *Term Rates*. Close Word and Excel.

Summary

- Office 95 pastes Word information that is separated by tabs into individual Excel worksheet cells. Text in a single block is pasted into the currently highlighted cell of the worksheet. Excel data that is copied to a Word document is automatically placed in a table.

- Excel data can be linked to a Word document using the Paste Special command. The document is automatically updated with changes made to the spreadsheet.

REVIEW ACTIVITIES

TRUE/FALSE

Circle T or F to show whether the statement is true or false.

T   F   1. A common integration operation is to paste numbers from a worksheet into a Word document.

T   F   2. When copying text from Word that is set up as a table, Excel will place the text in separate cells in the worksheet.

T   F   3. Linking is performed using the Copy Special command.

COMPLETION

Write the correct answer in the space provided.

1. What is the advantage of linking data?

   _____

   _____

2. What option do you choose in the Paste Special dialog box to link a Word document to Excel data?

   _____

INTEGRATION PROJECTS

Home Again Real Estate

PROJECT D

Prospective buyers often ask you how much the principal interest payments would be for a 30-year fixed rate mortgage for various priced houses, given a certain interest rate. To make this information easily available, you sketch out a Mortgage Calculator Chart (see Figure II-2) to estimate payments. Transfer this rough draft to an Excel worksheet and format as shown. After entering the formula in B4, fill down and right until the chart is complete. Save the worksheet as *Mortgage Chart.* Open *Letterhead* from Word. Copy and link the Mortgage Calculator Chart to the letterhead document. Save the file as *Mortgage Link* and print. Close all files.

FIGURE II-2

	A	B	C	D	E	F
1	Mortgage Calculator					
2	Principal and Interest Payments					
3		.065	.07	.075	.08	.085
4	$40,000	= PMT (B$3/12, 360, $A4)				
5	$45,000					
6	$50,000					
7	$55,000					
8	$60,000					
9	$65,000					
10	$70,000					
11	$75,000					
12	$80,000					
13	$85,000					
14	$90,000					
15	$95,000					

Format rows 4-15 for currency with zero decimals

PROJECT E

You choose to focus on listing houses in the Raintree residential sub-division. You have already gone door to door meeting the owners of each house and letting them know of the services you can provide if/when they decide to sell their homes. To maintain contact with them, you decide to send out a one-page newsletter each month. The newsletter will include general information about real estate that would be of interest, including topics such as interest rates, home improvement and maintenance, mortgages, and taxes. Use Word to create a two-column newsletter for the current month. Use information from actual real estate publications or make it up.

In the newsletter, you will keep the homeowners up to date on market trends in Raintree by providing price information about each house that has sold recently. Create an Excel worksheet for this purpose. Make *Address* the heading for column A and list down the column the addresses for seven houses that have sold within the past month. Make *List Price, Sale Price,* and *Difference* the headings for columns B through D. Get actual list prices from the newspaper or real estate guide, or make them up. Create a formula in column D to subtract column C from column B. Create an *Average* row after the address listings. In column B of the Average row, create a formula to average all the numbers in the column. Copy the formula to columns C and D. Save the worksheet as *House Prices*. Copy the worksheet and paste it in your newsletter. Save the newsletter as *Newsletter* and print. Close both files.

PROJECT F

Open *Mortgage Chart.* Add two more columns for 9% and 9.5% interest. Format them properly and copy the formulas from the appropriate cells to complete the chart. Open *Mortgage Link* and print the revised document. Save and close both files.

▼INTEGRATION SIMULATION

Java Internet Café

MARCH 5

You need to create a menu of coffee prices.

1. Open a new Excel worksheet.

2. Key the data in Figure II-3 into the worksheet and format as shown.

3. Change the width of columns A and C to 29, and columns B and D to 9.

4. Change the font to Arial 14 pt.

FIGURE II-3

	A	B	C	D
1	Coffee Prices			
2				
3	House coffee	$1.00	Café breve	$2.25
4				
5	Café au lait	$1.50	Café latte	$2.25
6				
7	Cappuccino	$1.75	Con panna	$2.50
8				
9	Espresso	$2.00	Espresso doppio	$2.75

5. Save the file as *Coffee Prices* on your Simulation template disk.

6. Highlight and copy A1 through D9.

7. Open Word and *Java Menu* from your Simulation template disk.

8. Insert one blank line below the *Menu* heading and paste link the worksheet.

9. Save as *Java Prices* on your Simulation template disk.

10. Switch to Excel.

11. Open *Computer Prices* from the Simulation template disk.

12. Highlight and copy A1 through B11.

13. Switch to Word and *Java Prices*.

14. Insert two blank lines after the coffee prices worksheet.

15. Paste link the *Computer Prices* worksheet.

16. Change the top and bottom margins to .75 inches.

17. Save and print *Java Prices*.

18. Close *Java Prices*. Switch to Excel and close *Coffee Prices* and *Computer Prices*.

MARCH 13

The menu you created has been very successful. However, your manager asks you to make a few changes.

1. Open *Coffee Prices* from your Simulation template disk.

2. Open *Computer Prices* from your Simulation template disk.

3. Make the changes to the *Coffee Prices* and *Computer Prices* worksheets as shown in Figure II-4.

4. Save and close *Coffee Prices* and *Computer Prices*.

5. Switch to Word and open *Java Prices* from your Simulation template disk.

6. Notice the file has been updated since you made changes to the two worksheet files. Correct the footer as shown on Figure II-4.

7. Save as *Java Prices Link* on your Simulation template disk.

8. Print and close.

FIGURE II-4

Java Internet Café

2001 Zephyr Street
Boulder, CO 80302-2001
303.555.JAVA JavaCafe@Cybershop.com

The Java Internet Café is a coffee shop with a twist. As you can see, there are seven computers on tables at the north side of the café. These computers provide high-speed Internet access to our customers. Whether you're a regular on the Net or a novice, our system is designed to allow you easy exploration of the World Wide Web. You've heard about it; now give it a try. Ask your server to help you get started.

Menu

Coffee Prices

House coffee	$1.00 *.75*	Café breve	$2.25
Café au lait	$1.50	Café latte	$2.25
Cappuccino	$1.75 *2.00*	Con panna	$2.50
Espresso	$2.00	Espresso doppio	$2.75

Computer Prices

Membership fee -- includes own account with personal ID, password, and e-mail address		$10 per month
28,800 bps Internet access (members) -- includes World Wide Web, FTP, Telnet, and IRC plus e-mail		$4 per hour
28,800 bps Internet access (non-members) -- includes World Wide Web, FTP, Telnet, and IRC		$6 per hour
Color scanner -- includes Internet access, use of software and the CD-ROM library		$5 per 1/2 hour
Laser printer -- inquire about duplexing capabilities		$.25 per page

Sit back, sip your coffee, and surf the net.

UNIT 4

MICROSOFT ACCESS

ACCESS BASICS

OBJECTIVES
When you complete this chapter, you will be able to:

1. Understand databases.
2. Start Access.
3. Open a database.
4. Identify parts of the Access screen.
5. Identify the database objects.
6. Create a database.
7. Create tables.
8. Enter records.
9. Close and exit Access.

Database Basics

Access is a program known as a ***database management system.*** A computerized database management system allows you to store, retrieve, analyze, and print information. You do not, however, need a computer to have a database management system. A set of file folders can be a database management system. Any system for managing data is a database management system. There are distinct advantages, however, to using a computerized database management system.

A computerized database management system (often abbreviated DBMS) is much faster, more flexible, and more accurate than using file folders. A computerized DBMS is also more efficient and cost-effective. A program like Access can store thousands of pieces of data in a computer or on a floppy disk. The data can be quickly searched and sorted to save time normally spent digging through file folders. For example, a computerized DBMS could find all the people with a certain ZIP code faster and more accurately than you could by searching through a large list or through folders. Computers can also quickly sort and arrange data, which saves time.

Starting Access

To start Access, click the Start button in the taskbar. A menu of choices appears. As with other Office 95 applications, you may use the New Office Document option at the top of the menu or point to the Programs option for a list of programs installed on your system. You can also use the Start a New Document button on the Microsoft Office Shortcut Bar. If you choose the Programs option on the Start menu, another menu of choices appears, as shown in Figure 11-1.

Move the mouse pointer into the Programs menu and click the Microsoft Access icon to load Access. After a few moments, the Access startup dialog box appears, as shown in Figure 11-2. The dialog box gives you the option of creating a new database or opening an existing one. You can also choose to use a Database Wizard to guide you through the process of creating a database.

FIGURE 11-1
Starting Access from the Programs menu.

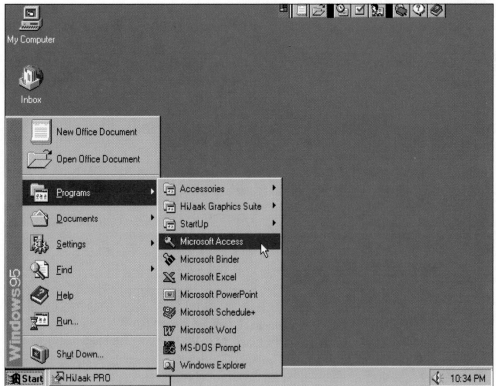

FIGURE 11-2
The Access startup dialog box allows you to open
an existing database or create a new one.

A C T I V I T Y

Starting Access

● ●

1. With Windows 95 running, click **Start** on the taskbar.

2. Point to **Programs** in the **Start** menu. The Programs menu appears.

3. Click **Microsoft Access** in the **Programs** menu. Access opens and the Access startup dialog box appears.

4. Leave the dialog box on the screen for the next activity.

Opening a Database

Y̲ou can open an existing database from the startup dialog box or from the File menu. To open a database from the startup dialog box, click the Open an Existing Database option and choose a database from the file list. To create a new database, click the Blank Database or Database Wizard option. If you choose Blank Database, you must manually create the database. If you choose the Database Wizard, you will be guided through the creation of the database. You will learn more about creating databases later in this chapter.

When a database opens, a tabbed window appears, as shown in Figure 11-3. Each tab represents a type of database object. You will learn about database objects later in this chapter.

FIGURE 11-3
A database is made up of database objects.

Opening a Database

1. If not already selected, click the **Open an Existing Database** option.

2. With the **More Files** option highlighted, click **OK.**

3. Use the Look in box to locate the template files for this book.

4. Open *Activity 11-2.* The database objects window appears.

5. Leave the database open for the next activity.

The Access Screen

Like other Office 95 applications, the Access screen has a title bar, menu bar, and toolbar. You may also have the Microsoft Office Shortcut Bar on the right end of the title bar. At the bottom of the screen is the status bar and taskbar. Figure 11-4 shows the Access screen with the *Activity 11-2* database open.

As you use Access, various windows and dialog boxes will appear on the Access screen. Unlike a word processor or spreadsheet, the Access screen does not have a standard document view. Instead, the screen changes based on how you interact with the database.

FIGURE 11-4
The Access screen is similar to other Office 95 applications.

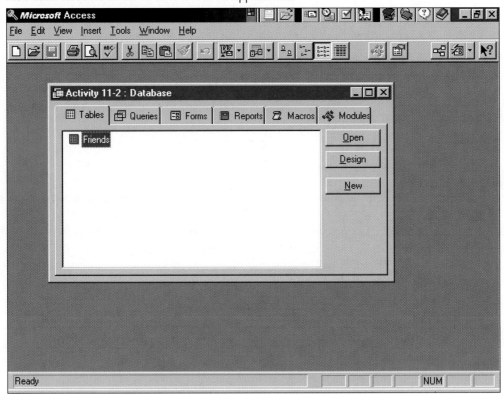

Database Objects

When a database is saved, the file that is saved contains a collection of objects. These objects work together to store data, retrieve data, display data, print reports, and automate operations. The database objects window has a tab for each type of object. Table 11-1 briefly explains the purpose of each type of object.

Table 11-1 makes it clear that the table is the most basic database object. Without a table, no data exists. In the activity that follows, you will explore the objects that make up the *Activity 11-2* database.

TABLE 11-1
Database objects.

OBJECT	DESCRIPTION
Tables	Tables store data in a format similar to that of a spreadsheet. All database information is stored in tables.
Queries	Queries search for and retrieve data from tables based on criteria supplied by the user. A query is a question you ask the database.
Forms	Forms allow you to display data in a custom format. You might, for example, create a form that matches a paper form.
Reports	Reports also display data in a custom format. Reports, however, are especially suited for printing and summarizing data. You can even perform calculations on data in a report.
Macros	Macros automate database operations by allowing you to issue a single command that performs a series of operations
Modules	Modules are like macros, but allow much more complex programming of database operations. Creating a module requires the use of a programming language.

ACTIVITY

11-3 Database Objects

1. The Tables section of the database objects window shows a table named *Friends*. The Friends table object is highlighted. Click the **Open** button. The table appears, as shown in Figure 11-5.

2. Choose **Close** from the **File** menu to close the table. The database objects window is visible again.

FIGURE 11-5
A table appears in a format similar to a spreadsheet.

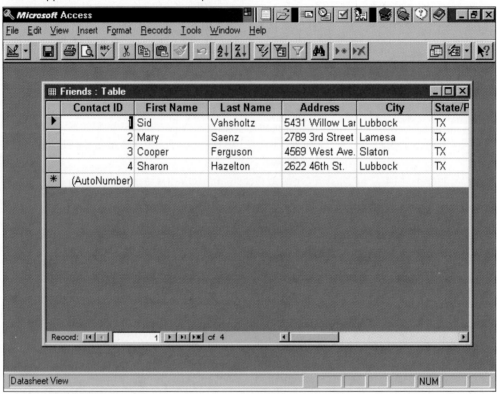

3. Click the **Queries** tab. There is one query object (named *City Query*). This query locates friends who live in Lubbock.

4. Click the **Open** button to activate the query. The query specified that only the city, first name, and last name be displayed.

5. After the query results appear, choose **Close** from the **File** menu.

6. Click the **Forms** tab. There is one form object (named *Form1*).

7. Click **Open** to display the form. The form appears as shown in Figure 11-6.

8. Choose **Close** from the **File** menu.

9. Click the **Tables** tab and open the Friends table again.

10. Leave the table on the screen for the next activity.

FIGURE 11-6
A form is often a more convenient way to enter data into a database.

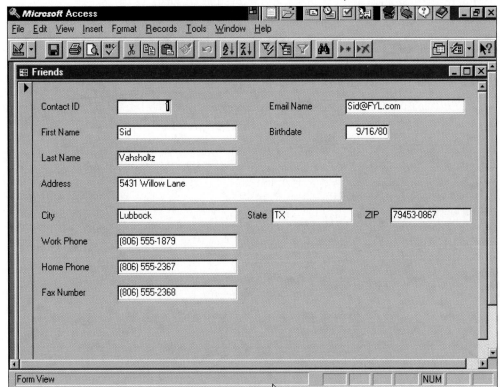

Database Terminology

There are four terms that are essential to working with databases. These terms relate to the way data is organized in a table. A *record* is a complete set of data. In the database you have been using in the activities, each friend is stored as a record. In a table, a record appears as a row, as shown in Figure 11-7.

Each record is made up of *fields.* For example, the first name of each friend is placed in a special field that is created to accept first names. In a table, fields appear as columns. In order to identify the fields, each has a *field name.*

The actual data that is entered into a field is called an *entry.* In the Friends database, for example, the first record has the name *Sid* as an entry in the First Name field.

FIGURE 11-7
A database is organized as records and fields.

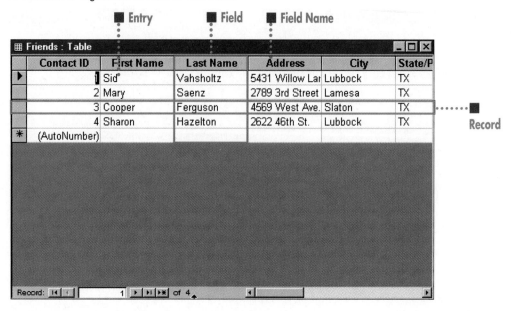

Designing a Database

Before creating a database, decide what data you need to store. You should divide the data into categories to create fields. For example, suppose you want to create a database of your favorite restaurants. Some fields to include would be the restaurant's name, address, and typical meal cost. An example of a record would be: KB's Diner (name), 1128 5th St. (address), and $5.50 (typical meal cost).

NOTE: *In many database management systems, data is stored using more than one table.*

Determine the type of data to be stored in each field and choose an appropriate *data type* for each field. The data type tells Access what kind of information can be stored in the field. Table 11-2 briefly describes the eight basic data types.

TABLE 11-2
Data types

DATA TYPE	DESCRIPTION
Text	The Text data type allows letters and numbers (alphanumeric data). A Text field can hold up to 255 characters. Data such as names and addresses is stored in fields of this type.
Memo	The Memo data type also allows alphanumeric data. A Memo field, however, can hold thousands of characters. Memo fields are used for data that does not follow a particular format. For example, you might use a Memo field to store notes about a record.
Number	The Number data type holds numeric data. There are variations of the Number type, each capable of storing a different range of values.
Date/Time	The Date/Time data type holds dates and times
Currency	The Currency data type is specially formatted for dealing with currency
Counter	The Counter data type is automatically incremented by Access for each new record added. Counters are used to give each record in a database a unique ID.
Yes/No	The Yes/No data type holds logical values. A Yes/No field can hold the values Yes/No, True/False, or On/Off.
OLE Object	The OLE Object data type is used for some of the more advanced features. It allows you to put graphics, sound, and even objects such as spreadsheets in a field.

Choosing the correct data type is important. For example, you might think a telephone number or ZIP code should be stored in a field with a Number data type. However, you should only use Number data types when you intend to do calculations with the data. You won't be adding ZIP codes. Numbers that will not be used in calculations are best stored as Text.

For the database of favorite restaurants mentioned earlier, the name of the restaurant and address would be stored in fields of Text type. The typical meal cost is an ideal candidate for the Currency type. Other possible fields are the date you last ate at the restaurant (Date type) and a Yes/No field type that specifies whether reservations are required.

Creating a Database

After you have designed your database, you can begin to create it. The first step is to create the file that will hold the database objects. Earlier in this chapter, you learned that the startup dialog box has options for creating a new database. One option is to create a new database manually. The other option is to use the Database Wizard to guide you through the process. We will create the database manually.

The first step of creating a database is easy. All you really do is give it a name.

ACTIVITY
11-4
Creating a Database

● ●

1. Choose **Close** from the **File** menu to close the table on your screen.

2. Choose **Close** from the **File** menu again to close the *Activity 11-2* database.

3. Choose **New Database** from the **File** menu. The New dialog box appears, as shown in Figure 11-8. Choose **Blank Database**, then **OK.** The File New Database dialog box appears.

FIGURE 11-8
The New dialog box allows you to create a new database.

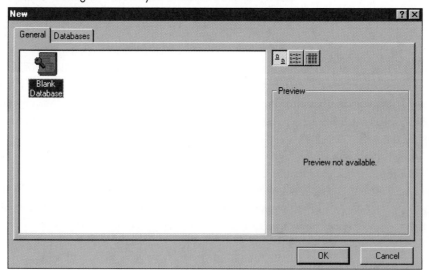

4. Locate the directory that contains your data files.

5. Key **Favorite Restaurants** as the file name and click **Create.** A database ob-jects window appears for the new data-base, but no objects exist yet.

6. Leave the window on the screen for the next activity.

Creating Tables

Because all other database objects rely on the existence of a data-base table, creating a table is the next step after creating a database. To create a table, click the New button from the Tables section of the database objects window. The New Table dia-log box will appear, as shown in Figure 11-9.

There are several ways to create a table, each of which is pro-vided as an option in the New Table dialog box. The most common way to create a table is using Table De-sign view. Therefore, in this chapter, you will use Table Design view to create a table.

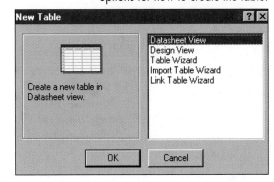

FIGURE 11-9
The New Table dialog box gives you options for how to create the table.

ACTIVITY

11-5 Creating a Table

1. With the Tables tab selected in the database objects window, click **New.** The New Table dialog box appears.

2. Click the **Design View** option and click **OK.** The Table Design window appears.

3. Key **Name** in the first row of the Field Name column. Press **Tab** (or **Enter**). The data type will default to Text, which is appropriate for the name of the restaurant. Press **Tab** to move to the next column.

4. Key **Name of Restaurant** in the De-scription column. Press **Tab** or **Enter** to move to the next row.

5. Enter the other fields and descriptions shown in Figure 11-10. All of the fields are Text type.

6. Leave the window open for the next activity.

FIGURE 11-10
Field data types default to Text type.

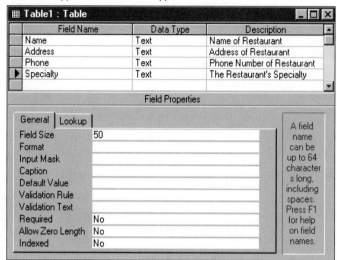

We are not finished creating fields yet. Next, you will enter two fields that have data types other than Text. To select a data type, click the arrow that appears in the Data Type column when the cursor is in that column. This button is called a list-box button. A drop-down menu appears allowing you to choose a data type.

A C T I V I T Y

Creating Fields of Various Types

1. Key **Last Visit** in the Field Name column and press **Tab.** This field is to be of type Date/Time.

2. Click the arrow in the Data Type field and choose **Date/Time** from the menu that appears, as shown in Figure 11-11. Press **Tab.**

3. Key **My Last Visit to the Restaurant** in the Description field. Press **Tab.**

4. Key **Reservations** in the Field Name column, choose **Yes/No** as the data type, and key **Are Reservations Required?** in the Description field.

FIGURE 11-11
Data types may be selected from a pop-up menu.

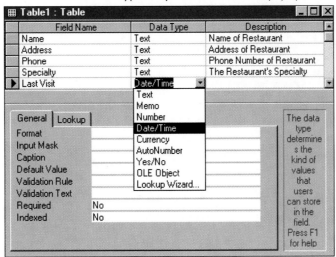

5. Choose **Save** from the **File** menu. Key **Restaurants** as the table name and click **OK.**

6. You will be asked if you want to create a primary key. The primary key is not necessary for a database as simple as this one. Click **No.**

7. Click the Close box to return to the database objects window. Note that your Restaurants table appears.

8. Leave the database objects window open for the next activity.

Modifying and Deleting Tables

Modifying a table is easy. Highlight the name of the table in the database objects window and click the Design button. The table appears in Table Design view again. You can make changes to the names of fields, data types, and descriptions. You can also add fields, or even delete a field by placing the cursor in the row you want to delete and choosing Delete Row from the Edit menu. When you finish changing fields, choose Save from the File menu.

You can delete an entire table by highlighting it in the database objects window and choosing Delete from the Edit menu.

11-7 Modifying a Table

1. With the Restaurants table highlighted in the database objects window, click the **Design** button. The table appears in Table Design view.

2. Scroll to the blank row below the other fields. Click in the blank row's Field Name column to place the cursor there.

3. Key **Meal Cost** in the Field Name column. Press **Tab.**

4. Choose **Currency** as the data type. Press **Tab.**

5. Key **Typical Meal Cost** as the description.

6. Choose **Save** from the **File** menu.

7. Choose **Close** from the **File** menu.

8. Leave the database objects window open for the next activity.

Navigating and Entering Records in Datasheet View

Once a table is created, you can enter records directly into the table using *Datasheet view*. In Datasheet view, the table appears in a form similar to a spreadsheet, as you saw earlier in the chapter. As with a spreadsheet, the intersection of a row and a column is referred to as a cell.

The techniques used to enter data in the table are familiar to you. Press Enter or Tab to move to the next field as you enter the data. The data types will be considered by the program as you enter the data. For example, you must enter a valid date in a Date/Time field and a number in a Number field.

You can use the mouse to move the cursor to a particular cell in the table. You can also use the keys in Table 11-3 to navigate through a table.

TABLE 11-3
Navigating in Datasheet view

KEY	DESCRIPTION
Enter, Tab, or right arrow	Moves to the following field
Left arrow or Shift+Tab	Moves to the previous field
End	Moves to the last field in the current record
Home	Moves to the first field in the current record
Up arrow	Moves up one record and stays in the same field
Down arrow	Moves down one record and stays in the same field
Page Up	Moves up one screen
Page Down	Moves down one screen

ACTIVITY

11-8 Entering Records

1. With the Restaurants table highlighted, click the **Open** button. The table appears in Datasheet view, as shown in Figure 11-12.

2. Key **Jose's** as the restaurant name. Press **Tab.**

3. Key **1267 Main St.** in the address field. Press **Tab.**

4. Key **555-8700** in the Phone field. Press **Tab.**

5. Key **Mexican** in the Specialty field. Press **Tab.**

6. Key today's date in the Last Visit field. Press **Tab.**

7. The Reservation field has a check box in it. Click the check box or press the spacebar to place a check in the box. Press **Tab.**

8. Key **6.99** as the typical meal cost. Press **Tab.**

9. Click the Close box or choose **Close** from the **File** menu. The records have been saved in the table automatically.

10. Leave the database open for the next activity.

FIGURE 11-12
The new table appears in Datasheet view.

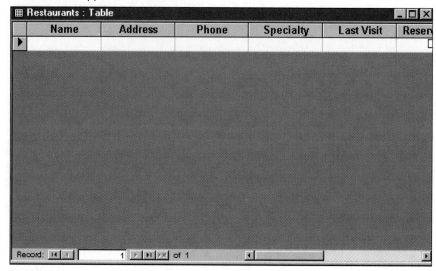

Exiting Access

As with other Office 95 applications, the File menu contains the Exit command. Exiting Access takes you back to the Windows 95 desktop. Remember to remove any floppy disks, and properly shut down Windows 95 before turning off the computer.

ACTIVITY

11-9 **Exiting Access**

1. Choose **Close** from the **File** menu. The database closes.

2. Choose **Exit** from the **File** menu. Access exits and the Windows 95 desktop appears.

Summary

- Access is a program known as a database management system. A computerized database management system allows you to store, retrieve, analyze, and print information. Start Access from the Programs menu.

- You can open an existing database from the startup dialog box or from the File menu. The Access screen has a title bar, menu bar, and toolbar. The Access screen, however, does not have a standard document view.

- A database is a collection of objects. The objects work together to store data, retrieve data, display data, print reports, and automate operations. The object types are tables, queries, forms, reports, macros, and modules.

- A record is a complete set of data. Each record is made up of fields. Each field is identified by a field name. The actual data that is entered into a field is called an entry.

- Before you create a database, you should decide what data you will store. You need to select an appropriate data type for each field. Creating a database creates a file that will hold database objects.

- To store data, a table must first be created. The Table Design window allows you to create fields and assign data types and descriptions to the fields. Once a table has been created, you may enter records.

- As in other Office 95 applications, the Exit command in the File menu exits the program.

• • • • • • • • • • • • • •

REVIEW ACTIVITIES

TRUE/FALSE

Circle T or F to show whether the statment is true or false.

T F **1.** A computerized DBMS is more efficient than paper filing.

T F **2.** Clicking the Start button on the taskbar is the first step in starting Access.

T F **3.** Opening a database automatically displays the data in the table.

T F **4.** Access has a standard document view that remains on the screen as long as a database is open.

T F **5.** A database file is a collection of database objects.

T F **6.** A record appears as a column in Datasheet view.

T F **7.** Fields are identified by field names.

T F **8.** The Number data type is the best data type for storing telephone numbers.

T F **9.** The New Database command creates a database file.

T F **10.** The File menu contains the Exit command.

COMPLETION

Write the correct answer in the space provided.

1. What do the tabs in a database objects window represent?

_____

2. List three types of database objects.

_____

_____

3. Which type of database object allows you to search for and retrieve data?

_____

4. What is the term for the actual data entered in a field?

_____

5. What data type is used to store logical values?

_____

6. What data type is used to store dollar amounts?

_____

7. What three pieces of information do you provide about fields in the Table Design window?

_____

_____

8. Datasheet view is similar to the format of what other type of application?

_____

9. Which keys can be used to enter data in Datasheet view and move to the next field?

_____

10. What appears after you exit Access?

_____

REINFORCEMENT APPLICATIONS

application 11-1

1. Select a type of collection and design a database to organize it. For example, you can design a database to keep track of a collection of baseball cards, business cards, comic books, insects, magazines, stamps, toy tractors, or whatever you like to collect.

2. Carefully consider the fields your database will need. Some possibilities may be description, value, date of issue, date of purchase, where purchased, etc.

3. Assign a data type to each field. Remember to use the Number, Currency, Yes/No, and Date/Time types where appropriate.

4. On paper, list your fields in a table that shows the field name, data type, and description.

application 11-2

1. Start Access.

2. Create the database you designed in Application 11-1. Give the database a name that accurately reflects its contents.

3. Use Table Design view to create the fields for the database. Save the table with an appropriate name.

4. Enter at least two records in the database using Datasheet view.

5. Exit Access.

MANIPULATING DATA AND USING FORMS

12

OBJECTIVES
When you complete this chapter, you will be able to:

1. Edit data in a table.

2. Select records and fields.

3. Cut, copy, and paste data.

4. Change the layout of a datasheet.

5. Create and use forms.

6. Understand field properties.

Editing Records

To make editing records easier, Access provides navigation buttons that are used to move around the datasheet. These buttons may not be necessary when working with databases as small as those in the previous chapter. As databases get larger, however, the navigation buttons become indispensable. Figure 12-1 identifies the locations of the navigation buttons.

The First Record and Last Record buttons at the bottom of the table window are used to move quickly to records at the top or bottom of the database. Buttons also are used to move to the next or previous record. To move to a specific record number, click the Record Number box and key a new number in the field. Press Tab to move to the record. The Move to Blank Record button moves to the blank record at the bottom of the database.

The current record is indicated by an arrow. Internally, the computer keeps track of the current record using a *record pointer*. When you move among records in Datasheet view, you are actually moving the record pointer.

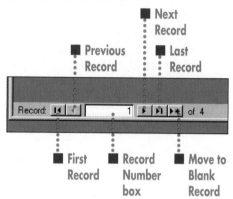

If you use a key such as Tab to move to a cell, Access highlights the contents of the cell when you select the field. As in a spreadsheet, you can replace the contents of the cell by keying data while the existing data is highlighted. If you click a cell with the mouse, the cursor appears in the cell, allowing you to edit the existing contents.

A C T I V I T Y

Editing Records in Datasheet View

1. Open *Activity 12-1.*

2. If the Tables section of the database objects window is not visible, click the **Tables** tab.

3. Click the **Calls** table and click **Open.** The table appears in Datasheet view. The purpose of this table is to keep a log of telephone calls.

4. Click the **Last Record** button at the bottom of the table to move the record pointer to the last record.

5. Click the **First Record** button to move the record pointer to the first record.

6. Click the **Next Record** button to move the record pointer to the next record. The current record should be the call to Christine Jimenez.

7. Suppose you entered 08:20 AM when you intended to enter 08:10 AM. Press **Tab** until the cursor is in the Call Time field.

8. Enter **08:10 AM** in the Call Time field and press **Tab.**

9. Leave the table on the screen for the next activity.

Undoing Changes to a Cell

There are two ways to undo changes to a cell. If the cursor is still in the cell you have accidentally changed, simply press Esc to restore the cell's original contents. If you have already entered the data in the cell, the Undo command in the Edit menu restores its contents. Remember, however, that the Undo command works only if you have not performed another operation since changing the cell.

Deleting Records

To delete an entire record, move to the record you want to delete and choose Delete Record from the Edit menu. A message box will appear, warning you that you are about to delete the record. Click Yes to permanently delete the record or No to cancel the deletion.

ACTIVITY

Deleting Records

1. Click the **Next Record** button to move the record pointer to the Gilbert Fern record.

2. Suppose you entered the record in the phone log and were interrupted before having the opportunity to place the call. Choose **Delete Record** from the **Edit** menu. A dialog box appears, asking if you really want to delete the record.

3. Click **Yes.** The record is deleted. Notice that the numbers in the Call ID field do not

renumber when a record is deleted. The reason is that the Call ID field is automatically assigned when the record is created, and does not change. In a later chapter, you will learn more about the use of automatically assigned fields.

4. Leave the table on the screen for the next activity.

Selecting Records and Fields

You can quickly select records and fields by clicking record and field selectors in the Table window, as shown in Figure 12-2. Clicking in the upper left corner of the datasheet selects all records in the database.

You can select multiple columns by clicking the field selector in one column, holding down the Shift key, and clicking the field selector in another column. The two columns, and all those in between, will be selected. You can use the same method to select multiple rows. You can also select multiple columns and rows by dragging across the column or row headings.

FIGURE 12-2
Record and field selectors allow you to quickly select records and fields.

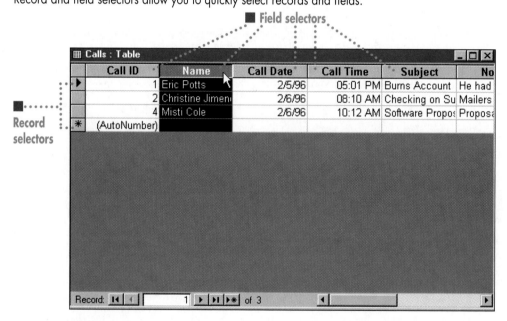

ACTIVITY

12-3 Selecting Records and Fields

1. Click the **Name** field selector to select the entire column.

2. Click the **Subject** field selector to select the column.

3. Select the **Name** field again.

4. Hold down the **Shift** key and click the **Call Time** field selector. The Name, Call Date, and Call Time fields are selected, as shown in Figure 12-3.

5. Click the record selector of the Eric Potts record.

6. Select the Misti Cole record.

7. Leave the table on the screen for the next activity.

FIGURE 12-3
The Shift key can be used in conjunction with the field selectors to select multiple columns.

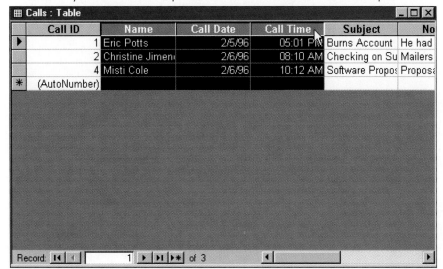

Cutting, Copying, and Pasting Data

In Access, you carry out Cut, Copy, and Paste functions the same as in other Office 95 applications. You can use the commands to copy and move data within a table or between tables. To cut or copy an entire record, click the record selector of the records you want to cut or copy and choose Cut or Copy from the Edit menu.

As a shortcut, you can select a record and click the right mouse button to display the shortcut menu, shown in Figure 12-4. The shortcut menu provides the Cut, Copy, and Paste commands in a convenient menu. There is also a command for adjusting row height, which you will learn about later in this chapter.

Using Cut, Copy, and Paste can be tricky sometimes. As in a spreadsheet, you must be aware that data pasted in the middle of a database will overwrite the existing data. If you want to copy an entire record and paste it into a table as a new record, use the Paste Append command in the Edit menu. As an alternative, highlight the blank record at the bottom of a table and choose Paste.

FIGURE 12-4
The shortcut menu provides easy access to the Cut, Copy, and Paste commands.

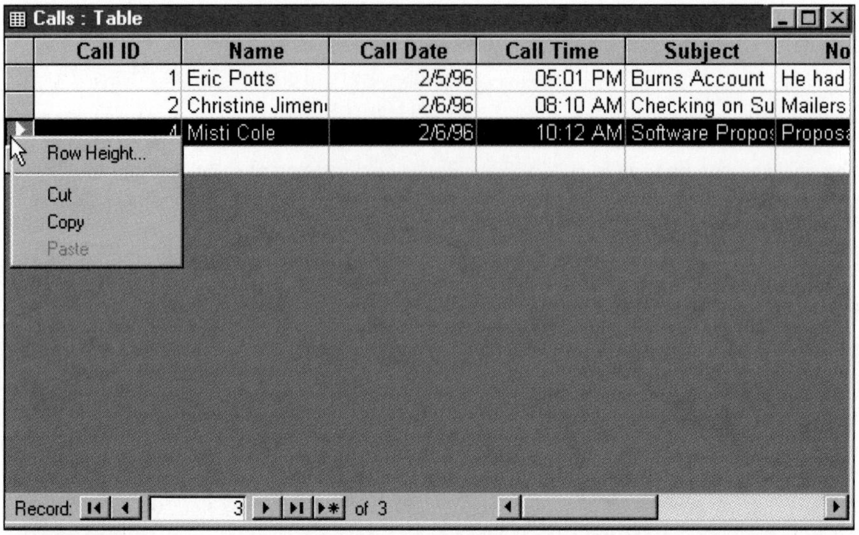

Call ID	Name	Call Date	Call Time	Subject	No
1	Eric Potts	2/5/96	05:01 PM	Burns Account	He had
2	Christine Jimen.	2/6/96	08:10 AM	Checking on Su	Mailers
4	Misti Cole	2/6/96	10:12 AM	Software Propo:	Propos:

Row Height...

Cut
Copy
Paste

Record: 14 ◄ 3 ► ►I ►* of 3 ◄ ►

ACTIVITY

12-4 Cutting, Copying, and Pasting

1. You were unable to get in touch with Eric Potts on February 5, so you try again on February 6. You decide to copy the first record to a new record to avoid re-keying some of the information. Select the Eric Potts record (Call ID 1).

2. Click the right mouse button. The shortcut menu appears.

3. Choose the **Copy** command from the shortcut menu.

4. Choose **Paste Append** from the **Edit** menu. The new record appears at the bottom of the database.

5. Change the date and time of the record at the bottom of the database to February 6 at 10:20 AM.

6. In the Notes field, enter the phrase **Plan to meet with Eric on Friday for lunch.**

7. Leave the table on the screen for the next activity.

Changing Datasheet Layout

There are a number of changes you may make to the datasheet layout, including changing row and column height, rearranging columns, and freezing columns.

Changing Row Height and Column Width

If you would like the data in your datasheet to have more room vertically, you can adjust the row height. Since all of the rows in the table must have the same height, to adjust row height, you can simply adjust the height of any row in the datasheet. Place the mouse pointer in the record selectors on the left end of the table. Position the pointer over a row border. You will know you have correctly positioned the pointer when it turns into a double arrow, as shown in Figure 12-5. Using the double arrow, drag the row border to adjust the row height.

You can use the shortcut menu to specify an exact row height. Select a row and click the right mouse button. Choose the Row Height command from the shortcut menu and enter a height for the row.

FIGURE 12-5
Adjusting the height of one row affects all rows in the datasheet.

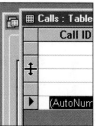

ACTIVITY

Adjusting Row Height

1. Place the cursor in the record selectors at the left end of the table. Position it on a row border. You will know you have the pointer correctly positioned when it changes to a double arrow.

2. Drag the row border down slightly to increase the height of the row. When you release the mouse button, all rows are affected by the change.

3. Select any record and click the right mouse button. The shortcut menu appears.

4. Choose **Row Height** from the shortcut menu.

5. Key **48** in the Row Height box and click **OK.** The row height increases to a height that allows the data in the Subject and Notes field to be read.

6. Leave the table on the screen for the next activity.

The column widths provided by default are often too wide or too narrow for a table's data. To adjust the column width, place the mouse pointer in the field selector, on the column's border. As when adjusting row height, the pointer changes to a double arrow. Columns can have individual widths. For example, a date field can be placed in a column narrower than that of an address field.

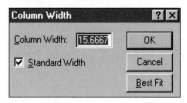

Accessing the shortcut menu while a field is selected provides a Column Width command, just as a Row Height command is available when a record is selected. The Column Width command accesses the Column Width dialog box, shown in Figure 12-6. When entering a column width in the Column Width dialog box, you have access to a feature called Best Fit. If you click the Best Fit button, an optimum column width for your data is selected for you.

NOTE: *Adjusting the column width does not change the data in the underlying table.*

ACTIVITY

Adjusting Column Width

1. Place the cursor in the field selectors at the top of the table.

2. Position the pointer on the right border of the Name field.

3. Drag to make the column wide enough to allow the name *Christine Jimenez* to fit on one line.

4. Select the **Call ID** field.

5. Click the right mouse button and choose the **Column Width** command from the shortcut

menu that appears. The Column Width dialog box appears.

6. Click **Best Fit.** The column narrows.

7. Use the **Best Fit** feature to adjust the width of the **Call Date** and **Call Time** fields.

8. Use the mouse to widen the Subject and Notes columns to about twice their current width.

9. Leave the table on the screen for the next activity.

Rearranging Columns

You may want to change the location of a field in Datasheet view. Access allows you to rearrange fields by dragging them to a new location. First click the field selector of the field you want to move. Then hold down the mouse button on the field selector and drag the field to the new location. A vertical bar will follow your mouse to show you where the field will be inserted. Release the mouse button to insert the field in its new location.

A C T I V I T Y

Rearranging Columns

● ●

1. Select the **Call Date** field by clicking its field selector.

2. Drag the **Call Date** field to the left until the vertical bar appears between the Call ID and Name fields. Release the mouse button.

The Call Date column appears between the Call ID and Name columns, as shown in Figure 12-7.

3. Leave the table on your screen for the next activity.

FIGURE 12-7
Columns can be rearranged simply by dragging them to new locations.

Call ID	Call Date	Name	Call Time	Subject	
▶ 1	2/5/96	Eric Potts	05:01 PM	Burns Account	He
2	2/6/96	Christine Jimenez	08:10 AM	Checking on Supplies	Ma
4	2/6/96	Misti Cole	10:12 AM	Software Proposal	Pro
5	2/6/96	Eric Potts	10:20 AM	Burns Account	Pla for
*	(AutoNu				

Record: ◄◄ ◄ 1 ► ►► ►* of 4

Freezing Columns

If a table has many columns, it may help to freeze a column or more to allow you to scroll to the columns that appear off the screen, while leaving the frozen columns on your screen. You have used a similar feature in spreadsheet applications.

To freeze columns, select the column or columns you wish to freeze and choose Freeze Columns from the Format menu. While the columns are frozen, you may scroll to see other columns, and the frozen columns remain on the screen.

To unfreeze columns, choose Unfreeze All Columns from the Format menu.

ACTIVITY

12-8 Freezing Columns

1. Select the **Call ID** column.

2. While holding down the **Shift** key, click the **Name** field. The Call ID, Call Date, and Name fields all appear highlighted.

3. Choose **Free̲ze Columns** from the **Fo̲rmat** menu.

4. Click the horizontal scroll arrows at the bottom of the table window to scroll to the Notes field. Notice that the frozen fields remain on the screen.

5. Choose **Unfre̲eze All Columns** from the **Fo̲rmat** menu.

6. Choose **C̲lose** from the **F̲ile** menu. You will be asked if you want to save changes to the layout of the table.

7. Click **Y̲es.** The database objects window is visible on the screen.

8. Leave the database open for the next activity.

Creating Forms

Datasheet view is good for many of the ways you work with a database. Often, however, a more convenient form is desired. For example, the form shown in Figure 12-8 places all of the important fields from the Calls table into a convenient and attractive layout.

Forms can be created manually by placing fields onto a blank form, arranging and sizing fields, and adding graphics. Access, however, provides a Form Wizard to make the process easier. Creating a form manually gives you more flexibility, but in most cases the Form Wizard can create the form you need quickly and efficiently.

FIGURE 12-8
Forms can make entering and editing data easier.

FIGURE 12-8
Forms can make entering and editing data easier.

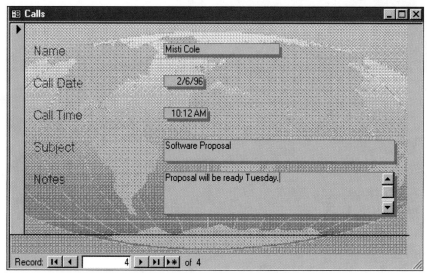

To create a form, click the Forms tab of the database objects window and click the New button. The New Form dialog box appears, as shown in Figure 12-9, giving you several options for creating the form. In this chapter, you will be concerned only with the Form Wizard option. The New Form dialog box also asks you to specify the table to use as a basis for the form. In more complex databases, you may have to choose among several tables or queries.

FIGURE 12-9
The New Form dialog box allows you to choose whether you want to create the form manually or with a Form Wizard.

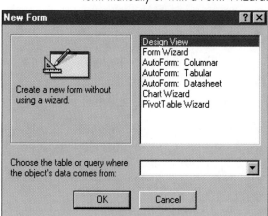

Starting the Form Wizard

1. Click the **Forms** tab.

2. Click **New.** The New Form dialog box appears.

3. Choose the **Form Wizard** option and the **Calls** database from the pop-up list.

4. Click **OK.** The Form Wizard dialog box appears, as shown in Figure 12-10.

5. Leave the Form Wizard dialog box on your screen for the next activity.

FIGURE 12-10
The Form Wizard dialog box first asks you to choose fields for the form.

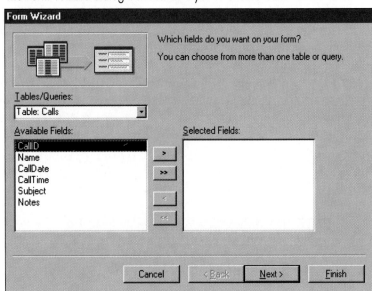

The next step is to choose the fields you want to appear in the form. To add a field to the form, click the field name in the Available Fields list and click the > button. To add all of the fields at once, click the >> button. If you plan to include almost all of the fields, click >> to include them all, then use the < button to remove the ones you do not want.

ACTIVITY

12-10 Choosing Fields for the Form

1. Click **>>**. All of the field names appear in the Selected Fields list.

2. Select the **CallID** field in the Selected Fields list.

3. Click **<**. The CallID field is moved back to the Available Fields list.

4. Click the **Next >** button. The Form Wizard dialog box changes to ask you to select a layout for the form, as shown in Figure 12-11.

5. Leave the dialog box open for the next activity.

FIGURE 12-11
The Form Wizard allows you to choose from three types of form layouts.

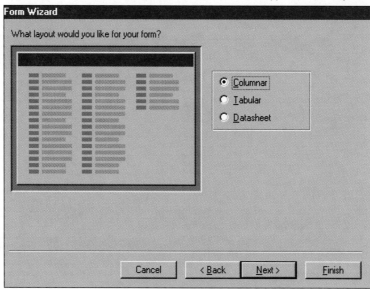

Three types of layouts are available when creating forms: Columnar, Tabular, and Datasheet. The Columnar layout is the most common. The form in Figure 12-12 is an example of a columnar layout. As data is entered, the cursor moves down the fields in the first column. When the user presses Tab in the field at the bottom of the first column, the cursor moves to the top of the next column.

FIGURE 12-12
The columnar layout is the most common form layout.

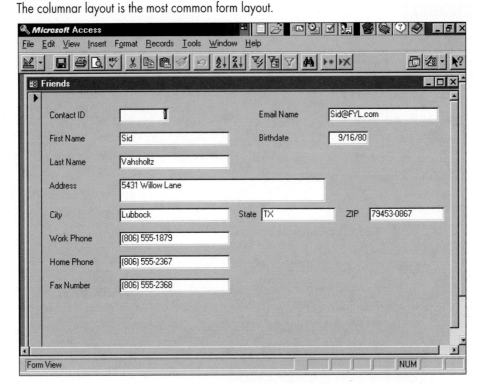

The Tabular and Datasheet layouts create forms similar to Datasheet view. Both layouts display data in a tabular form, giving you the ability to make a more attractive datasheet view. Figure 12-13 shows an example of a form created using a tabular layout.

FIGURE 12-13
A tabular layout allows you to create a form similar to Datasheet view, but with the ability to customize the view.

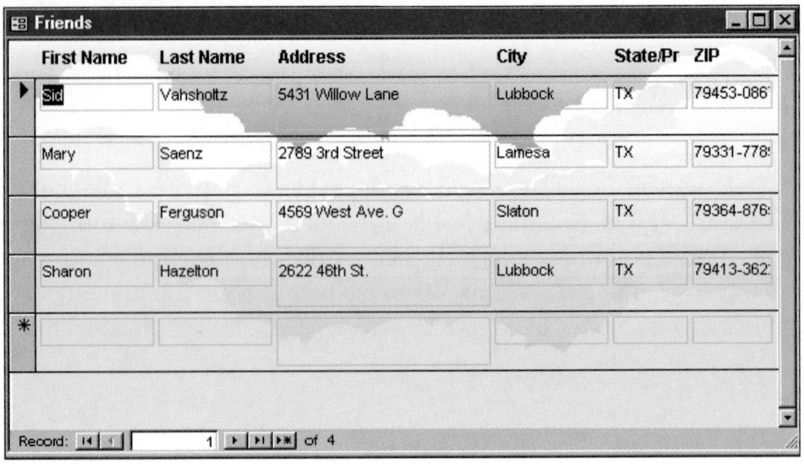

ACTIVITY

12-11

Choosing a Layout

1. If not already selected, click the **Columnar** option.

2. Click **Next >.** The dialog box then asks you to choose a style, as shown in Figure 12-14.

3. Leave the dialog box open for the next activity.

FIGURE 12-14
Choosing a style for a form can make a form more interesting.

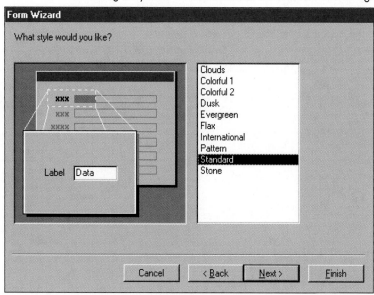

The style you select has no effect on the function of the form. Choosing a style allows you to personalize your form or give it flair. There are several styles from which to choose.

After you choose a style, you will be asked to name the form. The name you provide will appear in the Forms section of the database objects window. You are also given the option to begin using the form once it is created, or to modify it after the Form Wizard is done.

● ●

1. Click on the various styles to see how they look.

2. Choose the **International** style and click **Next >.** The final Form Wizard screen appears.

3. Key **My Form** and click **Finish.** Access will work for a minute or two creating your form. Finally, your form will appear, as shown in Figure 12-15.

4. Leave the form displayed for the next activity.

FIGURE 12-15
Your custom form appears when the Form Wizard is done.

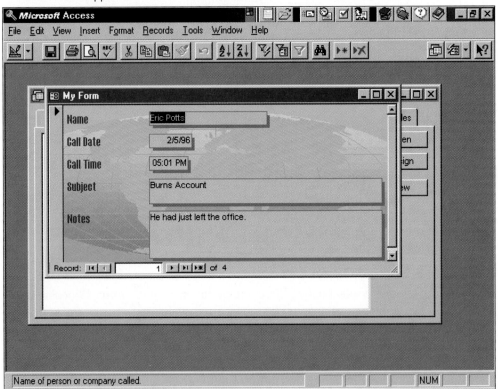

Using Forms

Using a form is basically the same as using Datasheet view. The same keys move your cursor among the fields, and at the bottom of the form are buttons like those that appear in Datasheet view, as shown in Figure 12-16. As with Datasheet view, you can move to a specific record by clicking in the Record Number box and entering the record number you want to see.

Table 12-1 summarizes the ways to move around when a form is displayed, including some keyboard shortcuts.

To add a new record, click the Next Record button until the blank record at the end of the database appears, or click the Add New Record button.

To edit an existing record, display the record and make changes in the fields of the form.

FIGURE 12-16
The controls at the bottom of the form allow
you to quickly move to the desired record.

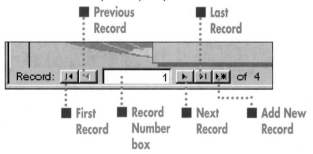

TABLE 12-1
Moving among records when a form is displayed.

TO MOVE TO THE ...	BUTTON	KEYBOARD SHORTCUT
First record	First Record button	Ctrl+Home
Last record	Last Record button	Ctrl+End
Next record	Next Record button	Page Down
Previous record	Previous Record button	Page Up

• •

1. Click the **Add New Record** button. A blank record appears in the form.

2. Enter the following information into the form:

   Name: Spencer Travel Agency

   Call Date: 2/6/96

Call Time: 04:18 PM

Subject: Reservations for flight to Orlando.

Notes: Flight 244
**   Leave 3:55 PM/**
**   Arrive 6:10 PM**

3. Close the database.

Field Properties

When you created fields in Chapter 11, you were concerned only with the field name, data type, and description. Now that you have created and used fields in a variety of situations, you should know about field properties. *Field properties* allow you to further customize a field beyond merely choosing a data type.

The field properties are specified in Table Design view, shown in Figure 12-17. There are many field properties available; we will look only at the most common. The available field properties vary depending on the selected data type.

Field Size

One of the most common field properties is Field Size. In fields of Text type, the Field Size is merely the number of characters allowed in the field. You can specify that it allow up to 255 characters.

In fields of Number type, the Field Size allows you to specify the internal data type Access will use to store the number. The available options are Byte, Integer, Long Integer, Single, Double, and Replication ID. If you have computer programming experience, the available field sizes may be familiar to you. If the options mean nothing to you, don't worry. There is an easy way to select the appropriate field size. If your field is to store whole numbers only, use Long Integer. If your field may be required to store fractional numbers, choose the Double field size.

FIGURE 12-17
Field properties are specified in Table Design view.

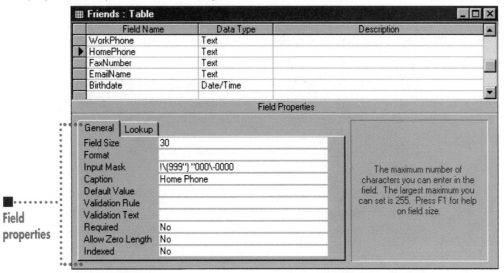

Field properties

Input Mask

An input mask allows you to control what kind of input will be allowed in the field. You can also specify characters that will be put into the field automatically. For example, you can specify that a phone number be formatted with area code in parentheses, and the rest of the number split by a hyphen.

Caption

The text you provide in the caption field property will be used in forms rather than the field name. For example, if the field name is *EmailName*, you could enter *E-mail address* in the caption field property. When you create a form that includes the field, the more descriptive name will appear as the field name.

Default Value

Another useful field property is Default Value. Use this field property when you have a field that usually contains the same value. For example, if most of the people in a database of names and addresses live in California, you can enter CA as the Default Value of the State field. The State field will automatically contain CA, unless you change it.

Required

The Required field property specifies whether the user must enter a value in the field. For example, an ID field may be required.

Decimal Places

Number and Currency fields have a field property called Decimal Places. This property usually adjusts automatically depending on the data in the field. You can specify a number of decimal places here to override the automatic setting.

Summary

■ Navigation buttons are used to move around the datasheet. They allow you to move to the first, last, previous, or the next record. You can also use a navigation button to add a new record.

■ You can replace the contents of a cell or edit the existing cell contents. There are two ways to undo a change to a cell. If the change has not yet been entered, you can press Esc to undo the change. If the change has already been entered, you can use the Undo command if you have not performed another operation since changing the cell.

■ To delete a record, use the Delete Record command. Entire records and fields can be selected by clicking the record and field selectors. Cut, Copy, and Paste are available in Datasheet view to move and copy data. The Paste Append command pastes a record at the end of the database.

■ There are a number of changes you may make to a datasheet. You can change the row height and column width. You can also rearrange and freeze columns.

■ Forms make it possible to organize the fields of a record into an arrangement that is more convenient than Datasheet view. The easiest way to create a form is to use the Form Wizard. You select the fields, the layout, and a style for the form, then the Form Wizard creates the form for you. Using a form is like using Datasheet view.

■ Field properties allow you to customize a field beyond merely choosing a data type. Some of the more common field properties are Field Size, Input Mask, Caption, Default Value, Required, and Decimal Places.

• • • • • • • • • • • • • •

REVIEW ACTIVITIES

TRUE/FALSE

Circle T or F to show whether the statement is true or false.

T   F   1. The navigation buttons move the cursor among the database fields.

T   F   2. If you click a cell with the mouse, the cursor appears in the cell.

T   F   3. The Esc key will undo a change that has been entered in a cell.

T   F   4. A record can be deleted using a command in the Edit menu.

T   F   5. The field selectors highlight an entire row in a datasheet.

T   F   6. Holding down the Alt key allows you to select more than one field.

T   F   7. In Access, you can use the Cut, Copy, and Paste commands.

T   F   8. Changing the height of one row changes the height of all datasheet rows.

T   F   9. Using a Form Wizard is the easiest way to create a form.

T   F   10. The Field Size field property specifies the number of characters allowed in a field.

COMPLETION

Write the correct answer in the space provided.

1. In Datasheet view, what indicates the current record?

_____

2. Briefly describe the two ways to undo changes in a cell.

_____

_____

3. What command is used to delete an entire record?

_____

4. In Datasheet view, how do you select an entire record?

_____

5. What special Paste command is available in Access to paste a new record?

_____

6. How do you access the shortcut menu?

_____

7. Why would you want to freeze columns in Datasheet view?

_____

_____

8. Which form layout is the most common?

_____

9. When using a form, what button causes the first record in the database to be displayed?

_____

10. What field property provides text that will be used in forms rather than the field name?

_____

REINFORCEMENT APPLICATIONS

application 12-1

1. Open *Application 12-1*.

2. Open the Friends table into Datasheet view.

3. Adjust the column widths of the fields to best fit the data.

4. Create a Columnar form for the Friends table using the Form Wizard. Do not include the work number, fax number, or birthdate in your form. Use any of the available styles. Name the form *My Columnar*.

5. Create a Tabular form for the Friends table. Include only the first and last names and e-mail address. Name the form *My Tabular*.

6. Close the database.

application 12-2

1. Open the database you created in Application 11-2.

2. Use the Form Wizard to create a Columnar form that includes the fields of your database. Choose an attractive style for the form.

3. Add a record to the table using the new form.

4. Close the database.

CHAPTER

FINDING AND ORDERING DATA

13

OBJECTIVES

When you complete this chapter, you will be able to

1. Find data in a database.

2. Query a database.

3. Use filters.

4. Sort a database.

5. Index a database.

Using Find

The Find command is the easiest way to quickly locate data in a database. The Find command allows you to search the database for specified information. There are several options that allow you flexibility in performing the search. These appear in the Find dialog box, shown in Figure 13-1.

You can access the Find dialog by choosing Find from the Edit menu, pressing Ctrl+F, or by clicking the Find button on the toolbar. The Find command is available only when a datasheet or form is displayed.

To search for data in a particular field, place your cursor in that field before choosing the Find command. Then make sure the Search Only Current Field option is chosen. To search all fields, make sure the Search Only Current Field option is *not* chosen.

Enter the data for which you are searching in the Find What box. Note that the Match Case check box gives you the option of a case-sensitive search. The Search text box has an arrow to the right that opens a pop-up list where you can specify whether you want to search up from the current record position, down from the current record position, or the entire table.

FIGURE 13-1

The Find dialog box allows you to quickly locate data in a database.

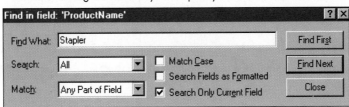

The Match text box also has a pop-up list that lets you choose what part of the field to search. If you want to exactly match the entire contents of a field, choose Whole Field in the Match pop-up list. More commonly, however, you will not want to enter the field's entire contents. For example, if you are searching a database of books for titles relating to antiques, you might want to search for titles with the word *antique* anywhere in them. In that case, you would choose Any Part of Field from the Match pop-up list. You can also specify that the search look only at the first part of the field by choosing the Start of Field option from the Match pop-up list. For example, the Start of Field option would be convenient if you need to search a table for people whose last name begins with *Mc*.

Click Find First to display the first record that matches the criteria you've specified in the Find What, Search, and Match boxes. Click Find Next to display the next record that matches the criteria. If Find reaches the bottom of the database before locating a match, you will be asked whether you want to continue from the top of the database.

ACTIVITY

 **Using Find**

1. Open *Activity 13-1*. A database that includes a table of products appears. The products represent the inventory of a small office supply store.

2. Open the **Products** table.

3. Place the cursor in the Product Name field of the first record.

4. Click the **Find** button on the toolbar. The Find dialog box appears.

5. Key **Stapler** in the **Find What** box.

6. Make sure **All** appears in the **Search** box. Choose **Any Part of Field** from the **Match** pop-up list.

7. The Match Case and Search Fields as Formatted options should not be selected. The Search Only Current Field option should be chosen.

8. Click the **Find First** button. Product 14 is selected, as shown in Figure 13-2.

9. Click **Find Next.** The next record (Product 15) is selected.

10. Click **Find Next** again. A message appears, telling you that the item was not found. There are only two staplers in the product line. Click **OK.**

11. Click **Close.** The Find dialog box closes.

12. Close the table and leave the database open for the next activity.

FIGURE 13-2
The Find First button finds the first record in the table that matches the specified criteria.

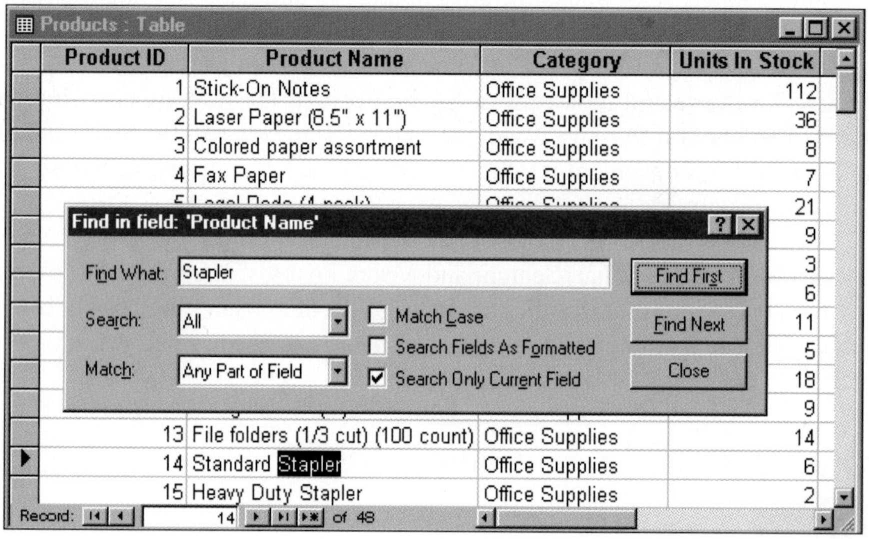

Using Queries

The Find command is an easy way of finding data. Often, however, you will need to locate data based on more complex criteria. For example, you may need to search for products with a value greater than $5. The Find command cannot do that. A special operation, called a *query,* will let you perform such a search and much more. Using a query, you can combine criteria to perform complex searches. For example, a query could locate products with a value greater than $5 of which fewer than three are in stock.

Queries allow you to "ask" the database almost anything about your data. In addition, queries can be made to display only the fields of interest to the search. For example, if you were querying a database of students to locate those with an average grade of 90 or better, you may want to display only the students' names and grades, rather than all the data in the table.

The first step in creating a query is to load the appropriate database and click the Queries tab of the database objects window. Then click the New button to create a new query. The New Query dialog box appears, as shown in Figure 13-3. The New Query dialog box gives you the option to create a query manually or to use one of several Query Wizards.

In this chapter, you will learn to create a query manually. The Design View option in the New Query dialog box allows you to do this.

FIGURE 13-3
The New Query dialog box allows you to choose if you want to create a query manually or use a Query Wizard.

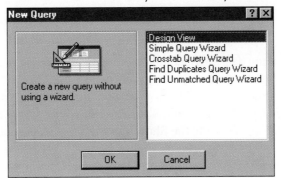

ACTIVITY
13-2 Creating a Query

1. Click the **Queries** tab of the database objects window.

2. Click the **New** button. The New Query dialog box appears.

3. Choose **Design View** if it is not already selected and click **OK.** The Show Table dialog

box appears, where you can choose a table for the query, as shown in Figure 13-4.

4. Leave the Show Table dialog box on the screen for the next activity.

FIGURE 13-4
The Show Table dialog box allows
you to choose a table for the query.

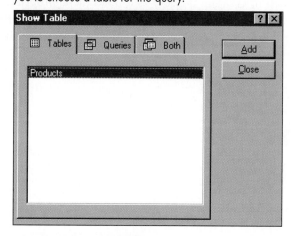

Because many databases include more than one table, the Show Table dialog box allows you to choose the table you want to use. The Add button adds the fields from the highlighted table to your new query. After you have added a table or tables, click the Close button to close the Show Table dialog box. The fields of the table chosen from the Show Table dialog box then appear in a small box in the Query window, shown in Figure 13-5.

The Query window is divided into two parts. The top part of the window shows the available tables and fields (only one table is shown in Figure 13-5). The bottom part shows the fields that will be searched and displayed in the query.

The bottom part of the Query window includes a grid that allows you to specify fields by which to search. The Field row is where you select a field to be part of the query. Click the down arrow to display the available fields. To search by more than one field, click in the next column of the Field row and choose another field. If you need to search by more fields than will fit in the window, the grid can be scrolled to expose additional columns.

The Table row allows you to choose from among the available tables. This is useful when working with multiple tables. The Sort row allows you to sort the results of the query (you will learn more about this later).

The Show check box determines whether the field is to be displayed in the query results. Normally, this will be checked. Occasionally, however, you may want to search by a field that does not need to appear in the query results.

Use the Criteria row to specify conditions for the search. For example, in Figure 13-5 the query specifies that only records whose Category field contains the words *Office Supplies* be included in the query results. You can specify more conditions using Or rows. When entering criteria that appear in the form of text, use quotation marks to enclose the text.

FIGURE 13-5
The Query window is where you actually create the query.

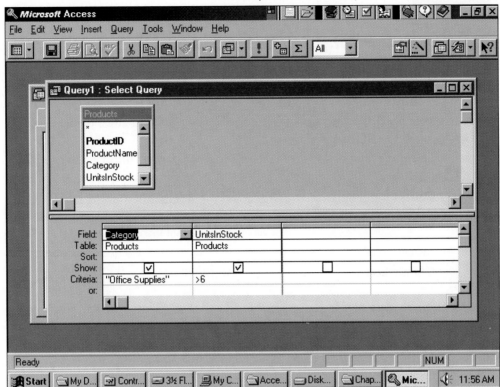

You can also use relational operators in the Criteria row. For example, in Figure 13-5 the UnitsInStock field is queried for records with more than (the > sign) six items in stock.

To create a query, you must supply three pieces of information: the fields you want to search, what you are searching for, and the fields you want to display with the results. Choose all of the fields you want to appear in the query. In the fields you want to search, enter search criteria. If you want to search a field but not display it, include the field and deselect the Show check box.

When you have entered the fields and criteria, you have some options for saving and running the query. To save the query, choose Save from the File menu. Saving a query, however, does not run the query. To run a query, close the Query window and run the query by opening it by name from the database objects window. You may also run the query from the Query window by choosing Run from the Query menu, or by clicking the Run button on the toolbar.

ACTIVITY

13-3 Creating a Query

●●●

1. Choose the **Products** table and click **Add.** The fields of the Products table appear in the Query window. Click **Close** to close the Show Table dialog box.

2. Choose **ProductName** from the first field pop-up list, as shown in Figure 13-6.

3. Click in the second column to activate the second field pop-up list.

4. Choose **UnitsInStock** from the pop-up list in the second column.

5. In the Criteria area of the second column, key **<3**. This will tell Access to display any records with fewer than three items in stock.

6. In the third column, choose the **RetailPrice** field.

7. Choose **Save** from the **File** menu. You are prompted for a name for the query.

8. Key **Reorder Query** and click **OK.**

9. Choose **Close** from the **File** menu.

10. Highlight **Reorder Query** and click **Open.** The results of the query appear, as shown in Figure 13-7.

11. Choose **Print** from the **File** menu. Make any necessary adjustments to the settings in the Print dialog box and click **OK.**

12. Close the Query view and leave the database open for the next activity.

FIGURE 13-6
Pop-up lists allow you to enter fields without keying the name of the field.

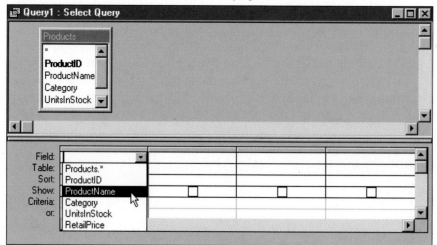

FIGURE 13-7
Opening a query applies its criteria to the database.

Reorder Query : Select Query		
Product Name	**Units In Stock**	**Retail Price**
Heavy Duty Stapler	2	$19.99
Letter Sorter	2	$7.99
Speaker Phone	2	$99.99
Fax Machine	2	$249.99
Cash Register	0	$229.00
Photocopier	1	$599.00
Typewriter	2	$149.99
Computer Desk	2	$299.99
Oak Office Desk	1	$399.99
Bookshelf	2	$89.99
Guest Chair	2	$199.00

Record: |◄ ◄ 1 ► ►| ►* of 11

Using Filters

Queries are very powerful and flexible tools. In many cases, however, less power is adequate. *Filters* provide a way to display selected records in a database more easily than using queries. Think of a filter as a simpler form of a query. A filter "filters out" the records that do not match the specified criteria. When you use a filter, all of the fields are displayed, and the filter cannot be saved for use again later. Other than that, most of the power of a query is available in a filter.

To create a filter, a table must be open. Then select Filter from the Records menu and choose Advanced Filter/Sort from the Filter pop-out menu. A Filter window like the one in Figure 13-8 will appear. Notice that the Filter window is

FIGURE 13-8
The Filter window is similar to the Query window.

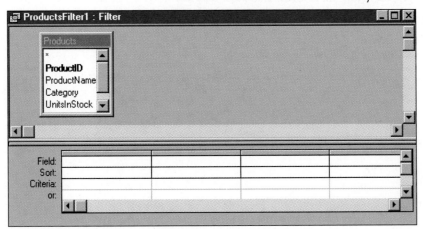

FIGURE 13-9
The Apply Filter button displays
the records specified by the filter.

Cancel × Apply Filter
button

very similar to the Query window. The table is automatically selected for you, so the Show Table dialog box does not appear. Also notice that there is no Show row to give you the choice of whether to display a field. All fields are displayed when you use a filter. In the Filter window, you select only those fields for which you want to enter criteria.

When you have included all of the field specifications, click the Apply Filter button on the toolbar, as shown in Figure 13-9. Clicking the Apply Filter button again removes the filter.

ACTIVITY

13-4 Using a Filter

1. Click the **Tables** tab of the database objects window.

2. Open the **Products** table in Datasheet view.

3. Choose **Filter** from the **Records** menu, then select **Advanced Filter/Sort** from the **Filter** pop-out menu. The Filter window appears.

4. The cursor appears in the Field area of the first column, along with an arrow indicating a pop-up list.

5. Choose **Category** from the pop-up list.

6. Key **"Business Machines"** in the Criteria row of the first column. (Include the quotation marks.)

7. Click the **Apply Filter** button on the toolbar. The filter is applied, and only the products in the Business Machines category are displayed, as shown in Figure 13-10.

8. Print the table with the filter applied.

9. Click the **Apply Filter** button again to remove the filter.

10. Leave the table on the screen for the next activity.

FIGURE 13-10

A filter hides all records that are not in the Business Machines category.

Product ID	Product Name	Category	Units In Stock	Retail Price
27	Scientific Calculator	Business Machines	3	$19.98
28	Basic Calculator	Business Machines	7	$3.99
29	Printing Calculator	Business Machines	3	$29.99
30	Speaker Phone	Business Machines	2	$99.99
31	Answering Machine	Business Machines	4	$49.99
32	Fax Machine	Business Machines	2	$249.99
33	Cash Register	Business Machines	0	$229.00
34	Photocopier	Business Machines	1	$599.00
35	Typewriter	Business Machines	2	$149.99
* (AutoNumber)				

Record: 14 ◄ 1 ► ►I ►* of 9 (Filtered)

Sorting

Sorting is an important part of working with a database. Often you will need records to appear in a specific order. For example, normally you may want a mailing list sorted by last name. But when preparing to mail literature to an entire mailing list, you may need the records to appear in ZIP code order. Access provides buttons on the toolbar to quickly sort the records of a table.

To sort a table, open the table and place the cursor in the field by which you want to sort. Then click either the Sort Ascending or Sort Descending button (see Figure 13-11). An *ascending sort* arranges records from *A* to *Z*, or smallest to largest. A *descending sort* arranges records from *Z* to *A*, or largest to smallest.

FIGURE 13-11
The Sort Ascending and
Sort Descending buttons
quickly arrange records.

■ **Sort Descending button**

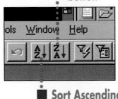

■ **Sort Ascending button**

Sorting Records

1. The **Products** table should be open in Datasheet view.

2. You want to sort the records from least in stock to most in stock. Place the cursor in the **Units In Stock** field.

3. Click the **Sort Ascending** button. The records appear in sorted order.

4. Now sort the records from most expensive to least expensive. Place the cursor in the **Retail Price** field.

5. Click the Sort Descending button. The products are sorted from most to least expensive.

6. Print the table and leave it open for the next activity.

Using the Sort Ascending and Sort Descending buttons is quick and easy. However, you will sometimes need to sort by more than one field. For example, suppose you want to sort the Products table by category, but within each category you want the items to appear from most to least expensive. To perform this kind of sort, you must create a filter.

To use a filter to sort, create a filter as you normally do, but select an ascending or descending sort for the desired field or fields by clicking the down arrow in the Sort row. If the filter window has information left from a previous query, you may need to click the cells with existing data and press the Backspace key to clear them.

Using a Filter to Sort

1. Choose **Filter** from the **Records** menu, then choose **Advanced Filter/Sort** from the **Filter** pop-out menu. A Filter window appears.

2. Choose the **Category** and **RetailPrice** fields as shown in Figure 13-12. In the Sort area, choose Ascending for the Category field and Descending for the RetailPrice field. You may have to clear some existing data from the filter window.

3. Click the **Apply Filter** button.

4. Scroll through the datasheet to see that the records have been sorted according to the specifications in the filter.

5. Print the table with the filter applied.

6. Leave the table open and the filter on for the next activity.

FIGURE 13-12
A filter allows you to sort a table by more than one field.

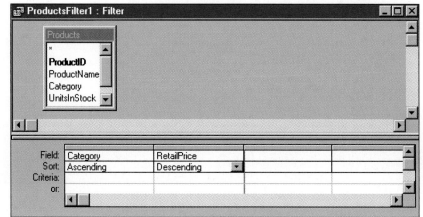

A filter can filter and sort at the same time. You can specify a sort order and a filter criterion in the same field. Applying the filter will filter the records *and* display them in sorted order.

ACTIVITY

13-7 Filtering Sorted Records

1. Choose **Advanced Filter/Sort** from the **Filter** pop-out menu on the **Records** menu. The filter used to sort the records appears.

2. Suppose you want to display only the products with a retail price greater than $100.

Key **>100** in the Criteria area of the Retail-Price column.

3. Click the **Apply Filter** button. Only ten of the records appear, as shown in Figure 13-13. The records are, however, sorted by retail price within the categories.

4. Print the table with the filter applied.

5. Click the **Apply Filter** button again to remove the filter. All of the records reappear.

6. Close the table. If prompted to save the design of the table, choose **No.** Close the database.

FIGURE 13-13
A filter can be used to filter records and sort at the same time.

Product ID	Product Name	Category	Units In Stock	Retail Price
34	Photocopier	Business Machines	1	$599.00
32	Fax Machine	Business Machines	2	$249.99
33	Cash Register	Business Machines	0	$229.00
35	Typewriter	Business Machines	2	$149.99
40	Oak Office Desk	Furniture	1	$399.99
39	Computer Desk	Furniture	2	$299.99
42	Executive Chair	Furniture	3	$259.99
43	Guest Chair	Furniture	2	$199.00
44	Desk Chair	Furniture	3	$189.99
45	4-Drawer Filing Cabinet	Furniture	4	$149.99
(AutoNumber)				

Record: 1 of 10 (Filtered)

Indexing

Indexing is an important part of database management systems. In small databases, indexes do not provide much benefit. Large databases, however, rely on indexing to quickly locate data. In an Access database, you can specify that certain fields be indexed. Access can find data in an indexed field faster than it can in one that is not indexed.

To index a field, go to Table Design view. For each field in design view, you can specify whether you want the field to be indexed.

If indexing improves speed, why not index all of the fields? The reason is that each indexed field causes more work and uses disk space when working with the table. You should be sure that the benefit of having the field indexed outweighs the added disk space and time that indexing causes. As a general rule, index fields only in large databases that are regularly used to locate records.

Summary

■ The Find command is the easiest way to locate data in a database. The Find command searches the database for specified information.

■ Queries allow more complex searches. A query allows you to search records using multiple and complex criteria, and to display selected fields. A query is saved so that it can be applied again later.

■ A filter is similar to a query; however, it displays all fields and cannot be saved. A filter can be used to sort records, or records can be sorted directly in a table without the use of a filter. Using a filter to sort records allows you to sort by more than one record.

■ Indexing is an important part of database management systems. Indexing allows records to be located more quickly, especially in large databases.

● ● ● ● ● ● ● ● ● ● ● ● ● ●

▼ REVIEW ACTIVITIES

TRUE/FALSE

Circle T or F to show whether the statement is true or false.

T   F   **1.** The Find command can search for data in all fields.

T   F   **2.** The Find command always matches the whole field.

T   F   **3.** The Find First button in the Find dialog box finds the first matching record.

T   F   **4.** Queries allow the most complex searches.

T   F   **5.** A query displays all fields in the table.

T   F   **6.** A query can be created using a Query Wizard.

T   F   **7.** Filters cannot be saved for later use.

T   F   **8.** Filters always display all fields.

T   F   **9.** An ascending sort arranges records from *Z* to *A*.

T   F   **10.** An indexed field can be searched more quickly than a non-indexed field.

COMPLETION

Write the correct answer in the space provided.

1. What is the easiest way to quickly locate data in a database?

   _____

2. What kind of search method must be used if you want to save the search for later use?

   _____

3. What three pieces of information must you supply when creating a query?

   _____

   _____

   _____

4. What dialog box allows you to choose a table for a query?

   _____

5. What menu is used to access the command that creates a filter?

   _____

6. What button is used to cause the result of a filter to be displayed?

_____

7. What button is used to sort records from largest to smallest?

_____

8. What must you do to sort a table by more than one field?

_____

9. What view allows you to index a field?

_____

10. Why is it not a good idea to index all fields?

_____

▼REINFORCEMENT APPLICATIONS

application 13 - 1

1. Open *Application 13-1*.
2. Use the Find command to locate the calculators in the product line.
3. Create a query that displays the products costing less than $20. Have the query display only the Product Name, Category, and Retail Price fields. Key in the query name **Less than $20**.
4. Print the results of the query, close the query, and reopen the complete products table.
5. Create a filter that displays furniture only, sorted from most to least expensive.
6. Print the table with the filter applied and close the database.

application 13 - 2

1. Open *Application 13-2*.
2. Use a query to display only the calls from 2/6/96. Display only the Name, Call Date, and Call Time fields.
3. Print the results of the query.
4. Close the database.

application 13 - 3

1. Open *Application 13-3*.
2. Sort the Friends table by Birthdate using the Sort Descending button.
3. Sort the Friends table by Last Name using the Sort Ascending button.
4. Close the table and database. There is no need to print.

application 13 - 4

1. Open the collection database you created in Application 11-2.
2. Create a filter that sorts your records by a field of your choice and filters out some of the records.
3. Print the table with the filter applied and remove the filter.
4. Create a query that asks a question of your database.
5. Print the results of the query.
6. Close the database.

REPORTS AND MACROS

CHAPTER

14

OBJECTIVES
When you complete this chapter, you will be able to:

1. Hide columns and print in landscape orientation.

2. Print from Form view.

3. Use the Report Wizards.

4. Modify a report.

5. Create and use macros.

Reports

Databases can become large as records are added. Printing the database from Datasheet view may not always be the most desirable way to put the data on paper. Creating a *database report* allows you to organize, summarize, and print all or a portion of the data in a database. You can even use reports to print form letters and mailing labels. Database reports are compiled by creating a report object. Figure 14-1 shows two examples of database reports.

Printing a database from Datasheet view, as you did in Chapter 13, is a form of a report. Printing from Datasheet view, however, offers you much less flexibility than does creating a report object. In this chapter, you will first learn more about printing from Datasheet view, then you will learn how to create report objects.

FIGURE 14-1
A database report allows flexible reporting of data.

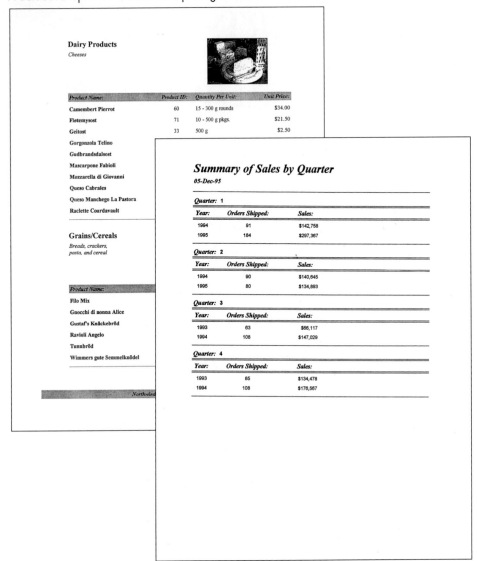

More about Printing from Datasheet View

Up to this point, you have printed databases from Datasheet view. Sometimes, however, the database may have more columns than will fit on the page. There are two ways to remedy the problem. You can print using landscape orientation or hide some of the columns.

Using Landscape Orientation

Landscape orientation prints the data sideways on the page. Because pages are longer than they are wide, printing in landscape orientation rather than portrait orientation allows more columns to be printed, as shown in Figure 14-2.

FIGURE 14-2

Landscape orientation allows more columns to fit on a page than portrait orientation.

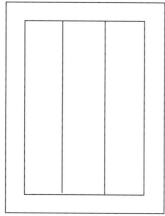

Portrait orientation

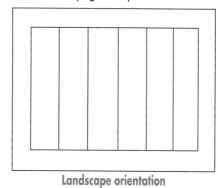

Landscape orientation

To print in landscape orientation, choose Page Setup from the File menu. The Page Setup dialog box appears. Click the Page tab, as shown in Figure 14-3. Click the Landscape Orientation option and click OK.

FIGURE 14-3

The Page Setup dialog box allows you to choose landscape orientation.

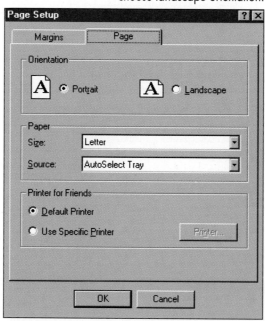

Printing in Landscape Orientation

1. Open *Activity 14-1*.

2. Open the Friends table.

3. Choose **Page Setup** from the **File** menu. The Page Setup dialog box appears.

4. Click the **Page** tab. The Page section of the dialog box appears.

5. Click the **Landscape** option and click **OK.**

6. Click the **Print** button on the toolbar. The datasheet will print in landscape orientation.

7. Leave the database open for the next activity.

Hiding Columns in Datasheet View

Hiding columns in Datasheet view can narrow the width of the datasheet enough to make it fit on one page. Of course, columns you hide will not appear on the printout. Therefore, hiding columns is helpful only when there are fields you don't need on the printout.

To hide a column, highlight it and choose Hide Columns from the Format menu. The column will completely disappear. To show hidden columns again, choose Unhide Columns from the Format menu. The Unhide Columns dialog box appears, as shown in Figure 14-4. The hidden columns do not have a check mark next to their names in the dialog box. Click the names of the hidden columns that you want to show and click Close.

FIGURE 14-4
The Unhide Columns dialog box allows you to choose the columns you want to be visible.

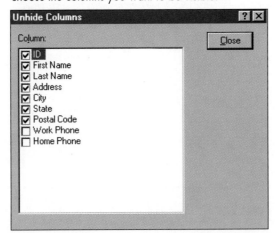

Hiding and Unhiding Columns

1. Choose **Page Setup** from the **File** menu.

2. Click the Page tab in the Page Setup dialog box.

3. Choose the **Portrait** Orientation option and click **OK.**

4. Highlight the **Home Phone** field.

5. With the Home Phone field highlighted, hold down the Shift key and click the **Work Phone** field. Both phone number fields are highlighted.

6. Choose **Hide Columns** from the **Format** menu. The columns disappear.

7. Print the datasheet. The remaining columns will fit on one page in portrait orientation.

8. Choose **Unhide Columns** from the **Format** menu. The Unhide Columns dialog box appears.

9. Click to place check marks next to the unchecked fields and click **Close.** The hidden columns reappear.

10. Choose **Close** from the **File** menu. A message appears, asking you if you want to save changes. Click **Yes.**

11. Leave the database on the screen for the next activity.

Printing from a Form

Another way to print database data is to print while a form is displayed, simply by choosing the Print command. Access will print as many records as it can fit on the page using the current form. In fact, Access will split records between pages. Therefore, printing from a form is not always the best way to print database data.

1. Click the Forms tab on the database objects window.

2. Open Form1.

3. Click the **Print** button on the toolbar.

4. Close the form.

5. Close the database and leave Access running for the next activity.

Report Objects

The Reports section of the database objects window is where you find *report objects.* A report object allows you to create reports that include selected fields, groups of records, and even calculations. As with other Access objects, you can create a report object manually or use a wizard. In this chapter, you will create a report using the Report Wizard. Then you will analyze what the Report Wizard creates to see how you could do it manually.

Using the Report Wizard

To create a report using the Report Wizard, click the Reports tab of the database objects window and click the New button. The New Report dialog box appears, as shown in Figure 14-5. There are several options for creating a new report.

To use the Report Wizard, choose Report Wizard from the list. Also choose the table or query from which you want to build the report. Choose a table if you want to include the entire table in the report. You can choose a query to include only certain data in the report. In many cases, you will want to create a query before creating a report.

Choosing Fields for the Report

The first Report Wizard window now appears, as shown in Figure 14-6. As with other wizards, the Report Wizard leads you through a series of windows

FIGURE 14-5

The New Report dialog box allows you to choose the method you want to use to create the report.

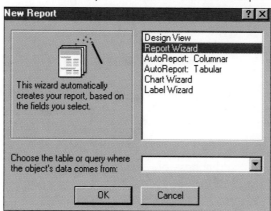

that ask you to specify information needed to create your report. The first window asks you to select fields for the report. You select these the same as when creating a form using the Form Wizard.

The screens that follow ask whether you want to group or sort the report, and what layout and style you desire. Finally, you will be asked to name the report.

FIGURE 14-6

The Report Wizard guides you through the steps of creating a database report.

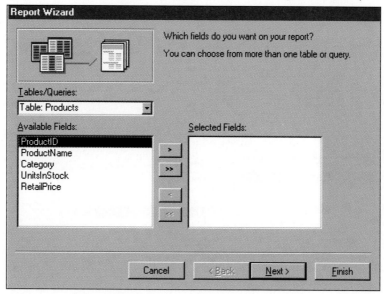

Starting the Report Wizard and Choosing Fields

1. Open *Activity 14-4*. The office products database you worked with in Chapter 13 appears again.

2. Click the **Reports** tab of the database objects window.

3. Click **New.** The New Report dialog box appears.

4. Choose **Report Wizard** from the list.

5. Choose **Products** from the pop-up list. Click **OK.** The first Report Wizard screen appears. The Report Wizard wants you to choose fields for the report.

6. Highlight **ProductName** in the **Available Fields** list. Click **>.** The Category field is now highlighted in the Available Fields list.

7. Click **>** three times to choose the Category, UnitsInStock, and RetailPrice fields for the Selected Fields list. Your screen should appear similar to Figure 14-7.

8. Click **Next>.** The Report Wizard now gives you the option to group the report.

9. Leave the Report Wizard on the screen for the next activity.

FIGURE 14-7
Choosing fields is an important early step in creating a report.

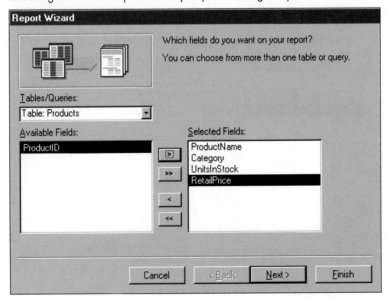

After fields have been selected, you may click the Finish button to create the report or continue working with the wizard to specify other options. The next options involve grouping and sorting the report.

Sorting and Grouping the Report

Grouping a report allows you to break it into parts based on the contents of a field. For example, you could break a report that lists your friends into parts that group the friends by city. In the report you are creating now, you will group the report by product category. To group a report, choose the fields by which you want to group from the Report Wizard screen shown in Figure 14-8.

FIGURE 14-8

The Report Wizard allows you to group the records in a report.

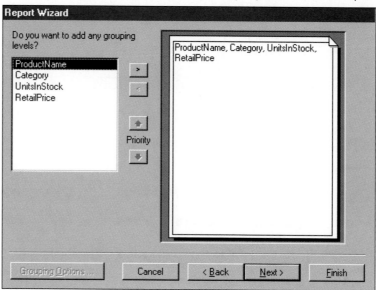

You can group by more than one field. When you do this, however, you must give the fields priority. For example, you could group friends by state first, then by city.

Sorting the report goes hand-in-hand with grouping. The screen shown in Figure 14-9 allows you to specify fields by which the report will be sorted. As you can see, you can sort by multiple fields.

FIGURE 14-9
Many reports are more useful if the records are sorted by one or more fields.

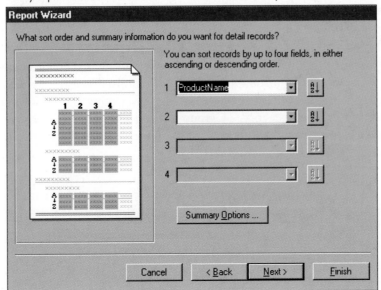

ACTIVITY

14-5

Grouping and Sorting the Report

1. Highlight **Category** and click **>.** Your screen should appear similar to Figure 14-10.

2. Click **Next >.** The Report Wizard now wants you to specify how you want the report sorted.

3. Choose **ProductName** as the first sort field by clicking the down arrow next to the number 1 box. We will sort by one field only.

4. Leave the sort screen displayed for the next activity.

FIGURE 14-10
Your report will be grouped by product category.

Report Wizard

Do you want to add any grouping levels?

ProductName
UnitsInStock
RetailPrice

>
<

Priority

Category

ProductName, UnitsInStock, RetailPrice

| Grouping Options ... | Cancel | < Back | Next > | Finish |

Summary Options

One of the most useful features of reports is the ability to create summaries within it. Each group of records in a report can be followed by totals, averages, or other summary information. The Summary Options dialog box allows you to specify summaries for fields in the report.

ACTIVITY

14-6 **Choosing Summary Options**

1. Click the **Summary Options** button. The Summary Options dialog box appears.

2. For the UnitsInStock field, click the Sum option. The report will total the UnitsInStock field.

3. For the RetailPrice field, click the **Min** and **Max** options.

4. Choose the **Calculate percent of total for sums** option. Your screen should appear similar to Figure 14-11.

5. Click **OK** to close the Summary Options dialog box.

6. Click **Next >.** The Report Wizard asks you to choose a layout and page orientation.

7. Leave the Report Wizard on the screen for the next activity.

FIGURE 14-11
The Summary Options dialog box allows you to specify
calculations to be included in the report.

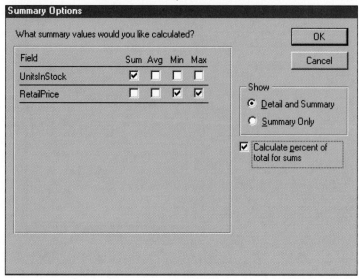

Layout and Style

Access provides several layout and style options for your report. The layout options let you choose how you want data arranged on the page. Figure 14-12 shows the screen in which the Report Wizard asks you to choose a layout.

Style options give you some control over the report's appearance. The style you choose tells the reader of the report something about the data being

FIGURE 14-12
Layouts control the alignment of data in a report.

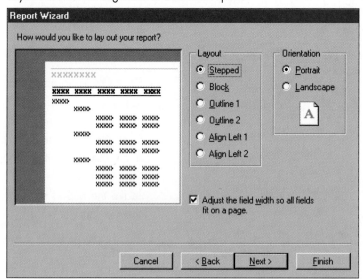

presented. Some reports may call for a formal style, while others may benefit from a more casual style.

Choosing Report Layout and Style

1. Highlight each of the available layouts. The sample shown on the screen should reflect the highlighted layout. When you have seen all of the options, choose **Stepped** as the layout.

2. Make sure that **Portrait** is chosen as the page orientation.

3. Click **Next >.**

4. Highlight each style to see the variety of options. Choose the **Corporate** style.

5. Click **Next >.** The final step in creating the report appears.

6. Leave the Report Wizard on the screen for the next activity.

The final step is naming the report. Use one that gives an indication of the report's output. For example, if a report from the database of your friends prints only those who live in your city, you might name the report *Local Friends*.

After you name the report, you have some additional options for what you want displayed when the Report Wizard completes its work. Most of the time you will want to preview the report you just created, so that is the default option. But you may choose to modify the report. You will get a brief look at how this is done later in this chapter.

Finishing the Report

1. Key **Category Report** as the name of the report.

2. Make sure the option to preview the report is selected and click **Finish.** After Access spends some time working, the report appears in a window, as shown in Figure 14-13.

3. Scroll through the report to see the various categories and summaries.

4. Click the **Print** button. The report prints.

5. Leave the report on the screen for the next activity.

FIGURE 14-13
Reports can be previewed on the screen before printing.

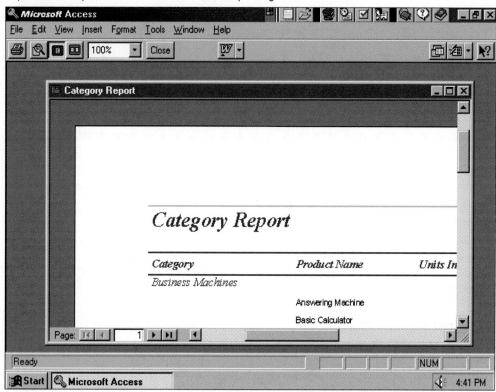

Modifying a Report

Any report, whether created manually or with the Report Wizard, can be modified from Design view. Design view shows the structure of a report. The report is divided into parts, called bands. Each band has a different purpose. Let's take a brief look at the bands that make up the report you created in the previous activities.

The first time you preview a report, Design view automatically appears when you close the preview. To access Design view again, click the Design button in the database objects window.

ACTIVITY

Design View

1. Click the **Close** button in the toolbar. The report screen appears in Design view, as shown in Figure 14-14.

2. Scroll down to see all of the bands in the report.

3. Leave the report in Design view for the next activity.

FIGURE 14-14
Design view allows you to make changes to a report.

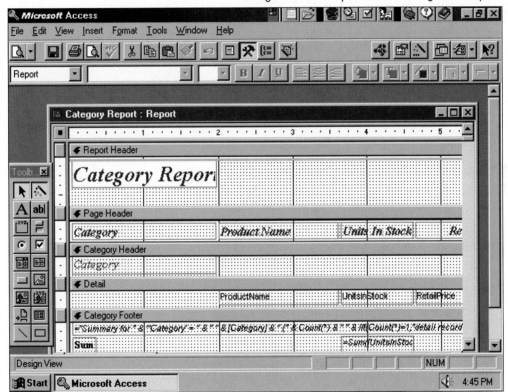

Table 14-1 summarizes the purpose of each band in the report.

In this chapter, you will not learn how to make changes to each of the bands. If you need to make a change to the contents of a band, use the online Help system for information on how to make those modifications.

TABLE 14-1

BAND	DESCRIPTION
Report Header	The contents of this band appear at the top of the first page of the report
Page Header	The contents of this band appear at the top of each page of the report
Category Header	The contents of this band appear at the top of each group. Because your report is grouped by Category, the band is called Category Header.
Detail	This band specifies the fields that will appear in the detail of the report.
Category Footer	The contents of this band appear at the end of each group. The summary options appear in this band.
Page Footer	The contents of this band appear at the end of each page of the report
Report Footer	The contents of this band appear at the end of the report

The Toolbox, shown in Figure 14-15, has tools that you can use to modify reports. The Label tool, for example, allows you to add text.

FIGURE 14-15
The Toolbox has the tools you need to modify reports.

Label tool

ACTIVITY

14-10

Modifying the Report

1. Click the **Label** tool in the Toolbox.

   A

2. Position the pointer in the Report Header to the right of the Category Report text and draw a text box as shown in Figure 14-16.

3. Key your name at the cursor that appears in the text box.

4. Choose **Close** from the **File** menu. A message appears asking if you want to save changes.

5. Click **Yes.** The database objects window appears.

6. With the name of the report highlighted, click **Preview.** The report appears on the screen.

7. If necessary, scroll to the right to see your name on the report.

8. Choose **Print** from the **File** menu. The Print dialog box appears.

9. In the Print Range portion of the dialog box, specify that you want to print only page 1. (Key **1** in the From and To boxes.) Click **OK.**

10. Close the report and leave the database open for the next activity.

FIGURE 14-16
The Label tool can be used to add text to a report.

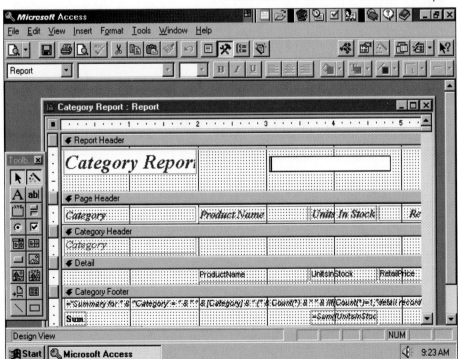

Macros

One of the nice features of professional database management systems such as Access is the ability to automate tasks that are performed often. This is done by creating an object called a macro. A *macro* is a collection of one or more actions that Access can perform on a database. You can think of a macro as a computer program you create to automate some task you perform with the database.

Creating macros can be challenging, and there is much detail to learn before becoming proficient at it. In this book, you will get just a taste of how macros work by analyzing an existing one and seeing it work.

To create a macro, click the Macros tab of the database objects window and click the New button. The Macro window appears, allowing you to specify the actions to be performed by the macro, as shown in Figure 14-17. The macro will execute the actions specified in the macro window, beginning with the first action listed.

FIGURE 14-17
The Macro window allows you to specify steps a macro is to follow.

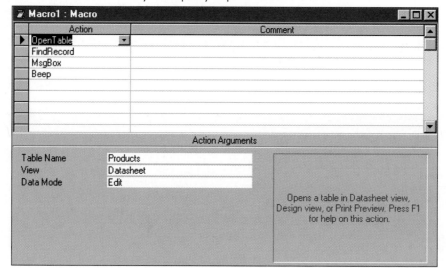

ACTIVITY

 **Creating a Macro**

1. Click the **Macros** tab of the database objects window. A macro has already been created for you and appears in the dialog box.

2. Because the macro already exists, click the **Design** button to see the actions in the macro.

3. Leave the macro window open for the next activity.

You can choose an action by clicking the down arrow in the action column. There are many actions from which to select; several perform advanced operations. The lower portion of the macro window shows the action arguments for the chosen action. Action arguments are specific information that Access needs in order to perform the specified action.

The macro created for you will open the Products table, find the first business machine in the table, present a message box, and beep. Let's add one more action to the macro: closing the table. When we have added the action that tells Access to close the table, we'll run the macro.

ACTIVITY

 **Adding to the Macro and Running**

1. Place the cursor in the Action column of the first blank row. An arrow indicating a pop-up list appears.

2. Click the arrow to display the pop-up list of legal commands.

3. Choose the **Close** command.

4. Choose **Close** from the **File** menu to close the Macro window. You will be asked if you wish to save the changes to the macro.

5. Click **Yes.** The database objects window is again visible.

6. With Macro1 highlighted, click the **Run** button. The Products table opens and the message box generated by the macro appears. Notice that the record pointer is on the first Business Machines record.

7. Click **OK** to dismiss the message. The computer beeps again because of the Beep command, and finally the table closes because of the command you added.

8. Close the database.

Summary

■ Database reports allow you to organize, summarize, and print all or a portion of the data in a database. Database reports are compiled by creating a report object.

■ When printing from Datasheet view, you may choose to print in landscape orientation to fit more columns on the page. You may also hide some of the table's columns. In addition, you can print records from Form view.

■ The easiest way to create a report object is to use the Report Wizard. When using the Report Wizard, you first choose the table from which the data is coming and what fields of that table you wish to include in the report. You can also choose to group the records and sort them. Summary options allow calculations to be performed for each group in the report.

■ The Report Wizard also allows you to choose a layout and style for your report. The layout controls the alignment of data in the report, while the style can give a report a casual look, a formal look, or something in between.

■ Reports are modified using Design view. Each report is divided into parts, called bands. Each band serves a unique purpose in generating the report.

■ Macros allow tasks you perform often to be automated. The Macro window allows you to create a macro object.

• • • • • • • • • • • • • •

REVIEW ACTIVITIES

TRUE/FALSE

Circle T or F to show whether the statement is true or false.

T   F   1. Portrait orientation allows more columns to be printed than landscape orientation.

T   F   2. The Hide Columns command causes a column of a table to disappear.

T   F   3. When printing from a form, only one record appears on each page.

T   F   4. Database reports are prepared by creating a report object.

T   F   5. The Report Wizard is the only way to create a report.

T   F   6. The Report Wizard always includes all fields in a report.

T   F   7. Grouping allows you to break a report into parts based on the contents of a field.

T   F   8. A summary option can be used to total a column in a report.

T   F   9. In Design view, the contents of the Report Header band appear at the top of each page of the report.

T   F   10. A macro can be used to automate a task in Access.

COMPLETION

Write the correct answer in the space provided.

1. Which dialog box allows you to change the page orientation?

2. What command is used to show hidden columns?

3. What command allows you to print from a form?

4. What section of the database objects window shows report objects?

5. List two summary options.

6. What options allow you to choose how you want data arranged on the page?

_____

7. What options are designed to give you control over the appearance of a report?

_____

8. What is the purpose of the Detail band in Report Design view?

_____

_____

9. Where do the contents of the Report Footer band appear in the report?

_____

10. Describe the steps necessary to access the Macro window.

_____

_____

REINFORCEMENT APPLICATIONS

application 14-1

1. Open the database you used to create the report in this chapter (*Activity 14-4*).
2. Use the Report Wizard to create a report that includes all fields, grouped by UnitsInStock.
3. Title the report **Products by Units in Stock.**
4. Print the report and close the database.

application 14-2

1. Open the database you created in Application 11-2.
2. Create a report that prints the information from your database. If possible, group the report by some field in your database.
3. Give the report an appropriate name and print it.

CREATING FORM LETTERS AND MAILING
LABELS USING ACCESS AND WORD

Moving and Copying Data Between Applications

Because Office 95 is an integrated program, you can easily move and copy data between applications. No matter which applications you are using, the data is automatically formatted so that it can be used in the destination file.

Word to Access

Suppose you have been given a list of names and addresses in a Word file. The names need to be entered into a database. Pasting into Access from Word is similar to pasting into a worksheet from Word. If the text from Word is set up as a table, with data separated by tabs, the database will separate the text into fields. Each line will be entered as a separate record. If the text is in a single block, all of the text will be pasted into the currently highlighted field.

Excel to Access

Pasting into an Access database from an Excel worksheet is essentially the same as pasting from a worksheet to a worksheet. The cells cut or copied from the worksheet will appear in the database, beginning with the highlighted entry.

Access to Excel

When you paste Access data into an Excel worksheet, the database records will be pasted into the worksheet rows, with each field entry in a separate column.

Access to Word

Data from an Access database is pasted into a Word document the same way Excel data is pasted into Word. The data is formatted with tabs when it enters the Word document. This feature could be used to create a table in Word, based on data from Access.

Form Letters

Another way to integrate Office applications is to print form letters. A *form letter* is a word processor document that uses information from a database in specified areas to personalize a document.

For example, you might send a letter to all of the members of a professional organization using a form letter. In each letter, the information is the same but the names of the recipients will be different. One letter may begin "Dear Mr. Conder" and another "Dear Ms. Whitlow."

Creating a Form Letter

To create form letters, you integrate information from a data source, such as an Access database, with a document from Word, called the main document. The *main document* contains the information that will stay the same in each form letter. The *data source* contains the information that will vary in each form letter. You insert the field names, or *merge fields,* in the main document where you want to print the information from the data source. The merge fields you place in the Word document are enclosed in angle brackets (<< Field Name >>). When the main document and the data source are merged, the merge fields in the main document are replaced with the appropriate information from the data source to create personalized form letters.

Word provides a Mail Merge Helper that makes it easy to create a form letter. To access the Mail Merge Helper dialog box, as shown in Figure III-1, choose the Mail Merge command from the Tools menu. There are three steps that you will complete in the Mail Merge Helper dialog box. To specify the main document, click Create in Step 1, click Form Letters, and then click Active Window. The active document (the one displayed on the screen) is now the main document. To specify a data source, click Get Data in Step 2, and click Open Data Source. When the Open Data Source dialog box appears, choose the file you want

FIGURE III-1
The Mail Merge Helper makes it easy to create form letters.

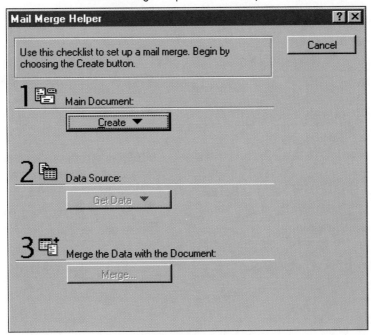

to use as the data source. If you want to query the database before merging, click the Query Options button. When you are ready to merge, click Merge in Step 3.

The Mail Merge toolbar, shown in Figure III-2, contains buttons to make the merging process easier. This toolbar is located above the ruler and below the Tip of the Day, but does not appear until you use the Mail Merge Helper. To insert merge fields, click the place in the main document where you want to insert information from the data source. Then click Insert Merge Field on the Mail Merge toolbar and click the appropriate field name. Insert all the merge fields you want until your main document is complete.

FIGURE III-2
The Mail Merge toolbar appears when you use the Mail Merge Helper.

ACTIVITY III-1 Creating Form Letters

1. Open the *Lakewood Parents* Access database from the Integration template disk. Open the *Fourth Grade* table.

2. Enlarge the *Fourth Grade: Table* window so all the fields and records are visible.

3. Open the *Lakewood Letter* Word document from the Integration template disk.

4. Choose **Mail Merge** from the **Tools** menu. The Mail Merge Helper dialog box appears, as shown in Figure III-1.

5. Click **Create**; then choose **Form Letters.**

6. Choose **Active Window.**

7. Click **Get Data;** then choose **Open Data Source.** The Open Data Source dialog box appears.

8. Click the down arrow to the right of the Files of type box. Click **MS Access Databases.**

9. Highlight *Lakewood Parents* and click **Open.** The Microsoft Access dialog box appears, as shown in Figure III-3.

10. With the Tables tab displayed, highlight *Fourth Grade* and click **OK.**

11. When the Microsoft Word dialog box appears, as shown in Figure III-4, choose **Edit Main Document.** The *Lakewood Letter* document appears on the screen.

12. Place your cursor on a line in between the date and the salutation.

13. Click the **Insert Merge Field** button on the Mail Merge toolbar. Insert Merge Field

FIGURE III-3
Choose the table you want to open from
the Microsoft Access dialog box.

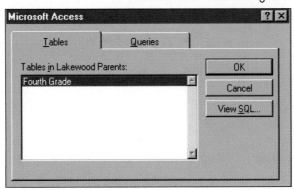

FIGURE III-4
The Microsoft Word dialog box appears when you have
not yet inserted merge fields into your main document.

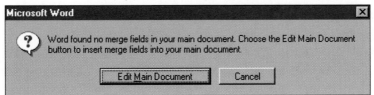

14. Click **Title** in the drop-down list.

15. Insert the rest of the merge fields shown in Figure III-5 using the same method. (Be sure to add spaces where necessary and include a comma between the City and State merge fields.)

16. Click the **Merge to New Document** button on the Mail Merge

toolbar. The data from the database is inserted into the merge fields to create the form letters in a new file.

17. Scroll down to see the form letters. Save the file as *Lakewood Form Letters* on your Integration template disk and close.

FIGURE III-5
Insert merge fields in your main document as shown.

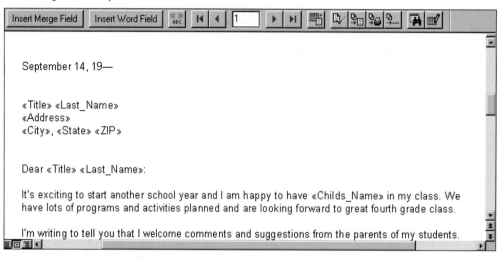

| Insert Merge Field | Insert Word Field | « » ABC | ⏮ ◀ | 1 | ▶ ⏭ | | | | | | | |

September 14, 19—

«Title» «Last_Name»
«Address»
«City», «State» «ZIP»

Dear «Title» «Last_Name»:

It's exciting to start another school year and I am happy to have «Childs_Name» in my class. We
have lots of programs and activities planned and are looking forward to great fourth grade class.

I'm writing to tell you that I welcome comments and suggestions from the parents of my students.

Using Query Options and Printing Form Letters

After the form letters have been created, they are ready to print. If you
don't want to print every letter, you can click the Query Options button in the
Mail Merge Helper. The Query Options dialog box will appear and you can
then filter out only the records you want to merge and print.

ACTIVITY

III-2 Using Query Options and Printing Form Letters

● ●

1. The *Lakewood Letter* document should be
open on your screen.

2. Click the **Mail Merge Helper**
button on the Mail Merge toolbar.
The Mail Merge Helper dialog box
appears.

3. Click the **Query Options** button in Step 3.
The Query Options dialog box appears.

4. You want to print only the letters to the parents of Riley Karr and Vanessa Pritchard. In
the Field box, click the down arrow. Click
Last Name.

5. The Comparison box should read *Equal to.*
In the Compare To box, key **Karr**.

6. In the And box, click the down arrow. Click
Or.

7. In the second Field box, click the down arrow. Click **Last Name.**

8. The Comparison box should read *Equal to.* In the Compare To box, key **Pritchard**. The Query Options dialog box should appear similar to Figure III-6.

9. Click **OK.** The Mail Merge Helper dialog box reappears.

10. Click **Merge.** The Merge dialog box appears.

11. Click **Merge.** The two form letters you wanted to print are created in a new file.

12. Save the file as *Print Form Letters* on your Integration template disk.

13. To print the form letters, choose **Print** from the **File** menu.

14. Click **OK.**

15. Close *Print Form Letters*. Save *Lakewood Letter* on your Integration template disk and close.

FIGURE III-6

The Query Options dialog box filters out the records you want to merge.

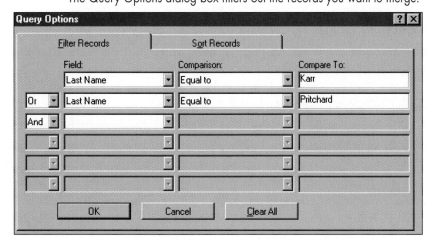

Mailing Labels

Office 95 makes it easy to create mailing labels from any data source that has name and address information. In this activity, creating mailing labels involves integrating the Word and Access applications. Creating mailing labels is very similar to creating form letters. The main difference is that mailing labels place information from more than one record on the same document page. This is because mailing labels usually come in sheets that have as many as 30 labels per page.

To create mailing labels, you will be using the Mail Merge Helper again. This time, choose Mailing Labels from the Create menu in the Mail Merge Helper dialog box. After specifying a main document and a data source, you can choose the label options you want, insert merge fields that contain the address information, and print your mailing labels.

Creating Mailing Labels

1. Open a blank Word document.

2. Choose **Mail Merge** from the **Tools** menu. The Mail Merge Helper dialog box appears.

3. Click **Create** and then click **Mailing Labels.**

4. Click **Active Window.**

5. Click **Get Data** and then click **Open Data Source.** The Open Data Source dialog box appears.

6. Click the down arrow to the right of the Look in box. With the Integration template disk in drive A, click **3_ Floppy (A:).**

7. Click the down arrow to the right of the Files of type box. Click **MS Access Databases.**

8. Highlight *Lakewood Parents* and click **Open.** The Microsoft Access dialog box appears.

9. With the Tables tab displayed, highlight *Fourth Grade* and click **OK.**

10. When the Microsoft Word dialog box appears, click **Set Up Main Document.** The Label Options dialog box appears, as shown in Figure III-7.

11. In the Printer Information box, be sure *Laser* is chosen and then choose the *Tray* option that you wish to use with your printer.

12. The Label Products box should have *Avery Standard* chosen. In the Product Number box, scroll down to highlight *5160 - Address.*

13. Click **OK.** The Create Labels dialog box appears.

FIGURE III-7
In the Label Options dialog box, you can choose
what size mailing labels you will be printing.

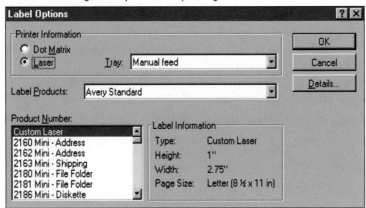

14. Click the Insert Merge Field button and insert merge fields into the Sample Label box, as shown in Figure III-8.

15. Click **OK.** The Mail Merge Helper reappears.

16. Click **Merge.** The Merge dialog box appears.

17. Click **Merge.** The labels are displayed in a new file.

18. Save the file as *Mailing Labels* on your Integration template disk.

19. Choose **Print** from the File menu.

20. Close *Mailing Labels.* Close the unsaved document without saving changes.

FIGURE III-8

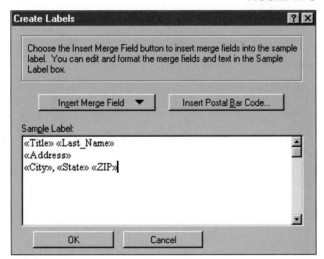

Summary

■ To create form letters, you integrate information from a data source with a main document. The merge fields in the main document are replaced with information from the data source.

■ Creating mailing labels is very similar to creating form letters. The Mail Merge Helper and Mail Merge toolbar make it easy to create form letters or mailing labels.

● ● ● ● ● ● ● ● ● ● ● ● ●

TRUE/FALSE

Circle T or F to show whether the statement is true or false.

T F 1. The data source contains the information that stays the same in each form letter.

T F 2. The Query Options dialog box provides a way to filter out only the records you want to merge and print.

T F 3. In the Label Options dialog box, you choose the data source you will be using for the mailing labels.

COMPLETION

Write the correct answer in the space provided.

1. What is a form letter?

_____

_____

2. Where are merge fields inserted?

_____

INTEGRATION PROJECTS

Home Again Real Estate

PROJECT G

Create a database in Access that contains the names and addresses of the fifteen people who live on Sycamore Street in the Raintree division. You can get names from a phone book or make them up. Include First Name, Last Name, Address, City, State, and ZIP fields. Save the database as *Raintree*. Create mailing labels for all the names in the database so you can use them to send out your newsletter. Save the labels as *Raintree Labels*. Print the labels and close the file.

PROJECT H

Add the names and addresses of fifteen more potential home buyers to the *Raintree* database. Save the database as *Prospective*. Open *Open House Letter*. Add an inside address by inserting merge fields that contain the appropriate information. Add the First Name merge field after the salutation. Merge the main document with the data source to create personalized form letters to send to each prospective buyer. Save the file as *Open House Form Letters*. Use the Query Option to filter out two of the letters and print them. Close *Open House Letter* and *Open House Form Letters*.

PROJECT I

Use the *Prospective* database to create mailing labels for all the prospective home buyers. Save the mailing labels as *Prospective Labels*. Print the labels and close both files.

INTEGRATION SIMULATION

Java Internet Café

MARCH 15

All membership fees for March were due on March 1. A few members have not paid their monthly dues. Your manager asks you to write a letter to the members as a reminder.

1. Open *Payment Late Letter* from the Simulation template disk.

2. Save as *Payment Late Merge Letter* to your Simulation template disk.

3. Open Excel and *Computer Prices* from the Simulation template disk.

4. Copy A1 through B11 and paste it between the first and second paragraphs of the *Payment Late Merge Letter.* Make sure there are two blank lines before and after the spreadsheet.

5. Close *Computer Prices* without saving and exit Excel.

6. Open Access and the *Java Members* database and the *Membership* table from the Simulation template disk.

7. David Stanley just paid his membership fee. Key $10.00 in the March Paid field of his record.

8. Add the following new member to the end of the database:

   Ms. Zellie Williams, 1290 Wood Crest Apt. 224, Boulder, CO 80302, March Paid = $10

9. Save the Layout and switch to Word.

10. Use the Mail Merge Helper to create form letters using the open database and Word document. Insert the merge fields as shown in Figure III-9.

FIGURE III-9

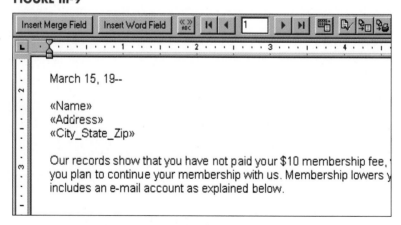

11. Use Query Options to create a query to merge the form letters for records with 0 in the March Paid field. (There should be three form letters.)

12. Save the new document as *Payment Late Form Letters* on your Simulation template disk.

13. Print the three form letters.

14. Close *Payment Late Form Letters*.

15. Save and close *Payment Late Merge Letter* and exit Word.

16. Close *Java Members* and exit Access.

MARCH 16

You need to create mailing labels for the form letters you just printed.

1. Open a blank Word document.

2. Use the Mail Merge Helper to create mailing labels for the three letters you just printed.

3. Use the *Java Members* database as the Data Source and the Active Window as the Main Document.

4. Choose the *Avery Standard 5162 - Address* labels.

5. Insert the merge fields Name, Address, and City_State_Zip onto the sample label.

6. Use Query Options to create a query to merge only the records with 0 in the March Paid field. Merge the data into a new document.

7. Highlight the labels and change the font size to 14 pt.

8. Save the labels document as *March Late Labels* on your Simulation template disk.

9. Print the labels and close.

10. Close the unsaved document without saving changes and exit Word.

11. Close *Java Members* and exit Access.

UNIT 5

MICROSOFT SCHEDULE+ AND MICROSOFT POWERPOINT

USING SCHEDULE+

OBJECTIVES
When you complete this chapter, you will be able to:

1. Start Schedule+.

2. Create a schedule.

3. Identify parts of the Schedule+ screen.

4. Add an appointment to the schedule.

5. Add a group meeting.

6. Add a special event.

7. Create a to do list.

8. Create a contact list.

9. Access an existing schedule.

10. Print a schedule, to do list, and contact list.

Introducing Schedule+

Schedule+ is a software program that helps you manage your time at work, as well as your personal time. By adding information such as appointments, meetings, and special events to an Appointment Book, you create a schedule of commitments. The Appointment Book information or schedule can be viewed in a daily, weekly, or monthly format.

In addition to your schedule, you can create a To Do List of projects and related tasks. Also, mailing and phone information can be entered into a Contact List of clients or people with whom you have meetings and appointments.

You can print a schedule, To Do List, and Contact List in various formats and page layouts.

Starting Schedule+

You open Schedule+ from the Programs menu. Depending on what settings the previous users of Schedule+ have chosen, a Group Enabling dialog box may appear. If you choose to work alone, the Schedule+ Logon box appears as in Figure 15-1.

In the User name box, you key your name as the owner of the schedule. When a new schedule opens, your name will appear at the top of the Schedule+ screen. After you click OK, the Microsoft Schedule+ dialog box appears.

FIGURE 15-1
The Schedule+ Logon box is where you key
your name as the owner of the schedule.

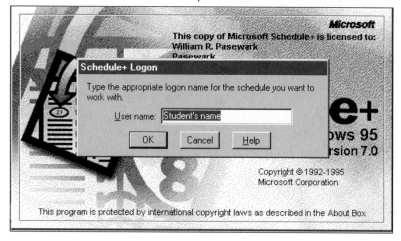

ACTIVITY

15-1 Starting Schedule+

1. With Windows 95 running, choose **Microsoft Schedule+** on the **Programs** menu. If the Group Enabling dialog box appears, click **No, work alone.**

2. Click **OK.** The Schedule+ Logon box appears as shown in Figure 15-1.

3. With the existing name highlighted (previous user) in the User name box, key **your name.**

4. Click **OK.** If you are not the previous user of Schedule+ on your computer, the Microsoft Schedule+ dialog box appears, as shown in Figure 15-2.

5. Leave the dialog box open for the next activity.

Creating a New Schedule

The Microsoft Schedule+ dialog box, shown in Figure 15-2, allows you to create a new schedule file or choose an existing one. When you want to create a new schedule file, choose the first option, *I want to create a new schedule file*, and click OK. You will learn how to access an existing schedule later in this chapter.

After you choose to create a new schedule, the Select Local Schedule dialog box appears as shown in Figure 15-3. You key the name of your schedule file in the File name box. In the Save in box, choose the drive where you want

FIGURE 15-2
The Microsoft Schedule+ dialog box allows you to create a new schedule file or open an existing one.

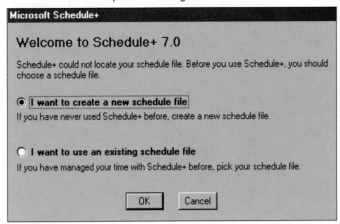

FIGURE 15-3
You name and save your schedule file using the Select Local Schedule dialog box.

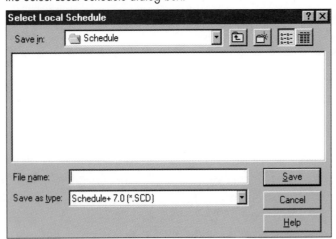

to save your file, then Save. Unless you choose another directory, Schedule+ will save your schedule in the MSOffice Schedule folder. In the workplace, this is the most convenient way to access your schedule. In this chapter, you will save your schedule to your data disk. This allows you to access your schedule from another computer and eliminates the use of space on your hard drive.

After saving, the Schedule+ screen (Figure 15-4) appears. This is where you enter your appointments, meetings, events, to do items, and contacts.

FIGURE 15-4
The Schedule+ screen is where you enter appointments, meetings, events, to do items, and contacts.

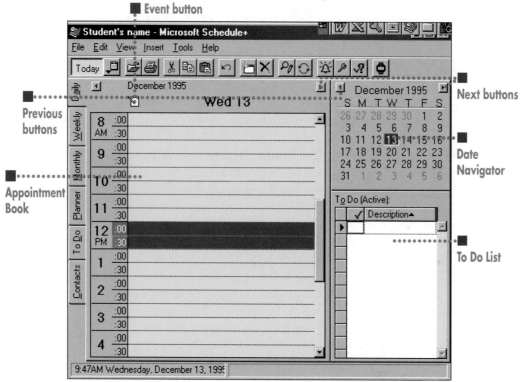

ACTIVITY

Creating a New Schedule

1. With the Microsoft Schedule+ dialog box displayed, click the option, **I want to create a new schedule file.**

2. Click **OK.** The Select Local Schedule dialog box appears as shown in Figure 15-3.

3. Place your data disk in drive A.

4. In the Save in box, choose drive A.

5. In the File name box, key the name of your schedule as follows: **Schedulexxx**. Key your initials to replace the last three *x*'s.

6. Click **Save.**

7. Your name will appear at the top of a new Schedule+ screen as shown in Figure 15-4.

8. Leave the schedule open for the next activity.

Identifying Parts of the Schedule+ Screen

You enter data for your schedule in the Schedule+ screen (shown in Figure 15-4). On the left side of the screen are six tabs that create different views of the schedule. The *Daily, Weekly,* and *Monthly* **tabs** display the schedule in those formats. The Daily tab is the default view. The *Planner* **tab** displays scheduled meetings and the names of the attendees. The *To Do* **tab** displays an extended view of all tasks and projects. The *Contacts* **tab** lists information about your contacts.

The *Appointment Book* is the highlighted area in the center of the screen. Appointments are entered and displayed here beside the appropriate times. Use the Next or Previous button to move to another day (or week or month).

Use the *Event* button, located directly above the Appointment Book, to enter special occasions such as birthdays or anniversaries. Schedule+ reminds you of the event by displaying it on the appropriate day.

Use the *Date Navigator,* the monthly calendar at the top right, to change dates by clicking directly on the requested date. To move quickly to Today or another date, click the right mouse button (also called right-clicking) in the Date Navigator to display a Date box and key the date. Click the Next or Previous button at the top of the Date Navigator to move to another month.

The *To Do (Active)* **List,** located at the bottom right, allows you to enter tasks and group them by project. Tasks and projects are maintained from this area or from the To Do tab.

The Schedule+ screen is described in more detail later in this chapter.

ACTIVITY

Displaying the Daily, Weekly, and Monthly Views of a Schedule

1. Using the **Date Navigator,** click on to-morrow's date. The daily schedule for to-morrow appears.

2. Click **Next** in the Date Navigator to move to the next month.

3. Click the **Weekly** tab to display a five day (Monday–Friday) schedule.

4. Click the **Previous** button to move to the previous week.

5. Click the **Monthly** tab to display a month of scheduled information.

6. Click **Next** to move one month ahead.

7. Click the **Daily** tab.

8. Right-click on the **Date Navigator.** A pop-up menu appears.

9. Click **Today** with the left mouse button to return quickly to today's schedule.

10. Leave the schedule open for the next activity.

Adding an Appointment

You add appointments to a schedule from the Daily schedule screen. Use the Date Navigator to choose the date for the appointment. In the Appointment Book, choose the appointment time by clicking on the start time and dragging through to the end time.

To enter the appointment information, choose Appointment from the Insert menu. The Appointment dialog box appears as shown in Figure 15-5. In the When box, check that the Start and End times and the date are correct. If necessary, click the up or down arrows to change the time. Select the All day option if the appointment is scheduled for the entire day. In the Description box, key a brief description of the appointment including the name of the person with whom you are meeting.

Other options within the Appointment dialog box further describe the appointment. If the option is chosen, its icon appears within the description. Key the location of the appointment in the Where box, which has a small building icon. The Set Reminder option has a bell icon and determines the number of

FIGURE 15-5
Enter appointment information in the Appointment dialog box.

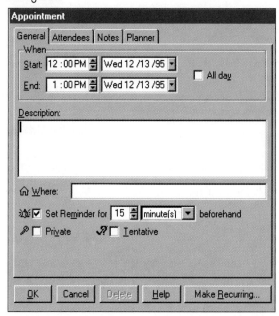

minutes (hours, days, weeks, or months) for Schedule+ to notify you before the appointment. The Private option has a key icon and prevents other users from viewing the appointment information. The Tentative option has a check mark and question mark icon and lets you know the time or place is questionable.

When you have entered all the necessary information about the appointment, click OK to return to the Appointment Book. You'll see the information in the ruled area next to the appointment time.

To edit an appointment, double-click its border. The Appointment dialog box appears for you to make changes. To delete an appointment, double-click the border and choose Delete. To reschedule an appointment, double-click the border and change the Start and End times and dates.

ACTIVITY

Adding an Appointment

● ●

1. Click tomorrow's date in the Date Navigator.

2. Highlight the appointment time by clicking on **12:00 p.m.** and dragging through to **1:00 p.m.** as shown in Figure 15-6.

3. Choose **Appointment** from the **Insert** menu. The Appointment dialog box appears as shown in Figure 15-5.

4. In the Description box, key **Lunch Appointment with John Cole**.

5. In the Where box, key **Corner Deli**.

6. Click the **Set Reminder** box to insert a check mark if it isn't chosen already.

7. Increase the minutes for the reminder from fifteen to thirty by clicking the up arrow until 30 appears in the box.

8. Click the **Private** box.

9. Click the **Tentative** box.

10. Click **OK.** The appointment information and icons appear on the Daily schedule screen.

11. Right-click on the **Date Navigator.** A pop-up menu appears.

12. Click **Today** to return quickly to today's schedule.

13. Leave the schedule open for the next activity.

FIGURE 15-6
Highlight the appointment time by clicking on 12:00 p.m. and dragging through to 1:00 p.m.

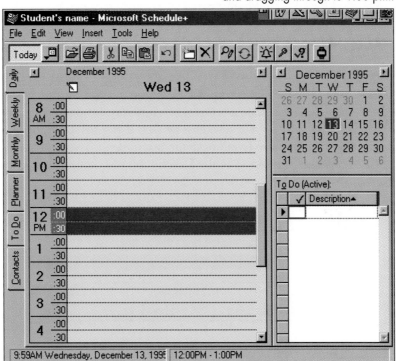

Adding a Group Meeting

A Group Meeting has more than one person attending. To schedule group meetings in Schedule+, you must first be on a network with other people who use Schedule+. Also, you must be working in a group-enabled mode and not working alone. At the beginning of this chapter, you chose to work alone. You must exit Schedule+ and start again in a group-enabled mode to schedule a group meeting.

To change an appointment into a meeting with others, edit the appointment and select the Attendees tab. Choose the Invite Others option and highlight the names of the people to attend the meeting. When you have finished, a Meeting Request screen appears to send a message through the network to the attendees. Remember, the Invite Others option appears only if you chose to work in a group-enabled mode.

To find free time for scheduling meetings, click the Planner tab. Your schedule over a three to four day period will display, with the busy times highlighted. If you are working in a group-enabled mode, you will also view the schedules of the other people using Schedule+.

Adding a Special Event

D uring the year, there are special events or occasions you may wish to remember. These might include a co-worker's birthday or anniversary.

You add an event to your schedule by first using the Date Navigator to choose the date. Then choose Event from the Insert menu. The Event dialog box appears as shown in Figure 15-7. In the Description box, key a brief description of the event.

FIGURE 15-7
Enter event information in the Event dialog box.

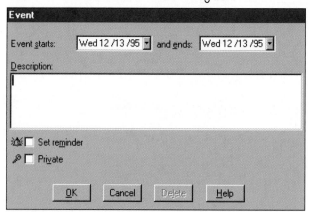

If you need a reminder, choose the Set Reminder option. Select the Private option to prevent other users from viewing the event. Choose OK when you are finished. The event icon—a pencil and note pad—along with the event information will be shown at the top of your Daily schedule.

ACTIVITY

 **Adding an Event**

1. Click on the date one week from today in the Date Navigator.

2. Choose **Event** from the **Insert** menu. The Event dialog box appears as shown in Figure 15-7.

3. In the Description box, key **John's Birthday**.

4. Click the **Set reminder** box if it's not already chosen.

5. Change *minute(s)* to *day(s)* by clicking the down arrow and choosing *day(s)*.

6. Change the number of day(s) from 15 to 1 by clicking the down arrow until 1 appears in the box.

7. Click the **Private** box.

8. Click **OK.** The event appears at the top of the Appointment Book.

9. Use the **Date Navigator** to return quickly to today's schedule.

10. Leave the schedule open for the next activity.

Creating a To Do List

A To Do List consists of tasks and projects to be done. A *task* is any activity you want to perform and monitor to its completion. A *project* is a group of related tasks. An example project might be Report Processing, with the related tasks of Sorting, Distribution, and Filing.

Adding a New Project

You can add a new project by right-clicking the To Do (Active) List at the bottom right of the screen and choosing New Project from the pop-up menu. The Project dialog box appears as shown in Figure 15-8. Key the name of your project in the Name box, and choose its priority using the up and down arrows.

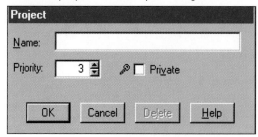

ACTIVITY

15-6 Adding Two Projects to Your To Do List

1. Right-click on the **To Do (Active)** List and choose **New Project** from the pop-up menu. The Project dialog box appears as shown in Figure 15-8.

2. In the Name box, key **Filing**.

3. Set the priority to **2** by clicking the down arrow.

4. Click **OK.**

5. To add the second project, right-click on the **To Do (Active)** List and again choose **New Project.**

6. In the Name box, key **Typing**.

7. Set the priority to **1** by clicking the down arrow.

8. Click **OK.**

9. To view the new projects, click the **To Do** tab located on the left side of the Daily Schedule screen. The projects appear listed by project.

10. Click the **Daily** tab to return to the Daily schedule screen.

11. Leave the schedule open for the next activity.

Adding a New Task

Remember that a project is a group of related tasks. You can add a task to a project by right-clicking on the To Do (Active) List and choosing New Task. The Task dialog box appears as shown in Figure 15-9. Key the task in the Description box, group the task to a project, set its priority, and set your reminder and private options. Then click OK.

FIGURE 15-9
Enter new tasks in the Task dialog box.

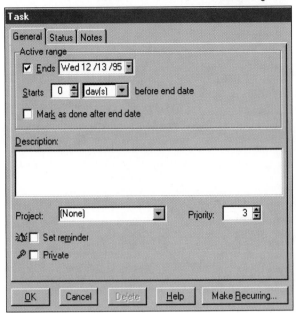

A C T I V I T Y

Adding Two Tasks to Your To Do List

1. To add the first task, right-click on the **To Do (Active)** List and choose **New Task** from the pop-up menu. The Task dialog box appears as shown in Figure 15-9.

2. In the Description box, key **Type Letters**.

3. In the Project box, click the down arrow and click **Typing.**

4. Click **OK.** The task will appear in the To Do (Active) List on the Daily schedule screen.

5. To add the second task, right-click on the **To Do (Active)** List and choose **New Task.** The Task dialog box appears.

6. In the Description box, key **File Daily Reports**.

7. In the Project box, click the down arrow and click **Filing.**

8. Click **OK.** The task will appear in the To Do (Active) box on the Daily schedule screen.

9. Leave the schedule open for the next activity.

Viewing the To Do List

To view the To Do List, click the To Do tab located at the left side of the Daily schedule screen. The To Do List will appear, grouped by project as shown in Figure 15-10. To select a different order or grouping, click and choose one of the options from the View menu as discussed in Table 15-1.

FIGURE 15-10
The To Do tab displays tasks grouped by project.

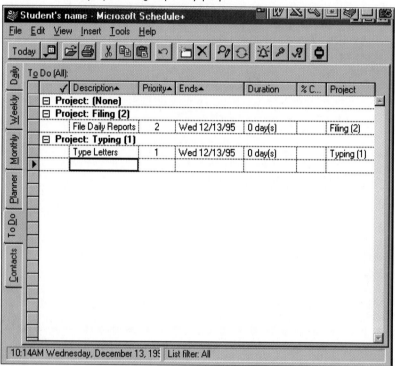

TABLE 15-1
View command options for a To Do List.

COMMAND	PURPOSE
Columns	To choose the columns to show in the To Do List
Group By	To group the projects and tasks up to three levels
Sort	To choose the order for the tasks to be listed; if Group By is used, the order will be within each group
Filter	To choose only specific tasks by completion date
Autosort	To sort the list automatically if a change is made
Sort Now	To sort the list now, if Autosort is not checked

ACTIVITY

15-8 Viewing and Grouping the To Do List by Priority

1. Click the **To Do** tab located on the left side of the Daily schedule screen. The To Do screen appears with the tasks grouped by project, as shown in Figure 15-10.

2. Choose **Group By** from the **View** menu. The Group by dialog box appears, as shown in Figure 15-11.

3. In the Group tasks by box, click the down arrow. A list of options to group by will appear.

4. Click **Priority** and click **OK.** The To Do screen appears with the tasks grouped by priority.

5. Click the **Daily** tab to return to the Daily schedule screen.

6. Leave the schedule open for the next activity.

FIGURE 15-11
The Group by dialog box allows you to view your To Do List in a different order.

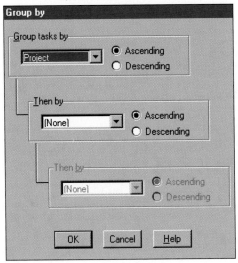

Creating a Contact List

A Contact List consists of mailing and phone information on clients or people with whom you have meetings and appointments. The list can be viewed in different sorted orders and groups by using the Contacts tab and View command.

Adding a Contact

To add a new client to your Contact list, click the Insert menu and choose Contact. The Contact dialog box appears as shown in Figure 15-12. Notice the four tabs at the top of the box. The Business tab includes mailing and other information, such as the contact's title and company name. The Phone tab has the business, fax, and other numbers. The Address tab has personal information, such as the home address and phone number. Notes is a box for keying additional information about the client. You can choose the appropriate tabs and key the information that is important for each contact.

FIGURE 15-12
Enter client information in the Contact dialog box.

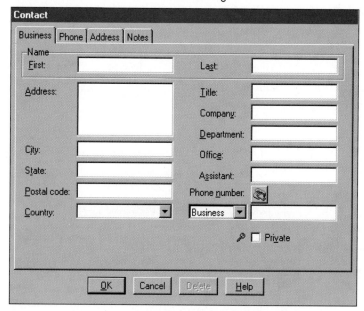

1. Choose **Contact** from the **Insert** menu. The Contact dialog box appears as shown in Figure 15-12. Click the Business tab if necessary.

2. In the First name box, key **Mark**.

3. Press **Tab.**

4. In the Last name box, key **Johnson** and press **Tab.**

5. In the Address box, key **1000 Airline Drive** and press **Tab.**

6. For the remaining boxes, key the information as shown in Figure 15-13.

FIGURE 15-13
To add the first contact, key the information from this figure.

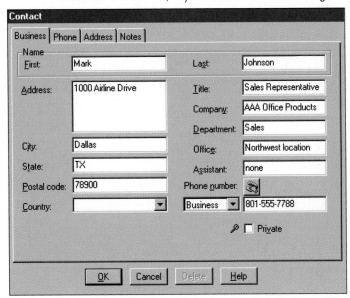

7. After completing the information, click **OK.** The Daily schedule screen appears.

8. Choose **Contact** from the **Insert** menu. The Contact dialog box appears.

9. To add a second contact, key the information as shown in Figure 15-14.

10. When finished, click **OK.** The Daily schedule screen appears.

FIGURE 15-14
To add the second contact, key the information from this figure.

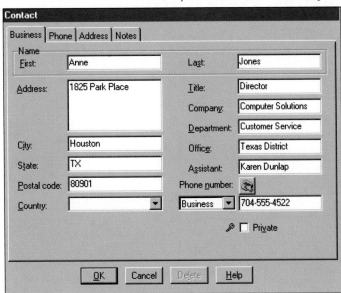

FIGURE 15-15
To add the third contact, key the information from this figure.

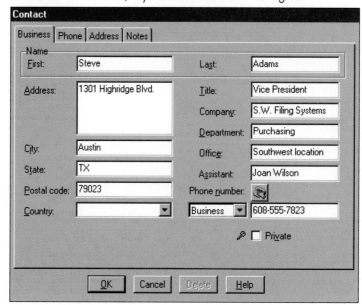

11. Choose **Contact** from the **Insert** menu. The Contact dialog box appears.

12. Add the third contact as shown in Figure 15-15.

13. When finished, click **OK.** The Daily schedule screen appears.

14. Leave the schedule open for the next activity.

Viewing the Contact List

To view the Contact list, click the Contacts tab located at the left side of the Daily schedule screen. The Contact list appears sorted by last name, as shown in Figure 15-16. To select a different order or grouping, click and choose one of the options from the View menu as previously discussed in Table 15-1.

FIGURE 15-16
The Contacts tab lists contacts sorted by last name.

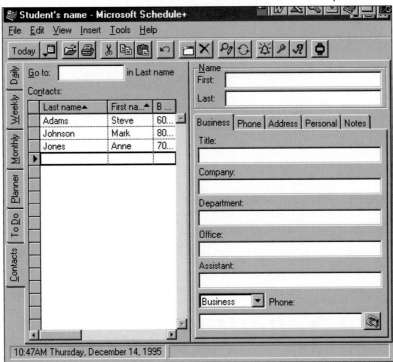

FIGURE 15-16
The Contacts tab lists contacts sorted by last name.

ACTIVITY

15-10 Viewing and Sorting the Contact List

1. Click the **Contacts** tab located on the left side of the Daily schedule screen. The Contact tab screen appears as shown in Figure 15-16.

2. Choose **Sort** from the **View** menu. The Sort dialog box appears as shown in Figure 15-17.

3. In the Sort contacts by box, click the down arrow. A list of options to sort by will appear.

4. Click **First name** and click **OK.** The Contacts tab screen appears with the Contacts sorted by first name.

5. Click the **Daily** tab to return to the Daily schedule screen.

6. Leave the schedule open for the next activity.

FIGURE 15-17
The Sort dialog box allows you to view your Contact List in a different order.

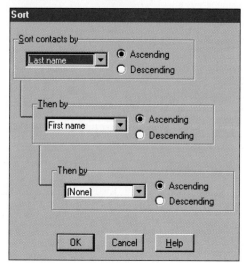

Exiting Schedule+

You quit Schedule+ by choosing Exit from the File menu. Always remove your data disk from the drive before leaving the computer.

ACTIVITY

 **Exiting Schedule+**

● ●

1. From the Daily schedule screen, choose **Exit** from the **File** menu.

2. Your schedule will close and the Microsoft Windows 95 screen appears.

3. Remove your data disk from drive A.

Accessing an Existing Schedule

The Schedule+ dialog box, as shown in Figure 15-18, allows you to create a new schedule file or choose an existing one. When you want to access an existing schedule file, choose the second option, *I want to use an existing schedule file*, and click OK.

After you choose to use an existing schedule, the Select Local Schedule dialog box appears as shown in Figure 15-19. Access the correct drive and highlight the name of your schedule file in the Look in box, then choose Open. The Schedule+ screen appears with your schedule file to update.

FIGURE 15-18

The Microsoft Schedule+ dialog box allows you to create
a new schedule file or open an existing one.

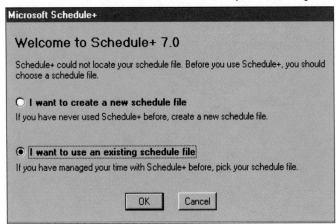

FIGURE 15-19

You access your existing schedule file using the
Select Local Schedule dialog box.

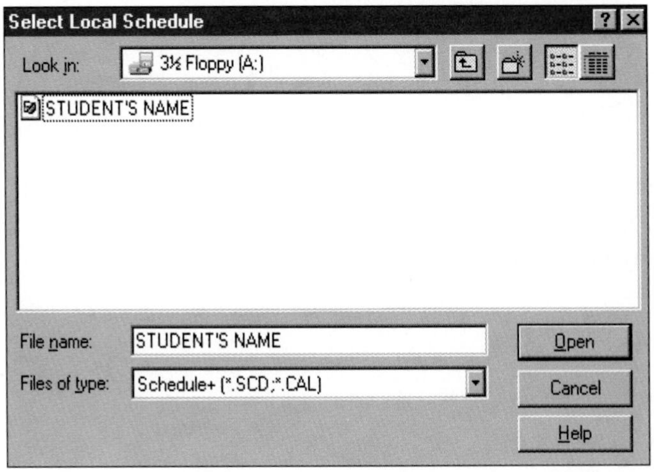

1. With Windows 95 running, start **Microsoft Schedule+.** If the Group Enabling dialog box appears, click **No, work alone.**

2. Click **OK.** The Schedule+ Logon box appears.

3. With the existing name highlighted in the User name box, key **your name**.

4. Click **OK.** The Microsoft Schedule+ dialog box appears.

5. Place the data disk with your saved schedule in drive A.

6. With the Welcome to Schedule+ dialog box displayed, click the option, **I want to use an existing schedule file.**

7. Click **OK.** The Select Local Schedule dialog box appears as shown in Figure 15-19.

8. Click your schedule name. The File name box updates with the chosen name.

9. Click **Open.**

10. The schedule with a Daily Reminder box listing your To Do items will display.

11. Leave the schedule open for the next activity.

Printing a Schedule, To Do List, and Contact List

You can print your schedule, To Do List, and Contact List in various formats and print layouts. Use the Date Navigator to choose the beginning date for the printed item.

To enter the print information, choose Print from the File menu. The Print dialog box appears as shown in Figure 15-20. In the Print layout box, choose one of the layout styles. See Table 15-2 for a description of each layout.

FIGURE 15-20

Enter print information in the Print dialog box.

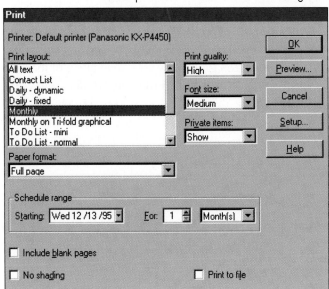

TABLE 15-2

Print layout options.

PRINT LAYOUT	DESCRIPTION OF PRINTED INFORMATION
All text	All the information in your schedule
Contact List	Your contact list
Daily–dynamic	Your daily appointments, without the To Do List
Daily–fixed	Your daily appointments, with the To Do List
Monthly	Your schedule, one month per page
Monthly on Tri-fold graphical	Your schedule by month with a one-year calendar in the center
To Do List–mini	Prints only the priority, task description, and due date
To Do List–normal	Prints only the priority, task description, start date, and end date
To Do List–text	Prints only the task description
Weekly–5 day	Prints a 5-day weekly schedule
Weekly–7 day	Prints a 7-day weekly schedule

In the Paper format box, you can choose to print the full page or choose the same manufacturer's format as your organizer. Display the formats by clicking the down arrow in the box.

In the Schedule range box, be sure the Starting date is correct. Also, choose the number of days, weeks, or months to print and click OK.

Click the Preview button to see how your schedule will look when printed. Choose the Cancel button to cancel the Print command.

ACTIVITY

15-13 Printing a Schedule

● ●

1. Choose **Print** from the **File** menu. The Print dialog box appears as shown in Figure 15-20.

2. In the Print layout box, click **Monthly.**

3. In the Paper format box, leave **Full page** as the selection.

4. Click **Preview.** Your schedule will display for you to preview.

5. Click **Zoom In** to get a closer look.

6. Click **Close** to exit Preview and return to the Print dialog box.

7. Click **OK.** Your schedule will print in a monthly format for one month beginning with tomorrow's date.

8. Exit Schedule+ by choosing **Exit** from the **File** menu.

Summary

- Schedule+ is a software program that helps you manage your time at work, as well as your personal time. The Schedule+ screen is where you enter appointments, meetings, events, to do items, and contacts.

- When adding an appointment, you can set a reminder to notify you minutes (hours, days, weeks, or months) before the appointment. To change an appointment into a meeting with others attending, you can edit the appointment and add attendees.

- During the year, there are special events or occasions you may wish to remember. You can add these to your schedule.

- You can create a To Do List consisting of tasks and projects. The Tasks are grouped into Projects and given a priority. You can also create a Contact List consisting of mailing and phone information on clients or people with whom you have meetings and appointments. These lists also can be sorted and viewed in different orders and groupings.

- You can print your schedule, To Do List, and Contact List in various formats and layouts.

● ● ● ● ● ● ● ● ● ● ● ● ● ●

REVIEW ACTIVITIES

TRUE/FALSE

Circle T or F to show whether the statement is true or false.

T F **1.** Parts of the Schedule+ screen include the Appointment Book and Date Navigator.

T F **2.** The Weekly, Monthly, and Yearly tabs on the Schedule+ screen display your schedule in those formats.

T F **3.** The Planner tab displays busy times for the next three to four weeks.

T F **4.** To enter appointment information, choose Appointment from the Insert menu.

T F **5.** You cannot reschedule an appointment.

T F **6.** To schedule a group meeting, you do not need to be on a network with the other people who use Schedule+.

T F **7.** Related tasks on your To Do List can be grouped into projects.

T F **8.** To view your Contact List, click the Contacts tab located at the left side of the Schedule+ screen.

T F **9.** In Schedule+ you can create a new schedule but you cannot access an existing one.

T F **10.** You can print your schedule, To Do List, and Contact List in various formats and layouts.

COMPLETION

Write the correct answer in the space provided.

1. What does Schedule+ help you to manage?

_____

2. What part of the Schedule+ screen contains a calendar for changing dates?

_____

3. What does the To Do tab display?

_____

4. How do you choose the time when adding a new appointment?

_____

5. When adding an appointment, what does the Private option prevent?

_____

6. How do you edit an appointment?

_____

7. What mode should you be working in to schedule a group meeting?

_____

8. What do you add to your schedule to remember a friend's birthday?

_____

9. Which menu allows you to select a different order or grouping for your To Do List?

_____

10. What type of information is contained within your Contact List?

_____

REINFORCEMENT APPLICATIONS

application 15 - 1

1. Start Schedule+.

2. Access your existing schedule from your data disk.

3. Use the Date Navigator to select tomorrow's date for a new appointment.

4. Highlight the appointment time from 2:00 p.m. to 4:00 p.m.

5. Add the appointment, *Training Session with Staff*.

6. Add the location of the appointment, *Training Room 5*.

7. Set a reminder for one hour before the appointment.

8. Print your schedule and choose Daily–dynamic as the print layout.

9. Exit Schedule+.

application 15 - 2

1. Start Schedule+.

2. Access your existing schedule from your data disk.

3. Use the Date Navigator to select the date one week from today for an event.

4. Add the event, *My Anniversary*.

5. Set a reminder for one day before the event date.

6. Print your schedule and choose Monthly as the print layout.

7. Exit Schedule+.

application 15 - 3

1. Start Schedule+.

2. Access your existing schedule from your data disk.

3. Use the Date Navigator to select tomorrow's date.

4. Add the task, *Type Invoices*.

5. Group the task with the *Typing* project.

6. Do not set a reminder.

7. Add another task, *File Time Sheets*.

8. Group the task with the *Filing* project.

9. Do not set a reminder.

10. Print your To Do List and choose To Do List–mini as the print layout.

11. Exit Schedule+.

POWERPOINT BASICS

CHAPTER

16

OBJECTIVES

When you complete this chapter, you will be able to:

1. Start PowerPoint.

2. Open an existing presentation.

3. Apply a design template.

4. Change a slide layout.

5. Add a slide to a presentation.

6. Change views and print.

7. Exit PowerPoint.

8. Create a new presentation.

9. Delete slides.

10. Add text to slides.

Introduction to PowerPoint

PowerPoint is an Office 95 application that can help you create a professional presentation. You can use PowerPoint to create slides, outlines, speaker's notes, and audience handouts. A presentation can include text, clip art, graphs, tables, charts, and even sound or video clips. Creating a presentation may seem like an intimidating prospect, but PowerPoint provides features such as templates and wizards to help make the process easier.

Starting PowerPoint

PowerPoint, like other Office 95 applications, is started from the desktop screen in Windows 95. One way to start PowerPoint is to click the Start button, select Programs, then choose Microsoft PowerPoint, as shown in Figure 16-1. After PowerPoint starts, a Tip of the Day may appear. Click OK to bring up the PowerPoint dialog box, as shown in Figure 16-2, where you can choose to create a new presentation or open an existing one. This dialog box also contains a Tip for New Users.

FIGURE 16-1
You can start PowerPoint from the Start menu.

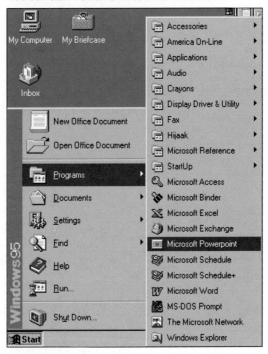

FIGURE 16-2
In the PowerPoint dialog box you can open an existing presentation or create a new one.

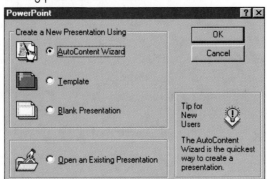

ACTIVITY

16-1 Starting PowerPoint

● ●

1. Click the **Start** button, click **Programs,** then choose **Microsoft PowerPoint** (see Figure 16-1). If you see a *What's New in Microsoft PowerPoint 95* screen, click the Close button.

2. PowerPoint starts. (If a Tip of the Day dialog box appears, click **OK.**)

3. The PowerPoint dialog box appears, as shown in Figure 16-2.

4. Leave the dialog box on the screen for the next activity.

Opening an Existing Presentation

When you want to open an existing presentation, choose the Open an Existing Presentation option in the PowerPoint dialog box. After you click OK, the File Open dialog box appears, where you locate and open the presentation. When you locate the presentation you want to open, a preview of the first slide displays. Choose Open and the first slide of the presentation will appear on the screen. To view the slides in a presentation, scroll up and down using the scroll bar.

You can go directly to the slide you want to view by moving the scroll box up or down until the label to the left of the scroll box shows the title and number of the correct slide (see Figure 16-3).

FIGURE 16-3
The label to the left of the scroll box displays the title and number of the slide currently on the screen.

Microsoft PowerPoint - Training Program

File Edit View Insert Format Tools Draw Window Help

Times New Roman | 24

Vision Statement

Slide: 2
Vision Statement

• To develop a comprehensive training program for new employees.

Slide 2 of 8 | Contemporary | New Slide... | Slide Layout...

Start | Microsoft PowerPoint... | 3:08 PM

ACTIVITY

16-2 Opening an Existing Presentation

1. With the PowerPoint dialog box on the screen, choose **Open an Existing Presentation.**

2. Click **OK.** The File Open dialog box appears.

3. Insert your template disk in drive A and locate *Activity 16-2.*

4. A preview of the first slide appears in the box to the right (see Figure 16-4).

5. Click **Open.** The presentation opens with the first slide displayed on the screen.

6. Click the down arrow at the bottom of the scroll bar on the right to scroll down and view each slide.

7. Go to the second slide by clicking the scroll box and moving it up until the label to the left reads *Slide: 2 Vision Statement,* as shown in Figure 16-3.

8. Leave the presentation open for use in the next activity.

FIGURE 16-4
In the File Open dialog box, you can preview the first
slide of your presentation before opening it.

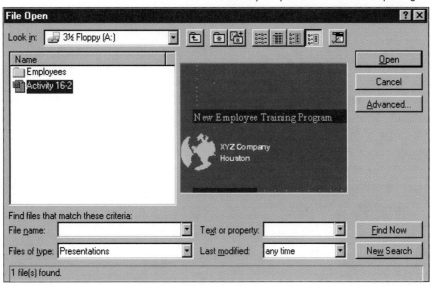

The Status Bar

he status bar, shown in Figure 16-5, appears just above the taskbar at the bottom of your screen. The first button on the status bar shows which slide is displayed. The second button indicates the design currently in use. The New Slide button provides a shortcut to the New Slide dialog box, where you can create new slides for your presentation. By clicking the Slide Layout button, you access the Slide Layout dialog box, which lets you chose the layout you want for the currently selected slide. You will learn more about designs, creating new slides, and changing slide layouts later in the chapter.

FIGURE 16-5
The status bar provides useful information and shortcuts.

Status
bar

Applying a Design Template

You can use a design template to change the appearance of your slides without changing the content. ***Design templates*** are predesigned graphic styles that can be applied to your slides. Using a design template, you can change the color scheme, font, formatting, and layout of your slides to create a different look.

To use a design template, access the Apply Design Template dialog box, shown in Figure 16-6, by double-clicking the design button on the status bar or choosing Apply Design Template from the Format menu. This dialog box contains the names of the different templates that come with the program. When you click the template in the Name box, the sample slide on the right changes to show the new design. Choose Apply to change all your slides to the new design.

FIGURE 16-6
You can access the Apply Design Template dialog box to use a design template.

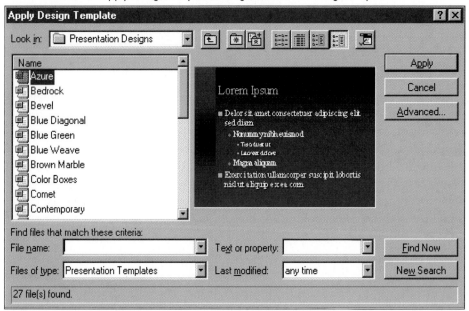

ACTIVITY

16-3 Applying a Design Template

● ●

1. Double-click the **Contemporary** button on the status bar. The Apply Design Template dialog box appears, as shown in Figure 16-6.

Contemporary

2. In the Name box on the left, click on **Bedrock** to highlight it. The sample slide changes to the Bedrock design.

3. Choose **Apply.** The presentation is displayed on your screen with a new design.

4. Scroll up and down to see that all the slides have been changed.

5. Save the presentation on your data disk as *XYZ Presentation*. Leave the presentation on your screen for the next activity.

Changing Slide Layout

When you want to easily change the layout of text or graphics on slides, you can use the program's preset layouts. PowerPoint includes twenty-four AutoLayouts for creating a new slide or changing the layout of an existing slide. The different layouts include placeholders for text, columns, bulleted lists, clip art, tables, organization charts, objects, graphs, and media clips. A *placeholder* reserves a space in the presentation for the type of information you want. Just click on a placeholder and replace it with your own information. You can choose the layout that best fits the need of a particular slide.

To change the layout for an existing slide, scroll to display the slide you want to change. Then, click the Slide Layout button on the status bar or choose Slide Layout from the Format menu. The Slide Layout dialog box contains small diagrams of the AutoLayouts. To change the layout, click a new layout and choose Apply.

16-4 Changing Slide Layout

• •

1. Display Slide 2.

2. Click the **Slide Layout** button on the status bar. The Slide Layout dialog box appears, as shown in Figure 16-7.

> Slide Layout...

3. Click on the first layout in the third row. The box to the right of the layout choices should say *Text & Clip Art.*

4. Choose **Apply.** The Vision Statement slide is displayed with the existing text and a placeholder for clip art, as shown in Figure 16-8.

5. Double-click the clip art placeholder. The Microsoft Clip Art Gallery 2.0 dialog box appears.

6. In the Categories box, scroll down to highlight *People,* as shown in Figure 16-9.

7. In the Pictures box, click the picture with the description, *Leadership,* as shown in Figure 16-10 with a box around it. (Your screen may not look exactly like the figure.) If that picture is not available, click another appropriate one.

8. Choose **Insert.**

FIGURE 16-7
You can change a slide layout by choosing one of the twenty-four AutoLayouts in the Slide Layout dialog box.

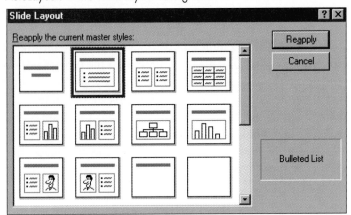

FIGURE 16-8
You can substitute your choice of clip art for the placeholder on the slide.

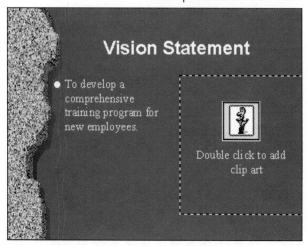

FIGURE 16-9
In the Categories box, choose the category of clip art that you want to view.

FIGURE 16-10
The Pictures box displays the clip art available in the category that is chosen.

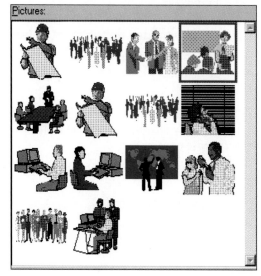

9. The Vision Statement slide is displayed with the clip art you chose. Click the clip art and drag to place it attractively on the slide if necessary.

10. Save the presentation and leave it on the screen for the next activity.

Adding a Slide

You can add a slide to a presentation by clicking the New Slide button on the status bar or the toolbar. This brings up the New Slide dialog box, which allows you to choose a layout for the new slide. The New Slide dialog box looks very similar to the Slide Layout dialog box and has the same twenty-four Auto-Layouts to choose from. When you choose a layout and click OK, the new slide is inserted into the presentation after the slide that is currently on the screen.

ACTIVITY

16-5 Adding a Slide

1. Display the sixth slide. The button on the left of the status bar should read *Slide 6 of 8*.

   New Slide...

2. Click the **New Slide** button on the status bar or on the toolbar. The New Slide dialog box appears.

3. Click the second layout in the first row if it is not already chosen. The box to the right of the layout choices should say *Bulleted List*.

4. Choose **OK.** A new slide with placeholders is displayed on the screen and the button to the left of the status bar now reads *Slide 7 of 9*.

5. Click on the slide in the box that reads *Click to add title*.

6. Key **Available Options**.

7. Click in the box that reads *Click to add text*.

8. Key **Equip each department to handle its own training.** Notice that PowerPoint automatically formats the bulleted item.

9. Press **Return,** then **Tab.** Pressing Tab automatically indents the text one more level.

10. Key the remaining text shown in Figure 16-11.

11. Save the presentation.

FIGURE 16-11
Key text to make your new slide appear as shown in this figure.

FIGURE 16-11
Key text to make your new slide appear as shown in this figure.

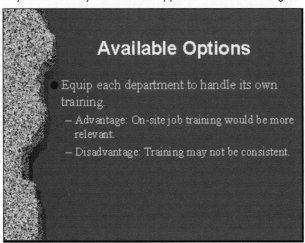

Changing Views and Printing

You can view a presentation five different ways. Each button on the bottom left of the screen, shown in Figure 16-12, corresponds with one of the five views. To change views, click the button for the view you want. You can also change views by choosing the view you want from the View menu.

You have been working in Slide view. This view displays one slide at a time and is useful for adding text or modifying the slide's appearance. Outline view shows the slide titles and main text in outline form. Slide Sorter view displays miniature versions of the slides on screen so that you can move and arrange them easily. Notes Pages view shows a slide on top with room on the bottom to create notes that can be used when giving the presentation. Using Slide Show view, each slide fills the screen and you can run your presentation on the computer as if it were a slide projector.

The Print dialog box gives you the option of printing your presentation in Slide view, Outline view, or Notes Pages view. You can also print handouts with either two, three, or six slides per page. You can choose to print all the

FIGURE 16-12
You can click a button to change the view of your presentation.

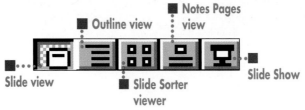

slides, only the current slide, or any combination of slides in your presentation. To be sure the slides will print on the page correctly, there is a Scale to Fit Paper option.

Changing Views and Printing

●●●

1. Click the **Slide Sorter View** button. The screen appears as shown in Figure 16-13.

2. Click on Slide 8 so that it is outlined in bold.

3. Click Slide 8 again and hold the mouse button down so that a little box is visible at the bottom of the pointer and a line appears between Slide 8 and Slide 9.

FIGURE 16-13
Slide Sorter view displays miniature versions of the slides on screen.

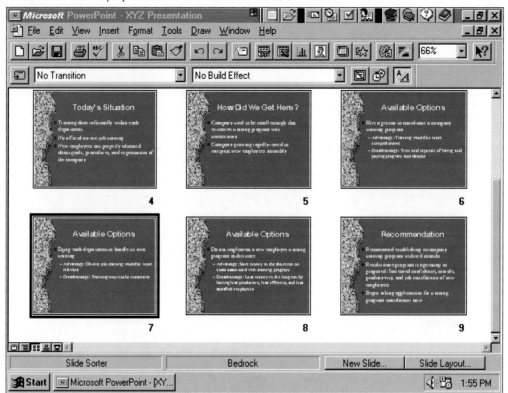

4. Still holding down the mouse button, drag the pointer up to Slide 5 so the line is now between Slide 5 and Slide 6.

5. Release the mouse button. Slide 8 moves to become Slide 6 and all other slides move down and are renumbered.

6. Choose **Outline** from the **View** menu. The presentation appears in the form of an outline.

7. Choose **Print** from the **File** menu. The Print dialog box appears.

8. In the Print what box, click the down arrow to the right and scroll down to choose Outline View. Click **OK.** The presentation prints in outline view.

9. Scroll up to the top of the outline and click on slide number 1 to highlight it.

10. Click the **Slide Show** button.

11. The first slide will appear on your screen as if you were giving a presentation. Click the left mouse button to advance through all the slides. When all the slides have been displayed, click the left mouse button to return to the Outline view.

12. Save the presentation and leave it open for use in the next activity.

Closing a Presentation and Exiting PowerPoint

When you want to close a presentation, choose Close from the File menu or click the presentation's Close box. To exit PowerPoint, choose Exit from the File menu or click the PowerPoint Close box in the upper right corner of the screen. If there are any unsaved changes to a presentation you have been working on, you will be asked if you want to save them before exiting.

ACTIVITY

Exiting PowerPoint

1. Choose **Close** from the **File** menu to close the presentation.

2. Choose **Exit** from the **File** menu to exit PowerPoint.

Creating a Presentation

From the PowerPoint dialog box that appears when you start Power-Point, you have three choices for creating a presentation: the AutoContent Wizard, a template, or a blank presentation. Using the *AutoContent Wizard,* you will be guided through a series of questions about the type of presentation, the style, the length, and the type of output you want. The wizard will then create a new presentation based on your answers. The templates that come with PowerPoint are already designed and formatted with certain colors, fonts, and layouts. If you decide to create a presentation using a template, you will be able to choose one that is right for the presentation you have planned. To start a presentation from scratch, choose the *blank presentation* option. This allows you to create a presentation using whatever layout, format, colors, and style you prefer. Unless you have a particular reason for creating a presentation from a blank document, it is easier to use the wizard or a template. You can always modify the presentation to suit your needs as you go along.

ACTIVITY

16-8 Creating a Presentation Using the AutoContent Wizard

1. Start PowerPoint and close the Tip of the Day dialog box if necessary.

2. With the PowerPoint dialog box on the screen, choose **AutoContent Wizard.**

3. Click **OK.** The AutoContent Wizard dialog box appears, as shown in Figure 16-14.

4. Read the screen, then click **Next >.**

5. Highlight the data in the What is your name? box and key **your name**. Press **Tab.**

6. Key **Copier Purchase for Office** in the What are you going to talk about? box. Press **Tab.**

7. Key **Mesa Foundation** in the Other information you'd like to display? box.

8. Click **Next >.**

9. Choose **Reporting Progress** as the type of presentation you're going to give. Click **Next >.**

10. Choose **Default** in the Select visual style for the presentation box.

11. Choose **30 minutes or less** in the How long do you want to present? box. Click **Next >.**

12. Choose **On-screen presentation** in the What type of output will you use? box.

FIGURE 16-14
The AutoContent Wizard helps you create a presentation quickly.

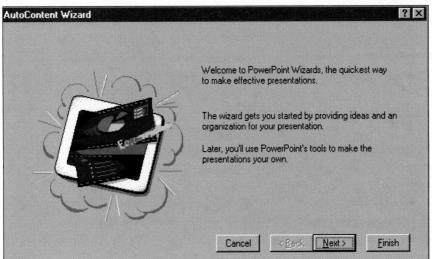

13. Choose **Yes** in the Will you print handouts? box.

14. Click **Next >.** Choose **Finish.** The first slide of your presentation appears on the screen.

15. Save the presentation as *Copier Presentation*.

Deleting Slides

A presentation created using the AutoContent Wizard includes a predetermined number of slides based on the type of presentation you chose. If you decide that a slide does not fit your presentation, you can easily delete it. With that slide displayed, choose Delete Slide from the Edit menu. If you accidentally delete the wrong one, immediately choose Undo Delete Slide from the Edit menu to restore the slide.

A C T I V I T Y

16-9 Deleting Slides

1. Display Slide 3, titled *Overall Status*.

2. Choose **Delete Slide** from the **Edit** menu. The slide is deleted.

3. Display Slide 5, titled *Component Two: Background* and delete it.

5. Save the presentation.

4. Display Slide 5, now titled *Component Two: Status* and delete it.

Adding Text to Slides

When the AutoContent Wizard helps you create a presentation, it creates placeholders on each slide that tell you what kind of information might go there. To replace a text placeholder, click on the text. A box appears around the text. You can then highlight the existing text and key your own text.

If you cannot see the text clearly, it is helpful to use the Zoom feature. Choose Zoom from the View menu to display the Zoom dialog box. There are preset percentages so that you can enlarge or reduce the size of the presentation on screen, or you can customize the percentage in the Percent box.

ACTIVITY

 **16-10** **Adding Text to Slides**

1. Display Slide 2. Click where it reads *Define the Subject*. A box appears around the text.

2. Highlight the existing text, then key **Office Copier Purchase**.

3. Click on the bulleted text. Highlight the first bulleted item, then key the text as it appears in Figure 16-15. Highlight the second bulleted item and do the same.

FIGURE 16-15
Key the text to make your slide appear as the figure does.

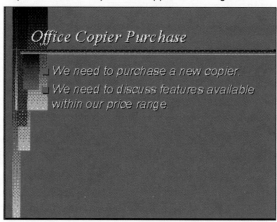

4. Use this method to replace the existing text on the remaining slides to make them look like those in Figure 16-16.

5. Save the presentation.

6. Display Slide 6.

7. Choose **Notes Pages** from the **View** menu.

8. Choose **Zoom** from the **View** menu.

9. In the Zoom dialog box, click **100%** and then click **OK.**

10. Scroll down if necessary and click where it reads *Click to add text.*

11. Key the text as shown in Figure 16-17.

12. Choose **Print** from the **File** menu. The Print dialog box appears.

13. In the Print range box, click **Current Slide.**

14. In the Print what box, scroll down to choose **Notes Pages.**

15. At the bottom of the dialog box, check **Scale to Fit Paper.**

FIGURE 16-16

3

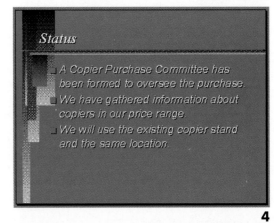

4

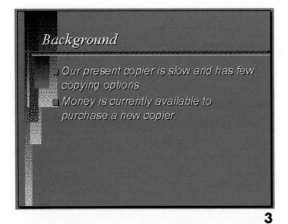

5

6

FIGURE 16-17
Slide notes can help you remember what to say during a presentation.

> Have Stephen talk briefly about information that has already been gathered.
>
> List specific copier features that need to be agreed upon.
>
> Hand out pamphlets and brochures that we currently have about new copiers.
>
> See if Monday the 23rd at 2:00 will work for everyone.

16. Click **OK.** Slide 6 prints in Notes Pages view.

17. Choose **Print** from the **File** menu. The Print dialog box appears. (If a dialog box appears with a message that PowerPoint is currently printing Copier Presentation, click the Print option.)

18. In the Print what box, scroll to choose **Handouts (6 slides per page).**

19. Click **OK.** The slides print on a single handout sheet.

20. Save and close the presentation.

21. Exit PowerPoint.

Summary

- PowerPoint is an Office 95 application that can help you create a professional presentation. When you start PowerPoint, you have the choice of opening an existing presentation or creating a new one.

- PowerPoint has helpful features that can make it much easier to create a presentation. You can use design templates to change the appearance of your slides. When you create a new slide or change the layout of an existing slide, there are twenty-four AutoLayouts to choose from. Clip art is available if you want to add pictures to your presentation.

- You can view your presentation five different ways: Slide view, Outline view, Slide Sorter view, Notes Pages view, and Slide Show. Each view has its own advantages. You can print in Slide view, Outline view, and Notes Pages view. You can also choose to print handouts with two, three, or six slides per page.

- There are three options for creating a presentation: the AutoContent Wizard, which creates a presentation for you with your help; templates, which are already designed and formatted; and blank presentations, which allow you to create a presentation from scratch.

- You can modify your presentation by deleting slides or adding text to slides. To close a presentation, choose Close from the File menu. To exit PowerPoint, choose Exit from the File menu.

• • • • • • • • • • • • • • •

REVIEW ACTIVITIES

TRUE/FALSE

Circle T or F to show whether the statement is true or false.

T   F   **1.** After PowerPoint starts, a Hint of the Week appears.

T   F   **2.** In the PowerPoint dialog box, you have the option of opening an existing presentation.

T   F   **3.** Applying a design template changes the content of your slides.

T   F   **4.** There are twenty AutoLayouts to choose from when you create a new slide or change the layout of an existing one.

T   F   **5.** The New Slide dialog box looks very similar to the Slide Layout dialog box.

T   F   **6.** You can view your presentation six different ways.

T   F   **7.** Notes Pages view shows miniature versions of the slides on screen.

T   F   **8.** To exit PowerPoint, you can choose Exit from the File menu.

T   F   **9.** To start a presentation from scratch, you choose the AutoContent Wizard option.

T   F   **10.** You can delete a slide by choosing Delete Slide from the Edit menu.

COMPLETION

Write the correct answer in the space provided.

1. What is one way to start PowerPoint?

   _____

2. Which dialog box allows you to preview the first slide of your presentation before opening it?

   _____

3. How do you access the Apply Design Template dialog box?

   _____

4. How can you go directly to a slide you want to change?

   _____

5. What does the New Slide dialog box allow you to do?

   _____

6. What does the button on the left of the status bar tell you?

_____

7. What view would you use to run your presentation on the computer as if it were a slide projector?

_____

8. What option would you choose in the PowerPoint dialog box to create a presentation that is already designed and formatted with certain colors, fonts, and layouts?

_____

9. How would you restore a slide that was accidentally deleted?

_____

10. How would you replace a text placeholder with text you want to add to a slide?

_____

_____

REINFORCEMENT APPLICATIONS

application 16-1

1. Start PowerPoint.

2. Open *Copier Presentation* from your data disk.

3. In Slide view on Slide 1, change the slide layout to Clip Art & Text.

4. Replace the clip art placeholder with the light bulb picture (Description: Idea Brainstorm) in the Cartoons category.

5. Apply the Blue Green design template to the presentation.

6. Switch to Slide Sorter view. Move Slide 5 so that it appears between Slide 2 and Slide 3.

7. Click on Slide 1. Switch to Slide Show view and run the presentation on your computer.

8. Switch to Outline view and print the presentation in outline form.

9. Save the presentation as *Copier Revised* and close it.

application 16-2

1. Open *XYZ Presentation*.

2. In Slide view, delete the slides with the titles Goal and Objective, Today's Situation, and How Did We Get Here? (currently Slides 3–5).

3. Go to Slide 2 and change the title from Vision Statement to Purpose.

4. Go to Slide 1 and switch to Notes Pages view. Key this text in the notes portion (zoom in if necessary): **Be sure everyone has handout.**

5. Print Slide 1 in Notes Pages view so that it fits on the page.

6. Print the entire presentation as a handout with six slides on a page.

7. Save the presentation as *XYZ Revised* and close it.

8. Exit PowerPoint.

EMBEDDING DATA USING POWERPOINT AND WORD

You have already learned that when you move data among applications by cutting or copying and pasting, Office 95 changes the format of the information you are moving so that it may be used in the destination file. Sometimes it is not possible to edit the information being pasted with the current application; instead, Office 95 *embeds* the information as an object. The embedded information becomes part of the new file, but it is a separate object that can be edited using the application that created it. For example, if you were copying a table from a Word document into a PowerPoint presentation, the data would be embedded since PowerPoint is not capable of editing it.

ACTIVITY

IV-1 Embedding Data

1. Open the *Copier Revised* presentation from your Integration template disk.

2. Switch to Slide View.

3. Display Slide 4.

4. Delete the second bulleted item.

5. Highlight the words *has few copying options* on the first bulleted item.

6. Key **requires too much maintenance.** Click elsewhere on the slide to close the text box.

7. Open Word and the *Copier Final Table* from the Integration template disk.

8. Highlight the table by placing the cursor in the table and choosing **Select Table** from the **Table** menu.

9. Choose **Copy** from the **Edit** menu.

10. Click **Microsoft PowerPoint** on the taskbar to display Slide 4 again.

11. Choose **Paste** from the **Edit** menu. Your slide should look similar to Figure IV-1.

12. Save the presentation as *Copier Final* on the Integration template disk and leave it on the screen for use in the next activity.

FIGURE IV-1
Slide 4 appears similar to the figure
when you embed a Word table.

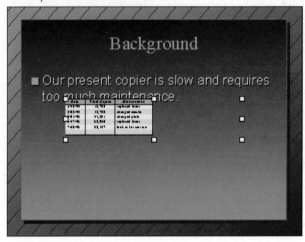

To make changes to the Word table embedded in the PowerPoint presentation, you would double-click on it. Word, the application that created the table, opens so that you can edit the table. When you finish and return to PowerPoint, the presentation includes the changes you made to the table.

Editing Embedded Data

1. Double-click on the table. The table is displayed in Word so you can edit it.

2. Click the handle in the middle of the right border and drag it to the left until it almost touches the right border of the table, as shown in Figure IV-2.

3. Click somewhere on the slide other than on the table. The table is no longer displayed in Word.

4. Click the bottom right handle and drag to enlarge the table until it is approximately the size shown in Figure IV-3. Drag the table to position it as shown if necessary.

5. Double-click on the table to display the table in Word.

6. In the last row, key **10-3-95** in the Date column, key **97,153** in the Total Copies column, and key **replaced master** in the Maintenance column.

7. Click somewhere on the slide other than on the table to exit Word. Click again on the slide to remove the handles from the table.

FIGURE IV-2

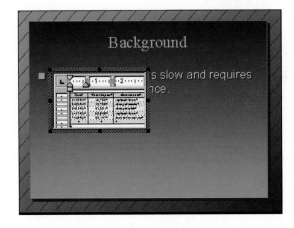

FIGURE IV-3

Background

■ Our present copier is slow and requires too much maintenance.

Date	Total Copies	Maintenance
3-12-94	16,722	replaced toner
8-28-94	32,720	changed master
2-21-95	45,281	changed plate
5-17-95	68,040	replaced toner
7-30-95	82,347	took in for service

8. Notice the information you keyed is now part of the table in the presentation.

9. Save the presentation.

10. Print Slide 4 and close the presentation. Exit PowerPoint and Word.

Summary

■ Embedding is another way to integrate data between applications. Information is embedded when the application that created the destination file is not capable of editing it.

■ To make changes to an embedded object, double-click on it to open the application that created it. Changes made when editing will be reflected in the destination file.

● ● ● ● ● ● ● ● ● ● ● ● ● ●

REVIEW ACTIVITIES

TRUE/FALSE

Circle T or F to show whether the statement is true or false.

T   F   1. Office 95 embeds information as a separate file.

T   F   2. Embedded information can be edited using the application that created it.

T   F   3. Changes made when editing embedded data will not be reflected in the destination file.

COMPLETION

Write the correct answer in the space provided.

1. If you were copying a table from a Word document into a PowerPoint presentation, why would the data be embedded instead of pasted?

   _____

   _____

2. How do you make changes to embedded information?

   _____

   _____

INTEGRATION PROJECTS

Home Again Real Estate

PROJECT J

When people come to your office wanting to list their home for sale with Home Again Real Estate, there is certain information you always need to give them. You decide it would be more interesting and attention-getting to provide this information in the form of a presentation. Create a presentation in PowerPoint that has at least four slides. Include the benefits of working with

Home Again Real Estate and how you are committed to helping clients sell their homes. Let the sellers know that an open house will be planned to showcase their homes. Open *House Table* from Word and embed it in the presentation to show the houses you've sold in the past month. Save the presentation as *Home Again Presentation*. Print the presentation in the form of handouts with six slides per page. Close the file.

▼ INTEGRATION SIMULATION

Java Internet Café

MARCH 20

Your manager asks you to create a presentation to show all new members.

1. Open PowerPoint and *Presentation-IB* from the Simulation template disk.

2. Save it on your Simulation template disk as *Internet Basics*.

3. Change the layout of Slide 4 to *Text & Clip Art*. Insert the clip art with the description *Happy Joy Laugh* from the Cartoons category.

4. Change the layout of Slide 9 to *Clip Art & Text*. Insert the clip art with the description *Love Flower* from the Plants category. Drag the text box handles to the left so that all text fits on the page.

5. Open Word and *Table* from the Simulation template disk.

6. Save it as *Equipment Table* on your Simulation template disk.

7. Center all headings in the table.

8. Select and copy the table.

9. Switch to PowerPoint.

10. Insert a new slide after Slide 11 with the *Title Only* layout.

11. Key **Computer Equipment** as the title.

12. Click on the slide to deselect the title.

13. Paste the table.

14. Drag the bottom right selection handle to increase the size of the table until it is approximately the same size as shown in Figure IV-4.

FIGURE IV-4

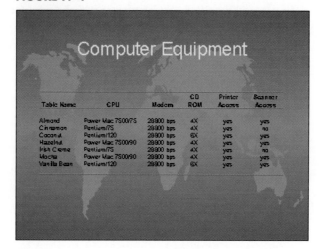

15. Double-click the table.

16. Change the *yes* to *no* in the first cell of the *Scanner Access* column.

17. Click on the slide.

18. Save and print *Internet Basics* as handouts, six slides per page.

19. Use the Slide Show view to view the entire presentation.

20. Close and exit PowerPoint.

21. Switch to Microsoft Word.

22. Save and close *Equipment Table* and exit Word.

SIMULATION

chapter 17

**Simulation—Great Day
Lawn Care Service**

SIMULATION— GREAT DAY LAWN CARE SERVICE

Throughout this book, you have learned to use Word, Excel, Access, PowerPoint, and Schedule+. This chapter is a simulation in which you will use each of these programs. The simulation, a business called Great Day Lawn Care Service, is operated by three friends.

OBJECTIVES
In this simulation, you will:

1. Use PowerPoint to create a presentation.

2. Use Word to create a form letter that will advertise Great Day Lawn Care's services.

3. Use Access to maintain address and billing information for customers.

4. Use Excel to calculate and maintain data on earnings and expenses.

5. Integrate Access and Word to create a billing form and form letter that will be sent to customers.

6. Use Schedule+ to keep track of your appointments and work schedule.

Background

You started Great Day Lawn Care Service last spring. You spent the warm months of the year (mid-May to mid-September) caring for ten lawns in the neighborhood. You offered the following services:

- Lawn mowing
- Edging

■   Hedge clipping

■   Watering

In September, several customers asked you about continuing your services the following year. In addition, a few neighbors of your current customers inquired about care for their lawns for the next year.

As the summer approaches, you are making plans to continue the lawn care. You know that if you increase the number of lawns you mow and edge, you will need some extra help. In fact, with two more workers, you could finish each job faster. Since you own two mowers and one edger, all machines could be operated simultaneously and each job would be completed in approximately one-third the time.

May 1

You have two friends, Tracy and Jordan, you are thinking of asking to help you in your business. You have been working on a presentation in PowerPoint to show them.

1. Open *Presentation* from the template disk.

2. Change the layout of slide 5 to Clip Art & Text.

3. Insert the clip art of the man scratching his head with the description *Confusion Dilemma* from the Cartoons category of the Microsoft ClipArt Gallery.

4. Insert a new slide after slide 6 with the Bulleted List layout. Key the title and text as shown in Figure 17-1. (After keying the advantages, press Shift + Tab to move text back one level to key the disadvantages.)

FIGURE 17-1

Option #2

● I can get Tracy and Jordan to join my business
   ■ Advantages
      – Together we could complete jobs faster
      – We would share profits and work
   ■ Disadvantages
      – Would there be enough lawns to mow?
      – Scheduling and billing would have to be managed carefully

5. Change the title of slide 8 to **Option #3.**

6. Change the title of slide 6 to **Option #1.**

7. Save as *GDLC Presentation.*

8. Display the first slide and then use Slide Show view to show the presentation.

9. Print the presentation as handouts, six to a page.

10. Save, close, and exit PowerPoint.

Tracy and Jordan agree to join you in business. The three of you will work together and split the profits (giving you a greater share since everyone will be using your equipment). You all begin a brainstorming session to solve the antici-pated problems of the new business.

Together you decide that Microsoft Office 95 can help you generate busi-ness, bill customers, and monitor profits.

May 3

The three of you compile the addresses that appear in Figure 17-2. Names are available for some of the addresses because they were your customers the pre-vious year. Other names are taken from mailboxes. If names are unavailable, the word Resident is used. All addresses are in the city of Smyrna, Georgia 30080.

Use these addresses to create a database that will supply addresses for the advertising letter and the billing form.

The three partners estimate a charge for their services based on the size of the lawn.

1. Create a new Access database named *Customers.* Create a new table using Design view. Define the following fields with the designated formats.

Field	Field Type	Description
Last Name	Text	Customer's Last Name
First Name	Text	Customer's First Name
Address	Text	Customer's Address
City, State, ZIP	Text	Customer's City, State, and ZIP
Fee	Currency	Amount to charge for this customer's lawn size

2. Save and name the table *Potential Customers.* (No primary key is needed.)

3. Open the table and enter the data shown in Figure 17-2 into the database and adjust the widths of the fields appropriately.

HINT: *You may use the Copy and Paste commands to enter Smyrna, GA 30080 into each entry of the City, State, and ZIP field.*

4. Save and close the table and the database file.

FIGURE 17-2

Last Name	First Name	Address	City, State, Zip	Fee
Dye	Allen	200 Thistle	Smyrna, GA 30080	$15.00
Dunsten	A.	201 Thistle	Smyrna, GA 30080	$20.00
Mata	Ricardo	203 Thistle	Smyrna, GA 30080	$15.00
Neman	John	204 Thistle	Smyrna, GA 30080	$22.00
Rigby	Eddy	205 Thistle	Smyrna, GA 30080	$22.00
Wolfe	James	206 Thistle	Smyrna, GA 30080	$22.00
Carter	John	207 Thistle	Smyrna, GA 30080	$15.00
Sanchez	Christina	208 Thistle	Smyrna, GA 30080	$15.00
Marcus	Lois	209 Thistle	Smyrna, GA 30080	$20.00
Lake	Jasmine	210 Thistle	Smyrna, GA 30080	$20.00
Torres	Ruben	211 Thistle	Smyrna, GA 30080	$20.00
Mueller	Anne	212 Thistle	Smyrna, GA 30080	$15.00
Resident		213 Thistle	Smyrna, GA 30080	$15.00
Roberts	Chad	214 Thistle	Smyrna, GA 30080	$15.00
Johnson	Virginia	215 Thistle	Smyrna, GA 30080	$15.00
Novack	D. K.	216 Thistle	Smyrna, GA 30080	$15.00
Keung	Y.	217 Thistle	Smyrna, GA 30080	$15.00
Schultz	Jason	218 Thistle	Smyrna, GA 30080	$15.00
Robinson	T. J.	219 Thistle	Smyrna, GA 30080	$15.00
Estes	Juanita	220 Thistle	Smyrna, GA 30080	$15.00
Reynolds	Clay	200 Kilt	Smyrna, GA 30080	$22.00
Richards	Della	201 Kilt	Smyrna, GA 30080	$22.00
Malcolm	R. J.	202 Kilt	Smyrna, GA 30080	$22.00
Patel	Nina	203 Kilt	Smyrna, GA 30080	$22.00
Cash	H. J.	204 Kilt	Smyrna, GA 30080	$22.00
Phillips	Paula	205 Kilt	Smyrna, GA 30080	$22.00
Moody	Mark	206 Kilt	Smyrna, GA 30080	$22.00
Harper	G. H.	207 Kilt	Smyrna, GA 30080	$22.00
Montoya	E. B.	208 Kilt	Smyrna, GA 30080	$22.00
Resident		209 Kilt	Smyrna, GA 30080	$22.00
Strawser	L. T.	210 Kilt	Smyrna, GA 30080	$22.00
Piper	Nate	211 Kilt	Smyrna, GA 30080	$20.00
Williams	R. B.	212 Kilt	Smyrna, GA 30080	$20.00
Hix	Jordan	213 Kilt	Smyrna, GA 30080	$20.00
Guy	D. P.	214 Kilt	Smyrna, GA 30080	$20.00
Carver	Alton	215 Kilt	Smyrna, GA 30080	$20.00
Ellis	J. B.	216 Kilt	Smyrna, GA 30080	$20.00

Liu	Lini	217 Kilt	Smyrna, GA 30080	$20.00
Lauer	Corey	218 Kilt	Smyrna, GA 30080	$20.00
Aslam	Ritu	219 Kilt	Smyrna, GA 30080	$20.00
Gibb	H. T.	220 Kilt	Smyrna, GA 30080	$20.00
Leon	Steven	200 Plaid	Smyrna, GA 30080	$15.00
Gold	Richard	201 Plaid	Smyrna, GA 30080	$15.00
Edge	A.V.	202 Plaid	Smyrna, GA 30080	$15.00
Shell	Charles	203 Plaid	Smyrna, GA 30080	$15.00
Valdez	Robert	204 Plaid	Smyrna, GA 30080	$20.00
Yarbrough	Frank	205 Plaid	Smyrna, GA 30080	$20.00
Sims	Trevor	206 Plaid	Smyrna, GA 30080	$20.00
Terrell	Kevin	207 Plaid	Smyrna, GA 30080	$20.00
Resident		208 Plaid	Smyrna, GA 30080	$20.00
Johnson	Veronica	209 Plaid	Smyrna, GA 30080	$20.00
Levine	Heather	210 Plaid	Smyrna, GA 30080	$20.00
Womack	David	211 Plaid	Smyrna, GA 30080	$15.00
Resident		213 Plaid	Smyrna, GA 30080	$15.00
Yapp	B. J.	214 Plaid	Smyrna, GA 30080	$15.00
Page	Misha	215 Plaid	Smyrna, GA 30080	$15.00
Taylor	Vicky	216 Plaid	Smyrna, GA 30080	$15.00
Sutton	Forrest	217 Plaid	Smyrna, GA 30080	$15.00
Smith	Charles	218 Plaid	Smyrna, GA 30080	$15.00
Ruff	Keesha	219 Plaid	Smyrna, GA 30080	$15.00

May 4

Tracy writes a form letter, shown in Figure 17-3, to advertise the services of Great Day Lawn Care Service. You design a letterhead template. The letter will be personalized by merging the names and addresses of potential customers in the database with the form letter.

1. Design a letterhead template for Great Day Lawn Care Service to be used with the letter in Figure 17-3. You can draw a graphic in Word or use clip art. Save it as a template in the MSOffice Letters & Faxes template category on your hard drive. Name it *Letterhead XXX*. (Replace the x's with your name or your initials.) Close the file.

2. Open *Letterhead XXX* as a new document and key the form letter into the file. Do not key the placeholders. Later you will put the placeholders in the form letter that will insert the appropriate field from the database file into the word processing file.

3. Save the file as *Form Letter* on your data disk and leave it on the screen.

FIGURE 17-3

CHAPTER 17: Simulation—Great Day Lawn Care Service

Great Day Lawn Care Service
221 Kilt Avenue
Smyrna, GA 30080
404-555-3894

May 4, 19—

«First_Name» «Last_Name»
«Address»
«City_State_ZIP»

Dear «First_Name» «Last_Name»

Great Day Lawn Care Service is a partnership of friends. We would like to care for your lawn on a weekly basis and perform the following services:

Lawn mowing
Edging
Hedging clipping
Watering

We are prepared to offer these services to you at a cost of «Fee» per week, billed monthly. We Are conscientious, guarantee all of our work, and will provide references in your neighborhood.

If you would like to employ our services, or if you have any questions, please contact us at 555-3894.

Sincerely,

Student's name   Tracy Ruthart   Jordan Perry

May 5

You only need to print the form letters for those for whom you don't have names, so you can distribute them door to door.

1. Use Word's Mail Merge Helper to merge the form letters with the *Customers* database. Choose the Active window for the Main document and open the *Customers* database and the *Potential Customers* table as the data source. Insert placeholders as shown in Figure 17-3.

2. Use the Mail Merge Helper's Query options to create a query to merge only those with Resident in the Last Name field to a new document named *Advertising Letters*. (There should be four records.)

3. Print the four form letters.

4. Save and close.

May 6

Anticipating a response to the letters, Jordan suggests that the billing information for the month of May be set up.

Create a worksheet to figure and track billing. Columns will be created to show the amount owed by each customer for each week. For example, 3-May will contain the amount owed for the third week in May. May Bill will contain the total amount owed by the customer for the month of May, and May Paid will contain the amount paid by the customer for the month of May.

1. Open a new Excel worksheet.

2. In A1, key **3-May**.

3. In B1, key **4-May**.

4. Save the worksheet as *Billing.*

5. In C1, key **May Bill**.

6. In D1, key **May Paid**.

7. Enter a formula in C2 to total the bill for May. It should contain the sum of the amounts in the 3-May and 4-May fields.

8. Copy the formula down to C61.

9. Save the document.

May 8

The following people (mostly former customers) have notified you that they would like to employ the services of Great Day Lawn Care Service.

Carver, Alton

Cash, H. J.

Guy, D. P.

Harper, G. H.

Phillips, Paula

Piper, Nate

Strawser, L. T.

Williams, R. B.

In addition, the residents of 209 Kilt (Tom Alfreds) and 213 Thistle (Lillian Spears) have employed Great Day Lawn Care Service.

1. Insert the following new fields in the *Customers* database:

Field	Data Type	Description
Cust	Yes/No	Is this a customer?
May Bill	Currency with 2 decimals	Amount owed for May

2. The residents of 209 Kilt and 213 Thistle were not known when the database was created. Edit the Last Name and First Name fields to show their correct names.

3. Indicate the people who are now customers by inserting a check mark in the Cust field box of your Access database. Since the database is large, you may want to use the Find command or sort the database alphabetically by last name to help you find customers.

4. Leave the database on your screen.

May 9

In anticipation of billing new customers, Jordan drafts a billing form to be put in a word processing file. A copy of the draft is in Figure 17-4.

FIGURE 17-4

Great Day Lawn Care Service

221 Kilt Avenue
Smyrna, GA 30080
404-555-3894

June 2, 19—

Charges for the Month of May
«First_Name» «Last_Name»
«Address»
«City_State_ZIP»

We have calculated your May bill based on our agreed amount of «Fee» per week. The total charge for May is «May_Bill».

Please make your check payable to "Great Day Lawn Care Service." Payment is due by June 10.

Thank you for your business.

1. Open *Letterhead XXX* as a new Word document and key the billing form into the file. Use the Mail Merge Helper to insert the appropriate place-holders from the *Potential Customers* table in the *Customers* database file.

2. Save the file as *Billing Form.*

May 10

Several more people have notified you that they would like to employ the services of Great Day Lawn Care Service for the summer:

Mata, Ricardo	**Gold, Richard**
Sanchez, Christina	**Edge, A.V.**
Lake, Jasmine	**Valdez, Robert**
Mueller, Anne	**Yarbrough, Frank**
Novack, D. K.	**Johnson, Veronica**
Robinson, T. J.	**Yapp, B.J.**
Lauer, Corey	**Page, Misha**

1. Indicate that these people are customers by inserting a check mark in the Cust field of the *Potential Customers* table.

May 12

An income statement will be prepared each month to report the profits of Great Day Lawn Care Service. Figure 17-5 is a draft of the income statement for the month of May. All three partners agree that the income statement will give them the information needed to evaluate the progress of their business venture.

1. Set up an income statement in Excel, as shown in Figure 17-5, for the month of May.

2. Save the file as *Income Statement--May.* Computed fields and amounts will be added to the income statement later.

FIGURE 17-5

	A	B	C	D
1	GREAT DAY LAWN CARE SERVICE			
2	INCOME STATEMENT			
3	FOR THE MONTH ENDING MAY 31, 19--			
4				
5	REVENUES			
6				
7	Collected Lawn Care Revenues			
8	Uncollected Lawn Care Revenues			
9				
10	TOTAL REVENUES			
11				
12	EXPENSES			
13				
14	Gasoline			
15	Mower Repair and Maintenance			
16	Trailer Repair and Maintenance			
17	Refreshments and Ice			
18	Computer Supplies			
19	Misc. Expenses			
20				
21	TOTAL EXPENSES			
22				
23	NET INCOME			
24				

May 14

More residents have notified you that they want the services of Great Day Lawn Care for the summer:

Dye, Allen

Richards, Della

Liu, Lini

Gibb, H. T.

The residents of 208 Plaid (Reginald Hinkle) and 213 Plaid (Misty Lobo) have employed the service.

1. The residents of 208 Plaid and 213 Plaid were not known when the database was originally created. Edit the Last Name and First Name fields to show their correct names.

2. Indicate that these people are customers by inserting a check mark in the Cust field of the *Potential Customers* table.

May 16

You want to be sure your equipment is in good shape before the summer begins. You take your lawn care equipment into the mower repair shop for servicing. The cost of servicing is $105.34. You also buy a new tire and brake light for the trailer. The total cost is $89.75.

1. Record the expense for Mower Repair & Maintenance in Column B of the *Income Statement--May* file. Record the trailer costs as Trailer Repair & Maintenance.

2. Format Column B for Currency with two decimals. The column should be right aligned.

3. Save the file.

May 19

You use Schedule+ to help manage your time. You need to insert two new contacts.

1. Open the *MySchedule* file from the template disk.

2. Go to May 19, 1997.

3. Insert the two contacts from Figures 17-6 and 17-7.

4. Close the file and exit Schedule+.

FIGURE 17-6

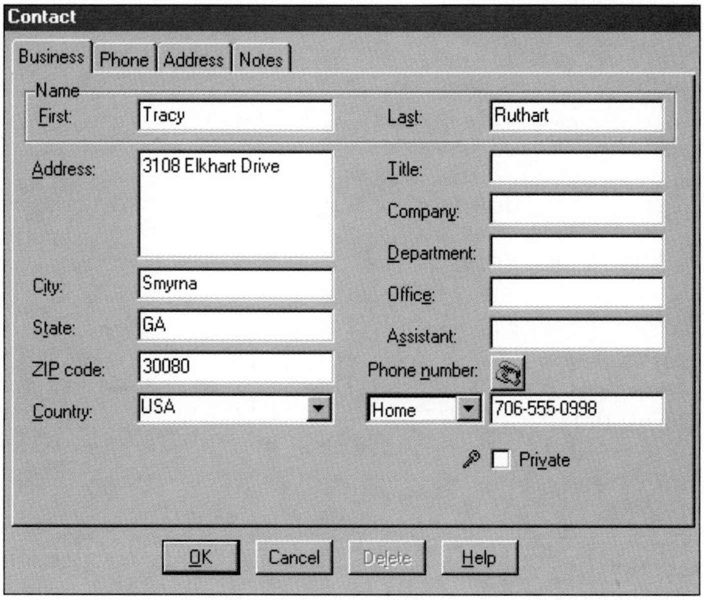

FIGURE 17-7

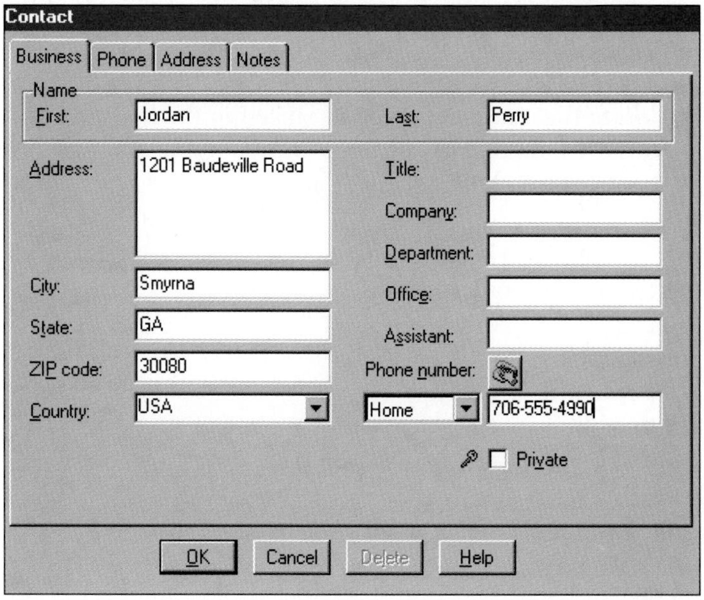

May 21

The lawns of the following customers have been serviced. The customers owe the amounts designated in the Fee field for the third week in May. A total of $10.13 was spent on gasoline to power the lawn care equipment; $15.12 was spent on refreshments and ice.

Dye	**Gold**
Mata	**Edge**
Sanchez	**Valdez**
Lake	**Yarbrough**
Mueller	**Johnson**
Novack	**Yapp**
Robinson	**Page**

1. In the database, create a filter to show only customers with a check mark in the Cust field.

2. Sort the Last Name field in Ascending order.

3. Switch to the worksheet *Billing* file, and insert three new columns to the left of column A.

4. Switch to the *Potential Customers* file. Copy the Last Name, Address, and Fee columns from the filter to the three new columns in the *Billing* file in that order.

5. In the *Billing* file, enter the amounts (listed in the Fee column) owed by the customers listed above in the 3-May column. Format D2 through D31 for currency with two decimal places.

6. In row 1, center and boldface the headings and change the cell color to None. Remove the borders from A1 through C31.

7. Save the file.

8. Switch to the *Income Statement--May* file and enter $10.13 in Column B for gasoline. Enter $15.12 in Column B for refreshments and ice.

9. Save the file.

May 24

The lawns of the following customers have been serviced. The customers owe the amounts designated in the Fee column for the third week in May. A total of $6.33 was spent on gasoline to power the lawn care equipment; $6.56 was spent on refreshments and ice.

1. Enter the amounts owed by each customer in the 3-May field of the *Billing* file.

Richards	**Carver**
Cash	**Liu**
Phillips	**Lauer**
Harper	**Gibb**
Strawser	**Alfreds**
Piper	**Hinkle**
Williams	**Lobo**
Guy	**Spears**

2.   Save the file.

3.   Add the amounts spent during this time for gasoline, and refreshments and ice to the existing amounts in the expenses column of the *Income Statement--May* file. The $10.13 in the gasoline account should be replaced with the formula =10.13+6.33. The $15.12 in the refreshments and ice account should be replaced with the cell formula =15.12+6.56.

4.   Save the file.

May 27

1.   Open the *MySchedule* file from the template disk.

2.   Create an appointment from 8 a.m. to 12:30 p.m. on May 27, 1997. In the Description box, key **Mow lawns** and in the Where box, key **Plaid St.** Do not set a reminder.

3.   Insert the following new tasks for May 27.

   Get gas (priority 1, do not set a reminder).

   Buy ice and refreshments (priority 2, do not set a reminder).

4.   Print out your To Do list for this day. Use the print layout To Do List - mini.

5.   Close the file and exit Schedule+.

May 28

The lawns of the following customers have been mowed and edged. The customers owe the amounts designated in the Fee column for the fourth week in May. A total of $10.18 was spent on gasoline to power the lawn care equipment; $6.78 was spent on refreshments and ice.

Dye	Sanchez
Mata	Lake
Richards	Mueller
Cash	Spears
Gold	Hinkle
Edge	Johnson
Valdez	Lobo
Yarbrough	Page

1. Enter the amounts owed by the customers in the 4-May column of the *Billing* file.

2. Format E2-G31 for currency with two decimals. Save the file.

3. Add the amounts spent during this time for gasoline, and refreshments and ice to the previously recorded amounts in the expenses column of the *Income Statement--May* file.

4. Save the file.

May 30

During May, $30.15 was spent on printer paper and $20.51 of miscellaneous expenses were incurred.

1. Record the amount for computer supplies and miscellaneous expenses to the *Income Statement--May* file under the appropriate account name.

2. Save the file.

May 31

The lawns of the following customers have been serviced, and they owe the amounts designated in the Fee column for the fourth week in May. A total of $3.76 was spent on gasoline to power the lawn care equipment; $6.90 was spent on refreshments and ice.

Novack	Liu
Robinson	Lauer
Phillips	Gibb
Harper	Yapp
Alfreds	Strawser

Piper	**Williams**
Guy	**Carver**

1. Enter the amounts owed by the customers in the 4-May column of the billing file. Save the file.

2. Add the amounts spent during this time for gasoline, and refreshments and ice to the previously recorded amounts in the expenses column of the *Income Statement--May* file.

3. Save the file.

June 2

The three partners decide to prepare bills for the month of May. The bills are printed and distributed door to door.

1. Switch to the *Potential Customers* database.

2. With the customers filter still in effect, sort in ascending order if it's not already. Copy the amounts in the May Bill column of the *Billing* file to the May Bill field of the *Potential Customers* database.

3. Open *Billing Form* in Word.

4. Merge with data from the *Potential Customers* database to a new document. Create a query in the Mail Merge Helper to merge only the billing forms for Spears and Novack. Name the new document *Spears and Novack Bills*.

5. Print the billing forms for Spears and Novack.

6. Save and close the new document and the database.

7. Save and close *Billing Form.*

June 3

The following customers were at home when the bills were distributed, and promptly paid the amounts due:

Dye	**Page**
Mata	**Guy**
Lake	**Lauer**
Novack	**Gold**

Robinson	Valdez
Cash	Yarbrough
Alfreds	Hinkle
Piper	Lobo
Williams	Yapp

Record the collection of these amounts in the May Paid column of the *Billing* worksheet.

June 8

The following customers have delivered checks to Great Day Lawn Care Service:

Phillips	Harper
Strawser	Liu
Sanchez	Johnson
Spears	Gibb

1. Record the collection of these amounts in the *Billing* worksheet in the May Paid column.

2. Save the file.

June 9

Tracy wonders about the unpaid bills. Calculate the amounts billed to the customers and the amounts actually received.

1. In the *Billing* file, clear F32 through F61.

2. In A33, key **Totals**.

3. Enter a formula in F33 to sum the May Bill column.

4. Copy the formula to G33.

5. In A35, key **Uncollected**.

6. In B35, enter a formula to subtract the total May Paid from the total of May Bill.

8. Boldface A33, A35, B35, F33, and G33.

9. Save, print, and close. (Set the print area to print only A1 through G35.)

June 10

Great Day Lawn Care Service has now compiled the data for its first month of operation. The partners want to know if they made a profit during May, so they obtain copies of the May income statement to assess their progress.

1. Switch to the file *Income Statement--May*. This file already contains updated expenses for May.

2. In B7, key **960** and in B8, key **144**.

3. In C10, enter a formula to total the Collected Lawn Care Revenues and the Uncollected Lawn Care Revenues.

4. In C21, enter a formula to total the expenses.

5. In C23, enter a formula to find the difference between the Total Revenues and Total Expenses.

6. If necessary, format column C for currency with two decimal places.

7. Save and print.

MICROSOFT BOOKSHELF '95

Microsoft Bookshelf '95 is an interactive CD-ROM reference tool that comes packaged with Microsoft Office Professional Edition. Bookshelf contains seven reference books:

■ The American Heritage Dictionary of the English Language, Third Edition

■ Roget's Thesaurus of English Words and Phrases

■ The Columbia Dictionary of Quotations

■ The Concise Columbia Encyclopedia, Third Edition

■ Hammond Atlas of the World

■ The People's Chronology

■ The World Almanac and Book of Facts '95

Bookshelf articles contain text, audio, animation and video, and/or pictures. You can use Bookshelf to research articles for reports and other projects. When you find articles or graphics you would like to use, you can copy them from Bookshelf and paste them into any Office 95 document.

Follow the instructions that came with the CD to install the necessary Bookshelf files if they aren't installed already.

ACTIVITY

 **Starting Bookshelf '95**

1. Insert the Bookshelf CD (Disc 2) in your CD-ROM drive.

2. Click **Start, Programs, Microsoft Reference, Microsoft Bookshelf '95.** The Bookshelf '95 Main Window and a Quote of the Day appears.

3. Click **Close** in the Bookshelf Daily dialog box.

4. Leave the Main Window on the screen for the next activity.

After starting Bookshelf '95, the Main window appears, as shown in Figure A-1.

The *menu bar* contains pull-down menus with commands, such as Print and Copy, that are similar to those in other Office 95 programs. The *Book bar*, located in the upper right of the screen, shows the seven reference books and an All Books icon. The open book tells you which book you're in. Use the *Tabbed lists* on the left of the screen to look for articles.

FIGURE A-1

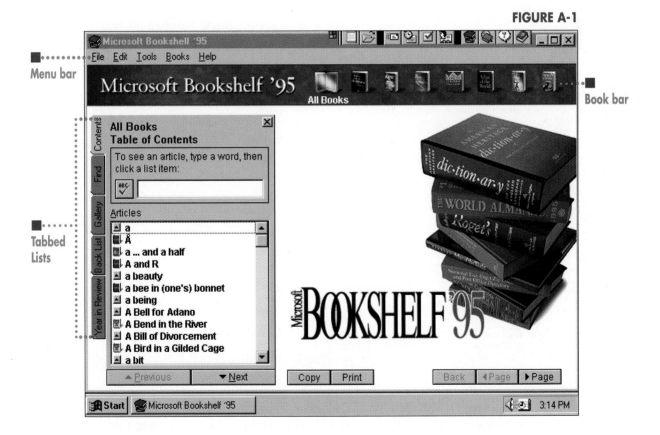

Menu bar

Book bar

Tabbed Lists

ACTIVITY

A-2 Finding Information and Exiting Bookshelf

1. Click the **Find** tab.

2. Key **endangered species** in the find box.

3. Click the **Find!** button. A list of articles appears below and the definition of endangered appears on the screen.

4. Click *endangered species*, the second item in the list. An article with a photo appears.

5. Click the arrow below the photo to start the video.

6. Read the article about endangered species.

7. Click the word *PESTICIDES* in colored type. The definition of pesticides is displayed.

8. Click the *yellow sound icon* beside the pesti-

cide heading to hear the correct pronunciation of the word.

9. Click the **Back** button at the bottom of the screen. You are returned to the *endangered species* article.

10. Click the **See Also** button at the bottom of the screen. A list of related articles appears in a box.

11. Close the box.

12. Click the fifth item in the list, *U.S. List of Endangered and Threatened Species*. A table appears.

13. Scroll through and read the table.

14. Choose **Exit** from the **File** menu.

Now that you've used a few of the features available in Bookshelf, you can continue exploring. For detailed help with using Bookshelf, choose Help Contents from the Help menu.

MICROSOFT ENCARTA '95

Encarta '95 is an interactive multimedia encyclopedia of 26,000 articles. It contains audio, graphics, video clips, a timeline of world history, and an atlas. You can use Encarta to research articles for reports and other projects—or just for fun.

Follow the User Guide instructions to install the necessary Encarta files if they aren't installed already.

ACTIVITY

 **B-1** Starting Encarta '95

1. Insert the Encarta '95 CD in your CD-ROM drive.

2. Click **Start, Programs, Microsoft Multimedia, Microsoft Encarta '95.** The Encarta '95 screen will appear and you will hear a series of music and sounds.

3. At the Encarta '95 screen, click **Enter.** The Main screen appears. A sample Main screen is shown in Figure B-1 (the screens may vary depending on the last article accessed).

4. Leave the Main screen displayed for the next activity.

FIGURE B-1

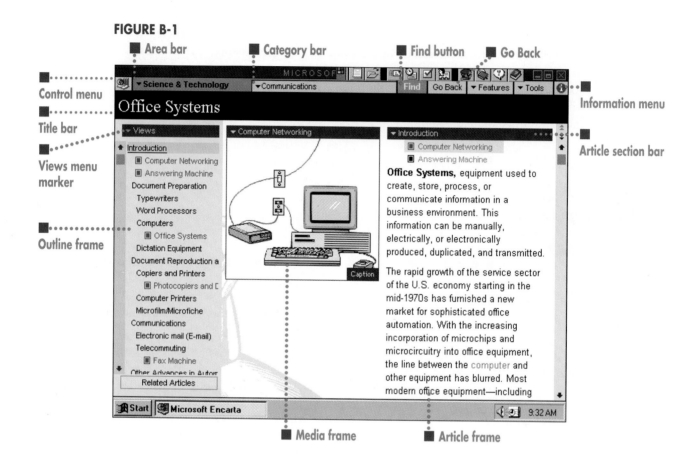

Area bar · **Category bar** · **Find button** · **Go Back**

Control menu

Title bar

Views menu marker

Outline frame

Information menu

Article section bar

Media frame · **Article frame**

The *Control menu* lets you change the size of the Encarta screen, switch programs, or quit Encarta. The *Area bar* shows the area of interest, and the *Category bar* shows the category within the Area. Click the *Find button* to open the Pinpointer (not shown), which searches Encarta for articles that interest you. The *Information menu* contains the Help files and printer setup. The *Article section bar* shows the heading of the article section on screen and the *Views menu marker* lets you show or hide media and outlines. The biggest part of the screen shows three sections, or frames. The *Outline frame* at the left shows an outline of the article and available media. The *Media frame* is in the middle, and shows the photos and other media related to the article. The *Article frame* on the right side of the screen displays the text.

 **Finding an Article and Closing Encarta '95**

1. Click the **Find** button. The Pinpointer appears.

2. Key **Office Systems** and press **Enter.** An article about office systems appears.

3. Click the **Views** menu marker. A drop-down menu appears.

4. Choose Main, Outline. The Main screen will look like Figure B-1.

5. Click on the word *Computer Networking,* at the top of the picture. A drop-down menu appears.

6. Choose **Enlarge** from the menu. The picture enlarges.

7. Click **Close** in the upper right corner of the graphic.

8. Click **Caption** below the graphic to read about computer networking.

9. Click **Caption** again.

10. Read the article about office systems in the Article frame.

11. Click the word **computer** that is in red type. Encarta switches you to an article about computers.

12. Enlarge the picture.

13. Click **Close** in the upper right corner of the graphic.

14. Click the **Go Back** button to return to the office systems article.

15. In the outline, click **Answering Machine.** A new article and graphic appears.

16. Enlarge the graphic.

17. Click the sound icon in the lower right corner. The sound begins.

18. Close the graphic.

19. Click the Control menu in the upper left corner of the screen.

20. Choose **Close Encarta.**

These are just a few of the features and options available in Encarta. To learn more, you can explore on your own, choose Help from the Information menu, or consult the *Microsoft Encarta '95 User's Guide.*

MICROSOFT EXCHANGE

Microsoft Exchange lets you send and receive electronic mail. You can create an address book that includes all the e-mail addresses of people you send mail to. You easily can choose a name from your address book and send that person a message. You can also include data in e-mail messages that was created in other applications.

To open Exchange, click Start, Programs, Microsoft Exchange. To use the program, follow the instructions to set up your profile.

When Exchange opens, the Microsoft Exchange Viewer, shown in Figure C-1, lists your personal folders. The Inbox contains new mail, and the Outbox holds messages you've sent until they are delivered. The Sent Items folder holds a copy of messages sent, and the Deleted Items folder contains messages deleted.

FIGURE C-1

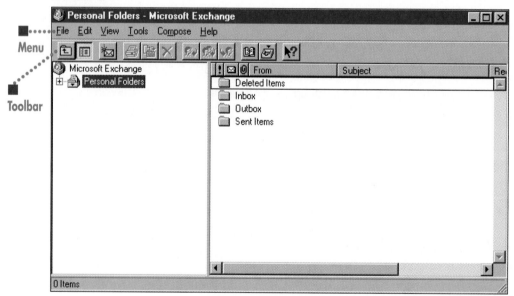

The *menu bar* has commands used to organize and access information. The *toolbar* contains tools for manipulating mail, such as sending, printing, and deleting.

Open the Inbox to see a list of mail you've received. Double-click each mail message to read it. A new screen will appear, like the one shown in Figure C-2.

To print the message, click the Print button. If you want to delete the message, click the Delete button. You can also move the e-mail to a new folder. If you want to reply to the sender, click the Reply to Sender button on the toolbar and a new message screen will appear where you can key the message.

To exit Exchange, choose Exit from the File menu. To learn more about Exchange, choose a topic from the Help menu.

FIGURE C-2

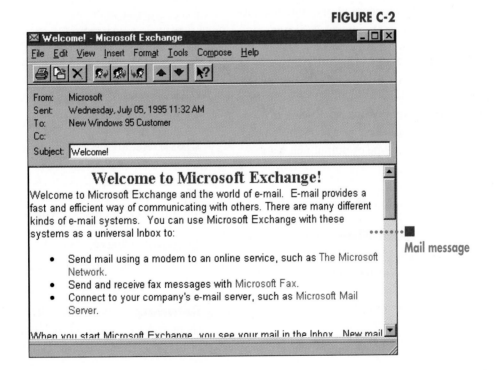

Mail message

GLOSSARY

A

Absolute Cell Reference Cell reference that does not adjust to the new cell location when copied or moved.

Active Cell A highlighted cell ready for data entry.

Appointment Book Located in the center of the Schedule+ screen, where appointments are entered and displayed beside the appropriate times.

Argument Value, cell reference, range, or text that acts as an operand in a function formula.

Ascending Sort A sort that arranges records from *A* to *Z* or smallest to largest.

AutoContent Wizard Option that creates a presentation for you depending on the style, length, and type of output you want.

B

Blank Presentation Option that lets you create a presentation from scratch using whatever layout, format, colors, and style you prefer.

C

Case Whether letters are capitalized or not; capital letters are uppercase, while others are lowercase.

Cell The intersection of a row and column in a worksheet.

Cell Note See *Note*.

Cell Reference Identifies a cell by the column letter and row number (for example, A1, B2, C4).

Chart Graphical representation of data contained in a worksheet.

Chart Sheet Area separate from the Excel worksheet in which a chart is created and stored; the chart sheet is identified by a tab near the bottom of the screen.

ChartWizard A five-step, on-screen guide that aids in preparing a chart from an Excel worksheet.

Clip Art Graphics that are already drawn and available for use in documents.

Clipboard A temporary storage place in memory.

Close Removing a document or window from the screen.

Close Button "X" on the right side of the title bar that closes a window.

Column Chart Chart that uses rectangles of varying heights to illustrate values in a worksheet.

Columns Appear vertically in a spreadsheet and are identified by letters at the top of the worksheet window.

Complex Formulas Formulas containing more than one operator.

Contacts Tab Displays information about your contacts, the people with whom you have meetings and appointments.

Cutting and Pasting Method of moving data from one location to another using commands in the menu bar or buttons in the toolbar.

D

Daily Tab The default view of the Schedule+ information, which displays a day of scheduled information.

Data Disk The disk on which you store your own documents.

Data Labels Values depicted by the chart objects (such as columns or data points) that are printed directly on the chart.

Data Series A group of related information in a column or row of a worksheet that is plotted on a worksheet chart.

Data Source Information stored in another application that is merged with a main document when creating form letters.

Data Type A specification that tells Access what kind of information can be stored in a field.

Database Management System Any system for managing data.

Database Report A report that allows you to organize, summarize, and print all or a portion of the data in a database.

Datasheet View A form similar to a spreadsheet that allows records to be entered directly into a table.

Date Navigator Located at the top right part of the Schedule+ screen, used to select dates by clicking directly on the requested date.

Default A setting used unless another option is chosen.

Descending Sort A sort that arranges records from Z to A or largest to smallest.

Design Templates Predesigned graphic styles that can be applied to your slides.

Desktop Space where you do your work.

Destination File The file you are moving data to when copying and moving data between applications.

Dialog Box A message box asking for further instructions before a command can be performed.

Dot Leaders A line of periods or dashes that precedes a tab.

Double-Clicking Pressing the left mouse button quickly two times in a row.

Drag and Drop A quick method for copying and moving text a short distance.

E

Embed Move information to a new file as a separate object that can be edited using the application that created it.

Embedded Chart Chart created within the worksheet; an embedded chart may be viewed on the same screen as the data from which it is created.

Endnote Printed at the end of your document, it is used to document quotations, figures, summaries, or other text that you do not want to include in the body of your document.

End-of-File Marker A horizontal line that shows the end of the document.

Entry The actual data entered into a field.

Equal Sign Tells Excel a function formula will be entered in a cell.

Event Button Located above the Appointment Book, allows you to add a special occasion.

F

Field Name A name that identifies a field.

Field Properties Specifications that allow you to customize a field beyond choosing a data type.

Fields Categories of data that make up records.

Filling Copies data into the cell(s) adjacent to the original.

Filter An easier-to-use type of query that cannot be saved and must display all fields.

Financial Function Used to analyze loans and investments.

Folder A place where other files and folders are stored on a disk.

Font Size Determined by measuring the height of characters in units called points.

Font Style Certain changes in the appearance of a font.

Fonts Designs of type.

Footer Text that is printed at the bottom of the page.

Footnote Printed at the bottom of each page of your document, it is used to document quotations, figures, summaries, or other text that you do not want to include in the body of your document.

Formatting Toolbar Contains buttons for changing character and paragraph formatting.

Form Letter A word processor document that uses information from a data source in specified areas to personalize a document.

Formula Equation that calculates a new value from values currently on a spreadsheet.

Formula Bar Appears directly below the toolbar in the worksheet; the formula bar will display a formula when the cell of a spreadsheet or entry of a database contains a calculated value.

Frame A special rectangle you draw that allows you to position a graphic.

Freezing Keeps row or column titles on the screen no matter where you scroll in the worksheet.

Function Formula Special formulas that do not use operators to calculate a result.

Function Name Identifies the operation to be performed.

G

Graphical User Interface (GUI) A way of interacting with a computer that involves selecting pictures that represent commands.

Graphics Pictures that help illustrate the meaning of the text or that make the page more attractive or functional.

Grid Snap An invisible grid on your screen that allows you to automatically align objects to the nearest grid line.

Gridlines Lines displayed through a chart that relate the objects (such as columns or data points) in a chart to the axes.

H

Handles Little squares that appear at the edges of the graphic that allow you to manipulate the selected object.

Hanging Indents A type of indent in which the first line is a full line of text and the following lines are indented.

Hardware Physical components of a computer.

Header Text that is printed at the top of each page.

Highlight The entry point of a worksheet; a highlighted cell is indicated by a dark border.

I

Icons Small pictures that remind you of each button's function.

Indent The space placed between text and a document's margin.

Indexing A feature of databases that allows a field to be more quickly searched.

Integrated Software Package A computer program that combines common tools into one program.

Integration Using more than one Office application to complete a project.

L

Legend A list that identifies a pattern or symbol used in an Excel worksheet chart.

Line Chart Chart that is similar to a column chart except columns are replaced by points connected by a line.

Line Spacing The amount of space between lines of text.

Linking Integrating data between applications so that it can be updated automatically.

M

Macro A collection of one or more actions that Access can perform on a database.

Main Document Contains the information that will stay the same in each form letter.

Margins Blank spaces around the top, bottom, and sides of a page.

Mathematical and Trigonometic Function Manipulates quantitative data in a worksheet.

Maximize Button Button at the right side of the title bar that enlarges a window to its maximum size.

Menu List of options from which to choose.

Menu Bar A row of titles located beneath the title bar at the top of the screen, each of which represents a separate pull-down menu.

Merge Fields Field names inserted in the main document that are automatically replaced with information from the data source when form letters are created.

Microsoft Office Shortcut Bar Located in the right portion of the title bar, the shortcut bar allows you to access other Office 95 documents quickly.

Minimize Button Button at the right side of the title bar that reduces a window to a button on the taskbar.

Mixed Cell Reference Cell reference containing both relative and absolute references.

Mnemonic An underlined letter that is pressed in combination with the Alt key to access items in the menu bar, pull-down menus, and dialog boxes.

Monthly Tab Displays a month of scheduled information.

Mouse Device that rolls on a flat surface and has one or more buttons on it used to interact with a computer.

My Computer Program to help you organize and manage your files.

N

Note Message that provides information concerning data in a cell that may be too large to enter into the cell; the note explains, identifies, or comments on information contained in the cell.

O

Open The process of loading a file from a disk onto the screen.

Operand Numbers or cell references used in calculations in the formulas of spreadsheets.

Operator Tells Excel what to do with operands in a formula.

Order of Evaluation Sequence of calculation in a spreadsheet formula.

Orphan The first line of a paragraph printed at the end of a page.

Overtype Allows you to replace existing text with the new text that is keyed.

P

Page Breaks Separate one page from the next.

Pane Contains separate scroll bars to allow you to move through that part of the document.

Pie Chart Chart that shows the relationship of a part to a whole.

Placeholder Space reserved in your presentation for information such as text, columns, clip art, and graphs.

Planner Tab Displays scheduled meetings and the names of the attendees.

Point and Click Method Constructs a cell formula in Excel by clicking on the cell you want to reference rather than keying the reference.

Pointer Indicates the position of the mouse.

Protecting Prevents inadvertent changes from being made to a worksheet; in a protected worksheet, data may not be added, removed, or edited until the protection is removed.

Pull-Down Menu A list of commands that appears below each title in the menu bar.

Q

Query A search method that allows complex searches of a database.

R

Random Access Memory (RAM) Temporary storage in a computer; data and programs stored in RAM are lost when the computer is turned off.

Range A selected group of cells in a worksheet; a range in a spreadsheet is identified by the cell in the upper left corner and the cell in the lower right corner, separated by a colon (for example, A3:C5).

Record A complete set of database fields.

Record Pointer The pointer which Access uses internally to keep track of the current record.

Recycle Bin Place to get rid of files or folders that are no longer needed.

Relative Cell Reference Cell reference that adjusts to a new location when copied or moved.

Report Object Allows you to create reports that include selected fields, groups of records, and calculations.

Restore Button Button at the right side of the title bar that returns a maximized window to its previous size.

Rows Appear horizontally in a worksheet and are identified by numbers on the left side of the worksheet window.

Ruler Allows you to quickly change indentions, tabs, and margins.

S

Sans Serif A font that does not have serifs.

Save The process of storing a file on disk.

Scale Resizing a graphic so that its proportions are correct.

Scatter Chart Chart that shows the relationship of two categories of data (sometimes called XY Chart).

Scroll Bars Located at the bottom and right sides of the window, allow you to move quickly to other areas of the document.

Scroll Box Small box in the scroll bar that indicates your position within the contents of the window.

Selecting Highlighting a block of text.

Serifs Small lines at the ends of the characters.

Shift-Clicking Holding down the Shift key while clicking the mouse.

Software Lists of instructions that computers follow to perform specific tasks; a program.

Sort Arranges a list of words or numbers in ascending order (*a* to *z;* smallest to largest) or in descending order (*z* to *a*; largest to smallest).

Source File The file you are moving data from when copying and moving data between applications.

Spreadsheet A grid of rows and columns containing numbers, text, and formulas; the purpose of a spreadsheet is to solve problems that involve numbers.

Standard Toolbar Contains word processing commands you can use by simply clicking the correct button.

Start Button on the taskbar that brings up menus with a variety of options.

Statistical Function Describes large quantities of data.

Status Bar A bar, located at the bottom of the editing screen, containing the document name, page and line numbers, and insertion point position.

T

Tabs Mark the place the insertion point will stop when the Tab key is pressed.

Taskbar Located at the bottom of the screen, it shows all open programs; the Start button lets you open programs on your computer.

Template (1) A file that contains page and paragraph formatting and text that you can customize to create a new document similar to but slightly different from the original. (2) Presentations that come with PowerPoint which are already designed and formatted with certain colors, fonts, and layouts.

Template Wizard Similar to a template, it asks you questions and creates a document based on your answers.

Thesaurus A useful feature for finding a synonym, or a word with a similar meaning, for a word in your document.

TipWizard Suggests tips to help you work faster and more efficiently.

Title Bar Where the name of the program is located.

To Do (Active) List Located at the bottom right part of the Schedule+ screen, allows you to enter tasks and group them by project.

To Do Tab Displays an extended view of all tasks and projects.

Toggle Key A key you can press to turn on a command and press again to turn off the command.

Trackball Alternative form of a mouse which has an embedded ball that the user rotates.

Triple-Clicking Pressing the left mouse button three times in a row quickly.

V

View Buttons At the lower left corner of the Word document window, these buttons allow you to quickly change between Normal, Page Layout, and Outline view.

W

Weekly Tab Displays a week of scheduled information.

Widow The last line of a paragraph printed at the top of a page.

Word Processing The use of a computer and software to produce written documents such as letters, memos, forms, and reports.

Word Wrap A feature that automatically wraps words around to the next line when they will not fit on the current line.

Workbook A collection of related worksheets in Excel.

Worksheet Computerized spreadsheet in Excel; a grid of rows and columns containing numbers, text, and formulas.

X

XY Charts Sometimes called *scatter charts,* these show the relationship between two categories of data.

INDEX

files, 23, 26, 49, 459
queries, 323
schedules, 374-375
worksheets, 174
scaling graphics, 105, 459
scatter charts, 240, 255, 459
Schedule+, 372
   Contact lists, 385-388
   exiting, 390
   group-enabled mode, 380
   starting, 373
   To do lists, 376, 381-384, 460
   window, 376
schedules
   appointments, 377-378
   creating, 374-375
   group meetings, 380
   opening, 391
   printing, 392-394
   saving, 374-375
   special events, 380-381
scroll arrows, 8
scroll bars, 8, 35, 37, 460
scroll box, 8, 460
searching
   databases, 318-319
   documents, 137-138, 139
   with filters, 325-326
   Help, 13
   with queries, 279, 320-323
selecting, 460
   cells, 161
   fields, 298
   objects, 96, 102
   records, 298
   text, 41-42

selection boxes, 102
sentence case, 64
serifs, 60, 460
setting
   print area, 196
   tabs, 73-74
shading, 107, 108
sharing data. See integration
sheet tabs, 158
shift-clicking, 41, 102, 460
Shortcut Bar, Microsoft Office, 21-22, 35, 36, 458
shortcut menus, 299, 302
slides
   adding text, 414
   AutoLayouts, 405
   creating, 408
   deleting, 413
   design templates, 404, 455
   layouts, 405
   placeholders, 405, 414, 459
   printing, 409-410
   viewing, 401
Slide Show view, 409
Slide Sorter view, 409
Slide view, 409
snap to grid, 104, 457
software, 3, 460
sorting, 460
   in filters, 328-329
   in reports, 343
   tables, 327-328
   in Word documents, 74-75
source files, 150, 460
special events, 380-381
spell checking, 133-134
   automatic, 46

splitting windows, 128-129
spreadsheets, 156-157, 460
   See also worksheets
standard toolbar, 35, 36, 460
Start button, 5, 460
starting
   Access, 275
   applications, 21-22
   Bookshelf '95, 446
   Encarta '95, 449
   PowerPoint, 400
   Schedule+, 373
   template wizards, 114
   Windows 95, 3-4
Start menu, 22
statistical functions, 222-223, 460
status bar, 35, 37, 460
   PowerPoint, 403
sums
   AutoSum, 214-215
   in reports, 345
switching between documents, 37, 125
synonyms, 135-136

T

Table Design view, 312-313
tables, 279
   creating, 285-286
   deleting, 287
   entering data, 288
   fields, 281, 456
   modifying, 287
   navigating through, 288-289, 295-296
   records, 281, 459

X